How Firm a Foundation in Scripture & Song

How Firm a Foundation in Scripture & Song

by John D. Morris

Master
Books

September 1999

ISBN: 0-89051-322-8
Library of Congress Number: 99-66474

Cover by Janell Robertson

Printed in the United States of America

Songs are used by permission from the following:

Selections 1, 2, 3, 4, 6, 7, 8, 9, 11, 12, 14, 15, and 16 — Sacred Music Services, P.O. Box 17072, Greenville, SC 29606; e-mail: smsoffice@aol.com.

Selections 5 and 17 — SoundForth Music, Greenville, SC 19614; e-mail: soundforth@6ju.edu; website: www.soundforth.com.

Selection 13 — The Wilds Music, P.O. Box 509, Taylors, SC 19687-0509; e-mail: music.sales@wilds.org; website: www.wilds.org.

To Sweet Dalta,
The godly woman who puts harmony
into the song of our lives.

Acknowledgments

This book was not written in the usual fashion — it grew out of prior publications with the help of a number of individuals. Their contributions are gratefully acknowledged.

♣ The staff of the Institute for Creation Research:
  - Mrs. Ruth Richards — associate editor of *Days of Praise* and a master at desktop publishing.
  - Mrs. Mary Thomas — my secretary; one of the few who can read my handwriting.
  - Miss Kathryn Stanley — who melded all the varied pieces into final form.
  - Dr. Henry Morris — my father, a source of great wisdom and a godly example.

♣ Miss Julie Cole — a talented musician who artfully arranged the words and music.

♣ Dr. Frank Garlock of Majesty Music — a lover of good Christian music and a family friend. I am honored by his gracious Foreword.

♣ Mr. Tim Fisher of Sacred Music Company — who produced the companion CD out of existing recordings.

♣ Bob Jones University musical groups — the original source of many of the recordings.

Contents

Foreword

Christian families are always looking for tools that will aid them in their desire to not only have regular family devotions, but to have them with meaning for the whole family. I believe *How Firm a Foundation — in Scripture and Song* will help them fulfill this desire.

As our three children were growing up, one of the things we always did as a part of our devotional time was to sing songs together. About the only time we could regularly have devotions as the children grew into their teen years was seven o'clock in the morning. And although you would never have known we were musicians if you had heard us sing at that hour, it was always a blessing to use music the first thing in the morning to meditate on the Word of God as it is contained in so many of the great hymns.

In fact, many of the hymns which I have written personally have come out of my own meditation on the Scripture-based words of the great hymnwriters of the past. The depth of thought and the dedication of heart of those writers is thrilling to contemplate as the words of their songs are assimilated into our spiritual beings through the medium of music.

As I looked over the list of hymns which Dr. Morris has chosen to include in this book, I was impressed not only by the variety of content of the songs chosen, but also by the wisdom he has shown in giving us hymns that have great poetry and music along with practical teaching that will aid us to live daily for the Lord. The gospel is clearly there, the comfort of God's presence is apparent, the challenge to live faithfully for our Lord is evident, and the sweetness that comes from great trial is obvious.

It was also interesting to notice that several of the hymns included in this book are ones that our whole church memorized during the 27 years that I was their minister of music. What a blessing it would have been to have had *How Firm a Foundation — in Scripture and Song* to give insight into the meaning of the hymn as the congregation memorized it.

I look forward to using *How Firm a Foundation — in Scripture and Song* as my wife and I have our devotions together, and I will give copies to the families of my three children so that they may use this devotional tool as they are seeking to raise my 13 grandchildren to serve the Lord.

— Frank Garlock

Introduction

Moses had led the children of Israel out of bondage in Egypt and through the 40 years of wilderness wandering. Together they had witnessed God's mighty hand at work in their deliverance and preservation. No one had ever experienced such direct intervention by God into the natural realm. No people had ever enjoyed such abundant blessing. And now Moses was about to exit his mortal body — his earthly ministry was nearly over.

Surely the people of Israel, God's chosen nation, would never forget God's awesome power displayed on their behalf. Surely they would never abandon their heritage, would they? If we were in their place, we certainly wouldn't — or would we?

Moses had reason to suspect that Israel would quickly turn their backs both on God and their place in His plans, but God had no doubt. He knew their hardheartedness and desire for selfish pleasure all too well, and He knew that they would soon slide away. In His omniscience He could see the rejection, apostasy, and hardship to come.

In order to give them every opportunity to remember and respond, He instructed Moses to rehearse their history in one final sermon (Deut. 31). In it Moses reiterated the law which they had been given (v. 9) and commanded them to gather at regular intervals to read it publicly and teach

13

their children (v. 10–12) "that their children, which have not known any thing, may hear, and learn to fear the Lord your God" (v. 13).

To further facilitate learning, God instructed Moses to write a song consisting of a summary statement on God's nature, His works, and their habitual rebellion. "And teach it the children of Israel: put it in their mouths, that this song may be a witness for me against the children of Israel. . . . It shall not be forgotten out of the mouths of their seed" (v. 19–21). God knew that His truth could be better committed to memory in song than through any other medium.

A similar situation confronts the English-speaking church. We, too, have a wonderful heritage. From Bunyon to Wesley to Mueller to Moody to Spurgeon, great wisdom has been accessible. Residents of English-speaking nations have been prolific Bible publishers, generous senders of missionaries, great prayer warriors, eloquent expositors, and stirring hymnwriters. Truly our spiritual heritage has been rich and deep. Surely we won't forget — or will we?

It doesn't take much awareness to notice that today's Church is in spiritual decline. Numerous surveys of church attendees have noted a lack of Bible knowledge and rejection of biblical absolutes for holy living, especially among the younger generation. The situational ethics taught in school has replaced God's law. While the Church of the present looks weak, the Church of the future looks gloomy indeed, unless our children can be made to remember and return.

This book addresses what I feel is one of the causes of (as well as a result of) this turning away, that of the replacement of the rich old hymns of days gone by with pleasant but sometimes trite choruses. Just as God designed Moses' hymn to instruct, remind, and warn the people of Israel, so the doctrinally sound great hymns of the faith instruct us of biblical truths, remind us of who God is and all He has done for us, and warn us of the wages of rejection.

Many of the popular choruses of today's churches focus on us — our feelings, our experiences, or our love for God. That they may minister to our spirit is not to be denied, but there is so much more. What about His nature, His works,

His love for us? To acknowledge Him for who He is and what He has done brings us into real praise.

To "worship Him" means to "declare His worth." Those who have grown up knowing only today's "worship choruses" may know some beautiful tunes and touching words, but do they know Him to whom they sing? Will the songs we teach them assist them in this endeavor?

Our Christian heritage in music has stood several generations in very good stead. Even when faced with a lack of good teaching, these doctrinally deep hymns allowed for growth and stability in the Christian life. Is this heritage worth saving? I think it is.

I was blessed to be born into a godly Christian home where there was never a lack of good teaching or a godly example. The churches we attended were always sound, and when there wasn't a good church, my father helped to start one. And always there was good music.

Of the six children in our family, I was the only one who had little training in music. While all the rest could play various instruments, I barely learned to play the guitar by ear. When I was in high school I sometimes played that guitar in our small church and even led the singing at times. I've always been around good Christian hymns and learned many of them by heart without even trying to.

And then came the days (as they so often come for children raised in godly homes) when I rejected what I knew to be true. Caught up in the rebellious mentality of the sixties, I purposely ran from the Lord. Living thousands of miles from home and almost never attending church, I surrounded myself with all the wrong influences.

But still, I was His child, and He drew me, sometimes gently, sometimes sternly, back to Him. One of the tools He used was music. Those hymns I had learned and which had become such a part of me, were still with me. Many times I would catch myself singing the words of truth. I tried to drown out those words of reminder, but there they were — they wouldn't leave, and eventually I listened.

And now things have come full circle. I have children of my own, and I'm trying to raise them in godliness. I'm seeing to it that they're also learning music — good music!

Finding a good church where God's word is taught has not always been easy. There's such a tendency to avoid doctrine and admonitions for a biblical lifestyle. And there is such pressure these days to limit the singing to shallow choruses. While this has a place, surely there's a better way.

Thankfully, God has blessed my young family with a wonderful church home where God's word is taught, honored, and obeyed. New believers enter the fellowship and grow strong — as they should. Children are being raised mighty in Spirit and strong in faith.

And the singing! Oh, how we love to sing! The choruses are not avoided, but mostly it's the hymns. I even get to select congregational songs and lead the singing. This means I get to choose my favorites! Our church family all knows my three favorite hymns, and they also know there's about 100 songs in my top ten.

Many times I tell a little history of the hymn — information about the author and the circumstances under which it was written. Often I call their attention to the words and give the scriptural significance. On Sunday evenings when things are less structured, I occasionally ask the congregation to quote Bible verses from which the hymn's words or thoughts are taken. In this way the songs aren't just sung by rote, they're sung from the heart. Our people have grown to love good hymns as much as I, and their love for the Lord behind the hymns has grown as well. The young people regularly participate too, with their singing and with their instruments, and I'm sure their walk with Him is on a surer foundation than it would have been otherwise.

Professionally, I'm a scientist for the Institute for Creation Research founded by my father, Dr. Henry Morris. Most of my scientific work deals with geology and its implications to the general subject of origins. Did we get here by creation or evolution? But while ICR is a scientific research think-tank, it is primarily a Christian organization engaged in the defense of Scripture, especially against the anti-scriptural and anti-God concept of evolution. Among other ministries, we publish a daily devotional booklet called *Days of Praise* which comes out quarterly. Each day's entry consists not of a mere devotional thought or testimony, but of a devotional

Bible study, something you can sink your teeth into. Nearly all of the studies are authored by ICR scientists, the majority by my father, but I've written quite a few since I joined the staff in 1984.

A few years ago, I used the words of one of my top three songs, "How Firm a Foundation," to organize the study. I identified the scriptural support for the song's phrases and concepts. Since the song has five verses, I ran this as a five-day series. The response was immediate and overwhelming, so much so that I've done this in each quarterly issue ever since. The songs selected were chosen for their scriptural content, and you'd be surprised how often the hymnwriter used or paraphrased the very words of Scripture in their songs, many times gathering several verses around a doctrinal theme. In this way, a favorite hymn becomes the impetus for Bible study.

Many readers have responded with appreciation. They enjoy seeing these wonderful hymns used in such a manner. Many have commented how the devotionals have been used by God in their lives, that the hymn selected for that quarter was just right to help meet a circumstance in their life at that moment. Quite a few have mailed in their favorites as suggestions. Some say as soon as they get the booklet, they thumb through to see which hymn appears, and then they "cheat" and read ahead.

Over the years, many wonderful hymns have been thus utilized to study Scripture, and now they have been incorporated into this book, in the order they appeared in *Days of Praise*. In doing so, it is hoped that you, too, will be encouraged in your Christian walk and faith. Perhaps you will choose to use this book in your daily quiet time with the Lord. Through it, I trust that others may be introduced to the worldwide ministry of ICR in addition to the daily devotional booklet, *Days of Praise*. Perhaps the most likely result is that these grand old hymns may be kept alive in your heart and memory, your church and children, for they are needed now more than ever. But most of all, I pray that in these studies the God to whom we sing would be glorified and His word honored.

How Firm a Foundation

Rippon's *Selection of Hymns*, 1787

Traditional American Melody
Caldwell's *Union Harmony*, 1837

1. How firm a foun - da - tion, ye saints of the Lord,
2. "Fear not, I am with thee; O be not dis - mayed,
3. "When through the deep wa - ters I call thee to go,
4. "When through fier - y tri - als thy path-way shall lie,
5. "The soul that on Je - sus hath leaned for re - pose

Is laid for your faith in His ex - cel - lent Word!
For I am thy God, and will still give thee aid;
The ri - vers of woe shall not thee o - ver - flow;
My grace, all suf - fi - cient, shall be thy sup - ply
I will not, I will not de - sert to his foes

What more can He say than to you He hath said,
I'll strength - en thee, help thee, and cause thee to stand,
For I will be with thee, thy trou - bles to bless,
The flames shall not hurt thee; I on - ly de - sign,
That soul, though all hell should en - deav - or to shake

To you who for ref - uge to Je - sus have fled?
Up - held by my right - eous, om - nip - o - tent hand.
And sanc - ti - fy to thee thy deep - est dis - tress.
Thy dross to con - sume, and thy gold to re - fine.
I'll nev - er, no nev - er, no nev - er for - sake."

1

How Firm a Foundation

The Institute for Creation Research started publishing *Days of Praise* in 1985. My father (who was then president of ICR) wrote all of the entries that first year, setting the tone for others to follow. It was decided that the booklet would be a "devotional Bible study," with each day's reading containing some "meat" from Scripture on which to chew and apply devotionally to the Christian life.

At the time he first started writing, I was on the faculty of geological engineering at the University of Oklahoma. I had entered graduate school there in 1975 and received the Ph.D. in 1980. When the department asked me to stay on the faculty, I accepted and remained until 1984, when I joined my father and the other scientists at ICR. He had already begun writing the first year's worth of devotionals, and after that first year I was asked to write as many as I could, in addition to my other duties.

It was difficult at first. To select a passage, do research on word meanings, find supporting Scripture, come to a resolution and apply it devotionally and personally — all in about 350 words — was a real challenge! Sometimes one devotional took many hours, but they were precious hours, times of personal growth and praise. They were spent in thankfulness that others would soon be reading and gaining similar benefit from my study.

The first hurdle to overcome was to choose a topic or verse to be studied. The way which works for me is to read books on theology or Bible commentaries. Remember, I am a scientist, not a theologian or a Greek scholar. Thus, I read what others have written until some verse or concept speaks to me or catches my attention. Then I do the necessary study, find cross references, make applications, and write.

My very first devotional followed from a study of the wonderful promise in Hebrews 13:5: "I will never leave thee, nor forsake thee." The verb tenses (so the commentaries pointed out) were extremely emphatic, a doubly strong assertion that He would never leave us, and a thrice-strong assertion that He would never forsake us. As I wrote, the words of the song "How Firm a Foundation" came to mind, especially its last verse. It became obvious that the verse was almost a literal translation of Hebrews 13:5. What a blessing!

When the devotional was typeset, much to my chagrin, it came out several lines too short to fill the page. What to do? Lines came hard back then. I had already said all I knew to say. In desperation, I asked and received permission to quote that verse of "How Firm a Foundation." This seemed to compliment the devotional and make a nice application. Once published, several letters of appreciation were received.

Just about that time my family took a vacation to our previous home in Norman, Oklahoma. We had been members of a wonderful church there, the Wildwood Community Church. These were years of spiritual growth, service, and fruitfulness, and I look back on them as sweet years. By default, I began leading the singing, and not long afterwards I was asked to serve as an elder. It had been our church home in every sense, so when we showed up unannounced that Sunday morning, Pastor Bruce Hess asked me to speak at the evening service, and I agreed.

That evening just before I was to speak, the congregation coincidentally sang "How Firm a Foundation." The song leader directed it a little differently, however. First he read a portion of Scripture which covered the same ground as verse one of the song, then the verse was sung. Then more Scripture related to verse two, which was sung, and so on to verse five for which Hebrews 13:5 was used. A seed was planted in my mind.

There was no immediate intention to use hymns in *Days of Praise*, but for the next several years I began to notice the scriptural content of hymns. It culminated in November 1991 — a five-day series in *Days of Praise* based on "How Firm a Foundation," and a tradition was born. It has since developed into a regular feature, one hymn per quarterly issue.

The hymn "How Firm a Foundation" has become one of my favorites — one of my top three, actually. When it was first published in 1787, it bore the title "Exceeding Great and Precious Promises," and that's the gist of the words. In some of the older hymnals, an additional verse is given before verse five. Since it was not included in the devotional, I'll add it here for completeness. It does add an extra dimension to the song.

> *Even down to old age, all my people shall prove*
> *My sovereign, eternal, unchangeable love;*
> *And when ivory hairs shall their temples adorn,*
> *Like lambs they shall still in my bosom be borne.*

Unfortunately, we know nothing of this hymn's author. Maybe that's best, for the words of its six verses cover every situation in every believer's life and show how God remains faithful. He allows and uses every event of our lives for our good and never, never forsakes us. ✺

How Firm a Foundation

Therefore leaving the principles of the doctrine of Christ, let us go on unto perfection; not laying again the foundation of repentance from dead works, and of faith toward God (Heb. 6:1).

Many of the grand old hymns of the faith are still treasured, even today. Their strength and enduring popularity lies in their use of music to teach scriptural truth, many times weaving in phrases from various scriptural passages to make a doctrinal point.

Such is the case with the hymn (of unknown authorship) normally entitled "How Firm a Foundation." Each verse contains unusually rich scriptural insights, using the words of Scripture, primarily built around the theme of the security of the believer.

The first verse is quite familiar:

How firm a foundation, ye saints of the Lord,
Is laid for your faith in His excellent word!
What more can He say then to you He hath said,
To you who for refuge to Jesus have fled?

Each Christian's pilgrimage begins at salvation. There at the Cross, through the foundational instruction of the word of God, we find everlasting life. We "have fled for refuge to lay hold upon the hope set before us: Which hope we have as an anchor of the soul, both sure and steadfast" (Heb. 6:18–19).

Once founded and anchored, we march on to maturity as stated in our text, using the "word of God" (Heb. 6:5) as our all-sufficient guide. He has told us therein all that we need to know to guide us through the days ahead, including the various perils and persecutions illumined in subsequent verses, all the while resting in Him for security, and ultimately realizing the "hope set before us" (Heb. 6:18).

Fear Not

Fear thou not; for I am with thee: be not dismayed; for I am thy God: I will strengthen thee; yea, I will help thee; yea, I will uphold thee with the right hand of my righteousness (Isa. 41:10).

The second verse of the hymn, "How Firm a Foundation," follows quite closely the words of our text.

Fear not, I am with thee; O be not dismayed,
For I am thy God, and will still give thee aid;
I'll strengthen thee, help thee, and cause thee to stand,
Upheld by my righteous, omnipotent hand.

The Christian should hold no illusions regarding his possible circumstances. Our Savior does not promise a life of ease or wealth or even acceptance. He does promise that He will be with us no matter what, and that He is just and powerful, able to deal rightly with any difficulty, and that we will be ultimately victorious with His help: "For I the Lord thy God will hold thy right hand, saying unto thee, Fear not; I will help thee" (Isa. 41:13).

The New Testament authors reflected this theme in many other passages as well. Paul prayed for the believers at Colosse, that they would be "strengthened with all might, according to his glorious power, unto all patience and longsuffering with joyfulness" (Col. 1:11). Christ promised: "These things have I spoken unto you, that in me ye might have peace. In the world ye shall have tribulation: but be of good cheer; I have overcome the world" (John 16:33).

We have no cause for fear, for our Savior subjected himself to far greater difficulties: "Consider him that endured such contradiction of sinners against himself, lest ye be wearied and faint in your minds" (Heb. 12:3). He is "the author and finisher of our faith" (Heb. 12:2). His victory is complete, and He is with us.

Deep Waters

When thou passest through the waters, I will be
with thee; and through the rivers, they shall not overflow thee: when thou walkest through the fire, thou
shalt not be burned; neither shall the flame kindle
upon thee (Isa. 43:2).

We live in a world that is plagued by the effects of sin
and the curse, where even the most godly Christian is subject to the ravages of disease, accident, old age, famine,
drought, and pestilence, and the sins and sinful choices of
others.

Many times our suffering is deserved, due to the consequences of our personal sin or improper choices. The conse-
quent suffering may be the direct result of our actions or
may be the chastisement of God to correct our behavior. God
may also bring difficulties into our lives to mold our character, making us more like His dear Son. Whatever the cause,
there are times when we must go through "deep waters."
But we do not face them alone, as the third verse of "How
Firm a Foundation" teaches:

When through the deep waters I call thee to go,
The rivers of woe shall not thee overflow;
For I will be with thee, thy troubles to bless,
And sanctify to thee thy deepest distress.

James begins his book on the effective Christian life by
discussing the benefits of trials: "Knowing this, that the trying of your faith worketh patience. . . . Blessed is the man
that endureth temptation [or trials]: for when he is tried, he
shall receive the crown of life" (James 1:3–12). Job reflects
the same triumphant attitude in our text as do other Scripture writers (e.g., 1 Pet. 1:7; Rom. 8:18; etc.) and as have
many saints down through the ages.

God has not promised to keep our lives free from times
of distress, but He has promised to be with us through them
and to use them to bring about our ultimate sanctification.

Fiery Trials

Beloved, think it not strange concerning the fiery trial which is to try you. . . . But rejoice, inasmuch as ye are partakers of Christ's sufferings; that, when his glory shall be revealed, ye may be glad also with exceeding joy. If ye be reproached for the name of Christ, happy are ye (I Pet. 4:12–14).

In addition to the normal distresses of life come outright persecution — direct opposition to the Christian and his faith by enemies of the Cross. Millions of Christians down through the ages have even suffered martyrdom for their testimony, and many are suffering today around the world.

Christ promised that we would be hated for our stand (John 15:18–21), but He also prayed for us, not that we would be spared the persecution, but that we would be victorious in it and sanctified through it. "The world hath hated them, because they are not of the world, even as I am not of the world. I pray not that thou shouldest take them out of the world, but that thou shouldest keep them from the evil. . . . Sanctify them through thy truth" (John 17:14–17). This is the message of the fourth verse of "How Firm a Foundation."

When through fiery trials thy pathway shall lie,
My grace, all-sufficient, shall be thy supply,
The flames shall not hurt thee, I only design,
Thy dross to consume, and thy gold to refine.

In His wisdom, He may choose to allow persecution to block life's pathway, but we will not face such opposition alone. His grace will supply our every need.

Heating gold above its melting point allows the denser gold to be separated from the frothy impurities (or dross), thus purifying the gold. Just so does God allow "fiery trials" in our lives, pushing us beyond the melting point, to "purify unto himself a peculiar people, zealous of good works" (Titus 2:14).

I Will Never Leave Thee

> Let your conversation be without covetousness; and be content with such things as ye have: for he hath said, I will never leave thee, nor forsake thee (Heb. 13:5).

This marvelous promise of security ought to serve to strengthen us in the face of any and all opposition. Our trust is in the Lord and His promises, in stark contrast to the preceding admonition to let our mindset "be without covetousness; and (to) be content with such things as (we) have."

A covetous spirit actually breaks the last of the Ten Commandments, and this warning tells us that such a spirit can afflict a Christian if he allows himself to become discontented with God's provision. The presence of God is far more precious than material possessions, and this should be enough.

Actually, the promise is even more emphatic in the original Greek. The word "leave," which means to uphold or sustain, is preceded by a twice-repeated negative. It literally means, "I will not, I will not cease to uphold you!" The word "forsake" implies forsaking one in a position of hopelessness, and it is preceded by a thrice-repeated negative: "I'll never, never, never abandon you in a hopeless state!"

Furthermore, this is a personal promise from Christ Jesus. The phrase, "He hath said," is in an intensive mode in Greek and could rightly be translated, "He, himself, hath said." Our Lord stakes His reputation on His ability to provide us security. No wonder "we may boldly say, The Lord is my helper, and I will not fear what man shall do unto me" (Heb. 13:6).

The last verse from the grand hymn, "How Firm a Foundation," now takes on new meaning.

> *The soul that on Jesus hath leaned for repose*
> *I will not, I will not desert to his foes.*
> *That soul, though all hell should endeavor to shake*
> *I'll never, no never, no never forsake.*

Hark! the Herald Angels Sing

Felix Mendelssohn-Bartholdy
Arr. by William H. Cummings

Charles Wesley

1. Hark! the her - ald an - gels sing, "Glo - ry to the new-born King;
2. Christ, by high - est heav'n a - dored, Christ, the ev - er - last - ing Lord:
3. Hail the heav'n - born Prince of Peace! Hail the Sun of Right-eous - ness!
4. Come De - sire of Na - tions, come! Fix in us Thy hum - ble home:

Peace on earth and mer - cy mild, God and sin - ners rec - on - ciled!"
Late in time be - hold Him come, Off - spring of a vir - gin's womb.
Light and life to all He brings, Ris'n with heal - ing in His wings.
Rise, the wom - an's con-quering Seed, Bruise in us the ser-pent's head.

Joy - ful all ye na - tions, rise, Join the tri - umph of the skies;
Veiled in flesh the God - head see, Hail th' in - car - nate De - i - ty!
Mild He lays His glo - ry by, Born that man no more may die;
Ad - am's like - ness now ef - face, Stamp Thine im - age in its place:

With th' an - gel - ic host pro - claim, "Christ is born in Beth - le - hem!"
Pleased as man with men to dwell, Je - sus, our Em-man - u - el.
Born to raise the sons of earth, Born to give them sec - ond birth.
Sec - ond Ad - am from a - bove, re - in - state us in Thy love.

Hark! the her - ald an - gels sing, "Glo - ry to the new-born King!"

2

Hark! The Herald Angels Sing

Christmas time was coming. Why not select a favorite Christmas carol? While many of our favorites shouldn't be examined too closely, some are rich in scriptural content. A quick browse through the Christmas section in my hymn book landed on "Hark! The Herald Angels Sing," by one of my favorite hymnwriters, Charles Wesley, who always wove deep doctrinal insights into his lyrics.

Wesley was born into a prominent, God-fearing family in England, the 18th of 19 children. His father was an Anglican clergyman while his mother provided much of the training, both academic and theological, for her children. (This has earned her a special place in the hearts of today's home-schooling moms.)

Always spiritually minded, Charles and his brother John sailed for America soon after they graduated from Oxford, to evangelize the Indians. Here he came face to face with his own meager relationship to God. He knew so much, but knew God so little. In contrast, Moravian missionaries with whom he fellowshiped had such sweetness in their walk and power in their ministries. He returned home in deep despair.

But soon, in a Moravian service, he fully met the Lord. Whether it was a conversion experience or a time of full surrender, God knows, but from that day Wesley served his Lord with great fervency and effectiveness. God granted much fruit in spite of vigorous persecution, even the birth of a new movement, the Methodists, stressing evangelism and personal holiness.

And his music! Oh, my, his music! Often the text of his hymns could serve as the lecture notes for a theology course. His desire was that Christians could sing their way into the greater knowledge of God that had eluded him so long.

And write he did! More than 6,500 hymns are attributed to him. Not all have remained in use, of course, but every hymn book, from every denomination, contains numerous "Wesley" hymns, five of which were studied in *Days of Praise* and included in this book. Be sure and look for the others: "And Can It Be That I Should Gain?" "Arise, My Soul, Arise" "Jesus, Lover of My Soul," and "Christ the Lord Is Risen Today." Other favorites: "O For a Thousand Tongues to Sing," "Love Divine, All Love Excelling," and "Rejoice — the Lord Is King!" History confirms the truth that God can mightily use a heart and mind firmly committed to Him.

In this hymn, Wesley probes the deep mystery of the incarnation of Christ. He incorporates into its words numerous scriptural phrases and concepts, braiding them into a majestic strand. Many scholars consider this one of the very best songs in the English language and certainly a favorite song of many at Christmas time throughout English-speaking countries. Even today, as unbelievers sing it as a Christmas "carol," they confront majestic truths. ✕

Hark! The Herald Angels Sing

And suddenly there was with the angel a multitude of the heavenly host praising God, and saying, Glory to God in the highest, and on earth peace, good will toward men (Luke 2:13–14).

Can we imagine how the shepherds felt that night? One moment they were sleepily watching their flock (Luke 2:8), and the next, they were confronted by "the angel of the Lord" (v. 9). Little wonder that they were "sore afraid." But the angel allayed their fears and announced the wonderful news that the long-awaited Messiah had just been born and that they were invited to go see Him (v. 10–12).

But before they could act, the sky was ablaze with "a multitude of heavenly host," singing and praising God in jubilation.

How could they have responded differently than "Let us now go even unto Bethlehem, and see this thing which is come to pass, which the Lord hath made known unto us. And they came with haste" (v. 15–16)?

The heralding angels deserve more than just a passing look. The Bible teaches that angels are not just inhabitants of heaven, but active participants in the affairs of earth. "Are they not all ministering spirits, sent forth to minister for them who shall be heirs of salvation?" (Heb. 1:14). They are continually at war with the fallen angels (e.g., Dan. 10:13) and aid us in our spiritual warfare (Eph. 6:12).

In our text, these angels constitute a "host," not a choir! They have not arrived from a perch in the clouds, but have assembled from their various duty stations and battlegrounds to celebrate the birth of their Creator, Jesus Christ. They had long been fascinated by God's plan of redemption (1 Pet. 1:12), and now rejoiced as it began to unfold.

Let us employ the favorite Christmas carol by Charles Wesley to focus our attention on this majestic event.

God and Sinners Reconciled

We pray you in Christ's stead, be ye reconciled to God. For he hath made him to be sin for us, who knew no sin; that we might be made the righteousness of God in him (2 Cor. 5:20–21).

In the beginning when God created Adam and Eve and placed them in the "very good" creation (Gen. 1:31), He gave them one rule to follow (Gen. 2:17). They were created to live forever in fellowship with Him, but disobedience to this rule would bring death.

As Creator, He had both the authority to set the rules over His creation and the penalty for breaking the rules, declaring "the wages of sin is death" (Rom. 6:23). A holy, sinless, ever-living God who abhors sin cannot allow disobedience in His presence, and a just God's nature demands a just punishment. Ever since the events of Genesis 3, God and humankind have been estranged, with the awful barrier of sin separating them. Man has been unable to restore fellowship with God on his own! Sin's penalty must be paid!

The angels were present at the creation of Adam and Eve, at their disobedience, and at God's withdrawal of fellowship with them. The angels have ever since been active on behalf of repentant sinners, but they were unable to bring about any permanent solution.

But finally it happened! God, the Creator who had been rejected by His creation, the righteous judge who demanded the penalty of death for sin, himself had come to pay that penalty, to redeem by His own death His fallen, rebellious creation, and the angels rejoiced.

Hark! the herald angels sing, "Glory to the new-born King;
Peace on earth, and mercy mild; God and sinners reconciled!"
Joyful all ye nations, rise, Join the triumph of the skies;
With the angelic hosts proclaim, "Christ is born in Bethlehem!"
Hark! the herald angels sing, "Glory to the newborn King!"

The Incarnate Deity

Christ Jesus: Who, being in the form of God, thought it not robbery to be equal with God: But made himself of no reputation, and took upon him the form of a servant, and was made in the likeness of men (Phil. 2:5–7).

The entire gospel message runs counter to the human mind. The Creator dying for the creation. The judge paying the penalty for the guilty. The immortal One dying. Sinless God substituting for human sinners. No human or devil ever could have thought of this scheme, and indeed, no such one did. This is evidenced by the works-oriented salvation offered by all cults and false religions, as conjured up by such sources.

But make no mistake! The babe in the manger was the Creator, holy and eternal! "Who is the image of the invisible God, the firstborn of every creature. . . . All things were created by him and for him . . . that in all things he might have the preeminence. For it pleased the Father that in him should all fulness dwell; And, having made peace through the blood of his cross, by him to reconcile all things unto himself" (Col. 1:15–20).

In order to qualify as a sacrificial substitute, He had to be born as a child into humankind, but without the inherited sin nature of His human parents. A virgin birth was therefore necessary.

He had to live a sinless life — a life without a penalty of its own to pay. He had to be fully human, but also fully God, so that His substitutionary death could apply to the sins of more than one guilty sinner. He had to be "God with us," the meaning of the precious title Emmanuel (Matt. 1:23), as prophesied years before (Isa. 7:14).

Christ, by highest Heav'n adored, Christ, the everlasting Lord:
Late in time behold Him come, Off-spring of a virgin's womb.
Veiled in flesh the God-head see, Hail th' incarnate Deity!
Pleased as man with men to dwell, Jesus our Emmanuel.
Hark! the herald angels sing, "Glory to the newborn King!"

The Prince of Peace

> For unto us a child is born, unto us a Son is given: and the government shall be upon his shoulder: and his name shall be called Wonderful, Counsellor, The mighty God, The everlasting Father, The Prince of Peace. Of the increase of his government and peace there shall be no end (Isa. 9:6–7).

There will come a time when the Creator's work of salvation will be complete, and we will fully realize the eternal life we now possess. Make no mistake! He has already assured the outcome of this work, but one day sin and its effects will be totally removed (Rev. 21:4–5), and the curse will be repealed (Rev. 22:3), for: "The last enemy that shall be destroyed is death. . . . Death is swallowed up in victory" (1 Cor. 15:26–54). He says, "Unto you that fear my name shall the Sun of righteousness arise with healing in his wings" (Mal. 4:2).

The fact that He was born into the human race qualified Him as a sacrifice for us. He had to be human (and a sinless human at that) to die for humans. The fact that He died freed us from paying sin's awful penalty ourselves, for He has paid it! But He also rose in triumph over sin and death, assuring us that we who have accepted His free gift of forgiveness and eternal life through the second birth (John 3:3, etc.) will also rise again just as He, the "firstfruits," did (1 Cor. 15:20).

Until that day arrives, we have glorious peace, for the Prince of Peace "made peace through the blood of his cross" (Col. 1:20). "Peace I leave with you, my peace I give unto you" (John 14:27).

Hail the heav'n-born Prince of Peace!
Hail the Sun of Righteousness!
Light and life to all He brings, Ris'n with healing in His wings.
Mild He lays His glory by, Born that man no more may die;
Born to raise the sons of earth,
Born to give them second birth.
Hark! the herald angels sing, "Glory to the newborn King!"

The Desire of Nations

> I will shake all nations, and the desire of all nations shall come: and I will fill this house with glory, saith the Lord of hosts (Hag. 2:7).

To think that the almighty sovereign Creator, the judge of all the earth, the righteous sacrifice for our sins, the conqueror of death, would take up residence in our own hearts! Through His work on the cross, He has done away with the need for an earthly temple at which to meet with man. Instead, "know ye not that ye are the temple of God, and that the Spirit of God dwelleth in you?" (1 Cor. 3:16).

This new and blessed relationship has been in view from the first. Immediately after pronouncing the penalty of death upon all creation (due to Adam and Eve's rejection of His authority over them), the Creator announced the ultimate solution to the problem which He would one day bring to pass. Speaking to Satan, God said: "I will put enmity between thee and the woman, and between thy seed and her seed; it shall bruise thy head, and thou shalt bruise his heel" (Gen. 3:15). And from that time on, the nation of Israel has been looking for the conquering seed of the woman who would return creation to its original created intent.

Adam's sin nature was passed on to all his descendants and likewise the unacceptability of sinful mankind to stand in the presence of a holy God. But his work in fulfillment of the prophecy above crushed Satan's hold on and claim over us. "For as in Adam all die, even so in Christ shall all be made alive" (1 Cor. 15:22). "Glory to the newborn King!"

Come Desire of Nations, come! Fix in us Thy humble home:
Rise, the woman's conquering Seed,
 Bruise in us the serpent's head;
Adam's likeness now efface, Stamp Thine image in its place:
Second Adam from above, Reinstate us in Thy love.
Hark! the herald angels sing, "Glory to the newborn King."

Hallelujah, What a Savior!

Philip P. Bliss

Philip P. Bliss

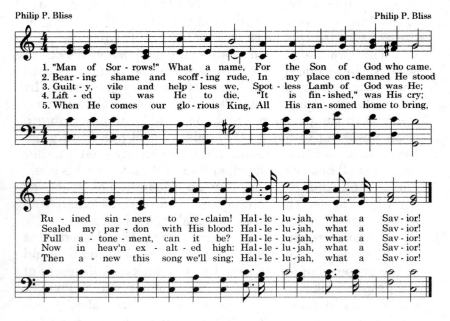

1. "Man of Sor - rows!" What a name, For the Son of God who came.
2. Bear - ing shame and scoff - ing rude, In my place con - demned He stood
3. Guilt - y, vile and help - less we, Spot - less Lamb of God was He;
4. Lift - ed up was He to die, "It is fin - ished," was His cry;
5. When He comes our glo - rious King, All His ran - somed home to bring,

Ru - ined sin - ners to re - claim! Hal - le - lu - jah, what a Sav - ior!
Sealed my par - don with His blood: Hal - le - lu - jah, what a Sav - ior!
Full a - tone - ment, can it be? Hal - le - lu - jah, what a Sav - ior!
Now in heav'n ex - alt - ed high: Hal - le - lu - jah, what a Sav - ior!
Then a - new this song we'll sing; Hal - le - lu - jah, what a Sav - ior!

3

Hallelujah, What a Savior!

God has blessed me with Dalta, whom I met in Oklahoma while attending graduate school. A wonderful wife, she loves the Lord and loves to minister to people. Soon after we were married, she got involved with a campus outreach called Friendship International, in which Christian ladies befriend the wives of international students, helping them learn English, crafts, and homemaking skills and telling them of Jesus, the One who came to all nations. Together we saw quite a few international students and families come to know the Savior.

Once each year a local church hosted Friendship Sunday, for which all the ladies in the group invited their "friends" to church. One year Dalta was hosting an elderly Korean lady, the mother of a graduate student. She spoke absolutely no English and could only communicate at all if she brought her five-year-old grandson along to the weekly meetings. Through his translation and vigorous hand signals, Dalta invited her to church on Sunday and to our apartment for lunch. When Sunday came she was ready, and with her was another Korean grandmother who also could speak no English, but they left the grandson at home.

I was leading singing in our church, so Dalta was on her own. Later when I met them at home for dinner, we had an awkward time of grinning and nodding as we passed the mashed potatoes. Afterwards, over a leisurely cup of tea, my wife whispered that they had carried what looked like a hymnal to church, written in Korean, and even seemed to be singing along with the congregation. Could they know the Lord? Could they be wanting to speak to us as much as we wanted to speak to them?

Spying two black leather books on the table, I grinned and nodded as I picked them up. Much to my delight, one was a Korean Bible, published by the American Bible Society. The other was indeed a hymn book, with subtitles in English for each hymn.

I pointed to one that I recognized and patted my chest, as if to say, "This is one of my favorites." They nodded and agreed, even humming a few notes. Then they pointed to a favorite, and we agreed and hummed a few bars. No words passed intelligently between us, but our spirits recognized each other.

We got out our hymnal and, with much deliberation, could cross between the two. Dalta spotted one of her favorites, and together we sang it to the ladies. They knew the song and were following along, with tears in their eyes.

Then, with the wavering voice of the elderly, they asked if they could sing to us. Their favorite? "Hallelujah! What a Savior." Now it was our turn to cry. What sweet fellowship we had that day trading testimonies in hymn. What a Savior, indeed!

Soon they returned to Korea, and we've had no contact since. But there will come a time of reunion, someday, when we can share more completely all that our Savior means to us. As the song says, "Then anew this song we'll sing; Hallelujah, what a Savior!" Until then, we'll treasure the memory of wordless, spirit-filled fellowship through song. ✼

Man of Sorrows

He is despised and rejected of men; a man of sorrows, and acquainted with grief: and we hid as it were our faces from him; he was despised, and we esteemed him not (Isa. 53:3).

The marvelous hymn of the last century, "Hallelujah, What a Savior!" provides in pithy but powerful form an insight into the work of our Lord and Savior, Jesus Christ, on the cross. Let us use its familiar verses to "think on these things" (Phil. 4:8).

> *Man of Sorrows!" What a name,*
> *For the Son of God, who came.*
> *Ruined sinners to reclaim!*
> *Hallelujah, what a Savior!*

The creation should have brought great joy to the Creator, "for thou hast created all things, and for thy pleasure they are and were created" (Rev. 4:11). But ever since the beginning, the "very good" creation has defied Him, bringing great grief. In the days of Noah, "it repented the Lord that he had made man on the earth, and it grieved him at his heart" (Gen. 6:6).

But even in the face of such sinful defiance, the rejected Creator, the very Son of God, came to "deliver them who . . . were all their lifetime subject to bondage. . . . To make reconciliation for the sins of the people" (Heb. 2:15–17).

Yet when He came, instead of receiving a liberator's welcome, He was again "despised and rejected" as in our text for today. He was ridiculed and slandered, hounded and hunted; his body was beaten and broken and hung on a cross. But through it all, "He hath borne our griefs, and carried our sorrows. . . . Was wounded for our transgressions . . . bruised for our iniquities . . . was oppressed and . . . afflicted" (Isa. 53:4–7), reclaiming ruined sinners.

Hallelujah, what a Savior!

Condemned in My Place

Likewise also the chief priests mocking him, with the scribes and elders, said, he saved others; himself he cannot save. If he be the King of Israel, let him now come down from the cross, and we will believe him. He trusted in God; let him deliver him now, if he will have him: for he said, I am the Son of God (Matt. 27:41–43).

Bearing shame and scoffing rude,
In my place condemned He stood —
Sealed my pardon with His blood:
Hallelujah, what a Savior!

Through the sham of a trial, they mocked Him and shamed Him. "They spit in his face, and buffeted him" (Matt. 26:67). They "platted a crown of thorns, (and) put it upon his head" along with a kingly robe, and "they bowed the knee before him, and mocked him, saying, Hail, King of the Jews!" (Matt. 27:29). They "scourged Jesus, (and) delivered him to be crucified" (v. 26). Finally, they stripped Him of His garments, hung Him naked on the cross, "And sitting down they watched him there" (v. 36). "They that passed by reviled him, wagging their heads" (v. 39).

Surely such treatment would be reserved for only the worst sinners, but Pilate called Him "this just person" (Matt. 27:24), not deserving of imprisonment or execution. Yet "they all condemned him to be guilty of death" (Mark 14:64).

He wasn't guilty, but I am, as are all of us. "For all have sinned" and "the wages of sin is death" (Rom. 3:23; 6:23). He chose to stand condemned where we belong, for God "hath made him to be sin for us, who knew no sin; that we might be made the righteousness of God in him" (2 Cor. 5:21).

We have thus been granted full pardon, "sealed unto the day of redemption" (Eph. 4:30).

Hallelujah, what a Savior!

The Spotless Lamb of God

Forasmuch as ye know that ye were not redeemed with corruptible things, as silver and gold . . . But with the precious blood of Christ, as of a lamb without blemish and without spot (1 Pet. 1:18–19).

Guilty, vile and helpless we,
Spotless Lamb of God was He;
Full atonement, can it be?
Hallelujah, what a Savior!

Before God, each individual stands as an absolutely guilty sinner. "There is none righteous, no, not one" (Rom. 3:10). Being more "good" than "bad" doesn't help. "For whosoever shall keep the whole law, and yet offend in one point, he is guilty of all" (James 2:10). "We are all as an unclean thing, and all our righteousnesses are as filthy rags [literally: used menstrual cloths]" (Isa. 64:6). We are altogether vile and worthless.

Furthermore, we are powerless to change our situation. Our sins demand the death penalty, "and without shedding of blood is no remission" (Heb. 9:22). Either the guilty party must die to pay sin's penalty, or a guiltless party must substitute and pay the penalty instead. And so, "when we were yet without strength, in due time Christ died for the ungodly. . . . God commendeth his love toward us, in that, while we were yet sinners, Christ died for us" (Rom. 5:6–8).

This transaction removes our sin from us. We now stand before a Holy God just as if we had never sinned and just as if we had always done right, "justified freely by his grace through the redemption that is in Christ Jesus" (Rom. 3:24).

"And not only so, but we also joy in God through our Lord Jesus Christ, by whom we have now received the atonement" (Rom. 5:11).

Hallelujah, what a Savior!

It Is Finished!

As Moses lifted up the serpent in the wilderness, even so must the Son of man be lifted up: That whosoever believeth in him should not perish, but have eternal life (John 3:14–15).

Lifted up was He to die,
"It is finished," was His cry;
Now in heav'n exalted high:
Hallelujah, what a Savior!

The people of Israel many times rejected God's plan and ways. Once their complaining brought deadly serpents into the camp as a judgment of God (Num. 21:5–7). In response to Moses' intercessory prayer, God said: "Make thee a fiery serpent, and set it upon a pole: and . . . every one that is bitten, when he looketh upon it, shall live" (v. 8).

This episode provides a clear illustration of our sinfulness and God's remedy. As in our text, those who look upon the cross of Christ with the eyes of faith, believing that His death provides a glorious remedy for our sin-wracked souls, will not only "live" but will have "eternal life."

While on that "pole," Almighty God died as "the propitiation for our sins: and not for ours only, but also for the sins of the whole world" (1 John 2:2). This infinitely difficult work had been initiated at the time when sin first entered into and thereby spoiled creation (Gen. 3). And as He completed His sacrifice, he cried out in "a loud voice" (Luke 23:46) the awesome victory cry: "It is finished: and he bowed his head, and gave up the ghost" (John 19:30).

But death does not end the story, for the grave could not hold the Creator of life. He rose in victory over death and the grave, thereby conquering sin, its power, and its penalty forever, for "when he had by himself purged our sins, sat down on the right hand of the Majesty on high" (Heb. 1:3).

Hallelujah, what a Savior!

When He Comes

For the Lord himself shall descend from heaven with a shout, with the voice of the archangel, and with the trump of God: and the dead in Christ shall rise first: Then we which are alive and remain shall be caught up together with them in the clouds, to meet the Lord in the air: and so shall we ever be with the Lord (1 Thess. 4:16–17).

When He comes our glorious King,
All His ransomed home to bring,
Then anew this song we'll sing;
Hallelujah, what a Savior!

The sacrificed, risen, and exalted Christ will one day return in glorious victory to the earth. The King of creation will restore His creation to its original created intent and reign over it in majesty: "The kingdoms of this world are become the kingdoms of our Lord, and of his Christ; and he shall reign for ever and ever" (Rev. 11:15).

Furthermore, as we see in the text above, we, whether alive or dead, shall be with Him when He returns and reigns — a cause of much rejoicing and singing throughout eternity. "And they sung a new song, saying, Thou art worthy . . . for thou wast slain, and hast redeemed us to God by thy blood out of every kindred, and tongue, and people, and nation; And hast made us unto our God kings and priests: and we shall reign on the earth" (Rev. 5:9–10).

Through His mighty work of redemption, we have been ransomed out of slavery to sin. Our sins have been washed away, we have been clothed in His righteousness and made fit to live forever with Him as His bride. "Alleluia: for the Lord God omnipotent reigneth. Let us be glad and rejoice, and give honor to him: for the marriage of the Lamb is come, and his wife hath made herself ready" (Rev. 19:6–7).

Hallelujah, what a Savior!

It Is Well With My Soul

Horatio G. Spafford

Philip P. Bliss

1. When peace like a riv-er, at-tend-eth my way, When
2. Tho Sa-tan should buf-fet, tho tri-als should come, Let
3. My Sin - O, the bliss of this glo-ri-ous thought-My
4. And Lord, haste the day when my faith shall be sight, The

sor-rows like sea bil-lows roll What-ev-er my lot, Thou hast
this blest as-sur-ance con-trol, That Christ hath re-gard-ed my
sin, not in part, but the whole, Is nailed to the cross, and I
clouds be rolled back as a scroll: The trump shall re-sound and the

taught me to say, It is well, it is well, with my soul.
help-less es-tate And hath shed His own blood for my soul.
bear it no more: Praise the Lord, Praise the Lord, O my soul!
Lord shall de-scend, E-ven so - it is well with my soul.

It is well with my soul; it is well, it is well with my soul!
It is well with my soul;

4

It Is Well with My Soul

My love affair with good hymns began, no doubt, in my youth, but it wasn't until I started leading the singing in church that the affair began to flower. In our church were many new Christians and many who had only known the music of the "Jesus People." I strummed my guitar and learned choruses from them, but desperately wanted them and all in attendance to go deeply into the grand hymns of the faith and worship God with their minds and spirits, not just singing the words.

One Sunday morning, the song, "It Is Well with My Soul," was scheduled. In announcing the number, the memory of a story I had once heard about that song came to mind. I told it as best I remembered, and a hush came across the auditorium. Many could be seen wiping tears, and then when we sang — from that day until now, this song has been in my "top three." For many Christians, it's their very favorite. Perhaps it's at its most meaningful when sung in times of distress or bereavement. The theme ought never to leave us, for no matter what the circumstance, "it is well with my soul."

Also, from that day to this, I've made it my business to learn the histories behind great hymns — the circumstances which led the author to write. These stories often "set the stage" for a hymn, softening hearts and preparing them for the message of the song. The testimonies of great Christians can live on in this way.

This song was born out of great grief and loss, greater than most will ever be called to bear. The author, Horatio Spafford, had been a successful lawyer in the frontier town of Chicago. His accumulated wealth and property had kept him from a full surrender to the Lord until meeting D.L. Moody, but from then on he had committed himself, his family, and his goods to his Savior. His love for God was tested and purified when his only son died suddenly in a tragic accident.

And then — the great Chicago fire of 1871 occurred, in which his wealth turned to ashes. With the little he had left, he decided to move his family to England and start over. Last minute developments kept him in Chicago, but his wife and four precious daughters went on ahead.

Sailing from New York on the *Ville de Havre*, the family expected the father to follow them on the next ship and join them in London. Suddenly, at two o'clock in the morning, disaster struck. In mid-ocean, their passenger liner collided with the iron sailing vessel *Lochearn* and quickly sank. In all, 226 lives were lost, including the four Spafford daughters. Mrs. Spafford was pulled from the ocean, barely conscious, and taken with the other survivors to England.

Mr. Spafford soon heard news reports of the tragedy, but knew nothing of his family's fate. Nine days after the crash, she cabled this brief message, "Saved alone."

Few of us will ever know how we would react under such circumstances. Mr. Spafford responded by penning the words which have become such a source of encouragement to many. Our confidence is in our Savior, and because of Him, "it is well with my soul."

Mr. Spafford wrote no other songs as far as I know, but he had a hand in identifying a possible site for the crucifixion of Christ some years later in Jerusalem. On a journey to that city, he had visited the British General Charles Gordon. From the general's window they could see, outside the city walls, a vertical rock outcropping with numerous crags. One afternoon, with the setting sun casting shadows across the cliff, they thought they could see the features of a human skull. Could this be Golgotha, "the place of a skull" (John 19:17), they wondered?

Upon investigation, they found that the road beneath the cliff dated from Roman times. Excavations soon revealed an empty tomb in a ruined garden nearby. Today, "Gordon's Calvary" and the garden tomb are a favorite of tourists.

Most archaeologists suspect that this is not actually the spot of Christ's death or resurrection, but it must have been a spot just like this. I was there in October 1971, and my life has never been the same. The full story follows, as the song "It Is Well with My Soul" is discussed. ✼

Peace Like a River

And the peace of God, which passeth all understanding, shall keep your hearts and minds through Christ Jesus (Phil. 4:7).

The beloved hymn, "It Is Well with My Soul," has been a source of much comfort to many. The hymn was written in memory of the author's four precious daughters who had just perished in a shipwreck as his wife was barely rescued. Through it all, the couple maintained faith in their Sovereign God and could say through their tears:

> *When peace like a river, attendeth my way,*
> *When sorrows like sea billows roll*
> *Whatever my lot, Thou hast taught me to say,*
> *It is well, it is well, with my soul.*

Our Lord has not promised us a life of ease, free from heartache and tragedy, but He has promised to be with us. "Yea, though I walk through the valley of the shadow of death, I will fear no evil: for thou art with me" (Ps. 23:4).

God's promise of provision to Israel applies in principle to us. "Fear not: for I have redeemed thee, I have called thee by thy name; thou art mine. When thou passest through the waters, I will be with thee; and through the rivers, they shall not overflow thee: when thou walkest through the fire, thou shalt not be burned; neither shall the flame kindle upon thee. For I am the Lord thy God, the Holy One of Israel, thy Savior" (Isa. 43:1–3). We can be content whatever comes, knowing He is with us.

The prerequisite for the "peace of God, which passeth all understanding" promised in our text is that we be anxious "for nothing; but in every thing by prayer and supplication with thanksgiving let your requests be made known unto God" (Phil. 4:6). "Thou wilt keep him in perfect peace, whose mind is stayed on thee" (Isa. 26:3).

Tho Satan Should Buffet

These things I have spoken unto you, that in me ye might have peace. In the world ye shall have tribulation: but be of good cheer; I have overcome the world (John 16:33).

The second verse of "It Is Well with My Soul" puts persecution and troubles in perspective.

Tho Satan should buffet, tho trials should come,
Let this blest assurance control,
That Christ hath regarded my helpless estate
And hath shed His own blood for my soul.

Paul was given "a thorn in the flesh, the messenger of Satan to buffet" him (2 Cor. 12:7). Almost every saint of every age could echo Paul's concerns, for trials come to each child of God. "Beloved, think it not strange concerning the fiery trial which is to try you" (1 Pet. 4:12). God had a purpose in Paul's life and He has one in ours, although Paul couldn't clearly see the purpose and at times we can't either. We can, however, "glory" as Paul did, or "rejoice" as Peter advises in response to the knowledge of God's loving oversight.

The persecution may never stop and may, in fact, result in serious loss — even death. But through it all we can have the controlling assurance that He has made our destiny certain, "For when we were yet without strength, in due time Christ died for the ungodly" (Rom. 5:6). "We see Jesus . . . for the suffering of death, crowned with glory and honor; that he by the grace of God should taste death for every man. . . . (Thereby) bringing many sons unto glory" (Heb. 2:9–10).

As our text reminds us, "In the world ye shall have tribulation." God may neither stop nor explain it, but He has "overcome" it by shedding His own blood for our souls.

"He that spared not his own Son, but delivered him up for us all, how shall he not with him also freely give us all things?" (Rom. 8:32).

Truly, "it *is* well with my soul."

Nailed to the Cross

Bless the Lord, O my soul, and forget not all his benefits: Who forgiveth all thine iniquities (Ps. 103:2–3).

When Christ was nailed to the cross as our atoning sacrifice, our sins — all of them — were nailed there as well. His death paid the entire penalty, "Having forgiven you all trespasses; Blotting out the handwriting of ordinances that was against us, which was contrary to us, and took it out of the way, nailing it to his cross" (Col. 2:13–14). This is the theme of the thrilling third verse of "It Is Well with My Soul."

> *My sin — O the bliss of this glorious thought —*
> *My sin, not in part, but the whole,*
> *Is nailed to the cross, and I bear it no more:*
> *Praise the Lord, praise the Lord, O my soul!*

"If we confess our sins, he is faithful and just to forgive us our sins, and to cleanse us from all unrighteousness" (1 John 1:9). On what basis? "The blood of Jesus Christ his Son cleanseth us from all sin" (v. 7). "Who his own self bare our sins in his own body on the tree, that we, being dead to sins, should live unto righteousness" (1 Pet. 2:24).

The fact that our sins are gone — "As far as the east is from the west, so far hath he removed our transgressions from us" (Ps. 103:12), and we bear them no more, gives us the courage, strength, and stamina to bear up, with His help, under the trials of this age — the theme of the song's first two verses.

If ever the circumstances of this present life threaten to overwhelm us, we can "Consider him that endured such contradiction of sinners against himself, lest ye be wearied and faint in your minds" (Heb. 12:3). The certainty of our future overrides any uncertainty in this life.

"It is well, it is well with my soul."

Faith Turned to Sight

That the trial of your faith, being much more precious than of gold that perisheth, though it be tried with fire, might be found unto praise and honor and glory at the appearing of Jesus Christ: Whom having not seen, ye love (1 Pet. 1:7–8).

As the resurrected Christ ascended into heaven, He promised to return and end this present age with all its trials and troubles. "Surely I come quickly" (Rev. 22:20), He said. The saints will eternally thereafter enjoy the presence of their Lord. Since "we walk by faith, not by sight" (2 Cor. 5:7) in this life, with much we don't yet understand, the prayer of each faithful saint has mirrored John's response to the Lord's promise, "Even so, come, Lord Jesus" (Rev. 22:20). The fourth and climactic verse of "It Is Well with My Soul" focuses on this coming event.

And Lord, haste the day when my faith shall be sight,
The clouds be rolled back as a scroll:
The trump shall resound and the Lord shall descend,
Even so — it is well with my soul!

For centuries faithful men and women have gazed upward, desiring to see "the heaven departed as a scroll when it is rolled together" (Rev. 6:14) at His return. Many have died in faith, and they now have fuller understanding, but they await the final resurrection. As the great day draws nearer, we should be all the more expectant. This hope of the Christian provides great comfort while we wait.

But on that day, "the Lord himself shall descend from heaven with a shout, with the voice of the archangel, and with the trump of God: and the dead in Christ shall rise first: Then we which are alive and remain shall be caught up together with them in the clouds, to meet the Lord in the air: and so shall we ever be with the Lord. Wherefore comfort one another with these words" (1 Thess. 4:16–18).

Until then, "it is well with my soul."

Faith Is the Victory!

John H. Yates

Ira D. Sankey

1. En - camped a - long the hills of light, Ye Chris - tian sol - diers rise, And
2. His ban - ner o - ver us is love, Our sword the Word of God; We
3. On ev' - ry hand the foe we find, Drawn up in dread ar - ray; Let
4. To him that o - ver - comes the foe, White rai - ment shall be giv'n; Be -

press the bat - tle ere the night, Shall veil the glow - ing skies. A - gainst the foe in
tread the road the saints a - bove, With shouts of tri - umph trod. By faith they like a
tents of ease be left be - hind, And on - ward to the fray. Sal - va - tion's hel - met
fore the an - gels he shall know, His name con - fessed in heav'n. Then on - ward from the

vales be - low Let all our strength be hurled; Faith is the vic - to - ry, we know,
whirl - wind's breath, Swept on o'er ev' - ry field; The faith by which they con - quered death,
on each head, With truth all girt a - bout, The earth shall trem - ble 'neath our tread,
hills of light, Our hearts with love a - flame; We'll van - quish all the hosts of night,

That o - ver - comes the world.
Is still our shin - ing shield. Faith is the vic - to - ry! Faith is the
And ech - o with our shout. Faith is the vic - to - ry! Faith is the
In Je - sus' con - qu'ring name.

vic - to - ry! Oh, glo - ri - ous vic - to - ry, That o - ver - comes the world.
vic - to - ry!

5

Faith Is the Victory

Many will remember how college life in the sixties was a war over belief systems fueled by a desire for lifestyles unshackled by accountability. Unfortunately, I was a casualty in that war, preferring temporal pleasure over obedience to the truth. I graduated in 1969 in civil engineering from Virginia Tech (where my father was on the faculty) and took a job in Los Angeles to get away from the restraints put on me by my godly parents.

Thankfully, God's reign includes even southern California. By 1971, God had fully wooed me back to himself and placed in me a desire to serve Him with my whole being, including my vocation. To a large extent, He caught my attention with the search for Noah's ark, the remains of which may still be on the mountains of Ararat in the modern country of Turkey. Before long I was heavily involved in that search. This soon rekindled a long-standing love for geology, and within a few years, I found myself in graduate school at the University of Oklahoma in their geological engineering program, preparing for a career defending the doctrines of recent creation and global flood.

Knowing that creation thinking had been deemed "politically incorrect" on the university campus, I determined to keep a low profile. I had heard of numerous graduate students who believed in creation, particularly in geology, biology, anthropology, and the like, whose degrees had been refused by aggressive evolutionary professors. Even though it would take at least five years to get a Ph.D., I decided to keep my creationism a secret until after I finished.

But God knew I would make a lousy undercover Christian, and my cover was blown on the very first day! He had given me a testimony of His grace, and a message of His creation, and He wanted others to hear. He knew I couldn't keep quiet and wouldn't allow me to try. Protecting me was a charge He took upon himself.

Engineering departments have their share of anti-Christians, but usually they don't exhibit nearly the venom that geology departments have, and that's where I took most of my courses. Soon it became obvious that I was in enemy territory, and you can imagine how my prayer life increased.

Often I would catch myself singing the words to "Faith Is the Victory." I needed daily victory — "Lord, please increase my faith." It may have been with this song that I first began to notice scriptural content in songs due to the fact that the chorus closely follows the easily recognizable 1 John 5:4: "This is the victory that overcometh the world, even our faith." Infrequent opportunities to lead singing in church gave me a desire to see familiar songs become meaningful again, and I remember pointing out some of the scriptural backing for "Faith Is the Victory" one Sunday evening. Before I knew it, this catchy tune with its insightful words had become my theme song for graduate school.

And God gave the victory. Not only did He protect me from excessive opposition and I eventually got the Ph.D., but He also gave me a wonderful ministry on campus with the other students and even with some of my professors. They even asked me to remain on the faculty after finishing.

Looking back, I see how both the Ph.D. and the following faculty position were God's design. I had originally intended to stay only for my master's degree, but He had other plans. My years in Oklahoma were ones of much growth and blessed fruitfulness, not to mention finding a godly wife. And the benefits continue, for without the credentials and the faculty experience, my present ministry would be impossible. He provides the victory, our duty is to faithfully follow His leading.

Faith in Him certainly overcame my little world. ⚘

Faith Is the Victory

For whatsoever is born of God overcometh the world: and this is the victory that overcometh the world, even our faith. Who is he that overcometh the world, but he that believeth that Jesus is the Son of God? (1 John 5:4–5).

The favorite hymn from the last century entitled "Faith Is the Victory" contains many allusions to scriptural concepts and passages. The theme, as is repeated in the chorus, is "Faith is the victory . . . O glorious victory, that overcomes the world."

The primary passage used for the source of this hymn is in our text, where we see that it is the Christian — the one "born of God" —who "believeth that Jesus is the Son of God" who "overcomes the world." The victory comes through faith.

Encamped along the hills of light, Ye Christian soldiers rise,
And press the battle ere the night, Shall veil the glowing skies.
Against the foe in vales below let all our strength be hurled;
Faith is the victory, we know, that overcomes the world.

This first verse harks back to several battles in the Old Testament where Israel, through faith in God, conquered many foes greater in number and better equipped than they. But the symbolism goes farther. The word for "world" is the Greek word *kosmos*, implying in context the world system of thought arrayed in opposition to God. "We know that we are of God, and the whole world [i.e., *kosmos*] lieth in wickedness" (1 John 5:19).

Strangely enough, Scripture here does not say that through faith we will overcome and gain the victory. Rather, it explains that faith itself is the victory. Evidently, with victorious faith, the overcoming is automatic.

"Ye are of God, little children, and have overcome them: because greater is he that is in you, than he that is in the world" (1 John 4:4).

Faith: Our Shining Shield

Above all, taking the shield of faith, wherewith ye shall be able to quench all the fiery darts of the wicked (Eph. 6:16).

The second verse of the well-known hymn "Faith Is the Victory" reflecting the teaching of 1 John 5:4, depicts the soldiers of light as they march into battle. Our commander-in-chief has erected His identifying banner over the troops, and His "banner over (us) is love" (Song of Sol. 2:4). How does love identify us? "For this is the love of God, that we keep his commandments" (1 John 5:3). "By this shall all men know that ye are my disciples, if ye have love one to another" (John 13:35). And, as they say, "Love conquers all."

His banner over us is love, Our sword the word of God;
We tread the road the saints above, With shouts of triumph trod.
By faith they like a whirl-wind's breath, Swept on o'er every field;
The faith by which they conquered death, Is still
*   our shining shield.*

The saints of yesteryear (some of whom are enshrined in Heb. 11), who in faith battled victoriously, give us great confidence. "Wherefore seeing we also are compassed about with so great a cloud of witnesses, let us lay aside every weight, and the sin which doth so easily beset us, and let us run with patience the race that is set before us, Looking unto Jesus the author and finisher of our faith" (Heb. 12:1–2).

Their armor and ours is listed in the classic passage of Ephesians 6:10–18. Our sword, identified as the "word of God" (v. 17), is "quick, and powerful, and sharper than any two-edged sword" (Heb. 4:12). Our faith is our shield (as in our text) which protects us from the wicked one.

But it's not over until it's over, and "The last enemy that shall be destroyed is death. . . . Death is swallowed up in victory" (1 Cor. 15:26–54). When it's over, our faith in the work and person of our Lord Jesus Christ will have provided a glorious and everlasting victory.

Onward to the Fray!

And it came to pass, when the people heard the sound of the trumpet, and the people shouted with a great shout, that the wall fell down flat, so that the people went up into the city, every man straight before him, and they took the city (Josh. 6:20).

The third verse of the hymn "Faith Is the Victory" portrays the attack-phase of the battle. The foe stands in dread array, also poised for the fight. The prepared troops attack without hesitation, with a well-formulated battle plan.

On every hand the foe we find, Drawn up in dread array;
Let tents of ease be left behind, And onward to the fray!
Salvation's helmet on each head, With truth all girt about:
The earth shall tremble 'neath our tread, And echo
  with our shout.

This last line recalls the episode in our text. The entire nation of Israel had marched for six days around the city of Jericho. On the seventh day they marched around the city seven times, and then the priests blew their trumpets, and the people shouted. What kind of battle plan was that?

But God had specifically instructed them to do it this way. They had seen Him work many stupendous miracles on their behalf, and their faith was great. Their unwavering obedience resulted in a glorious victory.

Today's warriors of faith have the same commander-in-chief and access to His mighty power. Furthermore, He provides the "whole armor of God, that ye may be able to withstand in the evil day, and having done all, to stand" (Eph. 6:13). "Stand therefore, having your loins girt about with truth" (v. 14). Faith must be faith in the truth. Faith in a lie will not stand. "And take [literally, receive] the helmet of salvation" (v. 17).

Each warrior, saved "by grace . . . through faith" (Eph. 2:8), immersed in truth and obedient to the commander, is assured of complete and overwhelming victory.

In Jesus' Conquering Name

Nay, in all things we are more than conquerors through him that loved us (Rom. 8:37).

The first verse of the well-loved hymn "Faith Is the Victory" describes preparation for the battle between the forces of light and darkness. The second verse tells of marching into battle, and the third, of the actual attack. For the soldier of faith, empowered by love and obedience to the commandments of God, the victory is assumed. The last verse relates the rewards of victory and a commitment to wise governing once the battle is over.

To him that overcomes the foe, White raiment shall be giv'n;
Before the angels he shall know, his name confessed in heav'n.
Then onward from the hills of light, Our hearts with love aflame;
We'll vanquish all the hosts of night, In Jesus' conq'ring name.

Jesus, when the apostle John saw Him in His present glorified, victorious state, made this promise to the churches: "He that overcometh, the same shall be clothed in white raiment; and I will not blot out his name out of the book of life, but I will confess his name before my Father, and before his angels" (Rev. 3:5).

Earlier, He had made a companion promise: "These things I have spoken unto you, that in me ye might have peace. In the world ye shall have tribulation: but be of good cheer; I have overcome the world" (John 16:33). In this life we will have battles to fight, but the ultimate victory has already been won.

As He left this world following His resurrection, He said: "Go ye therefore . . . and, lo, I am with you alway, even unto the end of the world" (Matthew 28:19–20). No wonder, then, as we see in our text, we are "more than conquerors" in every situation, as we battle in Jesus' conquering name.

"Thanks be unto God, which always causeth us to triumph in Christ" (2 Cor. 2:14).

And Can It Be

Charles Wesley

Thomas Campbell

1. And can it be that I should gain, An in - terest in the
2. 'Tis mys - tery all! the Im - mort - al dies! Who can ex - plain this
3. He left His Fa - ther's throne a - bove, So free, so in - fi -
4. Long my im - pris - oned spir - it lay, Fast bound in sin and
5. No con - dem - na - tion now I dread, Je - sus, and all in

Sav - ior's blood? Died He for me, who caused His pain? For me, who
strange de - sign? In vain the first - born ser - aph tries, To sound the
nite His grace! Emp - tied Him - self of all but love, And bled for
na - ture's night; Thine eye dif - fused a quick - 'ning ray, I woke, the
Him, is mine; A - live in Him, my liv - ing Head, And clothed in

Him, to death pur - sued? A - mazing love! How can it be, that
depths of love di - vine; 'Tis mer - cy all! Let earth a - dore! Let
A - dam's help - less race; 'Tis mer - cy all! Im - mense and free! For,
dun - geon flamed with light; My chains fell off, my heart was free, I
right - eous - ness di - vine, Bold I ap - proach th'e - ter - nal throne, And

thou, my God, should'st die for me? A - maz - ing love! How
an - gel minds in - quire no more. A - maz - ing love!
O my God, it found out me.
rose, went forth, and fol - lowed thee.
claim the crown, thru Christ, my own.

can it be, that thou my God should'st die for me?
How can it be, that thou my God should'st die for me?

6

And Can It Be

Experts on church hymnody recognize this hymn as one of the very finest in the English language. In it the author, Charles Wesley, once again filled his gripping lyrics with Scripture. As with many of his songs, this is a testimony, first expressing awe at Christ's sacrifice on our behalf, and second, of the transformation in the believer's life and destiny upon acceptance of His gift.

Evidence indicates that Wesley wrote the poem soon after his conversion. He acknowledges being bound in his own sin and his inherited sin nature. From the words, one might suspect that Wesley had been living a life of total debauchery before his salvation, but nothing could be further from the truth. Wesley was an ordained minister, living a very disciplined life as founder of the "Holy Club" of Oxford. It wasn't until later that he came to a personal faith in Christ after a powerless stint on the mission field. To all outward appearances he was a godly man, but inside, he knew his heart was imprisoned, chained in bondage to sin.

While enrolled in graduate school, I had the opportunity to speak in various area churches and was very thankful my self-imposed mandate of spiritual silence had been short-lived. One local pastor with whom I established a sweet friendship insisted on taking me to meet an elderly pastor in town, "Preacher" Hallock, without a doubt one of the godliest men on earth. I was given a book he had written on personal prayer, and it's still the best book I ever read on the subject. Not long after I met him, Preacher Hallock died at age 86 and was mourned by the entire Christian community. Perhaps no one has ever had such an impact in Central Oklahoma (particularly in Southern Baptist circles) as this man.

His testimony somewhat mirrors Charles Wesley's, for Preacher Hallock had been a preacher for many years before he knew Christ. He was never an outwardly "sinful" man, but a sinner before God in desperate need of salvation, nonetheless. His liberal teaching in Bible college and seminary had muddled his thinking, leading him into a life of works to gain entrance into heaven. When he was 40 years old, at a revival meeting in his own church, he had come to full recognition of his bondage and cried out to God for forgiveness and release. His life from then on was spent in proclamation of God's "amazing love."

Wesley's song presents something of a problem for congregational use. Each verse takes a long time to sing — and the song is five verses long! Which verses can be excluded? The answer? None of them, if the lyrics are to have continuity. Together they tell Wesley's story, and Hallock's story, and the story of many who sing it.

To church song leaders who might read this book, let me put a bug in your ear. In a meeting which has "flexibility," let me suggest that you sing the entire song. Then read a phrase and ask if anyone in the congregation or group can quote a Scripture verse which mirrors that thought. Try one phrase from each verse. Before you know it, many verses and Bible stories will come up.

I tried that one Sunday evening while writing the series for *Days of Praise*. Our people actually came up with some thoughts that I included. I do that often now, and people love it. Actually, they just love God's Word, and the hymns just provide an avenue to express that love. ✻

Can It Be?

> Christ also suffered for us. . . . Who his own self bare our sins in his own body on the tree, that we, being dead to sins, should live unto righteousness (1 Pet. 2:21–24).

Those who love good church music have come to love Charles Wesley's commitment to and knowledge of His Savior and the Scriptures, for he wove into his music and poetry deep insights which challenge and thrill us even today. This, one of his finest hymns, has unfortunately been much abridged in modern hymnals. Let us use its original five verses as an impetus to study the doctrinal themes expressed there:

> *And can it be that I should gain,*
> *An interest in the Savior's blood?*
> *Died He for me, who caused His pain?*
> *For me, who Him, to death pursued?*
> *Amazing love! How can it be,*
> *That thou, my God, should'st die for me?*

Even the Old Testament saints wondered why God loves man so. "What is man, that thou shouldest magnify him? and that thou shouldest set thine heart upon him?" (Job 7:17). The New Testament contains many similar expressions of wonder. "Behold, what manner of love [literally 'what a different kind of love'] the Father hath bestowed upon us, that we should be called the sons of God" (1 John 3:1). "God commendeth his love toward us, in that, while we were yet sinners, Christ died for us. . . . And not only so, but we also joy in God through our Lord Jesus Christ, by whom we have now received the atonement" (Rom. 5:8–11).

The point is, we were desperate sinners deserving His wrath. "But God, who is rich in mercy, for his great love [i.e., 'amazing love'] wherewith he loved us, Even when we were dead in sins, hath quickened us together with Christ, (by grace ye are saved;)" (Eph. 2:4–5). He has extended His amazing love to us, undeserving though we are.

The Immortal Dies

Now unto the King eternal, immortal, invisible, the only wise God, be honor and glory for ever and ever. Amen" (1 Tim. 1:17).

The second verse of "And Can it Be That I Should Gain?" poses and solves a great mystery:

> 'Tis mystery all! the immortal dies!
> Who can explain this strange design?
> In vain the first-born seraph tries,
> To sound the depths of love divine;
> T'is mercy all! Let earth adore!
> Let angel minds inquire no more.

Our text reminds us that God is immortal. And yet, "Christ died for our sins" (1 Cor. 15:3) in order to bring us salvation. If this astounds us (and it should), we can take solace in that we are not alone. "Of which salvation the prophets have inquired and searched diligently, who prophesied of the grace that should come unto you: Searching what, or what manner of time the Spirit of Christ which was in them did signify, when it testified beforehand the sufferings of Christ, and the glory that should follow. Unto whom it was revealed, that not unto themselves, but unto us they did minister the things . . . which things the angels desire to look into" (1 Pet. 1:10–12).

Think of it! The Creator, the author of life, has died to offer eternal life to His creation, for "all have sinned" (Rom. 3:23) and the "wages of sin is death" (Rom. 6:23). He died so that we don't have to die! This grand plan remains beyond our full grasp as it always was to the prophets and the angels.

The motive behind His plan is God's mercy. "Not by works of righteousness which we have done, but according to his mercy he saved us . . . which he shed on us abundantly through Jesus Christ our savior" (Titus 3:5–6).

"O the depth of the riches both of the wisdom and knowledge of God! how unsearchable are his judgments, and his ways past finding out!" (Rom. 11:33). Amazing love!

His Mercy Found Me

For by grace are ye saved through faith; and that not of yourselves: it is the gift of God (Eph. 2:8).

The third verse of the hymn which has drawn our attention, "And Can it Be That I Should Gain?" sets the stage for the implementation of His majestic plan.

He left His father's throne above,
So free, so infinite His grace!
Emptied himself of all but love,
And bled for Adam's helpless race;
T'is mercy all! Immense and free,
For, O my God, it found out me!

The plan involved the death of God the Son. The Creator dying for the creation. The righteous judge taking on himself the penalty of the condemned. The rejected Holy One becoming sin on behalf of the true sinner. The convicted ones, powerless to alter the situation, simply receiving the offered grace through faith (see our text — Eph. 2:8).

First, God had to take on himself the nature of the condemned and live a guiltless life so that He could die as a substitutionary sacrifice. To do so, God the Son had to leave His Father's throne. And, although "being in the form of God, thought it not robbery to be equal with God [i.e., was willing to give up His kingly status]: But made himself of no reputation [literally, 'emptied himself'], and took upon him the form of a servant, and was made in the likeness of men . . . and became obedient unto death, even the death of the cross" (Phil. 2:6–8).

Adam had rebelled against his Creator's authority, and all of mankind suffered. "By one man sin entered into the world, and death by sin; and so death passed upon all men, for that all have sinned" (Rom. 5:12). Yet, Christ's work on the cross changed all that. "For if through the offence of one many be dead, much more the grace of God, and the gift by grace, which is by one man, Jesus Christ, hath abounded unto many" (v. 15). Amazing love!

My Chains Fell Off

But ye are a chosen generation, a royal priesthood, an holy nation, a peculiar people; that ye should show forth the praises of him who hath called you out of darkness into his marvelous light (1 Pet. 2:9).

The fourth verse of Charles Wesley's great hymn, "And Can it Be That I Should Gain?" compares Peter's miraculous deliverance from prison with a sinner's deliverance from bondage to sin. "Peter was sleeping . . . bound with two chains. . . . And, behold, the angel of the Lord came upon him, and a light shined in the prison . . . And his chains fell off from his hands. And the angel said unto him . . . follow me" (Acts 12:6–8).

> *Long my imprisoned spirit lay,*
> *Fast bound in sin and nature's night;*
> *Thine eye diffused a quick'ning ray,*
> *I woke, the dungeon flamed with light:*
> *My chains fell off, my heart was free,*
> *I rose, went forth, and followed thee.*

The Bible teaches that before being delivered, "ye were the servants of sin [in bondage to sin], but ye have obeyed from the heart that form of doctrine which was delivered you. Being then made free from sin, ye became the servants of righteousness" (Rom. 6:17–18). We were powerless to gain freedom on our own.

But "God, who commanded the light to shine out of darkness, hath shined in our hearts, to give the light of the knowledge of the glory of God in the face of Jesus Christ" (2 Cor. 4:6), bringing freedom and life.

"For Christ also hath once suffered for sins, the just for the unjust, that he might bring us to God, being put to death in the flesh, but quickened [made alive] by the Spirit" (1 Pet. 3:18). "And you, being dead in your sins . . . hath he quickened together with him, having forgiven you all trespasses" (Col. 2:13). If He has done all this for us, how can we do less than follow Him and accept His amazing love?

Alive in Him

I am crucified with Christ: nevertheless I live; yet not I, but Christ liveth in me: and the life which I now live in the flesh I live by the faith of the Son of God, who loved me, and gave himself for me (Gal. 2:20).

The final verse provides a fitting climax:

No condemnation now I dread,
Jesus, with all in Him, is mine;
Alive in Him, my living Head,
And clothed in righteousness divine,
Bold I approach th' eternal throne,
And claim the crown, thru Christ, my own.

"There is therefore now no condemnation to them which are in Christ Jesus, who walk not after the flesh, but after the Spirit" (Rom. 8:1). "Who is he that condemneth?" Not Christ! "It is Christ that died, yea rather, that is risen again, who is even at the right hand of God, who also maketh intercession for us" (v. 34).

As in our text, we are now alive through Christ's work on the cross. This gives us a standing far beyond our comprehension. "For in him dwelleth all the fulness of the Godhead bodily. And ye are complete in him" (Col. 2:9–10).

The song calls Him our "living Head," and so He is. Peter calls Him a "living stone, disallowed indeed of men, but chosen of God, and precious. . . . The same is made the head of the corner" (1 Pet. 2:4–7).

In response to His love, we "put off concerning the former conversation [way of living] the old man. . . . And that ye put on the new man, which after God is created in righteousness and true holiness" (Eph. 4:22–24). Dressed in His righteousness, "Let us therefore come boldly unto the throne of grace, that we may obtain mercy, and find grace to help in time of need" (Heb. 4:16). "Henceforth there is laid up for me a crown of righteousness, which the Lord, the righteous judge, shall give me at that day" (2 Tim. 4:8).

Amazing love! How can it be, that thou, my God, should'st die for me?

I Am His, and He Is Mine

G. Wade Robinson

James Mountain

1. Loved with ev - er - last - ing love, Led by grace that love to know
2. Heav'n a - bove is soft - er blue, Earth a - round is sweet - er green;
3. Things that once were wild a - larms Can - not now dis - turb my rest;
4. His for - ev - er, on - ly His Who the Lord and me shall part?

Spir - it, breath - ing from a - bove, Thou hast taught me it is so!
Some - thing lives in ev' - ry hue Christ - less eyes have nev - er seen!
Closed in ev - er - last - ing arms, Pil - lowed on the lov - ing breast!
Ah, with what a rest of bliss Christ can fill the lov - ing heart!

O this full and per - fect peace, O this trans - port all di - vine
Birds with glad - der songs o'er - flow, Flowers with deep - er beau - ties shine,
O to lie for - ev - er here, Doubt and care and self re - sign,
Heav'n and earth may fade and flee, First - born light in gloom de - cline,

In a love which can - not cease, I am His and He is mine.
Since I know, as now I know, I am His and He is mine.
While He whis - pers in my ear - I am His and He is mine.
But while God and I shall be, I am His and He is mine.

In a love which can - not cease, I am His and He is mine.
Since I know, as now I know, I am His and He is mine.
While He whis - pers in my ear, I am His and He is mine.
But while God and I shall be, I am His and He is mine.

I Am His, and He Is Mine

How often we sing songs without really knowing what we're singing. It still happens to me, even though I make a conscious effort to notice the words. Very often I'll be singing along and a phrase jumps off the page at me, reinforcing some biblical concept.

Such a thing happened one morning in church. I was leading the congregation in singing "I Am His, and He Is Mine." I had even enjoined the others to notice the beautiful expressions of God's love for us and our response of love to Him and asked them to reflect on their own walk with this loving Savior. The music itself is moving, and the words are precious, and I was entering into a deeper love even as we sang. The Lord is so near; His love is so sweet. It's an intimate love, not unlike but far surpassing the closeness felt in a Christian marriage with "whispers in the ear."

When we came to the last line of the last verse, a deep realization of God's never-ending love came over me. "But while God and I shall be, I am His, and He is mine." In the song, the last line of each verse is repeated, and I was so overcome by this fact, I choked up and couldn't even sing it that second time. These thoughts were relayed to the others and we paused to more fully reflect on their significance.

And ever since, whenever we've sung this song, I remind them that it's in my top ten and that the last line is the best. And even though I know it's coming, I still choke up. Something about this musical reminder of a beautiful doctrine moves me.

Think about it. How long will God exist? Forever! How long will I exist? Forever! Thus, I am His, forever, and He is mine, forever. As long as either or both of us exist, our bond of love will last.

The first verse of the hymn speaks of that "everlasting love" and "perfect peace," the second of the provision of our loving Creator and provider. The third speaks of "wild alarms," but they are of no consequence, nestled in His "everlasting arms." The final verse caps it all off, with a blessed reminder that His love is unquenchable, and we are never to be separated from that love.

Allow a few words from Christ to close this discussion. The love between our God and us is not a love between equals; it is solely a gift of His graceful nature. The analogy between mindless sheep and a loving shepherd helps our understanding. He said in John 10:27–30: "My sheep hear my voice, and I know them, and they follow me: And I give unto them eternal life; and they shall never perish, neither shall any man pluck them out of my hand. My Father, which gave them me, is greater than all; and no man is able to pluck them out of my Father's hand. I and my Father are one." Thus, "while God and I shall be, I am His and He is mine."

Perhaps you need a full assurance or reassurance of God's enduring love. Maybe this song will be used by God's Holy Spirit to more firmly ground you in this truth. ✄

Everlasting Love

The Lord hath appeared of old unto me, saying,
Yea, I have loved thee with an everlasting love: therefore with lovingkindness have I drawn thee (Jer. 31:3).

Perhaps no doctrine in Scripture is as clearly stated as
that expressed in our text and in many other passages. God
loves us! His love is an "everlasting love" and compels Him
to act strongly and lovingly on our behalf. "Herein is love,
not that we loved God, but that he loved us, and sent his Son
to be the propitiation for our sins" (1 John 4:10). This theme
finds glorious expression in the grand hymn of the last century entitled "I Am His, and He Is Mine."

> *Loved with everlasting love,*
> *Led by grace that love to know*
> *Spirit, breathing from above,*
> *Thou hast taught me it is so!*
> *O this full and perfect peace,*
> *O this transport all divine —*
> *In a love which cannot cease,*
> *I am His and He is mine.*

Jesus prayed, "I in them, and thou in me . . . that the
world may know that thou hast sent me, and hast loved them,
as thou hast loved me. Father, I will that they also, whom thou
hast given me, be with me where I am" (John 17:23–24). The
Father will never allow us to part from Him or our Savior.

These precious facts are taught to us by the "inspired"
(literally "God-breathed") Scriptures (2 Tim. 3:16), and "the
Comforter . . . the Spirit of truth . . . (who) will guide (us)
into all truth" (John 16:7–13). He drew us to himself "in
love: Having predestinated us unto the adoption of children
by Jesus Christ to himself" (Eph. 1:4–5). "Behold, what
manner of love the Father hath bestowed upon us, that we
should be called the sons of God" (1 John 3:1). In His grace
we come to Him, experiencing sweet forgiveness and everlasting love. Cradled in the security of His undying love, we
have peace. "Thou wilt keep him in perfect peace, whose
mind is stayed on thee" (Isa. 26:3).

Appreciating God's Creation

And the Lord God planted a garden eastward in Eden; and there he put the man whom he had formed. And out of the ground made the Lord God to grow every tree that is pleasant to the sight, and good for food (Gen. 2:8–9).

Everything in the Garden of Eden was prepared for man's enjoyment. In the time between creation and the curse, Adam and Eve no doubt fully enjoyed the vegetation (Gen. 2:5, 9, 15, 16), the animals (v. 19–20), the atmosphere and the weather (v. 5–6), the rivers and the raw materials (v. 10–14), each other (v. 18, 21–25), and fellowship with God (Gen. 3:8). But soon they rebelled and were driven from the beautiful Garden (Gen. 3:24), and ever since, mankind's ability to enjoy creation has been shackled somewhat, for creation was distorted by sin, and the eyes of each one of us have become dull.

The second verse describes a partial reopening of the eyes of a believer upon salvation as a love gift from our Lord.

> *Heav'n above is softer blue,*
> *Earth around is sweeter green;*
> *Something lives in ev'ry hue*
> *Christless eyes have never seen!*
> *Birds with gladder songs o'erflow,*
> *Flowers with deeper beauties shine,*
> *Since I know, as now I know,*
> *I am His and He is mine.*

In His abundant love for His children, our Lord promises to supply all our needs once again. "Why take ye thought for raiment? Consider the lilies of the field, how they grow; they toil not, neither do they spin: And yet I say unto you, That even Solomon in all his glory was not arrayed like one of these" (Matt. 6:28–29). Creation's beauty waits to thrill us and instruct us. Our loving Father wills it so.

But creation will be fully restored soon, and "the desert shall rejoice, and blossom as the rose. It shall blossom abundantly, and rejoice even with joy and singing" (Isa. 35:1–2). He beckons us to join Him in His kingdom.

His Everlasting Arms

The eternal God is thy refuge, and underneath are the everlasting arms: and he shall thrust out the enemy from before thee (Deut. 33:27).

The third verse of Wade Robinson's love poem to his Lord, "I Am His, and He Is Mine," remembers former times of alarm, fear, and doubt, but testifies of the rest and peace in His love, cradled in the "everlasting arms" of the Savior.

Things that once were wild alarms
Cannot now disturb my rest;
Closed in everlasting arms,
Pillowed on the loving breast!
O to lie forever here,
Doubt and care and self resign,
While He whispers in my ear —
I am His and He is mine.

This verse reminds us of the evening when Jesus and His disciples were in a boat, and a violent storm arose. They awoke Jesus from His sleep and cried, "Master, carest thou not that we perish?" (Mark 4:38). Of course Jesus cared, for He loved them. So "He arose, and rebuked the wind, and said unto the sea, Peace, be still" (v. 39). To His disciples He said, "Why are ye so fearful? how is it that ye have no faith?" (v. 40). The time would come when they would need that faith and peace. They would learn to rest in His loving care.

The song also reminds us of the special loving relationship between Jesus and John, the beloved disciple. "Now there was leaning on Jesus' bosom one of his disciples, whom Jesus loved" (John 13:23). A deep intimacy with Him was John's, and can be ours if we will only pillow our head on Him. No passage expresses that intimacy as well as the Song of Solomon, using the analogy of husband and wife to reflect the self-sacrificing love between our Lord and His children. "I am my beloved's, and my beloved is mine" (Song of Sol. 6:3).

The affairs of this life interrupt our times of intimacy with Him, but there will be a day when we will "ever be with the Lord" (1 Thess. 4:17).

While God and I Shall Be

For I am persuaded, that neither death, nor life, nor angels, nor principalities, nor powers, nor things present, nor things to come, Nor height, nor depth, nor any other creature, shall be able to separate us from the love of God, which is in Christ Jesus our Lord (Rom. 8:38–39).

The final verse of this majestic hymn focuses on the unending love between the believer and God. As we read in our text, nothing can "separate us from the love of God."

His forever, only His —
   Who the Lord and me shall part?
Ah, with what a rest of bliss
   Christ can fill the loving heart!
Heav'n and earth may fade and flee,
   First-born light in gloom decline,
But while God and I shall be,
   I am His, and He is mine.

Resting in such supernatural love which lasts forever begets peace and rest even now. Our Savior beckons, "Come unto me, all ye that labor and are heavy laden, and I will give you rest" (Matt. 11:28).

Aspects of our present life may be temporary, but His love lasts forever. "The heavens shall vanish away like smoke, and the earth shall wax old like a garment . . . but my salvation shall be for ever" (Isa. 51:6). "And even to your old age I am he; and even to hoar hairs will I carry you" (Isa. 46:4).

Consider the last line of the verse: "But while God and I shall be, I am His and He is mine." As long as either God or the individual remains, their love will last. "But the Lord shall endure for ever" (Ps. 9:7). "He hath said, I will never leave thee, nor forsake thee" (Heb. 13:5). Thus, the Christian "will dwell in the house of the Lord for ever" (Ps. 23:6).

"I know them, and they follow me: And I give unto them eternal life; and they shall never perish, neither shall any man pluck them out of my hand" (John 10:27–28).

Immortal, Invisible, God Only Wise

Walter Chalmers Smith

Welsh Hymn Melody

1. Im - mor-tal, in - vis - i - ble God on - ly wise,
2. Un - rest-ing, un-hast-ing, and si - lent as light,
3. To all, life thou giv-est, to both great and small;
4. Great Fa-ther of glo - ry, pure Fa - ther of light,

In light in - ac - ces - si - ble hid from our eyes,
Nor want-ing, nor wast-ing, Thou rul - est in might;
In all life thou liv - est, the true life of all;
Thine an - gels a - dore thee, all veil - ing their sight;

Most bless-ed, most glo-rious, the An - cient of Days,
Thy jus-tice like moun-tains high soar - ing a - bove,
We blos-som and flour-ish as leaves on a tree,
All praise we would ren - der; O help us to see

Al - might - y, vic - to - rious, thy great Name we praise.
Thy clouds which are foun-tains of good - ness and love.
And wi - ther and per - ish but naught chang-eth thee.
'Tis on - ly the splen-dor of light hi - deth thee!

8

Immortal, Invisible, God Only Wise

Looking back on my early years, I regret not having taken full advantage of the opportunities afforded me in our Christian home. My father was well known in Christian circles, and especially in our town. People from all over would come to see him. It seems like he was always bringing missionaries or pastors or Christian workers over for dinner, during which their hearts and ministries would be shared. Since the evening meal in our home was a ritual which could not be avoided, I was there and listened. As an adult I've tried to reconstruct some of those conversations, and I've even been blessed to meet some of those dear people again.

My memory fails and I don't know why, but I remember asking many of those lovable, godly, fruitful Christians what the most plaguing sin was in their life. Maybe it was a teenage fascination with sin, but I wanted to know. As they grew more and more Christlike, as they matured in the Lord, what was the sin they couldn't conquer? I was struggling with sin then, and maybe I wanted to justify my own failures, but I was surprised at the consistent answer.

Can you guess? What would be the most grievous sin in the lives of humble, godly Christians? Pride. I couldn't see a lick of pride in them, but many responded that pride was a gruesome reality in their lives. Even as rebellion was growing in me, I realized the seriousness of pride and concluded that the more mature one gets in their Christian walk, the closer they got to the Lord, and the more they recognized their own shortcomings. The more they knew of God's worthiness, the more they felt their own worthlessness, and the more grievous pride became. The closer they got to the Light, the clearer they could see their own darkness and knew that pride in any quantity had no place.

Oh, that I would be ever more convicted of pride. He alone is worthy to be praised. Now, one of my goals as a father is to expose my children to godly Christians, particularly those whose lives are dedicated to serving Him. Frequent contact with those who put their walk with God in the top priority and the needs of others before their own served me well in my younger days, and I trust is having an effect on my children as well.

Usually it takes several days of intense study and writing to develop a devotional based on a hymn. "Immortal, Invisible, God Only Wise" had been the total focus of my mind for several days when we sang it that morning in church. I pointed out to the congregation that the entire song is essentially a list of the attributes of God and quoted a verse or two that bore that out.

Several of the hymn's lines refer to God in His blinding brilliance. Just as we are blinded when we look briefly at the sun, its blinding light hiding it from view, so we are blinded to God's full essence by the unfathomable light we do see. Reflecting on His splendor, we can see our own imperfections "and pour contempt on all our pride," as another hymn puts it.

In our church is a dear Jewish man, who as an adult had acknowledged Jesus Christ as his Messiah. The congregation had not been asked to stand as we sang, but before the first verse was completed he stood, in honor of the majestic One to whom he sang. Soon another stood and another, until all were on their feet.

I learned a lesson that day. Some songs must be sung on your feet, but with hearts and knees bowed and with any semblance of pride discarded. ✶

Immortal, Invisible, God Only Wise

Now unto the King eternal, immortal, invisible, the only wise God, be honor and glory for ever and ever. Amen (1 Tim. 1:17).

Many of the grand old hymns of the faith consist of the actual words and phrases of Scripture, either repeated verbatim or paraphrased and collected around a doctrinal theme. Such is the case for the stately hymn "Immortal, Invisible, God Only Wise," where we find, almost in list form, the attributes and character of God.

> *Immortal, invisible God only wise,*
> *In light inaccessible hid from our eyes,*
> *Most blessed, most glorious, the Ancient of Days,*
> *Almighty, victorious, Thy great Name we praise.*

Obviously, much of the source for this first verse comes from the benediction in our text above. God is both eternal and immortal. "I AM THAT I AM" (Exod. 3:14) He called himself. Later we read that the immortal One died but rose from the dead and now "ever liveth to make intercession for [us]" (Heb. 7:25).

Daniel called Him the "Ancient of days" and described Him with great splendor and brilliance (Dan. 7:9–14). Paul called Him "the blessed and only Potentate, the King of kings, and Lord of lords; Who only hath immortality, dwelling in the light which no man can approach unto; whom no man hath seen, nor can see: to whom be honor and power everlasting. Amen" (1 Tim. 6:15–16).

Note Daniel's testimony of praise: "Blessed be the name of God for ever and ever: for wisdom and might are his: And he changeth the times and the seasons: he removeth kings, and setteth up kings . . . and the light dwelleth with him" (Dan. 2:20–22).

The Unresting God

> Hast thou not known? hast thou not heard, that
> the everlasting God, the Lord, the Creator of the ends
> of the earth, fainteth not, neither is weary? there is
> no searching of his understanding (Isa. 40:28).

The second verse of the mighty hymn "Immortal, Invisible, God Only Wise" continues with a listing of some of His attributes. Of course, the full list of His attributes as recorded in Scripture would be very long, but many of them are pieced together here in this verse in a way which emphasizes God's mighty works on behalf of His creation and us, His children, and His utter self-sufficiency and power.

> *Unresting, unhasting, and silent as light,*
> *Nor wanting, nor wasting, Thou rulest in might:*
> *Thy justice like mountains high soaring above,*
> *Thy clouds which are fountains of goodness and love.*

As revealed in our text, God's power is inexhaustible; He needs neither rest nor refreshment. He is not like the impotent Baal, "peradventure he sleepeth" (1 Kings 18:27), unable to hear and unable to answer.

God needs nothing from us. "Who hath first given to him, and it shall be recompensed unto him again? For of him, and through him, and to him, are all things: to whom be glory for ever. Amen" (Rom. 11:35–36).

He never wastes His energy nor His actions. "For ever, O Lord, thy word is settled in heaven" (Ps. 119:89).

Several thoughts in the hymn are echoed by David's praise to his Lord. "Thy mercy, O Lord, is in the heavens; and thy faithfulness reacheth unto the clouds. Thy righteousness is like the great mountains; thy judgments are a great deep: O Lord, thou preservest man and beast. How excellent is thy lovingkindness, O God! therefore the children of men put their trust under the shadow of thy wings" (Ps. 36:5–7).

Naught Changeth Thee

For all flesh is like grass, and all the glory of man as the flower of grass. The grass withereth, and the flower thereof falleth away: But the word of the Lord endureth for ever (1 Pet. 1:24–25).

What comparison can be made between the unchanging, eternal Creator of life and frail, temporal man? Verse three of the beautiful hymn "Immortal, Invisible, God Only Wise" makes such a comparison, or rather, such a contrast.

To all, life thou givest, to both great and small;
In all life thou livest, the true life of all;
We blossom and flourish as leaves on a tree,
And wither and perish, but naught changeth thee.

As in nature today, life comes only from life, and in the beginning, the living Creator imparted life to otherwise inanimate chemicals. To the plants and non-conscious animals, He gave only biological life; but to the creatures, from the smallest to the greatest, He gave true life (i.e., breath, blood, and consciousness); and to men, His image. As Creator, He needs nothing from His creation: "Neither is worshipped with men's hands, as though he needed any thing, seeing he giveth to all life, and breath, and all things" (Acts 17:25). Furthermore, "In him we live, and move, and have our being" (v. 28).

But the creation was distorted by sin, and now death reigns over all life, "like grass which groweth up. In the morning it flourisheth, and groweth up; in the evening it is cut down, and withereth" (Ps. 90:5–6).

But God lasts forever. "Before the mountains were brought forth, or ever thou hadst formed the earth and the world, even from everlasting to everlasting, thou art God" (Ps. 90:2). He doesn't change. "Jesus Christ the same yesterday, and to day, and for ever" (Heb. 13:8). And, as we see in our text, neither does His word change.

Father of Glory, Father of Lights

I saw also the Lord sitting upon a throne, high and lifted up, and his train filled the temple. Above it stood the seraphims: each one had six wings; with twain he covered his face. . . . And one cried unto another, and said, Holy, holy, holy, is the Lord of hosts" (Isa. 6:1–3).

The fourth and concluding verse of the hymn "Immortal, Invisible, God Only Wise" continues to recognize the majesty of our great God. His splendor is so great that even the angels must hide their eyes from the brightness (as we see in our text) while they adoringly praise His purity.

> *Great Father of glory, pure Father of light,*
> *Thine angels adore thee, all veiling their sight;*
> *All praise we would render; O help us to see*
> *'Tis only the splendor of light hideth thee!*

All light and life, as well as all good things, come from God. "Every good gift and every perfect gift is from above, and cometh down from the Father of lights, with whom is no variableness, neither shadow of turning" (James 1:17).

He is not only the "Father of lights" dispelling each "shadow," He is also the "Father of glory." Paul prayed for you and me: "That the God of our Lord Jesus Christ, the Father of glory, may give unto you the spirit of wisdom and revelation in the knowledge of him: The eyes of your understanding being enlightened" (Eph. 1:17–18). As with the hymnwriter, we need His help to fully see and praise Him.

Thus in one hymn we are reminded that God is immortal, invisible, wise, light, blessed, glorious, the Ancient of days, almighty, victorious, unresting, unhasting, unwanting, not wasteful, mighty, just, life, unchangeable, the Father of glory, the Father of light, and adored by angels. Furthermore, He dwells in splendor, deserves our praise, rules in might, provides goodness and love, gives life, and enlightens our understanding.

Stand Up, Stand Up For Jesus

George Duffield

George J. Webb

1. Stand up, stand up for Je - sus, Ye sol - diers of the cross, Lift
2. Stand up, stand up for Je - sus, The trump-et call o - bey; Forth
3. Stand up, stand up for Je - sus, Stand in His strength a - lone; The
4. Stand up, stand up for Je - sus, The strife will not be long; This

high His roy - al ban - ner, It must not suf - fer loss; From
to the might - y con - flict, In this His glo - rious day. "Ye
arm of flesh will fail you - Ye dare not trust your own; Put
day the noise of bat - tle, The next the vic - tor's song; To

vic - tory un - to vic - tory, His ar - my shall He lead, Till
that are men, now serve Him," A - gainst un - numb - ered foes; Let
on the gos - pel ar - mor, Each piece put on with prayer; Where
him that o - ver - com - eth, A crown of life shall be; He

ev - ery foe is van - quished And Christ is Lord in - deed.
cour - age rise with dan - ger, And strength to strength op - pose.
du - ty calls or dan - ger, Be nev - er want - ing there.
with the King of glo - ry shall reign e - ter - nal - ly.

9

Stand Up, Stand Up
for Jesus

Many students of hymns have designated the hymn, "Stand Up, Stand Up for Jesus," as one of the most stirring challenges to the Christian Church that exists. No doubt it has spurred many on to more effective spiritual warfare, both offensive and defensive.

Almost every collection of hymn stories contains this one, and its story is gripping. Truth may be stranger than fiction, but could this story be true?

It involves a dynamic young minister named Dudley Tyng in Philadelphia in 1858, . Both his father and grandfather had been Episcopal pastors, and at the age of 29 he had taken over as rector of the wealthy, upscale Church of the Epiphany. The congregation had been accustomed to good teaching but not the confrontational style of young Dudley. He called them to holiness and to make a difference in the community. The issue of slavery was dominating civic affairs in those days, and he found it unbiblical and immoral and spoke out against it in no uncertain terms. As you might imagine, this ruffled some feathers, and before long some of the congregation were encouraging him to go elsewhere, which he did, planting a new church, the Church of the Covenant.

His forceful preaching brought him certain notoriety, and soon he began preaching noontime evangelistic meetings at the downtown YMCA, attended by factory workers on their lunch break. The meetings grew until on March 30, 1858, over 5,000 men were present. His text was Exodus 10:11, and his plea was, "Go now ye that are men, and serve the Lord." As he spoke he proclaimed: "I must tell my Master's errand, and I would rather that this right arm were amputated at the trunk, than that I should come short of my duty to you in delivering God's message!" The newspapers reported that 1,000 men were converted that day.

Unbelievably, just two weeks later his clothing was caught in some farm machinery, pulling his arm into the cogs, mangling it badly. Within a few days, shock and infection set in, forcing doctors to remove both arm and shoulder in a futile attempt to save his life.

Just before he died, he was asked for a final word. Clutching his father's hand he said "Stand up for Jesus; Father, stand up for Jesus. Tell all my brethren of the ministry, wherever you meet them, to stand up for Jesus." A reporter standing nearby wrote that he asked his wife to bring up their sons to be ministers of the gospel and to tell them to "Stand up for Jesus" in their lives and pulpits.

Dudley Tyng's friend and fellow pastor, George Duffield, wrote the words to this song after the funeral and read them in church the following Sunday. Soon they were put to music and have been sung by millions ever since. Pastor Tyng had a great ministry in life, but perhaps in death, his words have challenged even greater multitudes to "Stand up for Jesus."

We can't fully understand all that happens to us in this life. God has said that, "My thoughts are not your thoughts, neither are your ways my ways, saith the Lord. For as the heavens are higher than the earth, so are my ways higher than your ways, and my thoughts than your thoughts" (Isa. 55:8–9).

We can only rest in His knowledge and sovereign control over all things. He doesn't necessarily cause such horrible things to happen to His servants, but He does allow them. We live in a sin-cursed world, dominated by wrong choices, by ourselves and others, and the consequences of those wrong choices. While He doesn't always shield us from harm, He does use every circumstance to accomplish His purposes in our lives, to bring about Christlike character.

I suspect, if we could see things from His omniscient perspective, we would see the rightness of it all. We would agree that He had truly acted (or not acted) toward us in His undying love, and in every thing we would give Him thanks. One day we may be able to understand even life's heartaches from His point of view and praise Him for them. ✄

Stand Up for Jesus

Watch ye, stand fast in the faith, quit you like men, be strong (1 Cor. 16:13).

Many times Scripture compares this life to a battle, with the Christian a soldier warring against the foe. The well-loved hymn of the last century "Stand Up for Jesus" reflects this theme. It was inspired by the dying words of a young pastor, fatally injured in a tragic accident.

Stand up, stand up for Jesus,
Ye soldiers of the cross,
Lift high His royal banner,
It must not suffer loss;
From victory unto victory,
His army shall He lead,
Till every foe is vanquished
And Christ is Lord indeed.

"My son, be strong in the grace that is in Christ Jesus. . . . Thou therefore endure hardness, as a good soldier of Jesus Christ" (2 Tim. 2:1–3), Paul commanded his younger disciple. Among other things, a good soldier of Christ is to represent his leader well, seeing that no dishonor comes to Him or His banner. With Christ as commander-in-chief, the victory is assured, and one day God will "make thy foes thy footstool" (Acts 2:35). "God also hath highly exalted him, and given him a name which is above every name: That at the name of Jesus every knee should bow, of things in heaven, and things in earth, and things under the earth; And that every tongue should confess that Jesus Christ is Lord, to the glory of God the Father" (Phil. 2:9–11).

As David the great warrior-king lay dying, he exclaimed, "Thine, O Lord, is the greatness, and the power, and the glory, and the victory, and the majesty: for all that is in the heaven and in the earth is thine; thine is the kingdom, O Lord, and thou art exalted as head above all" (1 Chron. 29:11). How foolish not to "Stand Up for Jesus."

Ye That Are Men Now Serve Him

And the angel of the Lord appeared unto him, and said unto him, The Lord is with thee, thou mighty man of valour. . . . Go in this thy might, and thou shalt save Israel from the hand of the Midianites: have not I sent thee?" (Judg. 6:12–14).

At the noontime YMCA meeting just days before his death, Dr. Tyng' sermon text was Exodus 10:11: "Go now ye that are men, and serve the Lord," a theme repeated in the second verse of "Stand Up for Jesus," written in his memory.

Stand up, stand up for Jesus,
The trumpet call obey;
Forth to the mighty conflict,
In this His glorious day.
"Ye that are men, now serve Him,"
Against unnumbered foes;
Let courage rise with danger,
And strength to strength oppose.

This verse reminds us of the task facing Gideon following his commission into God's army, as given in our text. Israel was defenseless and outnumbered, but "the Lord said unto him, Surely I will be with thee, and thou shalt smite the Midianites as one man" (Judg. 6:16).

The chosen warrior-to-be obeyed, and "the spirit of the Lord came upon Gideon, and he blew a trumpet" (v. 34), thus gathering a fighting force soon to be pared down to only 300 choice men (Judg. 7:7). With these courageous men, God wrought a mighty victory, overcoming a well-armed fighting force numbering over 120,000. Truly it was "His glorious day."

In summary, we might remember the Lord's promise to Joshua, Israel's first general: "There shall not any man be able to stand before thee all the days of thy life . . . I will be with thee: I will not fail thee, nor forsake thee. . . . Only be thou strong and very courageous" (Josh. 1:5–7).

Let us follow his lead and "Stand Up for Jesus."

And Having Done All, Stand

Ye stand this day all of you before the Lord your God; your captains of your tribes, your elders, and your officers, with all the men of Israel . . . That thou shouldest enter into covenant with the Lord thy God, and into his oath, which the Lord thy God maketh with thee this day (Deut. 29:10–12).

The Old Testament soldier of national Israel needed physical armor and weapons, but more than that, he needed the covenant protection of the Lord. Today, the New Testament saint seldom must fight in the physical sense, but a much more intense fight is raging: "For we wrestle not against flesh and blood, but against principalities, against powers, against the rulers of the darkness of this world, against spiritual wickedness in high places" (Eph. 6:12). We are safe and victorious as long as we "put on the whole armor of God" (v. 11). The third verse refers to this cosmic battle:

> *Stand up, stand up for Jesus,*
> *Stand in His strength alone;*
> *The arm of flesh will fail you—*
> *Ye dare not trust your own;*
> *Put on the gospel armor,*
> *Each piece put on with prayer;*
> *Where duty calls or danger,*
> *Be never wanting there.*

Years ago the Assyrians came against God's people. King Hezekiah reminded them: "Be strong and courageous, be not afraid nor dismayed. . . . With him is an arm of flesh; but with us is the Lord our God to help us, and to fight our battles" (2 Chron. 32:7–8).

The source of our victory is the same. Our "gospel armor" includes "truth . . . righteousness . . . peace . . . faith . . . salvation . . . and . . . the word of God" (Eph. 6:14–17). When we don it "with prayer" (v. 18), we will "be able to withstand in the evil day, and having done all, to stand" (v. 13).

Share the victory! "Stand Up for Jesus."

The Victor's Song

> And Moses said unto the people, Fear ye not, stand still, and see the salvation of the Lord, which he will show to you to day.... The Lord shall fight for you, and ye shall hold your peace (Exod. 14:13–14).

This song encourages each Christian to join in the battle and "Stand Up for Jesus." He has already assured us of ultimate victory, and, in the meantime, leads us into each skirmish. He gives us the privilege of participating with Him in His victories. And, at times, as we see in our text, He tells us to simply "stand still" and watch Him work.

The final verse of this hymn relates the long war's end.

> *Stand up, stand up for Jesus,*
> *The strife will not be long;*
> *This day the noise of battle,*
> *The next the victor's song;*
> *To him that overcometh,*
> *A crown of life shall be;*
> *He with the King of glory*
> *Shall reign eternally.*

The strife will indeed be over soon, especially if we measure time on the scale of eternity. Until then, "our light affliction, which is but for a moment, worketh for us a far more exceeding and eternal weight of glory; While we look not at the things which are seen, but at the things which are not seen: for the things which are seen are temporal; but the things which are not seen are eternal" (2 Cor. 4:17–18).

And what are some of these eternal rewards? "Be thou faithful unto death, and I will give thee a crown of life.... He that overcometh shall not be hurt of the second death" (Rev. 2:10–11). And, speaking of our home in the eternal New Jerusalem, "the throne of God and of the Lamb shall be in it; and his servants shall serve him: And they shall see his face. ... And they shall reign for ever and ever" (Rev. 22:3–5).

What blessings await those who "Stand Up for Jesus."

My Faith Has Found a Resting Place

Lidie H. Edmunds

Norse Air
Arr. by William Kirkpatrick

1. My faith has found a rest-ing place, Not in de-vice nor creed;
2. E-nough for me that Je-sus saves, This ends my fear and doubt;
3. My heart is lean-ing on the Word, the writ-ten Word of God,
4. My great Phy-si-cian heals the sick, The lost He came to save;

I trust the ev-er-liv-ing One, His wounds for me shall plead.
A sin-ful soul I come to Him, He'll nev-er cast me out.
Sal-va-tion by my Sav-ior's name, Sal-va-tion thru' His blood.
For me His pre-cious blood He shed, For me His Life He gave.

I need no oth-er ar-gu-ment, I need no oth-er plea,

It is e-nough that Je-sus died, And that He died for me.

10

My Faith Has Found a Resting Place

The Sunday morning hymns must be selected at least several days in advance in order to be printed in the bulletin. Occasionally I'll make a spur-of-the-moment change as the service progresses, in response to the flow of the service, but that does not happen often.

On Sunday evening, however, the song selections aren't printed, and I usually come with several more selected than we can use. Frequently there's time for "favorites," selected by the congregation. Often if we have guests I'll ask for their favorite hymn and a testimony of explanation.

One such evening we had a guest speaker, an ex-Catholic priest who has a ministry to Catholics, encouraging these dear people to stop trusting in ritual and heritage and to turn to the Savior. Jesus Christ alone can grant forgiveness and salvation. Through Him we can know we have eternal life. We can go directly to God without any intermediary other than Jesus Christ our Savior. In Him and Him alone we have new life and assurance of our destiny. By grace alone, through faith alone, we are declared righteous by a holy and just God. Our salvation depends solely on His response to our faith-filled repentance, and not at all on our works of righteousness.

When this former Catholic priest told me his favorite hymn, it was so appropriate. I couldn't resist asking the others if they could guess his favorite, and many did. "I need no other argument, I need no other plea, It is enough that Jesus died, and that He died for me" was his predictable testimony in song. The chorus of "My Faith Has Found a Resting Place" says it all. No works of my own, no prayers of a relative, and no absolution from a priest make any difference. The death and blood of Christ is our only valid defense before our Holy God.

This song is one of the many that have made it into my "Top 10." (I tried to list my "Top 10" recently, but stopped when the list topped 30.) In order to arrive at such an "elite" status, a song must have an effective blend of words and music. As you'll see in the pages to follow, the words of "My Faith Has Found a Resting Place" are thrilling, and the music has just the right combination of highs and lows to enhance the words.

Remember, I don't know music in any formal sense, I just know what speaks to me. This music comes from a fully secular source, having been adapted from an old Norse folk song. But good music is good music, and this is good music. I even love to listen to it as an orchestral arrangement without the words (but I can't listen without singing the words to myself). In combination, however, words and music make a dynamic whole, fitting of the foundational doctrinal significance of the absolute sufficiency of Christ's atoning sacrifice. ✼

A Resting Place

Not by works of righteousness which we have done, but according to his mercy he saved us, by the washing of regeneration, and renewing of the Holy Ghost; Which he shed on us abundantly through Jesus Christ our Savior (Titus 3:5–6).

Certainly one of the most precious doctrines of all Scripture is that reflected in our text. Our salvation depends not on our own "works of righteousness," but upon His mercy and grace, given us freely through the atoning work of Jesus Christ our Savior.

The grand old hymn found in almost every hymnal, "My Faith Has Found a Resting Place," reflects this theme. Let us use its four verses and chorus to focus our study as well as our hearts.

My faith has found a resting place, Not in device nor creed;
I trust the ever-living One, His wounds for me shall plead.

Nothing we could do (i.e., device) or nothing we or our church could believe (i.e., creed) can provide a resting place for our faith. "For we which have believed [i.e., faith, same Greek word] do enter into rest. . . . For he that is entered into his rest, he also hath ceased from his own works" (Heb. 4:3–10). The only work which counts for anything is that which the ever-living One accomplished when He died on the cross. "Who his own self bare our sins in his own body on the tree, that we, being dead to sins, should live unto righteousness: by whose stripes [wounds] ye were healed" (1 Pet. 2:24). It is not so much our physical health in view here, but the healing of our sin-sick souls.

Since "Christ died for our sins" (1 Cor. 15:3), there is no more penalty to be paid. Since He rose from the dead, He conquered both sin and its power, and our faith can rest.

I need no other argument, I need no other plea,
It is enough that Jesus died, And that He died for me.

Enough For Me

Being justified freely by his grace through the redemption that is in Christ Jesus: Whom God hath set forth to be a propitiation through faith in his blood, to declare his righteousness for the remission of sins that are past (Rom. 3:24–25).

Jesus has done all that is necessary to bring us into right standing with a holy God, if we but believe and accept His free gift of salvation. Jesus saves! It is enough! "In whom we have redemption through his blood, the forgiveness of sins, according to the riches of his grace" (Eph. 1:7). The second verse of the great hymn "My Faith Has Found a Resting Place" further explains this truth:

Enough for me that Jesus saves, This ends my fear and doubt;
A sinful soul I come to Him, He'll never cast me out.

Jesus who loved us, said, "Him that cometh to me I will in no wise cast out" (John 6:37). There is no fear here, for "There is no fear in love; but perfect love casteth out fear" (1 John 4:18). Nor should there be any doubt in Him or His intentions, "In whom we have boldness and access with confidence by the faith of him" (Eph. 3:12). Furthermore, "Being confident . . . that he which hath begun a good work in you will perform it until the day of Jesus Christ" (Phil. 1:6).

The chorus of the hymn likewise presents a thrilling truth. It paints a picture of a courtroom and the interrogation of a defendant. When asked why one should be forgiven, granted eternal life and entrance into heaven, the argument or legal defense can be given that Jesus has died, and that is enough. No other legal defense or answer need be given. The plea has already been entered, and the court's findings are guaranteed, "justified freely by his grace."

I need no other argument, I need no other plea,
It is enough that Jesus died, And that He died for me.

Leaning on the Word

And this is the record, that God hath given to us eternal life, and this life is in his Son. . . . These things have I written unto you that believe on the name of the Son of God; that ye may know that ye have eternal life, and that ye may believe on the name of the Son of God" (1 John 5:11–13).

Our salvation does not find its basis in an emotional experience of the heart, although our emotional tendencies are God-given and not to be denied. Indeed, the salvation experience may be sweet and memorable, but all sorts of religions, non-religions, and cults have emotional experiences — like the Mormon's "burning of the bosom." But experiences alone are subjective and easy to be misinterpreted. Our faith should be a faith from the heart, and it should be founded on the written word of God. The third verse of our hymn, "My Faith Has Found a Resting Place," presents this timeless truth.

My heart is leaning on the Word, the written Word of God,
Salvation by my Savior's name, Salvation thru His blood.

The Bible, God's holy word, is a book about Jesus, and how God, through Jesus, deals with man. Much more could have been written: "But these are written, that ye might believe that Jesus is the Christ, the Son of God; and that believing ye might have life through his name" (John 20:31). "Neither is there salvation in any other: for there is none other name under heaven given among men, whereby we must be saved" (Acts 4:12). We were redeemed "with the precious blood of Christ, as of a lamb without blemish and without spot" (1 Pet. 1:19).

And this is sufficient! Nothing else needs to be done or said or paid! Christ's blood is enough! His word tells us so.

I need no other argument, I need no other plea,
It is enough that Jesus died, And that He died for me.

I Need No Other Argument

Who hath delivered us from the power of darkness, and hath translated us into the kingdom of his dear Son: In whom we have redemption through his blood, even the forgiveness of sins (Col. 1:13–14).

Each of the four verses of the majestic hymn "My Faith Has Found a Resting Place" repeats the theme that Christ's blood was shed on our behalf, and it is enough. Nothing else remains to be done. The final verse adds perspective to the other three:

My great Physician heals the sick, The lost He came to save;
For me His precious blood He shed, For me His life He gave.

Christ was certainly "the great physician," for He "went about all Galilee . . . healing all manner of sickness" (Matt. 4:23). But His ministry was not only to the physically ill, for as He said, God "hath sent me to heal the brokenhearted, to preach deliverance to the captives" (Luke 4:18). His mission was a deeper one — that of healing the sin-sickness of the soul. "They that are whole have no need of the physician, but they that are sick: I came not to call the righteous, but sinners to repentance" (Mark 2:17). "For the Son of man is come to seek and to save that which was lost" (Luke 19:10).

As we read in our text, "We have redemption through his blood," and through His blood alone. As a result, we have "forgiveness of sins," we are "delivered from the power of darkness," and we are given a home in "the kingdom of his dear Son."

And there we will join in singing "a new song, saying, Thou art worthy . . . for thou wast slain, and hast redeemed us to God by thy blood out of every kindred, and tongue, and people, and nation" (Rev. 5:9). He has done it all, and He has done it "for me!"

I need no other argument, I need no other plea,
It is enough that Jesus died, And that He died for me.

The Old Rugged Cross

George Bennard

George Bennard

1. On a hill far a-way stood an old rug-ged cross, The em-blem of
2. Oh, that old rug-ged cross, so de-spised by the world, Has a won-drous at-
3. In the old rug-ged cross, stained with blood so di-vine, A won-drous
4. To the old rug-ged cross I will ev-er be true, Its shame and re-

suf-fering and shame; And I love that old cross where the dear-est and best
trac-tion for me; For the dear Lamb of God left His glo-ry a-bove
beau-ty I see, For t'was on that old cross Je-sus suf-fered and died
proach glad-ly bear; Then He'll call me some day to my home far a-way,

For a world of lost sin-ners was slain.
To bear it to dark Cal-va-ry. So I'll cher-ish the old rug-ged
To par-don and sanc-ti-fy me. cross, the
Where His glo-ry for-ev-er I'll share.

cross, Till my tro-phies at last I lay down; I will cling to the
old rug-ged cross,

old rug-ged cross, And ex-change it some day for a crown.
cross, the old rug-ged cross,

11

The Old Rugged Cross

Another song which has just the right melding of words and music is George Bennard's sensitive hymn, "The Old Rugged Cross." Every survey of favorite hymns places this one as perhaps the best loved of 20th century hymns.

We usually use it in my church during communion, singing it as either the bread or cup is being passed. Its moving melody and touching words encourage all to "remember" His death on our behalf. Surely everyone loves this song. Not so.

Once one of our people came with a concern. Is this not idolatry to "cherish" the cross, and promise to "ever be true" to the cross? Does this not take away from our devotion to the Christ of the cross? This was a new thought to me and needed resolution.

After study, meditation, and consultation with others, here are my thoughts and conclusion.

First, hymnwriters may experience "inspiration" in their writing, as an artist would be inspired, but they are not inspired in the same way that the Scriptures are inspired. The Scriptures came as "holy men of God spake as they were moved by the Holy Ghost" (2 Pet. 1:21). Thus, "All Scripture is given by inspiration of God, and is profitable for doctrine, for reproof, for correction, for instruction in righteousness:

That the man of God may be perfect, throughly furnished unto all good works" (2 Tim. 3:16–17).

Second, hymns are basically poems put to music. They may contain deep theological truth, but they will never stand up to the scrutiny with which we analyze Scripture. Poets are allowed to take poetic license to create a mood or impression, and when put to music, a spiritual poem can be most moving. Even scriptural "poems," like the psalms, contain allegories and word pictures which must not be taken too literally. God is not "a rock" for instance. He is a strong, enduring place of refuge, yes, but not limestone or granite. The true, "literal" interpretation recognizes the allegory or parable and discerns the proper meaning and application. We must never take them farther than intended.

Third, God has given us minds, but He has also given us emotions and a love for music, ordaining the use of both. We can enjoy hymns and allow them to lead us into worship and truth, but we must never mistake the words of a majestic hymn or the words of a godly pastor for the words of God. Nor should we piously deny them their proper — if imperfect — function, for then there would be no music nor preaching. Thus, in my *Days of Praise* devotionals, I never try to "exegete" a song, but I employ its words and structure to lead back to Scripture. And in our singing we must never place the song or its words on too high of a pedestal, but use the song, words, and music to lead us into true worship.

The author of this hymn was a deeply spiritual man, having studied the Scriptures relative to the cross for many years. He had had a seed thought for the song, and had even written the hauntingly beautiful melody before the words finally came. It was while conducting a series of revival meetings during which he preached of the true meaning of Christ's love as shown on Calvary (during which many knelt at the cross for salvation), that he himself was overtaken by the cross's importance. Soon the words came that would inspire the hearts of many. ✄

The Old Rugged Cross

God forbid that I should glory, save in the cross of our Lord Jesus Christ, by whom the world is crucified unto me, and I unto the world (Gal. 6:14).

As we ponder the crucifixion of our Lord Jesus Christ, a fuller understanding should bring us to an ever-deeper reliance on and identification with Him. To assist us in examining the work of Christ on the cross, let us use the beloved hymn, "The Old Rugged Cross." Here we will find its words reflecting a deep and abiding love for Christ and His cross. Let's start with its chorus:

> *So I'll cherish the old rugged cross,*
> *Till my trophies at last I lay down;*
> *I will cling to the old rugged cross,*
> *And exchange it some day for a crown.*

Our text reminds us that there is not worth in any deed of our own, including even a full adherence to the law of Moses (Gal. 6:12–13). Only through the cross and the salvation by grace made possible by the cross do we have any standing before God. We must cherish the cross and cling to it! Thus, we can say with Paul, that this "world is crucified unto me, and I unto the world" — its sinful allurements and the recognition of men of no value.

"Henceforth there is laid up for me a crown of righteousness, which the Lord, the righteous judge, shall give me at that day: and not to me only, but unto all them also that love his appearing" (2 Tim. 4:8). All our legitimate accomplishments, those true trophies or "crowns of rejoicing" (1 Thess. 2:19) done in His power and for His glory will be cast before His throne (Rev. 4:10) in recognition of His worth and kingship. His cross made it all possible.

So I'll cherish the old rugged cross.

On a Hill Far Away

And he bearing his cross went forth into a place called the place of a skull, which is called in the Hebrew Golgotha (John 19:17).

The Hebrew word *golgotha* and the Latin word *calvarie* actually mean "skull." The Romans had selected a place of execution outside Jerusalem (Heb. 13:12) but near the city (John 19:20), near a public highway (Matt. 27:39), and easily visible from some distance away (Mark 15:40). This has led many to speculate that it was on a hill, as in the first verse of the well-loved hymn, "The Old Rugged Cross."

> *On a hill far away stood an old rugged cross,*
> *The emblem of suffering and shame;*
> *And I love that old cross where the dearest and best*
> *For a world of lost sinners was slain.*

Truly His cross involved great suffering: "Christ also suffered for us. . . . Who his own self bare our sins in his own body on the tree, that we, being dead to sins, should live unto righteousness: by whose stripes ye were healed" (1 Pet. 2:21–24). Likewise, it involved great shame: "Christ hath redeemed us from the curse of the law, being made a curse for us: for it is written, Cursed is every one that hangeth on a tree" (Gal. 3:13). But this suffering and shame was not in vain, for as we see in both passages above, it was on our behalf. "Greater love hath no man than this, that a man lay down his life for his friends" (John 15:13).

However, God's dearest and best, indeed God's "only begotten son" (John 3:16) was slain, not so much for "friends," but for enemies! A world of lost sinners put Him on the cross. "But God commendeth his love toward us, in that, while we were yet sinners, Christ died for us. . . . When we were enemies, we were reconciled to God by the death of his Son" (Rom. 5:8–10).

So I'll cherish the old rugged cross.

Dark Calvary

Now from the sixth hour there was darkness over all the land unto the ninth hour (Matt. 27:45).

The second verse of the grand old hymn, "The Old Rugged Cross," contains much truth, rich and deep.

Oh, that old rugged cross, so despised by the world,
Has a wondrous attraction for me;
For the dear Lamb of God left His glory above
To bear it to dark Calvary.

The world despises the cross and the One on the cross. "He is despised and rejected of men; a man of sorrows, and acquainted with grief: and we hid as it were our faces from him; he was despised, and we esteemed him not" (Isa. 53:3). But yet, even in His bloodied and broken form, there is a wondrous attraction, for "surely he hath borne our griefs, and carried our sorrows. . . . He was wounded for our transgressions, he was bruised for our iniquities: the chastisement of our peace was upon him; and with his stripes we are healed" (v. 4–5).

His death substituted for ours, He was the sacrificial "Lamb of God, which taketh away the sin of the world" (John 1:29). This Lamb is none other than God the Son, who willingly "took upon him the form of a servant, and was made in the likeness of men . . . and became obedient unto death, even the death of the cross" (Phil. 2:7–8).

Remarkably, even God the Father "despised" Him as He hung on the cross, for God is holy, and for our sakes had "made him to be sin for us, who knew no sin; that we might be made the righteousness of God in him" (2 Cor. 5:21). The apex of Christ's suffering came, as we see in our text, when God the Father separated himself from His beloved Son, "forsaking" (Matt. 27:46) Christ to suffer for three hours the awful pangs of hell which we deserved.

So I'll cherish the old rugged cross.

Stained with Blood So Divine

But when they came to Jesus, and saw that he was dead already . . . one of the soldiers with a spear pierced his side, and forthwith came there out blood and water (John 19:33–34).

As with many of the great hymns, the verses of "The Old Rugged Cross" tell a story when considered in sequence. The first verse states the general doctrine of the cross; the second speaks of the necessity of the incarnation to accomplish the cross's purpose; the third, quoted below, gives details of the crucifixion and what it accomplished; and the last verse rehearses the results, both now and in the future.

In the old rugged cross, stained with blood so divine,
A wondrous beauty I see,
For t'was on that old cross Jesus suffered and died
To pardon and sanctify me.

That old rugged cross was stained with blood, as is obvious from our text. But this blood was special, for "ye know that ye were not redeemed with corruptible things, as silver and gold. . . . But with the precious blood of Christ, as of a lamb without blemish and without spot: Who verily was foreordained before the foundation of the world" (1 Pet. 1:18–20).

The divine Lamb of God suffered and died on the cross. "In whom we have redemption through his blood, even the forgiveness of sins" (Col. 1:14), "that he might sanctify the people with his own blood" (Heb. 13:12).

But the old rugged cross was not the only thing stained that day, for "the blood of Jesus Christ . . . cleanseth us from all sin" (1 John 1:7). The saints in heaven are portrayed as having "washed their robes, and made them white in the blood of the Lamb" (Rev. 7:14). "Come now, and let us reason together, saith the Lord: though your sins be as scarlet, they shall be as white as snow" (Isa. 1:18).

So I'll cherish the old rugged cross.

I Will Ever Be True

Looking unto Jesus the author and finisher of our faith; who for the joy that was set before him endured the cross, despising the shame, and is set down at the right hand of the throne of God (Heb. 12:2).

The concluding verse of our song, "The Old Rugged Cross," contains a commitment to follow Christ in this life and looks forward to life with Him in eternity.

To the old rugged cross I will ever be true,
Its shame and reproach gladly bear;
Then He'll call me some day to my home far away,
Where His glory forever I'll share.

When coupled with the preceding scriptural verse, our text mirrors these thoughts: "Let us lay aside every weight, and the sin which doth so easily beset us, and let us run with patience the race that is set before us" (Heb. 12:1). In this life, we have both the victorious examples of many that have gone before (Hebrews 11) and Christ himself. Both He and they have suffered joyfully, and so can we: "Beloved, think it not strange concerning the fiery trial which is to try you . . . But rejoice, inasmuch as ye are partakers of Christ's sufferings; that, when his glory shall be revealed, ye may be glad also with exceeding joy. If ye be reproached for the name of Christ, happy are ye" (1 Pet. 4:12–14).

Once Christ fully "endured the cross," He rose from the dead in victory over death to take His rightful place "at the right hand of the throne of God." He now calls us to be "crucified with Christ" (Gal. 2:20), "in whom we have redemption through his blood, the forgiveness of sins" (Eph. 1:7). He'll call us some day to himself, where we shall "sit together in heavenly places in Christ Jesus" (Eph. 2:6), "and so shall we ever be with the Lord" (1 Thess. 4:17).

So I'll cherish the old rugged cross.

Arise, My Soul, Arise

Charles Wesley

Lewis Edson

1. A - rise, my soul, a - rise; Shake off thy guilt - y fears;
2. He ev - er lives a - bove; For me to in - ter - cede,
3. Five bleed - ing wounds He bears, Re - ceived on Cal - va - ry.
4. The Fa - ther hears Him pray, His dear A - noint - ed One;
5. My God is rec - on - ciled; His par - doning voice I hear.

The bleed - ing Sac - ri - fice in my be - half ap - pears:
His all - re - deem - ing love, His pre - cious blood to plead;
They pour ef - fect - ual prayers; They strong - ly plead for me.
He can - not turn a - way The pres - ence of His Son.
He owns me for His child; I can no lon - ger fear.

Be - fore the throne my Sure - ty stands, Be - fore the throne my
His blood a - toned for all our race His blood a - toned for
"For - give him, oh, for - give," they cry, "For - give him, oh, for -
His Spir - it an - swers to the blood, His Spir - it an - swers
With con - fi - dence I now draw nigh, With con - fi - dence I

Sure - ty stands, My name is writ - ten on His hands.
all our race And sprin - kles now the throne of grace.
give," they cry, "Nor let that ran - somed sin - ner die."
to the blood, And tells me I am born of God.
now draw nigh, And, "Fa - ther, Ab - ba, Fa - ther," cry.

12

Arise, My Soul, Arise

Charles Wesley wrote many songs. All which have maintained their popularity are full of deep spiritual insights and loaded with Scripture. Such is the case with "Arise, My Soul, Arise," but although it's in nearly every modern hymnal, I have never heard it sung outside our little church. People need to be reminded of its existence, for it truly is a song worth singing.

Actually, I did hear it sung once, not in a church, but believe it or not, by my wife's hairdresser. Carol had lived a very rough and sinful life. While working as a licentious blackjack dealer in Las Vegas, she had heard the gospel and the freedom from bondage to sin which it offered. Claiming Christ's atoning sacrifice as applicable to her sins, she was radically and permanently changed.

We met her at Christian Heritage College where my wife taught part time. Carol was working as a hairdresser and taking Bible courses — learning all she could about her Lord, preparing for a lifetime of ministry to those in darkness, similar to that from which she had been delivered. They soon became close friends.

Oh, how Carol loves the Lord! And how she loves good Christian music, having left the worldly music scene in which she had been trapped. She joined us on a long drive one day, crossing a seemingly endless desert. As the sharing of

Scripture and the trading of testimonies eventually turned to singing favorite hymns, she suggested her favorite, "Arise, My Soul, Arise." We had never heard it, but she knew every verse. As she sang I had difficulty understanding its meaning. Only more careful thought allowed the message to come clear.

The scene of the song is God's throne, where Christ is interceding to the Father on our behalf. While Scripture does assure us that this interchange actually does take place, we seldom actually think about it in concrete terms. Evidently Charles Wesley did.

In the song, the sinner is encouraged to truly believe that the transaction of forgiveness can take place, and the believer is challenged to truly believe that his sins are gone and new life is his. It's quite a remarkable song!

One can envision the young Charles Wesley penning this song as his own personal testimony. Years of doubting God's love and forgiveness finally vanished before the truth of Christ's redeeming love and completely sufficient atoning sacrifice, allowing him to approach the Father's throne with confidence.

Two different musical scores are used for this song. One is an old Norman melody adapted by Daniel Towner and the other composed by Lewis Edson. To me the latter fits the dignified words better, and I prefer it. So does Carol. ❧

Arise, My Soul, Arise

Let us therefore come boldly unto the throne of grace, that we may obtain mercy, and find grace to help in time of need (Heb. 4:16).

Let us use the five verses of this beautiful old hymn, seldom sung anymore, to focus our thoughts.

Arise, my soul, arise; Shake off thy guilty fears;
The bleeding sacrifice in my behalf appears:
Before the throne my surety stands, (repeat)
My name is written on His hands.

At first reading, the theme of the song seems unclear, until we recognize that the sinner is being enjoined to come to salvation and by the power of the sacrificial blood shed on his behalf, receive forgiveness and eternal life.

Because "Christ . . . hath given himself for us an offering and a sacrifice to God" (Eph. 5:2) "we have peace with God through our Lord Jesus Christ: By whom also we have access" (Rom. 5:1–2) to the Father, who alone has the power to forgive our sins. We have no need to fear rejection, for "we have an advocate with the Father, Jesus Christ the righteous" (1 John 2:1).

As we see in our text, we can arise and "come boldly unto the throne of grace," where God the Father reigns. We have assurance of access because our "surety of a better testament" (Heb. 7:22) is "a great high priest, that is passed into the heavens, Jesus the Son of God" (Heb. 4:14), and "who is (seated) on the right hand of the throne of the Majesty in the heavens" (Heb. 8:1). Here He requests the Father's "mercy and . . . grace" on our behalf, for He knows us by our names which are already "written in the Lamb's book of life" (Rev. 21:27) "from the foundation of the world" (Rev. 17:8).

For Me to Intercede

Wherefore he is able also to save them to the uttermost that come unto God by him, seeing he ever liveth to make intercession for them (Heb. 7:25).

The second verse of the moving old hymn "Arise, My Soul, Arise" speaks of Christ's intercessory work on our behalf and the basis on which His prayers are accepted.

He ever lives above; For me to intercede,
His all-redeeming love, His precious blood to plead.
His blood atoned for all our race (repeat)
And sprinkles now the throne of grace.

Our text contains the primary thought that Christ is our intercessor, pleading with the Father to save us from our sins, for which the penalty has been paid by His "sacrifice . . . for this he did once, when he offered up himself" (Heb. 7:27). It is "the precious blood of Christ, as of a lamb without blemish and without spot" (1 Pet. 1:19) which pleads for our forgiveness. He does this for us because He "loved us, and washed us from our sins in his own blood" (Rev. 1:5) as we come to God in repentant faith.

Because Jesus was himself a fully righteous man, He could die on another's behalf; because He was fully God the Son, His death was sufficient to pay the penalty for the whole human race. "Jesus Christ the righteous: And he is the propitiation for our sins: and not for ours only, but also for the sins of the whole world" (1 John 2:1–2). "Thou art worthy . . . for thou wast slain, and hast redeemed us to God by thy blood out of every kindred, and tonue, and people, and nation" (Rev. 5:9).

Only in this way can we come "to the general assembly and church of the firstborn, which are written in heaven, and to God the Judge of all, and to the spirits of just men made perfect, And to Jesus the mediator of the new covenant, and to the blood of sprinkling" (Heb. 12:23–24).

Forgive Him, Oh Forgive

Who his own self bare our sins in his own body on the tree, that we, being dead to sins, should live unto righteousness: by whose stripes ye were healed (I Pet. 2:24).

The third verse of the majestic hymn by Charles Wesley, "Arise, My Soul, Arise," relates how the crucified but risen intercessor, Christ, pleads with the Father to save a sinner, and why His prayers are heard.

Five bleeding wounds He bears, Received on Calvary.
They pour effectual prayers; They strongly plead for me.
"Forgive him, oh, forgive," they cry, (repeat)
"Nor let that ransomed sinner die."

When Jesus was crucified, they "pierced [His] hands and feet" (Ps. 22:16) and "pierced his side" with a spear (John 19:34). After His resurrection His disciples would view these five wounds (John 20:27). It was from these wounds that His blood flowed, "and without shedding of blood [there] is no remission" of sins. "So Christ was once offered to bear the sins of many" (Heb. 9:22–28). Our text for today declares that it was His "stripes" (literally, "wounds") which heal us of our deadly sin sickness. His death provides life and health and righteousness.

If "the effectual fervent prayer of a righteous man availeth much" (James 5:16), surely the pleadings of Christ, a perfectly righteous "Man," are of infinite strength. "Neither pray I for these alone [His disciples], but for them also which shall believe on me through their word . . . [that they] be with me where I am" (John 17:20–24).

As a truly repentant sinner comes in faith to God seeking forgiveness for his sins, Christ pleads, "Forgive him, oh, forgive."

"For there is one God, and one mediator between God and men, the man Christ Jesus; who gave himself a ransom for all" (1 Tim. 2:5–6).

His Spirit Answers to the Blood

But if the Spirit of him that raised up Jesus from the dead dwell in you, he that raised up Christ from the dead shall also quicken your mortal bodies by his Spirit that dwelleth in you (Rom. 8:11).

The fourth verse of the precious old hymn, "Arise, My Soul, Arise," speaks of God the Father answering the request of God the Son and granting salvation to a repentant sinner, adopting him into His family.

The Father hears Him pray, His dear Anointed One;
He cannot turn away The presence of His Son.
His Spirit answers to the blood, (repeat)
And tells me I am born of God.

As Christ the Messiah (which literally means "the anointed One") hung on Calvary's tree, God the Father turned away, unable in His holiness to look upon Christ as He bore "the sins of many" (Heb. 9:28). "My God, my God, why hast thou forsaken me?" (Ps. 22:1) He cried in His agony. But once God's righteous justice was satisfied, the Father turned back and answered Christ's prayer, even from the horns of the altar, as it were (Ps. 22:21). "I and my Father are one," Christ had said (John 10:30), and once sin's penalty was paid, there would be no more separation.

When a sinner comes to God, claiming the blood of Christ as a full payment for his sins, and Christ himself prays for the sinner's full forgiveness and acceptance, the Father cannot turn away, for "He loved us, and sent his Son to be the propitiation for our sins" (1 John 4:10).

In our text, the same Spirit which raised up Christ grants the spiritually dead sinner new life and declares him to be born of God. "Marvel not that I say unto thee, Ye must be born again (John 3:7)," literally, "born from above." "Behold, what manner of love the Father hath bestowed upon us, that we should be called the sons of God" (1 John 3:1).

Father, Abba, Father

They are the sons of God. For ye have not received the spirit of bondage again to fear; but ye have received the Spirit of adoption, whereby we cry, Abba, Father (Rom. 8:14–15).

This great hymn concludes in the fifth verse with a stirring testimony of the joy of salvation.

My God is reconciled; His pardoning voice I hear.
He owns me for His child; I can no longer fear.
With confidence I now draw nigh, (repeat)
And, "Father, Abba, Father," cry.

"If any man be in Christ, he is a new creature: old things are passed away; behold, all things are become new. And all things are of God, who hath reconciled us to himself by Jesus Christ" (2 Cor. 5:17–18). As our text explains, once we have received the Spirit of adoption, we are the sons of God — He owns us as His child. We who formerly were estranged from our Creator have been reconciled to Him, for He is "reconciled" to the fact that His Son's death allows Him to pardon our sins. The close-knit ties are strong, "for he hath said, I will never leave thee, nor forsake thee" (Heb. 13:5).

Now that He is our Father, we have direct access to Him. "Draw nigh to God, and he will draw nigh to you" (James 4:8). As an earthly father desires the best for his children, "how much more shall your Father which is in heaven give good things to them that ask him?" (Matt. 7:11). "And this is the confidence that we have in him, that, if we ask any thing according to his will, he heareth us: And . . . we know that we have the petitions that we desired of him" (1 John 5:14–15).

This father/child relationship goes deep. The term "Abba, Father" reflects a most sensitive and loving bond, perhaps best rendered "O Sweet Daddy."

"We pray you in Christ's stead, be ye reconciled to God" (2 Cor. 5:20).

A Mighty Fortress Is Our God

Martin Luther
Trans. by Frederick H. Hedge

Martin Luther

1. A might-y for-tress is our God, A bul-wark nev-er fail - ing;
2. Did we in our own strength con-fide, Our striv-ing would be los - ing;
3. And though this world, with dev-ils filled, Should threat-en to un - do us,
4. That word a-bove all earth-ly powers, No thanks to them, a-bid - eth;

Our help-er He, a - mid the flood Of mor-tal ills pre - vail - ing:
Were not the right Man on our side, The Man of God's own choos - ing:
We will not fear, for God hath willed His truth to tri - umph through us:
The Spir-it and the gifts are ours Thro' Him who with us sid - eth:

For still our an - cient foe Doth seek to work us woe; His craft and power are
Dost ask who that may be? Christ Je-sus, it is He, Lord Sa - ba - oth, His
The Prince of Dark-ness grim - We trem-ble not for him; His rage we can en -
Let goods and kin - dred go, This mor-tal life al - so; The bod - y they may

great, And, armed with cru-el hate, On earth is not his e - qual.
name, From age to age the same, And He must win the bat - tle.
dure, For lo, his doom is sure, One lit - tle word shall fell him.
kill: God's truth a - bid-eth still, His king - dom is for - ev - er.

13

A Mighty Fortress Is Our God

Martin Luther, the father of the Reformation, wrote this song. In his lifetime he, among other things, translated the Bible into German so that the common man could have access to it. As a Catholic monk, he defied the pope and the established church, denying their claim of sole arbitrator of forgiveness and salvation. He opened the way for women to more directly participate in worship and study. And, in direct application to this present context, he reintroduced congregational singing to the Church, a source of great joy and encouragement to all. Eventually he compiled a complete hymn book and is personally credited with 37 hymns. This hymn was written in 1529.

The great reformer (as some call him) was a man of unusual insight. Today, theologians and pastors can read commentaries of those that have gone before, but Luther and the other reformers were starting "on the ground floor." The Church owes them all a debt of gratitude.

Regarding music, he once said: "The devil hates music because he cannot stand gaiety," and "Satan can smirk, but he cannot laugh; he can sneer, but he cannot sing." This led one writer to conclude that "Luther translated the Bible into German so God could speak directly to the people in His

Word and provided the hymnal so that the people could answer God in their songs."

Martin Luther was also a man much persecuted, even being excommunicated by the pope, thus breaking all ties and allegiance to his former training and church. Furthermore, there was governmental abuse resulting even in the death of many fellow dissenters from the established order, and, of course, direct satanic opposition. But he was a man who was willing to stand alone if need be. Through his work, the light of truth was beginning to shine, exposing the darkness, and Satan, the prince of darkness, must oppose such a work.

Even though he was a great man who accomplished great things, he was still just a man, subject to discouragement and even occasional bouts of severe depression. In one such lengthy bout, he turned to Scripture for his consolation and found Psalm 46 of great comfort and inspiration. He focused his energies and prayers on resisting Satan's deceptions in his own mind, and from that victorious battle came the words to "A Mighty Fortress Is Our God."

This powerful hymn has now been translated into practically every major language, sometimes more than once. There are about 60 translations of it in English alone.

Try reading the words to this song as you would a paragraph, and you'll discover that none of the verses can be omitted when sung. It forms one continuous thought, almost a run-on sentence. The most powerful rendition of it I ever heard was at a recent ICR Graduate School graduation ceremony. The soloist sang without accompaniment, almost "preaching" the song rather than "singing" it. Together, this loose paraphrase of Psalm 46 buoys the Christian spirit and proclaims great hope to all.

Some have attributed the music to Luther himself, but others have noted its similarity to an old German folk song, probably sung in taverns. But despite its source, its melodic rises and falls fit the tenor of the song, reminiscent of a mighty army on the march. Its triumphant sound stands in marked contrast to the dull and mystical chants practiced in the Roman Church. Seems fitting for a declaration of victory over Satan's devices, does it not? ✖

A Mighty Fortress Is Our God

God is our refuge and strength, a very present help
in trouble. Therefore will not we fear (Ps. 46:1–2).

Martin Luther, the central figure in the Reformation,
was keenly aware of spiritual warfare. His journal entries
inform us of his continual battle against evil forces and that
Psalm 46 was a great comfort to him. As he meditated on the
words of our text, the thrust of a mighty song was born which
openly declared victory in the great battle. We have come to
know this song as "A Mighty Fortress Is Our God." Let us
use its four verses to focus our thoughts on that victory.

A mighty fortress is our God, a bulwark never failing;
Our helper He, amid the flood Of mortal ills prevailing:
For still our ancient foe Doth seek to work us woe;
His craft and power are great,
*   And, armed with cruel hate,*
On earth is not his equal.

The battle to be fought is "not against flesh and blood,
but against principalities, against powers, against the rulers of the darkness of this world, against spiritual wickedness in high places" (Eph. 6:12). Satan, along with his hench-
men, is an ancient foe, "a roaring lion," as it were, "seeking
whom he may devour" (1 Pet. 5:8). But there is no need for
alarm, "the Lord of hosts is with us; the God of Jacob is our
refuge" (Ps. 46:11). He "is our refuge and strength," a bul-
wark never failing. "For this purpose the Son of God was
manifested, that he might destroy the works of the devil" (1
John 3:8).

Only God could accomplish this victory, for Satan is "the
prince of this world" (John 14:30), "the prince of the power
of the air" (Eph. 2:2). No man on earth is his equal.

But how did the Son of God gain the victory? By taking
on himself "flesh and blood," and dying a substitutionary
death, "that through death he might destroy him that had
the power of death, that is, the devil" (Heb. 2:14).

The Right Man on Our Side

Behold, Satan hath desired to have you, that he may sift you as wheat: But I have prayed for thee, that thy faith fail not (Luke 22:31–32).

Our Lord warned Peter — Satan wanted him to fall, and fall he would (v. 34), but Christ had prayed for him that victory would come. The second verse of Martin Luther's grand hymn, "A Mighty Fortress Is Our God," reflects our vulnerable position on our own and our invincibility on His side.

Did we in our own strength confide,
Our striving would be losing;
Were not the right man on our side,
The man of God's own choosing:
Dost ask who that may be? Christ Jesus it is He,
Lord Sabaoth, His name, From age to age the same,
And He must win the battle.

After revealing a list of many thrilling blessings to the child of God, Paul asks: "What shall we then say to these things? If God be for us, who can be against us?" (Rom. 8:31). Furthermore, nothing, neither "principalities, nor powers" nor any thing else in all creation is "able to separate us from the love of God, which is in Christ Jesus our Lord" (Rom. 8:38–39). With Him on our side, Satan cannot win in the battle for our minds or destinies. But if we rely on our own strength, we cannot win.

The term Lord Sabaoth might confuse us until we recognize that this is not the sabbath, or seventh day. *Sabaoth* is the Hebrew word for "hosts," in particular the "host of heaven." The term "Yahweh Sabaoth" or Lord Sabaoth occurs some 300 times in the Old Testament, and constitutes a most majestic name for God. "For thy Maker is thine husband; the Lord of hosts is his name; and thy Redeemer the Holy One of Israel; The God of the whole earth shall he be called" (Isa. 54:5). This is none other than "Jesus Christ the same yesterday, and to day, and for ever" (Heb. 13:8).

Christ Jesus — Creator (Col. 1:16), sustainer (v. 17), Redeemer (v. 20). He must win the battle.

His Doom Is Sure

Ye are of your father the devil, and the lusts of your father ye will do. He was a murderer from the beginning, and abode not in the truth, because there is no truth in him. When he speaketh a lie, he speaketh of his own: for he is a liar, and the father of it (John 8:44).

The third verse of the Reformation hymn, "A Mighty Fortress Is Our God," focuses on the certain end of Satan. God has willed a mighty triumph through His truth.

And though this world, with devils filled,
*   Should threaten to undo us,*
We will not fear, for God hath willed
*   His truth to triumph through us:*
The Prince of Darkness grim — We tremble not for him;
His rage we can endure, For lo, his doom is sure,
One little word shall fell him.

When Satan was cast from heaven, fully a third of the angels fell with him (Rev. 12:4), such that a "legion" of them could inhabit one individual (Mark 5:9). They are evidently everywhere doing Satan's bidding, giving him the power to accomplish his malevolent desires.

But God has other plans for His children. He desires "to turn them from darkness to light, and from the power of Satan unto God, that they may receive forgiveness of sins" (Acts 26:18). He desires us to "resist the devil" (James 4:7), and not "give place to the devil" (Eph. 4:27).

He also has plans for Satan, including "everlasting chains under darkness" (Jude 6), and "everlasting fire, prepared for the devil and his angels" (Matt. 25:41). Just one little word and Satan will be "cast into the lake of fire and . . . tormented day and night for ever and ever" (Rev. 20:10).

Jesus, anticipating His coming execution, spoke of it in triumphant terms. This had been His Father's will all along. "Now," He said, "shall the prince of this world be cast out. And I, if I be lifted up from the earth, will draw all men unto me" (John 12:31–32), and now the battle is His.

His Kingdom Is Forever

Let us lay aside every weight, and the sin which doth so easily beset us, and let us run with patience the race that is set before us, Looking unto Jesus the author and finisher of our faith; who for the joy that was set before him endured the cross, despising the shame, and is set down at the right hand of the throne of God (Heb. 12:1–2).

The four verses of "A Mighty Fortress Is Our God" could be considered one long statement, with each verse building directly on the one before. This final verse describes our tools and comportment while in the battle, and the final victory.

That word above all earthly powers,
  No thanks to them, abideth;
The Spirit and the gifts are ours
  Thro' Him who with us sideth:
Let goods and kindred go, This mortal life also;
The body they may kill: God's truth abideth still,
His kingdom is forever.

As soldiers in the King's army, we have certain God-given abilities and possessions, most notably the indwelling Spirit of God and the empowering gifts of the Spirit. "If any man have not the Spirit of Christ, he is none of his" (Rom. 8:9). "Now there are diversities of gifts, but the same Spirit" (1 Cor. 12:4).

We should "fear not them which kill the body, but are not able to kill the soul" (Matt. 10:28). Our focus should be on Him, "denying ungodliness and worldly lusts" (Luke 9:60–62) even goods and kindred if need be, but "we should live soberly, righteously, and godly, in this present world; Looking for that blessed hope, and the glorious appearing of the great God and our Savior Jesus Christ" (Titus 2:12–13).

As of yet the battle continues. "To him that overcometh will I grant to sit with me in my throne," promises the risen Christ, "even as I also overcame, and am set down with my Father in his throne" (Rev. 3:21). "And so shall we ever be with the Lord" (1 Thess. 4:17).

Thou Didst Leave Thy Throne

Emily E. S. Elliot

Timothy R. Matthews

1. Thou didst leave thy throne And thy king - ly crown When thou cam - est to earth for me; But in Beth - le - hem's home was there found no room For thy ho - ly na - tiv - i - ty. O come to my heart, Lord Je - sus, There is room in my heart for thee.

2. Heav - en's arch - es rang When the an - gels sang, Pro - claim - ing thy roy - al de - cree; But of low - ly birth Didst thou come to earth, And in great hu - mil - i - ty. O come to my heart, Lord Je - sus, There is room in my heart for thee.

3. The fox - es found rest, And the birds their nest In the shade of the for - est tree; But thy couch was the sod, O thou Son of God, In the des - erts of Gal - i - lee. O come to my heart, Lord Je - sus, There is room in my heart for thee.

4. Thou cam - est, O Lord, with the Liv - ing Word That should set thy peo - ple free; But with mock - ing scorn And with crown of thorn They bore thee to Cal - va - ry. O come to my heart, Lord Je - sus, There is room in my heart for thee.

5. When the heavens shall ring And the an - gels sing At thy com - ing to vic - to - ry, Let thy voice call me home, Say - ing, "Yet there is room, There is room at My side for thee." My heart shall re - joice, Lord Je - sus, When thou com - est and call - est for me!"

14

Thou Didst Leave Thy Throne

Emily Elliot was born into a dedicated and musical Christian family of Brighton, England, in 1836. Her father was a minister of the evangelical wing of the Anglican Church and her aunt, Charlotte Elliot, the author of the much-loved hymn, "Just As I Am." From an early age she gave herself to the ministry of service to the less fortunate, from rescue missions to street children to bedridden invalids. Some 48 of her hymns were published in a book of hymns entitled *Under the Pillow*, designed especially for saints confined in hospitals and nursing homes.

The beautiful song "Thou Didst Leave Thy Throne" contains five verses, each of which consist of doctrinal and scriptural content, while the chorus is pure devotional application. This Christmas hymn was written principally for the children in her father's church, to help them learn more fully the Christmas story and message. From personal experience with the children of my own family, I know that it still accomplishes its mission. Let me tell you of an innovative use of it.

My older sister and her husband, with their three boys, have served their entire married lives in missions, with lengthy stays in the jungles of New Guinea and the Philippines, translating the Bible into tribal languages and bringing the Good News to those in desperate need who would otherwise have never heard it. They raised their three boys in substantial isolation from the trappings of American Christendom and had to devise original ways to teach them things that we assume children will learn by osmosis here. In just that way, she used this hymn to emphasize the necessity of personal salvation.

At Christmas time, using the journey of Mary and Joseph to Bethlehem as a backdrop, she would station her husband and two older boys behind various curtains in their primitive home. With her youngest, then a toddler, she would go to the first door, behind which was the father, and ask: "Is there any room here for me and my baby?" The answer: "No, no room in here." Then he would join them in their journey to the second door. "Is there any room here for me and my baby? Any room at all?" "No, there's no room here. You'll have to go somewhere else." Then the four would go to the last room. "Is there any room here? Please let us come in." "No, you can't come in. There's no room for you here."

Finally, as parents and all three boys were together, they would sing "O come to my heart, Lord Jesus, There is room in my heart for thee." I suspect that this teaching tool was probably more effective than yearly Christmas pageants. ✄

Thou Didst Leave Thy Throne

Christ Jesus: Who, being in the form of God, thought it not robbery to be equal with God: But made himself of no reputation, and took upon him the form of a servant, and was made in the likeness of men (Phil. 2:5–7).

This lovely Christmas carol tells the story of Christ's incarnation, birth, life, and death, ending with hope for the future and assurance of salvation. We should note the little word, "but," for each of the first four verses pivots on it, while it is conspicuously absent in the fifth.

Thou didst leave thy throne And thy kingly crown
When thou camest to earth for me;
But in Bethlehem's home Was there found no room
For thy holy nativity.

Our text sets forth how God the Son set aside His kingly crown and came to earth as a man, to live a sinless life and die a perfect sacrifice. The passage continues, "And being found in fashion as a man, He humbled himself, and became obedient unto death, even the death of the cross" (Phil. 2:8).

The song declares that He did this for "me," and so He did, for "Christ Jesus came into the world to save sinners; of whom I am chief" (1 Tim. 1:15). "Neither is there salvation in any other: for there is none other name under heaven given among men, whereby we must be saved" (Acts 4:12).

His status was kingly and His mission gracious, but His birth in Bethlehem was very lowly from a human perspective. "And she [Mary] brought forth her firstborn son, and wrapped him in swaddling clothes, and laid him in a manger; because there was no room for them in the inn" (Luke 2:7). Nevertheless, we can make room for Him.

O come to my heart, Lord Jesus, There is room in my heart for thee.

Heaven's Arches Rang

And suddenly there was with the angel a multitude of the heavenly host praising God, and saying, Glory to God in the highest, and on earth peace, good will toward men (Luke 2:13–14).

When Christ came to earth for His first advent, many angels serving in God's mighty army ("host") of "ministering spirits" (Heb. 1:14) briefly left their posts and battle stations to gather above the shepherd's field in Bethlehem and joined in mighty chorus to praise God for the wondrous plan of redemption now underway. The second verse of the well-loved Christmas carol, "Thou Didst Leave Thy Throne," echoes this event.

> *Heaven's arches rang When the angels sang,*
> *Proclaiming thy royal decree;*
> *But of lowly birth Didst thou come to earth,*
> *And in great humility.*

Yes, the King had been born, but the angel said to the shepherds, "Ye shall find the babe [the King] wrapped in swaddling clothes, lying in a manger. . . . And they came with haste, and found Mary, and Joseph, and the babe lying in a manger" (Luke 2:12–16).

Jesus continued that life of humility, "For ye know the grace of our Lord Jesus Christ, that, though he was rich, yet for your sakes he became poor, that ye through his poverty might be rich" (2 Cor. 8:9), expanding it into a lifestyle of service and example.

"Ye call me Master and Lord: and ye say well; for so I am. If I then, your Lord and Master, have washed your feet; ye also ought to wash one another's feet. For I have given you an example, that ye should do as I have done to you" (John 13:13–15).

O come to my heart, Lord Jesus, There is room in my heart for thee.

The Foxes Found Rest

Are not five sparrows sold for two farthings, and not one of them is forgotten before God? (Luke 12:6).

The third verse of "Thou Didst Leave Thy Throne" discusses the human condition of our Savior in His life on earth. From outward appearances, He and His disciples were frequently homeless and penniless without any of the comforts we consider necessary.

> *The foxes found rest, And the birds their nest*
> *In the shade of the forest tree;*
> *But thy couch was the sod, O thou Son of God,*
> *In the deserts of Galilee.*

As we see in the text verse above, even the sparrows have a home, but not Him. Likewise, "A certain scribe came, and said unto him, Master, I will follow thee whithersoever thou goest. And Jesus saith unto him, the foxes have holes, and the birds of the air have nests; but the Son of man hath not where to lay his head" (Matt. 8:19–20).

God has graciously provided for all of His creation, but the Son of God chose to suffer deprivation and hardship so that He can fully minister to us even now, completely identifying with each and every human problem. "Forasmuch then as the children are partakers of flesh and blood, he also himself likewise took part of the same. . . . For in that he himself hath suffered being tempted, he is able to succor [help] them that are tempted" (Heb. 2:14–18).

There was a point at which Christ had somewhere "to lay his head." On the cross, after He had completed all that was necessary to accomplish our salvation, He cried out with a loud voice, "It is finished: and he bowed his head, and gave up the ghost" (John 19:30). The Greek verb "to bow" is the same as "to lay."

O come to my heart, Lord Jesus, There is room in my heart for thee.

The Living Word Came

And the Word was made flesh, and dwelt among us, (and we beheld his glory, the glory as of the only begotten of the Father,) full of grace and truth (John 1:14).

The life of any individual without Christ is marked by bondage — bondage to sin and its penalty, death. "But when the fullness of the time was come, God sent forth his Son, made of a woman, made under the law, To redeem [free from bondage] them that were under the law" (Gal. 4:4–5). His Son, of course, is none other than Jesus Christ, identified as the living "Word made flesh" in our text.

The fourth verse of "Thou Didst Leave Thy Throne" reflects this transaction.

> *Thou camest, O Lord, with the Living Word*
> *That should set thy people free;*
> *But with mocking scorn And with crown of thorn*
> *They bore thee to Calvary.*

His creation should have welcomed Him gladly, gratefully accepting this free redemption from bondage, but, instead, they "stripped him, and put on him a scarlet robe. And when they had platted a crown of thorns, they put it upon his head, and a reed in his right hand: and they bowed the knee before him, and mocked him, saying, Hail, King of the Jews!" (Matt. 27:28–29).

Then they bore Him "to the place, which is called Calvary, there they crucified him" (Luke 23:33).

This work of liberation and freedom from bondage merits our lifelong thankfulness and devotion, for His death bought our freedom. "Stand fast therefore in the liberty wherewith Christ hath made us free, and be not entangled again with the yoke of bondage" (Gal. 5:1). As freed slaves, we are free to say,

O come to my heart, Lord Jesus, there is room in my heart for thee.

The Heavens Shall Ring

> Death is swallowed up in victory. O death, where is thy sting? O grave, where is thy victory? . . . Thanks be to God, which giveth us the victory through our Lord Jesus Christ (1 Cor. 15:54–57).

The final verse of the stirring song "Thou Didst Leave Thy Throne" looks to the future, when all that has gone before will come to culmination.

Christ's birth, life, and death will find full and final expression in ultimate and eternal victory.

> *When the heavens shall ring And the angels sing*
> *At thy coming to victory;*
> *Let thy voice call me home, Saying, "Yet there is room,*
> *There is room at My side for thee."*

As we noted in verse two, the angelic host proclaimed His first coming to the startled shepherds in the field. At His second coming, this "innumerable company of angels" will be joined by "the general assembly and church of the firstborn, which are written in heaven . . . and to the spirits of just men made perfect" (Heb. 12:22–23), all gathered around the throne of God.

Together we will thank Him and serve Him and sing His praises forever.

There is no "but" in this final verse of the hymn. "For all the promises of God in him are yea, and in him Amen, unto the glory of God by us" (2 Cor. 1:20).

Notice, instead, the precious reminder that while God's attention envelops all of redeemed mankind, yet He still focuses on each individual. When the time comes, He will personally welcome each of us to His side. "My sheep hear my voice, and I know them, and they follow me: And I give unto them eternal life; and they shall never perish" (John 10:27–28).

My heart shall rejoice, Lord Jesus, when thou comest and callest for me!

According to Thy Gracious Word

James Montgomery

Arthur Cottman

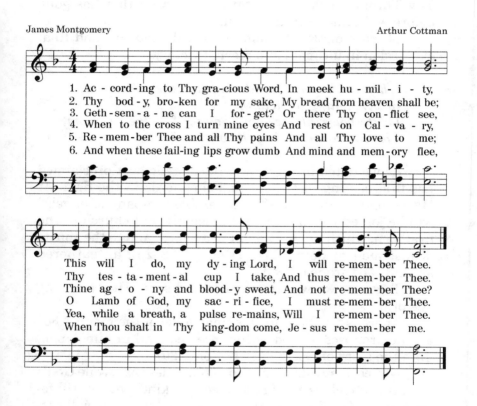

1. Ac - cord-ing to Thy gra-cious Word, In meek hu - mil - i - ty,
2. Thy bod - y, bro-ken for my sake, My bread from heaven shall be;
3. Geth - sem - a - ne can I for - get? Or there Thy con - flict see,
4. When to the cross I turn mine eyes And rest on Cal - va - ry,
5. Re - mem-ber Thee and all Thy pains And all Thy love to me;
6. And when these fail-ing lips grow dumb And mind and mem-ory flee,

This will I do, my dy - ing Lord, I will re-mem-ber Thee.
Thy tes - ta - ment-al cup I take, And thus re-mem-ber Thee.
Thine ag - o - ny and blood-y sweat, And not re-mem-ber Thee?
O Lamb of God, my sac - ri - fice, I must re-mem-ber Thee.
Yea, while a breath, a pulse re-mains, Will I re-mem-ber Thee.
When Thou shalt in Thy king-dom come, Je - sus re-mem-ber me.

15

According to Thy Gracious Word

I'm a small-church guy. While mega-churches minister to many, I prefer a church home where we can be involved, where my family is missed if we're not there, and where we can be an integral part of the ministry.

The small church where my family now attends, and at which I serve as elder and song leader, was started as a church plant in 1992. There had been a good church in the building before, but a long series of unfortunate occurrences led to the church closing and the building standing empty for several years. The members all dispersed, except, that is, for a handful of "veteran" Christian ladies, who continued to meet weekly and pray that God would once again raise up a Bible-teaching witness in that modest facility.

At long last their prayers were answered, and a godly young man agreed to plant a church. He, too, was a man of prayer and joined with the ladies to ask God's blessing. Together they formed a praying nucleus, and God has granted their requests.

I had been impressed with this young man as a student in two scientific apologetics classes I had taught in Bible college and had kept up with him. When we were able to join him, there were about 20 people attending, including the ladies and several new Christians.

In choosing a church, I first look for good biblical teaching, which was present. But as much as I like good singing, this isn't a requirement — it's icing on the cake! As it turns out, the music ministry at this little church plant had room, shall we say, for growth.

A small, out-of-tune piano remained from before, but it didn't come with a pianist. Phyllis (one of the "praying" ladies) could play a little, mostly with just one hand. She loves her Lord and serves Him with a whole heart and did what she could, but her prayers, however, turned to asking God to send talented musicians.

When I came, I was no help, since liking music doesn't mean you know music. One week when Phyllis was away, I offered to play my guitar and lead the singing and took over the role of leading from then on. Meanwhile, Phyllis kept playing as best she could and praying for musically minded Christians. Since then, God has blessed abundantly through new members and young people who have grown into ministry-mindedness, including each of my three teenagers. Now we have so many good pianists, good violinists, horn blowers, organists, and soloists that music is a church strength. Now she should pray for a song director that can read music!

Phyllis does what I sometimes do — uses a hymnal in her own personal quiet time with God. Over the months she grew to love my hymn studies in *Days of Praise* and suggested I consider this communion hymn, "According to Thy Gracious Word." It was new to me, but I soon grew to love it. It was written by the beloved hymnwriter James Montgomery. Born of missionary parents, he was an outspoken advocate of both foreign and home missions throughout his life and even spent time in prison for his opposition to slavery. His biblical wisdom and spiritual maturity were acknowledged by all who knew him. This hymn of remembrance reveals his deep understanding of the Cross and our need to always "remember" the transaction completed there. ✀

I Will Remember Thee

The Lord Jesus . . . took bread: And when he had given thanks, he brake it, and said, Take, eat: this is my body, which is broken for you: this do in remembrance of me. . . . This cup is the new testament in my blood: this do ye, as oft as ye drink it, in remembrance of me (1 Cor. 11:23–25).

The occasion of our text is, of course, the last supper Christ ate with His disciples before He was betrayed and crucified, dying a sacrificial death for our sins. At this meal He instituted the precious ordinance of communion, to be regularly observed by Christians, during which we are to "remember" His death in a special way.

A touching communion hymn entitled "According to Thy Gracious Word" helps focus our thoughts on Christ's ordeal.

According to thy gracious word,
In meek humility,
This will I do, my dying Lord,
I will remember thee.

The Greek structure of the verb "do" (used twice in our text), signifies a command to continue "doing" this action as an integral part of one's lifestyle. We are to make it a habit to regularly observe the "Lord's Supper," as it has come to be known, when we "come together" (1 Cor. 11:33) with other Christians. His gracious word has told us to do so, and we must obey.

But this should not be done in meaningless rote but, as our song says, in meekness and humility. Those who do so "unworthily [literally, 'in an unworthy manner'], shall be guilty of the body and blood of the Lord" (v. 27). A careful self-examination (v. 28) should reveal all unconfessed sin, to be followed by true repentance and forgiveness. Then we can fully "remember" Him.

Thy Testamental Cup I Take

And he took bread, and gave thanks, and brake it, and gave unto them, saying, This is my body which is given for you: this do in remembrance of me. Likewise also the cup after supper, saying, This cup is the new testament in my blood, which is shed for you (Luke 22:19–20).

The sensitively written second verse of the song speaks of the communion elements and their meaning to us.

Thy body, broken for my sake,
My bread from heaven shall be;
Thy testamental cup I take,
And thus remember thee.

In the Book of Hebrews we read that "it is not possible that the blood of bulls and of goats should take away sins" (Heb. 10:4), even though the covenant of God with the people of Israel included many such sacrifices. These were merely "a shadow of good things to come" (v. 1), pointing toward the ultimate and fully sufficient sacrifice of the sinless and undeserving Son of God on the cross. He has said, for this purpose "a body hast thou prepared me" (v. 5), and "I come . . . to do thy will, O God" (v. 7).

This divinely "prepared" body was "broken" on the Cross. He was battered and brutalized, scourged, and spit upon, mocked and pierced for our sake, taking upon himself the punishment due us. The bread partaken of on the communion table helps us never to forget.

The cup symbolized His blood, shed for us, as His very life poured out in sacrifice. Our text speaks of the new testament, or new covenant, by which He has, of His own will, committed himself to us and sealed the covenant with His blood. He has done all that was necessary — the only thing we can do is simply believe, partake of His testamental cup — and remember.

Can I Forget?

And they came to a place which was named Gethsemane: and he saith to his disciples, Sit ye here, while I shall pray. . . . My soul is exceeding sorrowful unto death: tarry ye here, and watch (Mark 14:32–34).

The prayerful agony of our Lord in Gethsemane's garden on the night of His betrayal is reflected in the third verse of this stirring communion hymn, written in the mid-1800s.

Gethsemane can I forget?
Or there thy conflict see,
Thine agony and bloody sweat,
And not remember thee?

Actually, this verse asks a question: Lord, how could I ever forget the intense events of that night?

A mighty war was waged that night, a great conflict of soul. "And he went forward a little, and fell on the ground, and prayed that, if it were possible, the hour might pass from him. And he said, Abba, Father, all things are possible unto thee; take away this cup from me: nevertheless not what I will, but what thou wilt" (Mark 14:35–36). In His humanity, He certainly shrank from the torturous death before Him, but in His Spirit, pure and undefiled as it was, He recoiled from the world of sin — my sin and your sin about to become His — and the infinite separation between the Holy Father and the sin-laden sacrifice which would follow. His agony was so great that the physician Luke records that "His sweat was as it were great drops of blood falling down to the ground" (Luke 22:44), a rare but extremely painful response of the brow to intense emotional struggle as pore after pore burst until His entire forehead was one gaping wound.

When we acknowledge that this struggle was for our eternal welfare, and that He struggled alone as His disciples slept, how could we not remember?

To the Cross I Turn My Eyes

Looking unto Jesus the author and finisher of our faith; who for the joy that was set before him endured the cross, despising the shame, and is set down at the right hand of the throne of God (Heb. 12:2).

The mere thought of the Cross should evoke in our hearts an ever-deepening thankfulness for the eternal work accomplished there. This is the theme of verse four of the hymn.

> *When to the cross I turn mine eyes*
> *And rest on Calvary,*
> *O Lamb of God, my sacrifice,*
> *I must remember thee.*

"And when they were come to the place, which is called Calvary, there they crucified him" (Luke 23:33). The Roman occupiers of Israel executed many, sometimes for the slightest of offenses. They invented the hideous execution method of crucifixion, which had been prophesied in great detail in Psalm 22. In all likelihood, many had been executed at Calvary, some no doubt undeserving, but none like this!

For the One to whom we turn our eyes is none other than the Lamb of God. "Behold the Lamb of God, which taketh away the sin of the world" (John 1:29), a "lamb without blemish and without spot" (1 Pet. 1:19), "the Lamb slain from the foundation of the world" (Rev. 13:8).

But the death of the Lamb takes on infinite proportions when we recognize that His death was a sacrificial death for us. For "Christ also suffered for us. . . . [He] who did no sin, neither was guile found in his mouth . . . Who his own self bare our sins in his own body on the tree, that we, being dead to sins, should live unto righteousness" (1 Pet. 2:21–24).

"God forbid that I should glory, save in the cross of our Lord Jesus Christ" (Gal. 6:14). And God forbid that we should fail to remember.

Remember Thy Love to Me

That Christ may dwell in your hearts by faith; that ye, being rooted and grounded in love, May be able . . . to know the love of Christ, which passeth knowledge (Eph. 3:17–19).

Christ's sacrificial love for us was remarkable. "Greater love hath no man than this, that a man lay down his life for his friends" (John 15:13), but "Christ died for the ungodly. . . . God commendeth his love toward us, in that, while we were yet sinners, Christ died for us" (Rom. 5:6, 8). The fifth verse of the grand old communion hymn we are studying remembers that love.

> *Remember thee and all thy pains*
> *And all thy love to me;*
> *Yea, while a breath, a pulse remains*
> *Will I remember thee.*

The gospels give graphic portrayals of the physical suffering endured by Christ on the cross, but a prophetic passage equally explicit is found in Isaiah, where we read that because of His treatment, "His visage was so marred more than any man" (Isa. 52:14). He had "no form nor comeliness . . . no beauty" (Isa. 53:2). In His sacrificial role He was "despised and rejected of men; a man of sorrows, and acquainted with grief" (v. 3). Why did He endure all this? "He was wounded for our transgressions, he was bruised for our iniquities: . . . the Lord hath laid on him the iniquity of us all" (v. 5–6).

How should we react? Certainly by accepting His free gift of forgiveness based on the truth that our sins are already paid for, but also with a heart of loving remembrance throughout our entire lives.

And on into eternity! "Behold, what manner of love the Father hath bestowed upon us, that we should be called the sons of God" (1 John 3:1). Our adoption into His family lasts forever, as will our remembrance of His love and work.

Jesus, Remember Me

And thou shalt love the Lord thy God with all thy heart, and with all thy soul, and with all thy mind, and with all thy strength: this is the first commandment (Mark 12:30).

Each verse in this hymn has encouraged us to "remember" various aspects of Christ's atoning death on Calvary. The final verse looks to the future, when age or illness or even death saps our strength and mind. Surely we will "remember" Him throughout eternity, but there's more.

And when these failing lips grow dumb
And mind and memory flee,
When thou shalt in thy kingdom come,
Jesus remember me.

Paul wrote, "That if thou shalt confess with thy mouth the Lord Jesus, and shalt believe in thine heart that God hath raised him from the dead, thou shalt be saved" (Rom. 10:9). Those who have "confessed" him have been saved; granted eternal life. This life lasts for all time, even in times of physical frailty. Jesus said, "Whosoever therefore shall confess me before men, him will I confess also before my Father which is in heaven" (Matt. 10:32).

Jesus even prayed for us, "Father, I will that they also, whom thou hast given me, be with me where I am" (John 17:24). Furthermore He said, "I am the resurrection, and the life: he that believeth in me, though he were dead, yet shall he live" (John 11:25).

The hymn's last two lines remind us of the words of the repentant thief on the cross next to Jesus. "Lord, remember me when thou comest into thy kingdom" (Luke 23:42). The response? "Today shalt thou be with me in paradise" (v. 43).

We have no fear, even of death, for He shall remember us!

Deeper and Deeper

Oswald J. Smith

Oswald J. Smith

1. In-to the heart of Je - sus, deep - er and deep - er I go,
2. In-to the will of Je - sus, deep - er and deep - er I go,
3. In-to the cross of Je - sus, deep - er and deep - er I go,
4. In-to the joy of Je - sus, deep - er and deep - er I go,
5. In-to the love of Je - sus, deep - er and deep - er I go,

Seek-ing to know the rea - son why He should love me so—
Pray-ing for grace to fol - low, seek-ing His way to know;
Fol - low-ing through the gar - den, fac - ing the dread-ed foe—
Ris - ing with soul en - rap - tured far from the world be - low;
Prais-ing the One who brought me out of my sin and woe;

Why He stooped to lift me up from the mir - y clay,
Bow - ing in full sur - ren - der low at His bless-ed feet,
Drink - ing the cup of sor - row, sob - bing with brok - en heart;
Joy in the place of sor - row, peace in the midst of pain,
And through e - ter - nal a - ges grate - ful - ly I shall sing;

Sav-ing my soul, mak-ing me whole, Though I had wan-dered a - way.
Bid-ding Him take, break me and make, Till I am mold-ed and meet.
"Oh, Sav-iour, help! Dear Sav-iour, help! Grace for my weak-ness im - part."
Je - sus will give, Je - sus will give, He will up - hold and sus - tain.
"Oh, how He loved! Oh, how He loved! Je - sus, my Lord and my King."

16

Deeper and Deeper

Dalta and I have been led to home school our children, and it has been a real blessing in our home. The children have flourished, both spiritually and academically, and we are glad for the "home-school movement" and thankful for the many like-minded friends who have supported us in this endeavor.

For a number of years we used the curriculum developed by Bill Gothard's Institute in Basic Life Principles. Monthly "wisdom booklets" form the core of this curriculum, designed to foster godly character and personal Bible study habits. Each "wisdom booklet" includes one hymn, and students are given the task of researching its history and the life of the author, resulting in a written research paper. Combining academic tasks with scriptural and spiritual projects is an excellent way to learn. Since I have gathered books on such subjects over the years, our young people may have had an easier time of this than most, but the exercise was good for them.

One such featured hymn was Oswald J. Smith's, "Deeper and Deeper." Dr. Smith, long-time pastor of the large People's Church of Toronto, Canada, is recognized as one of the greatest evangelical pastors and missions advocates of our century. Over the many years of his ministry, he wrote numerous fine songs which you would recognize, but he considered this one his most profound. It was also one of his very first.

A young man of 21, he was to preach one Sunday morning in 1911. As he walked, a tune began to form in his mind. Keeping time with his footsteps, he added the words, "Into the heart of Jesus, deeper and deeper I go," to the first line. The entire tune was crystal clear, but no matter how hard he tried, the other words which he added didn't seem to fit. No matter, his joy was great as he preached that morning, praying he could remember the tune until he could write it down. This was accomplished that afternoon. But the words came hard, requiring three long years of life applications to complete.

In his memoirs, written years later, he wrote: "The writing of the hymn afforded me much joy, nor has it ever grown old. I still love it and always will, for it was the child of my youth. It proves conclusively that God can impart His deepest truths to the heart of the young, for I doubt if I have ever written anything more profound since.

I learned this new-to-me song with my children, and the church learned it the next Sunday night. As it turned out, my father was guest speaker that evening, doing a series of sermons on the Book of Genesis. In addition to his other interests, he has had a long-standing love affair with good hymns, but even he didn't know this one. It's a moving song, entreating the believer to go deeper into the heart, the will, the cross, the joy, and the love of Jesus. That evening it forced its way into my "top ten," and simultaneously became one of his favorites. He had his own Sunday school class learn it the very next Sunday morning, for none of those dear saints knew it either. ✄

Deeper and Deeper

That ye, being rooted and grounded in love, May be able to comprehend with all saints what is the breadth, and length, and depth, and height; And to know the love of Christ, which passeth knowledge, that ye might be filled with all the fulness of God (Eph. 3:17–19).

Every sincere Christian longs for a deeper relationship with Christ, driving them to more effective prayer and Bible study and service. The rich old hymn "Deeper and Deeper" reflects this heart cry.

Into the heart of Jesus, deeper and deeper I go,
Seeking to know the reason why He should love me so —
Why He stooped to lift me up from the miry clay,
Saving my soul, making me whole,
Though I had wandered away.

"Behold, what manner of love the Father hath bestowed upon us, that we should be called the sons of God" (1 John 3:1). God's infinite grace is "a mystery" to us, "But God hath revealed them unto us by his Spirit" (1 Cor. 2:10).

These mysteries were revealed by the Spirit primarily to the writers of the New Testament who wrote them down for our instruction through the empowerment of the Spirit (2 Pet. 1:19–21). Only in His revelation to us can we hope to understand something of His love and mercy and grace, but only through a close heart-walk with him in the Spirit can we know His heart. "The Lord searcheth all hearts, and understandeth all the imaginations of the thoughts: if thou seek him, he will be found of thee" (1 Chron. 28:9).

We who had wandered away from Him were saved and made whole, for "God commendeth his love toward us, in that, while we were yet sinners, Christ died for us" (Rom. 5:8). "He brought me up also out of an horrible pit, out of the miry clay" (Ps. 40:2). He did this all out of a heart of love.

God grant us an ever deeper knowledge of His heart.

Surrender to His Will

I beseech you therefore, brethren, by the mercies of God, that ye present your bodies a living sacrifice, holy, acceptable unto God, which is your reasonable service. And be not conformed to this world: but be ye transformed by the renewing of your mind, that ye may prove what is that good, and acceptable, and perfect, will of God (Rom. 12:1–2).

To be a true follower of Christ, we must know His will and submit to it. Our text informs us that His will has ever deeper stages, but once a saint sacrifices his own body and mind, and submits his will to His, we will "prove" it to be "perfect." The second verse echoes this thought.

Into the will of Jesus, deeper and deeper I go,
Praying for grace to follow, seeking His way to know;
Bowing in full surrender low at His blessed feet,
Bidding Him take, break me and make,
  Till I am molded and meet.

God may give a Christian a burden to accomplish a task or a life's work and then open and shut doors to make it possible. Discerning His will has never been easy, but we must seek earnestly to know it and follow it. "O the depth of the riches both of the wisdom and knowledge of God! how unsearchable are his judgments, and his ways past finding out! For who hath known the mind of the Lord?" (Rom. 11:33–34) are the verses just prior to our text.

The key, then, to knowing God's will is full surrender to it, whatever it may be, starting with obedience. "If a man love me, he will keep my words" (John 14:23). To be useful to Him, we must be broken of our own pride and self-will, then remolded as He desires. "If a man therefore purge himself from these, he shall be a vessel unto honor, sanctified, and meet for the master's use, and prepared unto every good work" (2 Tim. 2:21).

God grant us an ever deeper submission to His will.

The Fellowship of the Cross

That I may know him, and the power of his resurrection, and the fellowship of his sufferings, being made conformable unto his death (Phil. 3:10).

The third verse of the precious hymn "Deeper and Deeper" speaks of the suffering which the Christian will encounter if mature in Christ and effective in His service.

Into the cross of Jesus, deeper and deeper I go,
Following through the garden, facing the dreaded foe —
Drinking the cup of sorrow, sobbing with broken heart;
"Oh, Savior, help! Dear Savior, help!
Grace for my weakness impart."

But this suffering, while not welcome from a human perspective, still is not a thing to be avoided or refused. As our text explains, we are privileged to experience "the fellowship of his sufferings." He did so willingly, but not without asking God to "remove this cup [of sorrow] from me: nevertheless not my will, but thine, be done" (Luke 22:42). His suffering included betrayal and arrest and finally crucifixion, dying with a broken heart, but purchasing our eternal life with His death. By "fellowshiping" in His sufferings, we identify with His death, share His reproach, and follow His example. We, through His death, pass through death into a new life of victory over sin and death (1 Pet. 4:13).

Therefore, we accept and even welcome sufferings as a gift from God. "For unto you it is given in the behalf of Christ, not only to believe on him, but also to suffer for his sake" (Phil. 1:29). Paul said, "We ourselves glory in . . . all your persecutions and tribulations . . . that ye may be counted worthy of the kingdom of God" (2 Thess. 1:4–5). Of course, suffering isn't easy, and we need our Savior's help and grace to "endure" (James 5:10–11). But we have the promise that "if we suffer, we shall also reign with him" forever (2 Tim. 2:12).

May God grant us a deeper fellowship in the Cross.

The Joy of Jesus

Jesus Christ: Whom having not seen, ye love; in whom, though now ye see him not, yet believing, ye rejoice with joy unspeakable and full of glory (1 Pet. 1:7–8).

Because of Christ, we "rejoice with joy unspeakable," and the deeper we know Him, the more our joy. The fourth verse of our study hymn speaks of this joy. It was written by a young man whose life in the years to come was marked by a deep and fruitful walk with God.

Into the joy of Jesus, deeper and deeper I go,
Rising with soul enraptured far from the world below;
Joy in the place of sorrow, peace in the midst of pain,
Jesus will give, Jesus will give,
*   He will uphold and sustain.*

Joy is, of course, part of "the fruit of the Spirit" (Gal. 5:22) of Christ, who had prayed to His Father, "Now come I to thee . . . that they might have my joy fulfilled in themselves" (John 17:13). Most specifically, "we have peace with God through our Lord Jesus Christ . . . and rejoice in hope of the glory of God" (Rom. 5:1–2). In joy we rise over the lure of sin and the world. "Blessed are they whose iniquities are forgiven, and whose sins are covered" (Rom. 4:7).

The joy of the Lord is not predicated on external circumstances. "As sorrowful, yet alway rejoicing; as poor, yet making many rich; as having nothing, and yet possessing all things" (2 Cor. 6:10). And "I am filled with comfort, I am exceeding joyful in all our tribulation" (2 Cor. 7:4).

The last line is well supported in the writings of David, where the Lord provides this joy. "Though he [a good man] fall, he shall not be utterly cast down: for the Lord upholdeth him with his hand" (Ps. 37:24). "Cast thy burden upon the Lord, and he shall sustain thee: he shall never suffer the righteous to be moved" (Ps. 55:22).

May God grant us an even deeper joy in Jesus.

Oh, How He Loved

In this was manifested the love of God toward us, because that God sent his only begotten Son into the world, that we might live through him. Herein is love, not that we loved God, but that he loved us, and sent his Son to be the propitiation for our sins (1 John 4:9–10).

The final verse of Oswald J. Smith's touching hymn enjoins us to enter into God's love and sing of it throughout eternity.

Into the love of Jesus, deeper and deeper I go,
Praising the One who brought me out of my sin and woe;
And through eternal ages gratefully I shall sing;
"Oh, how He loved! Oh, how He loved!
Jesus, my Lord and my King."

The word "deep," or "depth," in Scripture comes from the Greek word *bathos*, from which is derived several English nautical terms and includes the concept of the deep ocean. Thus, probing "deeper and deeper" into the heart, the will, the cross, the joy, and now the love of Jesus takes on proper proportion. Each is immense, beyond our conception.

We should continually acknowledge, as does the song, that His love brought us out of our sinful condition which had totally separated us from Him. "But God, who is rich in mercy, for his great love wherewith he loved us, Even when we were dead in sins, hath quickened us [made us alive] together with Christ, (by grace ye are saved)" (Eph. 2:4–5). "In this was manifested the love of God toward us, because that God sent his only begotten Son into the world, that we might live through him. . . . We love him, because he first loved us" (1 John 4:9–19).

We will have the opportunity to sing of that love throughout eternity, because "in the ages to come he might [will] shew the exceeding riches of his grace in his kindness toward us through Christ Jesus" (Eph. 2:7).

May God grant us an ever-deepening love of Jesus.

He Ransomed Me

Julia H. Johnston

J. W. Henderson

1. There's a sweet and bless-ed sto-ry Of the Christ who came from glo-ry,
2. From the depth of sin and sad-ness To the heights of joy and glad-ness
3. From the throne of heav'n-ly glo-ry—Oh, the sweet and bless-ed sto-ry!
4. By and by with joy in-creas-ing, And with grat-i-tude un-ceas-ing,

Just to res-cue me from sin and mis-er-y; He in lov-ing-kind-ness sought me,
Je-sus lift-ed me, in mer-cy full and free; With His pre-cious blood He bought me,
Je-sus came to lift the lost in sin and woe In-to lib-er-ty all-glo-rious,
Lift-ed up with Christ for-ev-er more to be; I will join the hosts there sing-ing,

And from sin and shame hath bro't me, Hal-le-lu-jah! Je-sus ran-somed me.
When I knew Him not, He sought me, And in love di-vine He ran-somed me.
Tro-phies of His grace vic-to-rious, Ev-er-more re-joic-ing here be-low.
In the an-them ev-er ring-ing, To the King of Love who ran-somed me.

Hal-le-lu-jah, What a Sav-ior! Who can take a poor lost sin-ner, Lift him

from the mi-ry clay and set him free; (Hal-le-lu-jah!) I will ev-er tell the sto-ry,

shout-ing Glo-ry, glo-ry, glo-ry, Hal-le-lu-jah! Je-sus ran-somed me.

17

He Ransomed Me

This song I know nothing about, neither the hymn's history nor the author, Julia Johnston, except that she also wrote the marvelous anthem, "Grace Greater Than All Our Sin," both of which are in my top ten. I do know the Lord, however, and how "He rescued me from sin and misery," as this hymn puts it. Please allow me to use this hymn to tell my story.

My years in college were a time of miserable failure for me. I was a Christian and knew it. I clearly remember the time when, at age five or six, in my father's lap, I acknowledged my sin before God and asked Him to forgive me for His Son Jesus' sake. As a young man, I never doubted God or His word, nor could I ever discard the sure knowledge that I was His child. But, I did run from Him, eventually turning my back completely on the Lord and the things I knew to be true. Thankfully, He didn't turn His back on me.

Some may wonder if there's any hope for a Los Angeles bachelor living the rebellious lifestyle of the sixties, but God is creative. He graciously and wisely brought into my life several individuals who were involved in the search for Noah's ark and used this captivating adventure to draw me back to himself.

Before I knew it, I had applied and been accepted for an August 1971 expedition to Mount Ararat! I was generally athletic, but I had never climbed a real mountain before, so I knew I had to get in shape. This meant eliminating some of the harmful, sinful habits I had adopted. About that time my mother (who had been diligently praying for me) gave me a Bible and in tears asked me to read it. Partly to placate her, and partly to prepare for this "religious" adventure, I agreed.

As the sinful practices lessened, it seemed like a fog was lifting. The Bible began to make sense once again, and I read it avidly. But the Lord knew I wasn't ready. While my thoughts were shifting, my heart remained in the world.

Thankfully, the expedition that summer was canceled, but my interest remained high. I took a leave of absence from my job and used all the money I had to join a Bible-Science Holy Land tour in October, scheduled to spend three days at Mount Ararat. Imagine my disappointment when an early storm covered the entire area with two feet of snow as we arrived. I couldn't even see the mountain.

Think of it. Here I was, gone halfway around the world, spent my entire net worth, feeling God's tug on my heart and expectantly following, thinking He was leading me to be involved in the search for the ark, and now nothing.

I spent that entire night pacing the floor of a nearby primitive "hotel," asking God to somehow show himself to me, to let me know His will. In His grace He answered, through circumstances, the words of the others, and through a firm inner assurance, that He did want me to return to Ararat to continue the search for the ark. But most of all He wanted me. He wanted me to put childish pleasures behind me and embrace Him fully, to serve Him and follow Him wherever He would lead.

I had my answer. I was ready to go home, but the tour had just started. We journeyed from there to western Turkey and followed Paul on his missionary journeys. We went to Egypt and Lebanon, each stop reinforcing the accuracy of Scripture.

Next, a week-long stay in Israel. We walked where Jesus walked, saw where Gideon had fought the Midianites, and where Abraham had pitched his tents. If ever I had doubted Scripture, I believed now. The Bible was not only true, it was *really* true! These things actually happened!

Our tour climaxed at a hillside just outside Jerusalem's city walls, a possible site for our Lord's crucifixion. In the rock cliffs, at the base of the hill, one can see the shape of a skull. Could it be the actual site?

Looking up at the hillside I realized it didn't matter if this was the exact spot of Christ's death. What really mattered was that Christ had truly died! For me! He suffered the agonizing death penalty for my sins! His blood was shed so that I could be ransomed — from bondage to sin!

As these thoughts overwhelmed me, I fell to my knees in repentance. Through tears and sobs I pleaded for His forgiveness and cleansing and to restore to my life harmony with Him. I asked for strength to live for Him in victory over wrong choices.

And there, at the foot of Calvary, He answered. He not only forgave my past, but He gave me a new direction and message for my life, and He has promised never to leave me. As our song says, "Glory! Hallelujah! Jesus ransomed me." ✄

Hallelujah! Jesus Ransomed Me

For there is one God, and one mediator between God and men, the man Christ Jesus; Who gave himself a ransom for all, to be testified in due time (1 Tim. 2:5–6).

The concept of being ransomed, or redeemed, or delivered, comprises a major Bible theme and finds full development in the New Testament where "the Son of man came not to be ministered unto, but to minister, and to give his life a ransom for many" (Matt. 20:28). First let us look at the chorus of this song which was written early in this century:

Hallelujah, What a Savior!
Who can take a poor lost sinner,
Lift him from the miry clay and set him free;
I will ever tell the story, shouting Glory, glory, glory,
Hallelujah! Jesus ransomed me.

The chorus is broken into three thoughts: the miserable state of the sinner, Christ's ransoming work, and the ransomed sinner's response. To be sure, the poor sinner is lost, but "the Son of man is come to save that which was lost" (Matt. 18:11), lost in sin and under sin's penalty of death. "But God commendeth his love toward us, in that, while we were yet sinners, Christ died for us" (Rom. 5:8).

"He brought me up also out of an horrible pit, out of the miry clay, and set my feet upon a rock" (Ps. 40:2). Sin is not just a horrible pit. Jesus said, "Whosoever committeth sin is the servant of sin" and needs to be ransomed. But, "If the Son therefore shall make you free, ye shall be free indeed" (John 8:34–36). Jesus said to one such freed servant of sin, "Go home to thy friends, and tell them how great things the Lord hath done for thee" (Mark 5:19). "To him be glory both now and for ever" (2 Pet. 3:18). Hallelujah! Jesus ransomed me.

A Sweet and Blessed Story

That which we have seen and heard declare we unto you, that ye also may have fellowship with us: and truly our fellowship is with the Father, and with his Son Jesus Christ. . . . and the blood of Jesus Christ his Son cleanseth us from all sin (1 John 1:3–7).

Those of us who have been ransomed are compelled to tell others. Our fellowship with the Father and with the Son must be shared. The prerequisite for such fellowship — and our main message — is that "the blood of Jesus Christ . . . cleanseth us from all sin." The first verse of the wonderful old hymn rehearses this truth.

There's a sweet and blessed story
Of the Christ who came from glory,
Just to rescue me from sin and misery;
He in lovingkindness sought me,
And from sin and shame hath bro't me,
Hallelujah! Jesus ransomed me.

The blind man, who could now see, testified: "One thing I know, that, whereas I was blind, now I see. . . . If this man were not of God, he could do nothing" (John 9:25–33). Indeed, He was "of God," for "When the fullness of the time was come, God sent forth his Son . . . To redeem [or rescue] them that were under the law" (Gal. 4:4–5).

Some who need rescuing don't realize it. They may think they "have need of nothing; and knowest not that thou art wretched, and miserable, and poor, and blind, and naked" (Rev. 3:17). Others recognize that they have been brought "into captivity to the law of sin which is in my members. O wretched man that I am! who shall deliver me from the body of this death?" (Rom. 7:23–24).

God sought us out in lovingkindness, "hath saved us, and called us with an holy calling, not according to our works, but according to his own purpose and grace, which was given us in Christ Jesus before the world began" (2 Tim. 1:9).

Hallelujah! Jesus ransomed me.

From the Depths to the Heights

Out of the depths have I cried unto thee . . . If thou, Lord, shouldest mark iniquities, O Lord, who shall stand? But there is forgiveness with thee (Ps. 130:1–4).

The fact that we have been forgiven of our grievous sin is remembered in verse two of this well-loved hymn.

From the depth of sin and sadness
To the heights of joy and gladness
Jesus lifted me, in mercy full and free;
With his precious blood He bought me,
When I knew Him not, He sought me,
And in love divine He ransomed me.

"There is none that doeth good, no, not one. . . . Their throat is an open sepulchre . . . Whose mouth is full of cursing and bitterness: Their feet are swift to shed blood" (Rom. 3:12–15). "Every man is tempted, when he is drawn away of his own lust, and enticed. Then when lust hath conceived, it bringeth forth sin: and sin, when it is finished, bringeth forth death" (James 1:14–15). A sad state indeed.

Yet we are promised that we may "rejoice with joy unspeakable and full of glory: Receiving the end of your faith, even the salvation of your souls" (1 Pet. 1:8–9). Such heights of joy and gladness are available only to those who have been lifted out of their sinful state and made alive or "quickened, who were dead in trespasses and sins" (Eph. 2:1). It was "according to his mercy he saved us . . . shed on us abundantly through Jesus Christ our Savior" (Titus 3:5–6).

We "were not redeemed [or ransomed] with corruptible things. . . . But with the precious blood of Christ" (1 Pet. 1:18–19). What makes this transaction even more remarkable is that we didn't deserve it, didn't want it, and were even "enemies of the cross of Christ" (Phil. 3:18). Yet He paid the ransom price anyway. "When we were enemies, we were reconciled to God by the death of his Son" (Rom. 5:10).

Hallelujah! Jesus ransomed me.

From the Throne of Heavenly Glory

> Who, being in the form of God . . . made himself
> of no reputation . . . and became obedient unto death,
> even the death of the cross (Phil. 2:6–8).

Our text explains that our Lord and Savior Jesus Christ voluntarily left heaven to die on our behalf. Verse three of this doctrinally rich hymn begins with the same thought.

From the throne of heav'nly glory —
Oh, the sweet and blessed story!
Jesus came to lift the lost in sin and woe
Into liberty all-glorious,
Trophies of His grace victorious,
Evermore rejoicing here below.

Truly this is a sweet and blessed story. "For ye know the grace of our Lord Jesus Christ, that, though he was rich, yet for your sakes he became poor, that ye through his poverty might be rich" (2 Cor. 8:9). The story becomes even more blessed when we recall just how lost in sin and woe we were. "Now the works of the flesh are manifest, which are these; Adultery, fornication, uncleanness, lasciviousness, idolatry, witchcraft, hatred, variance, emulations, wrath, strife, seditions, heresies, envyings, murders, drunkenness, revellings, and such like" (Gal. 5:19–21). Nothing about us was worth ransoming.

And yet despite all this, "Christ Jesus came into the world to save sinners" (1 Tim. 1:15). We have the promise that one day the entire creation "shall be delivered from the bondage of corruption into the glorious liberty of the children of God" (Rom. 8:21).

Paul wrote, "By the grace of God I am what I am" (1 Cor. 15:10), a trophy of His grace. "Being justified by his grace, we should be [are] made heirs" (Titus 3:7); "heirs of God, and joint-heirs with Christ" (Rom. 8:17) of the kingdom which He left to become our Savior.

Hallelujah! Jesus ransomed me.

Singing with the Hosts

And they sing the song of Moses the servant of God, and the song of the Lamb, saying, Great and marvelous are thy works, Lord God Almighty; just and true are thy ways, thou King of saints (Rev. 15:3).

Verse four speaks of the Christian hope, the ultimate realization of our full ransom.

By and by with joy increasing,
  And with gratitude unceasing,
Lifted up with Christ forever more to be;
I will join the hosts there singing,
  In the anthem ever ringing,
To the King of Love who ransomed me.

In this life we may go through "fiery trials," but they will be over by and by. Rather "rejoice, inasmuch as ye are partakers of Christ's sufferings; that, when his glory shall be revealed, ye may be glad also with exceeding joy" (1 Pet. 4:12–13). "Giving thanks unto the Father. . . . Who hath delivered [or ransomed] us from the power of darkness, and hath translated us into the kingdom of his dear Son: In whom we have redemption through his blood, even the forgiveness of sins" (Col. 1:12–14).

The work of Christ lifted us up out of bondage to sin, "And hath raised us up together, and made us sit together in heavenly places in Christ Jesus" (Eph. 2:6), "and so shall we ever be with the Lord" (1 Thess. 4:17).

What shall we do there? Among other things, as we see in our text, we will sing. Moses' "song" was written on the far shore of the Red Sea and celebrated their ransom from Egypt and protection from their enemies. "The Lord is my strength and song, and he is become my salvation" (Exod. 15:2).

We'll also sing "a new song," a song of ransom. "Thou art worthy . . . for thou wast slain, and hast redeemed us to God by thy blood" (Rev. 5:9).

He redeemed us, but Hallelujah! Jesus ransomed me!

Crown Him With Many Crowns

Matthew Bridges
Godfrey Thring

George J. Elvey

1. Crown Him with man - y crowns, The Lamb up - on His throne;
2. Crown Him the Son of God Be - fore the worlds be - gan,
3. Crown Him the Lord of life, Who tri - umphed o'er the grave,
4. Crown Him the Lord of love! Be - hold His hands and side,
5. Crown Him the Lord of peace, Whose peace a scep - ter sways
6. Crown Him the Lord of Heav'n! One with the Fa - ther known,

Hark! how the heaven - ly an - them drowns All mu - sic but its own!
And ye, who tread where He hath trod, Crown Him the Son of man,
And rose vic - to - rious in the strife For those He came to save.
Rich wounds, yet vis - i - ble a - bove, In beau - ty glo - ri - fied.
From pole to pole, that wars may cease, And all be prayer and praise!
One with the Spir - it through Him giv'n From yon - der glo - rious throne.

A - wake my soul and sing Of Him who died for thee,
Who ev - ery grief hath known That wrings the hu - man breast,
His glo - ries now we sing Who died and rose on high,
All hail, Re - deem - er, hail! For thou hast died for me;
His reign shall know no end, And round His pierc - ed feet
To Thee be end - less praise, For Thou for us hast died;

And hail Him as thy match - less King Through all e - ter - ni - ty.
And takes and bears them for His own, That all in Him may rest.
Who died, e - ter - nal life to bring, And lives that death may die.
Thy praise shall nev - er, nev - er fail through - out e - ter - ni - ty.
Fair flowers of Par - a - dise ex - tend Their fra - grance ev - er sweet.
Be Thou, O Lord, through end - less days A - dored and mag - ni - fied.

18

Crown Him with Many Crowns

It's my conviction that the grand old hymns should be retained in the consciousness of our churches. We shouldn't let them die. But to sing them all takes a concentrated effort.

I've worked out a system whereby, in the course of a year, we never sing a song twice, on Sunday morning at least. This last year, including songs from special events and communion, we sang a total of 232 different songs. But our hymnal contains over 800! Some of them I don't know at all. Obviously some will never be sung.

On Sunday evenings we like to sing our favorites, and usually the more up-tempo songs. Recently our church has launched a program to learn some of the songs we don't know, but in a year, we could hardly learn 20 or 30 in this fashion. In spite of our best efforts, we are losing many cherished treasures.

Most of the songs which become favorites, known by all, are those with complimentary words and music. It's best if both can thrill the soul. Together they make a good package.

That's not always the case. To this musical illiterate, the music to "Crown Him with Many Crowns" just doesn't do it. It kind of lumbers along in an uninspiring way. Maybe others enjoy it more than I do, but I just don't care for it.

Except for the words — these do move me, for they powerfully exalt my Lord in many aspects of His work and essence. It starts with His being in eternity past, goes to His work of creation, then redemption, then resurrection. It deals with His grace in our lives today and in national affairs, His sovereignty and His throne in heaven.

How can we refrain from crowning Him Lord and Master as we reflect on who He is and all He has done?

This is another song whose history is lost, at least as far as I have been able to find. It does have two authors, but they appear not to have collaborated, for the verses are attributed to one or the other. Perhaps these were two separate poems combined by one of them or a third author at a later time. Furthermore, you'd be surprised how many variants of this song are in print. Of the many hymn books I have checked, none had the same verses in the same order. Some included a sixth verse (in various places). But, it does belong with the rest, and seems to be a fitting climax to the song, for it crowns Him on His eternal throne, in His role as part of God's Triune nature.

> *Crown Him the Lord of heaven;*
> *One with the Father known,*
> *One with the Spirit thru Him giv'n*
> *From yonder glorious throne,*
> *To thee be endless praise,*
> *For Thou for us hast died;*
> *Be Thou, O Lord, thru endless days*
> *Adored and magnified. %*

Crown Him with Many Crowns

The four and twenty elders fall down before him that sat on the throne, and worship him that liveth for ever and ever, and cast their crowns before the throne, saying Thou art worthy, O Lord, to receive glory and honor and power: for thou hast created all things, and for thy pleasure they are and were created (Rev. 4:10–11).

As Christians, we are promised crowns of various sorts. Those we have ministered to are our "crown of rejoicing" (1 Thess. 2:19), our "joy and crown" (Phil. 4:1). We have the "crown of righteousness" (2 Tim. 4:8) for service to the Lord. If we endure, we will "receive the crown of life" (James 1:12) and the "crown of glory" (1 Pet. 5:4). These crowns are "incorruptible" (1 Cor. 9:25), lasting for eternity. But of what use will crowns be in glory?

Our text answers the question: We will willingly cast our "crowns" — our accomplishments performed in service of Him — at His feet as an act of worship, for all we are and have done has been a gift from the almighty sovereign Creator/Savior. We can crown Him King of our lives. This grand old hymn relates this and reminds us to look ahead.

> *Crown Him with many crowns,*
> *The lamb upon His throne;*
> *Hark! how the heavenly anthem drowns*
> *All music but its own!*
> *Awake my soul and sing*
> *Of Him who died for thee,*
> *And hail Him as thy matchless King*
> *Through all eternity.*

There will come that day when we form "a great multitude . . . before the throne, and before the Lamb" (Rev. 7:9) singing "the song of the Lamb, saying, Great and marvelous are thy works" (Rev. 15:3). The theme of our song will be that "God commendeth his love toward us, in that, while we were yet sinners, Christ died for us" (Rom. 5:8).

Crown Him with many crowns!

Crown Him the Son of God

But these are written, that ye might believe that Jesus is the Christ, the Son of God; and that believing ye might have life through his name (John 20:31).

This hymn was written in the late 1800s, a time of rampant skepticism. Vital Bible doctrines were abandoned by many, including the Creator's kingship over creation and its inhabitants. The need remains to crown Him King in all areas of life. Note the hymn's second verse:

> *Crown Him the Son of God*
> *Before the worlds began,*
> *And ye, who tread where He hath trod,*
> *Crown Him the Son of man,*
> *Who every grief hath known*
> *That wrings the human breast,*
> *And takes and bears them for His own,*
> *That all in Him may rest.*

Jesus Christ, God the Son, possessed great glory given by God the Father "before the foundation of the world" (John 17:24). Then, even though "all things were made by him" (John 1:3), "God sent forth his Son, made of a woman, made under the law, To redeem them that were under the law, that we might receive the adoption of sons" (Gal. 4:4–5).

While in human form, Jesus preferred to call himself the "Son of man" and chose to live a life of poverty and suffering. "The Son of man hath not where to lay his head" (Matt. 8:20). He chose to suffer these things so that He could fully identify and empathize with our problems. "For we have not an high priest which cannot be touched with the feeling of our infirmities; but was in all points tempted like as we are, yet without sin" (Heb. 4:15).

Thankfully, because "He hath borne our griefs, and carried our sorrows . . . and the Lord hath laid on him the iniquity of us all" (Isa. 53:4–6), we can be forgiven and find rest in Him. "Let us therefore come boldly unto the throne of grace, that we may obtain mercy, and find grace to help in time of need" (Heb. 4:16).

Crown Him the Lord of Life

> For the wages of sin is death; but the gift of God is
> eternal life through Jesus Christ our Lord (Rom. 6:23).

Verse three speaks of life — eternal life — made possible by the death of the Creator of life. This was followed by His retaking life and returning in victory from the grave. The hymn expresses it well.

> *Crown Him the Lord of life,*
> *Who triumphed o'er the grave,*
> *And rose victorious in the strife*
> *For those He came to save.*
> *His glories now we sing*
> *Who died and rose on high,*
> *Who died, eternal life to bring,*
> *And lives that death may die.*

As in our text, eternal life is a "gift of God," made possible "by the appearing of our Savior Jesus Christ, who hath abolished death, and hath brought life and immortality to light through the gospel" (2 Tim. 1:10). The penalty for sin had to be paid, and so "Christ died for our sins" (1 Cor. 15:3). But in order to fully vanquish death and offer forgiven sinners eternal life, He "rose again the third day" (v. 4), "Wherefore he is able also to save them to the uttermost that come unto God by him, seeing he ever liveth to make intercession for them" (Heb. 7:25).

Then, "When he had by himself purged our sins, [He] sat down on the right hand of the Majesty on high" (Heb. 1:3). "Death is swallowed up in victory. O death, where is thy sting? O grave, where is thy victory? . . . Thanks be to God, which giveth us the victory through our Lord Jesus Christ" (1 Cor. 15:54–57).

Although eternal death has been vanquished, we still face physical death. Yet there will soon come a day when "God shall wipe away all tears from their eyes; and there shall be no more death, neither sorrow, nor crying, neither shall there be any more pain: for the former things are passed away" (Rev. 21:4).

Crown Him the Lord of Love

For I am persuaded, that neither death, nor life, nor angels, nor principalities, nor powers, nor things present, nor things to come, Nor height, nor depth, nor any other creature, shall be able to separate us from the love of God, which is in Christ Jesus our Lord (Rom. 8:38–39).

God's great love for us moved Him to extend His grace to us. This love was not a sentimental, feel-good "love" as the term is used today but was sacrificial on our behalf. "Greater love hath no man than this, that a man lay down his life for his friends" (John 15:13). The fourth verse speaks of this.

Crown Him the Lord of love!
Behold His hands and side,
Rich wounds, yet visible above,
In beauty glorified.
All hail, Redeemer, hail!
For thou hast died for me;
Thy praise shall never, never fail
Throughout eternity.

Soon after Christ rose from the dead, He appeared to His disciples who were "glad, when they saw the Lord" (John 20:20). But doubting Thomas was not present and demanded to see proof before he believed. Several days later Jesus reappeared and desired to remove all stumbling blocks to faith. "Reach hither thy finger, and behold my hands; and reach hither thy hand, and thrust it into my side: and be not faithless, but believing. And Thomas answered and said unto him, My Lord and my God" (John 20:27–28). One day all the world will see those yet-visible wounds, for "they shall look upon me [Christ] whom they have pierced" (Zech. 12:10). Our Redeemer deserves all praise from redeemed sinners: "For all have sinned, and come short of the glory of God; Being justified freely by his grace through the redemption that is in Christ Jesus" (Rom. 3:23–24). This praise will never end, "that God in all things may be glorified through Jesus Christ, to whom be praise . . . for ever and ever" (1 Pet. 4:11).

Crown Him the Lord of Peace

Now the Lord of peace himself give you peace always by all means. The Lord be with you all (2 Thess. 3:16).

Isaiah's great prophecy of Christ's first advent identified "His name [as] . . . Wonderful, Counsellor, The mighty God, The everlasting Father, The Prince of Peace" (Isa. 9:6). The peace He brings is personal as we see in our text. "Therefore being justified by faith, we have peace with God through our Lord Jesus Christ" (Rom. 5:1). But it is also effective in society at large, a fact borne out in verse five.

> *Crown Him the Lord of peace,*
> *Whose peace a scepter sways*
> *From pole to pole, that wars may cease,*
> *And all be prayer and praise!*
> *His reign shall know no end,*
> *And round His pierced feet*
> *Fair flowers of Paradise extend*
> *Their fragrance ever sweet.*

"Thy throne, O God, is for ever and ever: a scepter of righteousness is the scepter of thy kingdom" (Heb. 1:8). The King of this kingdom is none other than our Lord and Savior Jesus Christ. As the angel announced the birth of Christ, he prophesied: "And he shall reign over the house of Jacob for ever; and of his kingdom there shall be no end" (Luke 1:33). "And he shall judge among the nations, and shall rebuke many people: and they shall beat their swords into plowshares, and their spears into pruninghooks: nation shall not lift up sword against nation, neither shall they learn war any more" (Isa. 2:4).

Perhaps the best thing about His eternal, righteous, peaceful kingdom is that we will be there. "To him that overcometh will I give to eat of the tree of life, which is in the midst of the paradise of God" (Rev. 2:7). "Who is he that overcometh the world, but he that believeth that Jesus is the Son of God?" (1 John 5:5). We can overcome because He overcame, and now offers us eternal peace.

Crown Him the Lord of Heaven

> God that made the world and all things therein,
> seeing that he is Lord of heaven and earth, dwelleth
> not in temples made with hands (Acts 17:24).

While all three Persons of the Trinity participated in creation (for their Person and purpose is unified), the primary agent through which the Trinity's purpose was accomplished was none other than God the Son. "All things were created by him, and for him" (Col. 1:16). The final, climatic verse reflects this unity while focusing on the implementing work of Christ. The great Creator became our Savior and deserves our allegiance as Lord of heaven.

> *Crown Him the Lord of heav'n;*
> *One with the Father known,*
> *One with the Spirit through Him giv'n*
> *From yonder glorious throne.*
> *To thee be endless praise,*
> *For thou for us hast died;*
> *Be thou, O Lord, through endless days*
> *Adored and magnified.*

Jesus prayed, "O Father, Lord of heaven and earth" (Matt. 11:25), but then He ascended "up into heaven, and sat on the right hand of God" (Mark 16:19). Throughout His earthly ministry He taught "I and my Father are one" (John 10:30).

He also promised His disciples that the Holy Spirit, "the Comforter [would] come, whom I will send unto you from the Father" (John 15:26). Paul added that the Spirit would take up residence in the Christian. "What? know ye not that your body is the temple of the Holy Ghost which is in you, which ye have of God?" (1 Cor. 6:19).

Our response to all that our Lord has done for us should be to worship Him — to adore and magnify Him — for all eternity. We will join the "four and twenty elders [and] fall down before him that sat [sits] on the throne, and worship him that liveth for ever and ever, and cast their [our] crowns before the throne, saying Thou art worthy, O Lord" (Rev. 4:10–11).

No Blood, No Altar Now

Horatius Bonar

Anon.
& Alfred B. Smith

1. No blood, no al-tar now. The sac-ri-fice is o'er!
2. We thank thee for the blood, The blood of Christ thy Son:
3. We thank thee for the grace, Des-cend-ing from a-bove,
4. We thank thee for the hope, So glad, and sure, and clear;
5. We thank thee for the crown Of glo-ry and of life;

No flame, no smoke as-cends on high. The Lamb is slain no more;
The blood by which our peace is made, our vic-to-ry is won:
That ov-er-flows our wid-est guilt, E-ter-nal Fa-ther's love.
It holds the droop-ing spir-it up Till the bright dawn ap-pear;
'Tis no poor with-er-ing wreath of earth, Man's prize in mor-tal strife;

But rich-er blood has flowed from no-bler veins,
Great vic-to-ry o'er hell, and sin and woe
Love of the Fa-ther's ev-er-last-ing Son
Fair hope! with what a sun-shine does it cheer
'Tis in-cor-rup-ti-ble as is the throne,

To purge the soul from guilt, and cleanse the red-dest stains.
That needs no sec-ond fight, and leaves no sec-ond foe.
Love of the Ho-ly Ghost, Je-ho-vah, Three in One
Our rough-est path on earth, our drear-iest de-sert here.
The king-dom of our God and His in-car-nate Son.

19

No Blood, No Altar Now

I am on the road a good deal of the time speaking at creation seminars and other meetings around the country. This means I miss Sunday morning services in my church fairly often.

In most churches finding a substitute to lead the singing wouldn't present a big problem, but of the people available in our church, most know less about song leading than I do, and remember, I can't read music. My only qualifications are that I love the Lord, love good music, and can, to some degree, carry a tune.

The fellow who usually fills in for me is a retired Navy mechanic named Harold, a lovely Christian gentleman with a deep knowledge of Scripture and a rich tenor voice. Unfortunately, he can't read music either. Together, we've tried to learn the difference between 3/4 and 4/4 time.

But Harold knows hymns. He knows probably every hymn in the book, including some nobody ever heard.

I usually select the songs printed in the bulletin, but if Harold gets a hankering to sing a certain song, he'll just make the change, even if the pianist doesn't know the song. So when I get back to town, the people have learned songs I don't know and which, on Sunday evening, they might request and want me to lead. Talk about crisis time!

Just such a song is Horatius Bonar's song "No Blood,

No Altar Now," a song with a lot of words and a beautiful but somewhat unpredictable tune. After an initial bumbling time of panic, I've grown to love it.

Dr. Horatius Bonar began his ministry in the staunchly Calvinistic Presbyterian Church of Scotland, authorized and controlled by the government. Among their strongly held beliefs was that acceptable church music could only be taken directly from the Psalms. Bland tunes were attached to these words and no instruments such as pianos or organs were permitted.

In the mid-1800s, an evangelical revival began to sprout within the Church, and among the most influential leaders was the dynamic young preacher and hymnwriter, Dr. Bonar. He was known as a gifted speaker, with his doctrinaire Calvanism moderated by a deep concern for the lost and a pre-millennial view of prophecy. He established himself as a leader in the Free Church movement, writing numerous books and gospel tracts which enjoyed wide usage. His love for the Scriptures comes through in his hymns, such as this one and others, including "I Heard the Voice of Jesus Say" and "Not What These Hands Have Done."

Interestingly enough, while Bonar wrote approximately 600 fine hymns, he wasn't able to use them in his own church until his later years, since his congregation still felt comfortable with the old Psalms only. The newer ones were thought to either be blasphemous or coarse, mentioning such "undignified" themes as the "blood" of Christ.

Nevertheless, his gospel hymns were used far and wide, and Dr. Bonar is credited with opening the door for the evangelistic team of D.L. Moody and Ira Sankey to use newly written, triumphant gospel songs on their crusades throughout Scotland. He even wrote several specifically for their meetings. His impact in many areas is still felt today. ✼

No Blood, No Altar Now

> Neither by the blood of goats and calves, but by his own blood he entered in once into the holy place, having obtained eternal redemption for us (Heb. 9:12).

Our text verse contains the kernel truth of Christianity, that Christ, God the Son, shed His own blood on our behalf and thereby "obtained eternal redemption for us." In Old Testament times the high priest needed to make animal sacrifices continually for the sins of the people, but Christ only needed to do it "once," fully satisfying God's holy justice. Our hymn, seldom used these days, reflects this theme.

> *No blood, no altar now.*
> *The sacrifice is o'er!*
> *No flame, no smoke ascends on high.*
> *The Lamb is slain no more;*
> *But richer blood has flowed from nobler veins,*
> *To purge the soul from guilt,*
> *And cleanse the reddest stains.*

Since all of animalkind suffer under the effects of the curse, "it is not possible that the blood of bulls and of goats should take away sins" (Heb. 10:4). A richer blood was needed. Thus we "were not redeemed with corruptible things . . . But with the precious blood of Christ, as of a lamb without blemish and without spot" (1 Pet. 1:18–19). As fully God and sinless man, He could pay sin's penalty and "purge your [our] conscience from dead works to serve the living God" (Heb. 9:14).

"Come now, and let us reason together, saith the Lord: though your sins be as scarlet, they shall be as white as snow; though they be red like crimson, they shall be as wool" (Isa. 1:18).

The sacrifice is over — the penalty is paid. Reason dictates that we accept the forgiveness offered, and when we do, our guilt will be removed, our garments washed "white in the blood of the Lamb" (Rev. 7:14).

The Blood-Bought Victory

> And, having made peace through the blood of his cross, by him to reconcile all things unto himself; by him, I say, whether they be things in earth, or things in heaven (Col. 1:20).

There was a time for all of us corporately and individually when we "were without Christ . . . aliens . . . strangers . . . having no hope, and without God in the world" (Eph. 2:12). Our situation and our choices doomed us, "but now in Christ Jesus ye who sometimes were far off are made nigh by the blood of Christ. For he is our peace" (v. 13–14). The second verse of this thoughtful hymn expounds on this great victory.

> *We thank thee for the blood,*
> *The blood of Christ, thy Son:*
> *The blood by which our peace is made,*
> *Our victory is won:*
> *Great victory o'er hell, and sin, and woe*
> *That needs no second fight,*
> *And leaves no second foe.*

His victory consisted of multiple battles. On an individual basis, we that were "alienated and enemies in your [our] mind by wicked works, yet now hath he reconciled. In the body of his flesh through death, to present you [us] holy and unblamable and unreprovable in his sight" (Col. 1:21–22).

On a grander scale, "Death is swallowed up in victory. O death, where is thy sting? O grave, where is thy victory? . . . Thanks be to God, which giveth us the victory through our Lord Jesus Christ" (1 Cor. 15:54–57). "He hath put all enemies under his feet. The last enemy that shall be destroyed is death" (v. 25–26) through His resurrection from the dead. In the final battle, "death and hell were cast into the lake of fire" (Rev. 20:14).

Christ's death on the cross assured the victory, but we are still occupied in personal struggles. As we press on, our hearts are strengthened by the sure knowledge that "It is finished" (John 19:30), and no more sacrifice is needed.

Grace from Above

For all have sinned, and come short of the glory of God; Being justified freely by his grace through the redemption that is in Christ Jesus: Whom God hath set forth to be a propitiation through faith in his blood (Rom. 3:23–25).

Our sins had separated us from our sinless, Holy Creator/God, erecting an impenetrable barrier. "But where sin abounded, grace did much more abound" (Rom. 5:20). In His grace, God the Father sent God the Son to accept our guilt upon himself and pay our penalty. Thus, in Him "we have redemption through his blood, the forgiveness of sins, according to the riches of his grace" (Eph. 1:7). The third verse reminds us of this love and grace.

We thank thee for the grace,
Descending from above,
That overflows our widest guilt,
Eternal Father's love.
Love of the Father's everlasting Son
Love of the Holy Ghost,
Jehovah, Three in One

The love which called us and saved us issued forth from each Person of the Triune Godhead, and in unity each played a crucial role in implementing it. Consider the Father's part, extended through His Son. "God commendeth his love towards us, in that, while we were yet sinners, Christ died for us" (Rom. 5:8). Who can "separate us from the love of God, which is in Christ Jesus our Lord" (Rom. 8:39)? Likewise, "Who shall separate us from the love of Christ?" (Rom. 8:35). Even now we may appropriate the "love of the Spirit" (Rom. 15:30).

Each Person of the Trinity, while comprising the whole yet inseparable from each other, acts in concert with the others in character and purpose, especially in this matter of our salvation. "The grace of the Lord Jesus Christ, and the love of God, and the communion of the Holy Ghost, be with you all" (2 Cor. 13:14).

A Sure Hope

According to his mercy he saved us, by the washing of regeneration, and renewing of the Holy Ghost; Which he shed on us abundantly through Jesus Christ our Savior; That being justified by his grace, we should be made heirs according to the hope of eternal life (Titus 3:5–7).

This moving song delineates the fact that Christ Jesus has died the perfect sacrifice, abundantly providing all that is necessary for God to justly wash our sins away. As our text reveals, His grace justified or declared us righteous, making us heirs of His kingdom and granting to us the certain hope of everlasting life. The fourth verse explains:

We thank thee for the hope,
So glad, and sure, and clear;
It holds the drooping spirit up
Till the bright dawn appear;
Fair hope! with what sunshine does it cheer
Our roughest path on earth,
Our dreariest desert here.

Today's common usage of the word "hope" limits it merely to the state of "wish," "desire," or "expectation." Not so for the Greek word *elpis*, meaning a confident expectation; a future certainty. Paul writes of the "hope of eternal life, which God, that cannot lie, promised before the world began . . . That blessed hope, and the glorious appearing of the great God and our Savior Jesus Christ; Who gave himself for us" (Titus 1:2–2:14).

This hope, far more than a view of a certain future, provides stability and confidence in these present unsteady days. Since He himself has promised us this hope, and since it is "impossible for God to lie, we might have a strong consolation, who have fled for refuge to lay hold upon the hope set before us: Which hope we have as an anchor of the soul, both sure and stedfast" (Heb. 6:18–19). The facts are in. Jesus has died, our sins are forgiven, and our hope is sure!

The Crown of Glory and Life

Blessed be the God and Father of our Lord Jesus Christ, which according to his abundant mercy hath begotten us again unto a lively hope by the resurrection of Jesus Christ from the dead, To an inheritance incorruptible, and undefiled, and that fadeth not away, reserved in heaven for you (1 Pet. 1:3–4).

The final verse of this rich old hymn praises God for the final sacrifice for sin, accomplished by our Lord Jesus Christ. It unfolds the ultimate blessings to the believer.

We thank thee for the crown
Of glory and of life;
'Tis no poor withering wreath of earth,
Man's prize in mortal strife;
'Tis incorruptible as is the throne,
The kingdom of our God
And His incarnate Son.

Our struggles in life are compared to that of an athlete, striving "to obtain a corruptible crown; but we an incorruptible" (1 Cor. 9:25). Our goal is not a victor's wreath; instead, "when the chief shepherd shall appear, ye shall receive a crown of glory that fadeth not away" (1 Pet. 5:4), "the crown of life, which the Lord hath promised to them that love him" (James 1:12).

Note the deep thought in the hymn. These crowns are as incorruptible as "the throne of the Majesty in the heavens" (Heb. 8:1), for "flesh and blood cannot inherit the kingdom of God; neither doth corruption inherit incorruption" (1 Cor. 15:50). They are ours because of the incorruptible Jesus and His work.

"Let us lay aside every weight, and the sin which doth so easily beset us, and let us run with patience the race that is set before us, Looking unto Jesus the author and finisher of our faith; who for the joy that was set before him endured the cross, despising the shame, and is set down at the right hand of the throne of God" (Heb. 12:1–2).

The Solid Rock

Edward Mote

William B. Bradbury

1. My hope is built on noth - ing less Than Je - sus' blood and right - eous - ness;
2. When dark - ness veils His love - ly face, I rest on His un - chang - ing grace;
3. His oath, His cov - e - nant, His blood Sup - port me in the whelm - ing flood;
4. When He shall come with trum - pet sound O may I then in Him be found,

I dare not trust the sweet - est frame, But whol - ly lean on Je - sus' name.
In ev - ery high and storm - y gale My an - chor holds with - in the veil.
When all a - round my soul gives way, He then is all my hope and stay.
Dressed in His right - eous - ness a - lone Fault - less to stand be - fore the throne.

On Christ, the sol - id Rock, I stand - All oth - er ground is

sink - ing sand, All oth - er ground is sink - ing sand.

20

The Solid Rock

Being in the earth sciences, I love what I call "geology" hymns, and there are quite a few: "Rock of Ages," "My Anchor Holds," "A Shelter in the Time of Storm," etc. But I like "The Solid Rock" the best. In fact, it rounds out my "top three," with "It Is Well with My Soul" and "How Firm a Foundation."

Actually, the song took me by surprise as I taught Sunday school one morning. To emphasize a point regarding the sufficiency of Christ, I blurted out (unplanned but with great enthusiasm), "On Christ the solid rock I stand, all other ground is sinking sand." It stuck with the class and with me, and now I catch myself humming that tune more often than any other.

I discovered that the song originally had a different title: "The Immutable Basis of a Sinner's Hope." And that's the key to tying it in to Scripture. The song consists of a list of objective truths on which the believer can base his faith: Jesus' blood, His righteousness, His name, His unchanging grace, His oath, His covenant, His blood. Upon this rock we can stand firm.

Edward Mote, the hymn's author, converted to Christ as an adult. Raised in the home of poor, ungodly parents, he simply had not ever heard there was a God. At the age of 16, he apprenticed to be a cabinetmaker and learned the trade from a God-fearing man. At the insistence of his master, he began attending church and eventually gave his life to Christ. In time he became a fruitful preacher.

On his deathbed, Pastor Mote exclaimed to the church deacons gathered around, "I think I am nearing port, but the truths I have preached I am living upon, and they will do to die upon. Ah! The precious blood! The precious blood which takes away all my sins; it is this which makes peace with God."

The song brings back a very special memory for me. Less than one year after my full surrender to the Lord at the foot of Mount Calvary, I led an expedition team of five men to Mount Ararat in search of Noah's ark, the first of my 13 trips to that fabled mountain. Each expedition has been filled with danger and adventure, but this first expedition was marked by God's mighty hand of deliverance and provision on numerous memorable occasions.

It all culminated on August 3, 1972, when two other climbers and I were ascending a near-vertical glacial slope at the 14,000-foot elevation. Suddenly a storm came over the top of the mountain; first snow, then hail, then lightning. It was not just lightning strikes, we were actually up in the thunderhead! We tried scrambling for safety, but there was no refuge.

Suddenly, the lightning struck the ledge on which we had gathered, literally blowing us out into the air. I landed about 100 feet away and tumbled head over heels down the steep, ice-covered slope, with my heavy pack still strapped to my back. When I finally stopped, I found to my horror that I was totally paralyzed from the waist down. Calling to the others, I discovered they were also badly injured.

God taught me a lot that day. I learned of His sovereign control of every situation, of His comfort in times of distress, of the secure position of a believer even in the face of death. I learned something of His mighty power to act in accordance with His divine will, even to heal a broken body. I learned that He can even restore paralyzed limbs in response to a prayer of submissive faith.

Four hours after the lightning had struck us, but still in a major blizzard, three battered and weary pilgrims began climbing back up the mountain, back up over the slope from which we had been hurled, up to where the glacier was flat and we could pitch our tent and gain shelter from the storm. Suddenly, just as the last tent peg was pounded in, the storm broke, and we were bathed in blue sky and sunlight from a setting sun.

Very few people have ever climbed so high on Mount Ararat, but I am certain no one has ever had such a wonderful time singing hymns and praising God as we did that evening. One song we sang with great gusto was "The Solid Rock." God had brought us through the "high and stormy gale" and, just like Noah, had placed our feet on the stable rocks of a mighty mountain.

But even more dear to us that evening than the physical provision He had given was our absolute certainty of His eternal provision for us. We have an immutable basis for our hope, standing on "Christ, the solid Rock." ✄

The Solid Rock

> Whosoever cometh to me, and heareth my say-
> ings, and doeth them, I will shew you to whom he is
> like: He is like a man which built an house, and digged
> deep, and laid the foundation on a rock: and when
> the flood arose, the stream beat vehemently upon that
> house, and could not shake it: for it was founded upon
> a rock (Luke 6:47–48).

Throughout Scripture, the analogy of a rock is used to
represent our God. We understand a rock to be a place of
safety, a lasting place, a refuge, a sure foundation. "The Lord
is my rock, and my fortress, and my deliverer; my God, my
strength, in whom I will trust" (Ps. 18:2). "Unto thee will I
cry, O Lord my rock" (Ps. 28:1). "The Lord is my defense;
and my God is the rock of my refuge" (Ps. 94:22).

This rock theme has surfaced time and again in Christian hymns, and why not? "O come, let us sing unto the Lord:
let us make a joyful noise to the rock of our salvation" (Ps.
95:1). Obviously, the "rock theme" we are thinking about
here has nothing to do with modern rock music as it is known
— not even so-called Christian rock — but only of this great
"rock of our salvation."

Perhaps the most loved "rock" song is the grand old
hymn "The Solid Rock." The chorus reads:

> *On Christ the solid Rock I stand*
> *All other ground is sinking sand*
> *All other ground is sinking sand.*

Our Lord Jesus Christ reminds us in our text that we
lay a good foundation for our lives when we follow His teach-
ings.

"For other foundation can no man lay than that is laid,
which is Jesus Christ" (1 Cor. 3:11). "The foundation of God
standeth sure" (2 Tim. 2:19). Since our foundation stands,
we are able "to stand [even] against the wiles of the devil"
(Eph. 6:11).

Building on the Foundation

Being justified freely by his grace through the redemption that is in Christ Jesus: Whom God hath set forth to be a propitiation through faith in his blood, to declare his righteousness for the remission of sins (Rom. 3:24–25).

"According to His abundant mercy [our Lord] hath begotten us again unto a lively hope by the resurrection of Jesus Christ from the dead, To an inheritance incorruptible, and undefiled, and that fadeth not away, reserved in heaven for you" (1 Pet. 1:3–4).

A "hope" in Scripture is much more than a "wish" for the future. It is absolute certainty, since it is based on absolute facts of the past. The Christian's hope is based on the finished work of Christ on the cross and His resurrection from the dead. Those who are born again are "kept by the power of God" (v. 5). Thus, our "inheritance" is "reserved in heaven."

The first verse of the beautiful old hymn "The Solid Rock" speaks of this hope and the foundation upon which it is built.

> *My hope is built on nothing less*
> *Than Jesus' blood and righteousness;*
> *I dare not trust the sweetest frame,*
> *But wholly lean on Jesus' name.*

We do not base our hope on "works of righteousness which we have done, but . . . his mercy . . . regeneration, and renewing of the Holy Ghost" (Titus 3:5). Nor do we "trust in uncertain riches, but in the living God" (1 Tim. 6:17). Because of our sin, we have "the sentence of death in ourselves, that we should not trust in ourselves, but in God which raiseth the dead" (2 Cor. 1:9).

Our confidence, our "hope," is well founded only when we wholly lean on Jesus' name, for we are all sinners but now are "washed . . . sanctified . . . [and] justified in the name of the Lord Jesus" (1 Cor. 6:11).

An Anchor of the Soul

We . . . have a strong consolation, who have fled for refuge to lay hold upon the hope set before us: Which hope we have as an anchor of the soul, both sure and stedfast, and which entereth into that within the veil (Heb. 6:18–19).

For those who have tasted God's free gift of forgiveness, gaining salvation and life with the Savior for all eternity, an amazing peace and security awaits. A good analogy is that of a ship in a dreadful storm, cast about in the darkness and nearing unseen danger. But to find the safe harbor is to find a refuge.

The second verse of this precious hymn tells of the Christian's secure haven.

> *When darkness veils His lovely face,*
> *I rest on His unchanging grace;*
> *In every high and stormy gale*
> *My anchor holds within the veil.*

Into each Christian's life comes, from time to time, hardship and heartache, trials and tribulation. Some may even encounter persecution. "For unto you it is given [literally 'graced'] in the behalf of Christ, not only to believe on him, but also to suffer for his sake" (Phil. 1:29).

The certain knowledge of eternal life which we possess gives us the courage to face life's difficulties and be victorious over them. Our faith, our steadfast, secure hope, is in "Jesus the author and finisher of our faith; who for the joy that was set before him endured the cross, despising the shame, and is set down at the right hand of the throne of God" (Heb. 12:2).

Jesus has entered into the presence of God, and "He hath said, I will never leave thee, nor forsake thee" (Heb. 13:5). Thus, we are assured of access. As our text reveals, our "anchor of the soul" is anchored "within the veil," in the presence of God for all eternity.

His Oath, His Covenant, His Blood

Now [may] the God of peace, that brought again from the dead our Lord Jesus, that great shepherd of the sheep, through the blood of the everlasting covenant, Make you perfect in every good work to do his will (Heb. 13:20–21).

This favorite old hymn, written in 1834, was entitled "The Immutable Basis of a Sinner's Hope" when first published. This title more directly describes verse three.

His oath, His covenant, His blood
Support me in the whelming flood;
When all around my soul gives way,
He then is all my hope and stay.

With Israel, God had made a covenant, but now we have a new covenant. At His last supper with His disciples, Jesus said, "This cup is the new testament [same word as covenant] in my blood, which is shed for you" (Luke 22:20). The covenant is unbreakable, for it is "impossible for God to lie" (Heb. 6:18).

The fact that our sins are forgiven gives us the sure hope of a life with Him in heaven. This certain knowledge buoys us along in times of trouble. If God has given us His oath, and sealed His covenant with His blood, how can we doubt?

The hymn speaks of His ministry to us in times of darkest despair — that He becomes our "stay." This word was used in David's psalm of deliverance to mean protector or support. "They prevented me in the day of my calamity: but the Lord was my stay" (Ps. 18:18), protected by His covenant. He provides all that we need.

His covenant with us is unconditional and immutable. It can never be annulled. Our response should be to submit to Him, and if we do, as we see in our text, He will "make [us] perfect in every good work to do his will" (Heb. 13:21).

Faultless Before the Throne

That I may win Christ, And be found in him, not having mine own righteousness, which is of the law, but that which is through the faith of Christ, the righteousness which is of God by faith (Phil. 3:8–9).

We have seen that our hymn rehearses the many facets of our foundation rock, that on which we base our sure hope of His acceptance. Verse four has His ultimate return in view and the standing we shall have in Him before the Father.

> *When He shall come with trumpet sound*
> *O may I then in Him be found*
> *Dressed in His righteousness alone*
> *Faultless to stand before the throne.*

"For the Lord himself shall descend from heaven with a shout, with the voice of the archangel, and with the trump of God: and the dead in Christ shall rise first: Then we which are alive and remain shall be caught up together with them in the clouds, to meet the Lord in the air: and so shall we ever be with the Lord" (1 Thess. 4:16–17).

Our holy God demands nothing less than absolute purity, but even "all our righteousnesses are as filthy rags" (Isa. 64:6) in His sight. But when we enter His presence, we shall have "washed their [our] robes, and made them white in the blood of the Lamb" (Rev. 7:14).

As our text explains, when we are "found in him," our righteousness is really Christ's, and when God the Father sees us, He sees instead Christ's sinlessness imputed to us. This is "the immutable basis of a sinner's hope."

"Now unto him that is able to keep you from falling, and to present you faultless before the presence of his glory with exceeding joy, To the only wise God our Savior, be glory and majesty, dominion and power, both now and ever. Amen" (Jude 24–25).

Jesus, Lover of My Soul

Charles Wesley   Simeon B. Marsh

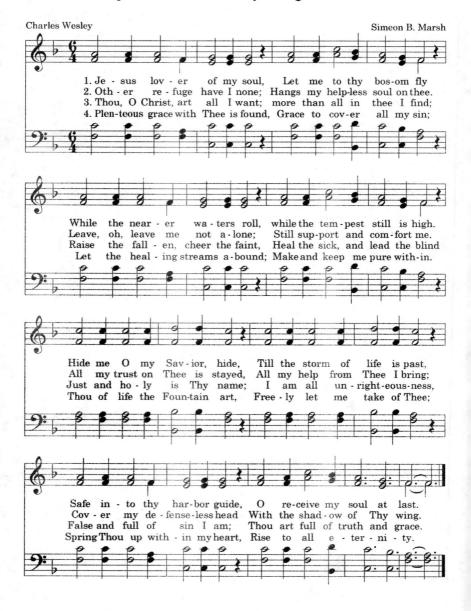

1. Je - sus   lov - er   of my soul,   Let me to thy   bos-om fly
2. Oth - er   re - fuge have I none; Hangs my help-less soul on thee.
3. Thou, O Christ, art   all I want;   more than all in   thee I find;
4. Plen-teous grace with Thee is found, Grace to cov - er   all my sin;

While   the near - er   wa - ters roll,   while the tem - pest still is high.
Leave,   oh, leave me   not a - lone;   Still sup-port and com - fort me.
Raise   the fall - en, cheer the faint, Heal the sick, and lead the blind
Let   the heal - ing streams a - bound; Make and keep me pure with-in.

Hide me O my   Sav - ior, hide,   Till the storm of   life is past,
All   my trust on   Thee is stayed,   All my help   from   Thee I bring;
Just and ho - ly   is Thy name;   I am all   un - right-eous-ness,
Thou of life the   Foun-tain art,   Free - ly let   me   take of Thee;

Safe in - to thy   har-bor guide,   O   re-ceive my soul at last.
Cov - er   my de - fense-less head With the shad - ow of   Thy wing.
False and full of   sin I am;   Thou art full of truth and grace.
Spring Thou up with - in my heart, Rise to all   e - ter - ni - ty.

21

Jesus, Lover of My Soul

One song which was difficult for me to analyze was Charles Wesley's "Jesus, Lover of My Soul." Twice I tried to write, but the more I delved into the words, the more I realized that I knew too little of the love of Jesus. The words spoke of a depth beyond my experience. How could my thoughts even be relevant?

Finally, I purposed in my heart to complete the study — and what a blessing! It's a simply written song, with over 80 percent of the words consisting of only one syllable, but profound in thought. Time spent in study was well spent, for it was spent in Scripture.

In it Christ is presented as lover, refuge, supporter, comforter, helper, wing, healer, leader, just, holy, truth, grace, fountain, and spring. The author presents himself as helpless, hopeless, frightened, trusting, defenseless, fallen, faint, sick, blind, unrighteous, false, full of sin — in all cases portrayals grounded in God's Word.

That such a God could love such a hopeless sinner is nothing short of grace. No human could love in such a way. Oh, that we might come to a fuller experience of that love.

Charles Wesley wrote "Jesus, Lover of my Soul" just two years after his dramatic conversion. His head knowledge had become heart knowledge, and the love of God flowed from his pen.

The certain circumstances under which the hymn was written are evidently lost to history, for several competing stories have come down to us. One such story relates that a vicious storm hit the boat on which Wesley was returning from the mission field, and all aboard feared they would be lost. Wesley at the time, remember, had no personal relationship with God, nor assurance of his salvation. The nearness of death engraved itself deeply on his heart and led eventually to the song, after his heart made full peace with God, and he tasted of His love. Others add that in the midst of the storm, a frightened little bird flew in his window looking for refuge. The bird found it in Wesley's coat, next to his heart, and led to the words "let me to thy bosom fly." Others yet see the song as an allegory of Wesley's own search for God's love and how he found sweet refuge in the Lord.

A final story, which names people and places (thus adding credibility to its authenticity), remembers the opposition that the Wesley brothers faced while teaching their new doctrines, so different from that of the Anglican church. In place of ritual and infant baptism, they taught the necessity of personal, knowledgeable salvation and holy living. The bitter antagonism which gushed from those opposed to the "methods" of the Wesleyan "methodists," erupted all too often in violence.

Once Charles Wesley was caught and beaten by an angry mob. Escaping from them, he hid under a farmer's hedge, with the angry shouts of his searching abusers all around him. His thoughts settled on his Savior's loving protection, and the idea for a song was born. He wrote it, so the story goes, on the very next day.

Many consider this one of the finest songs in the English language, and it is included in almost every hymn book with variations in both words and music. Its musical style may evoke memories of previous generations, but the love of Jesus is timeless. ✻

Jesus, Lover of My Soul

I am persuaded, that neither death, nor life, nor angels, nor principalities, nor powers, nor things present, nor things to come, Nor height, nor depth, nor any other creature, shall be able to separate us from the love of God, which is in Christ Jesus our Lord (Rom. 8:38–39).

Charles Wesley wove into his lyrics the very words and thoughts of Scripture. Such it is with this deeply moving hymn. Let us use its four verses to direct our thoughts to our Lord and Savior, His love for us, and our love in return.

Jesus lover of my soul,
Let me to thy bosom fly
While the nearer waters roll,
While the tempest still is high.
Hide me O my Savior hide
Till the storm of life is past,
Safe into thy harbor guide,
Oh, receive my soul at last.

"Now there was leaning on Jesus' bosom one of his disciples, whom Jesus loved" (John 13:23). How often do we lean on Jesus' bosom and partake of that intimate agape love? There we find safety both in this life and the life to come, for Jesus himself "is in the bosom of the Father" (John 1:18), and He asks, "Father, I will that they also, whom thou hast given me, be with me where I am" (John 17:24).

Safe in His arms of love we find shelter from the flood and tempest. "For in the time of trouble he shall hide me in his pavilion: in the secret of his tabernacle shall he hide me; he shall set me up upon a rock" (Ps. 27:5). "For thou hast been a strength to the poor, a strength to the needy in his distress, a refuge from the storm, a shadow from the heat" (Isa. 25:4).

Jesus, the lover of the soul, paid the ultimate sacrifice and is even now preparing an eternal safe haven for you and me, the objects of His love. He promised, "If I go and prepare a place for you, I will come again, and receive you unto myself; that where I am, there ye may be also" (John 14:3).

In the Shadow of His Wings

Fear thou not; for I am with thee: be not dismayed; for I am thy God: I will strengthen thee; yea, I will help thee; yea, I will uphold thee with the right hand of my righteousness (Isa. 41:10).

Verse two deals with life's trials and tribulations and begins by presenting our Savior as "our refuge and strength, a very present help in trouble" (Ps. 46:1).

> *Other refuge have I none;*
> *Hangs my helpless soul on thee.*
> *Leave, oh, leave me not alone;*
> *Still support and comfort me.*
> *All my trust on thee is stayed,*
> *All my help from thee I bring;*
> *Cover my defenseless head*
> *With the shadow of thy wing.*

In the perils and persecutions of life, we may be helpless on our own, but in love He beckons us to "the throne of grace, that we may obtain mercy, and find grace to help in time of need" (Heb. 4:16). Our soul need not hang in jeopardy.

Because "He hath said, I will never leave thee, nor forsake thee . . . we may boldly say, The Lord is my helper, and I will not fear what man shall do unto me" (Heb. 13:5–6).

"There is none like unto the God of Jeshurun, who rideth upon the heaven in thy help, and in his excellency on the sky. The eternal God is thy refuge, and underneath are the everlasting arms" (Deut. 33:26–27). Help from none other is needed. "Thou, O Lord, art a shield for me; my glory, and the lifter up of mine head" (Ps. 3:3).

As His sacrificial death drew near, Jesus' heart nearly broke over Israel's rejection of His love. "How often would I have gathered thy children together, even as a hen gathereth her chickens under her wings, and ye would not!" (Matt. 23:37). We dare not reject His loving provision. We can pray with David, "Keep me as the apple of the eye, hide me under the shadow of thy wings" (Ps. 17:8). The one to whom we pray will answer, for He is Jesus, the lover of the soul.

Thou, O Christ, Art All I Want

Thou wilt keep him in perfect peace, whose mind
is stayed on thee: because he trusteth in thee (Isa. 26:3).

These touching stanzas reveal Charles Wesley's response of love to Christ's gracious love. One can discern a progression in the verses mirroring a Christian's growth in Christ. Verse three seems to reflect the walk of a maturing believer who desires a full and fruitful oneness with Christ.

> *Thou, O Christ, art all I want;*
> *More than all in thee I find;*
> *Raise the fallen, cheer the faint,*
> *Heal the sick, and lead the blind*
> *Just and holy is thy name;*
> *I am all unrighteousness,*
> *False and full of sin I am;*
> *Thou art full of truth and grace.*

Paul's prayer for his growing converts was, "That ye, being rooted and grounded in love, May be able to comprehend with all saints what is the breadth, and length, and depth, and height; And to know the love of Christ, which passeth knowledge, that ye might be filled with all the fulness of God" (Eph. 3:17–19). He stated his own testimony thus: "I count all things but loss for the excellency of the knowledge of Christ Jesus my Lord" (Phil. 3:8).

In His earthly ministry, Christ lovingly came to "Heal the sick, cleanse the lepers, raise the dead, cast out devils" (Matt. 10:8). He didn't just do this for those who followed Him, but for those who needed it, whether or not they responded in love, and indeed, before long, those whom He had befriended turned on Him and demanded He die a sinner's execution. But He was sinless — "The word was made flesh . . . full of grace and truth" (John 1:14).

Even though He had the power to avoid Calvary, His love was so great that He willingly accepted a sacrificial death for those who sent Him there. "Christ also hath once suffered for sins, the just for the unjust, that he might bring us to God" (1 Pet. 3:18). Truly, He is the lover of the soul.

The Fountain of Life

And the Spirit and the bride say, Come. And let him that heareth say, Come. And let him that is athirst come. And whosoever will, let him take the water of life freely (Rev. 22:17).

Charles Wesley wrote this hymn only two years after he, having personally drank of the Fountain of life, tasted in his soul the love of Jesus. His fourth verse speaks of the mature Christian's desire for purity and victory over sin and looks forward to the ultimate victory in eternity.

> *Plenteous grace with thee is found,*
>   *Grace to cover all my sin;*
> *Let the healing streams abound;*
>   *Make and keep me pure within.*
> *Thou of life the fountain art,*
>   *Freely let me take of thee;*
> *Spring thou up within my heart,*
>   *Rise to all eternity.*

Our maturing in Christ begins at the time of repentance and forgiveness, and no matter the depth of our sin, His love can conquer it, for "the grace of our Lord was exceeding abundant with faith and love which is in Christ Jesus. . . . Christ Jesus came into the world to save sinners; of whom I am chief" (1 Tim. 1:14–15). Indeed, "the blood of Jesus Christ . . . cleanseth us from all sin" (1 John 1:7).

"Behold, what manner of love the Father hath bestowed upon us, that we should be called the sons of God . . . Every man that hath this hope in him purifieth himself, even as he is pure" (1 John 3:1–3). Thus, His gracious love for us becomes the agent of pure living in our lives.

The love of Jesus Christ is like "a well of living waters" (Song of Sol. 4:15). This well is freely open to all, as we see in our text. Jesus, the lover of the soul, who says "Come," also says, "Whosoever drinketh of the water that I shall give him shall never thirst; but the water that I shall give him shall be in him a well of water springing up into everlasting life" (John 4:14).

Joy to the World

From Psalm 98
Isaac Watts

George F. Handel

1. Joy to the world, the Lord is come! Let earth re-
2. Joy to the earth! the Sav-ior reigns! Let men their
3. No more let sins and sor-rows grow, Nor thorns in-
4. He rules the world with truth and grace, And makes the

ceive her King; Let ev-er-y heart pre-pare Him room,
songs em-ploy; While fields and floods, rocks, hills, and plains
fest the ground; He comes to make His bless-ings flow
na-tions prove The glo-ries of His right-eous-ness,

And heaven and na-ture sing. And heaven and na-ture
Re-peat the sound-ing joy. Re-peat the sound-ing
Far as the curse is found. Far as the curse is
And won-ders of His love. And won-ders of His

1. And heaven and na-ture sing.

1. And

sing. And heaven, and heaven and na-ture sing.
joy. Re-peat, re-peat the sound-ing joy.
found. Far as, far as the curse is found.
love. And won-ders, won-ders of His love.

heaven and na-ture sing.

22

Joy to the World

So far in this book we have studied four hymns by the great hymn writer, Charles Wesley, and one more is to follow. While he is perhaps the greatest English hymn writer ever, the term "Father of English Hymnody" goes to Isaac Watts, author of many hymns still sung today, such as, "When I Survey the Wondrous Cross," "Jesus Shall Reign," and "Joy to the World."

Isaac Watts was a true scholar, excelling in numerous fields including theology and linguistics. Substantially home-schooled, he exhibited these aptitudes from his youth. Biographers have documented that at age 5 he learned Latin, and Greek at age 9. At 11 he learned to speak French and at 13 he learned Hebrew, all at the hand of his church-deacon father. A critic of the government-established church, Enoch Watts spent numerous spells in jail. It was then that Isaac's mother tutored him in poetry and music.

All this led to Isaac's study of philosophy and theology, which, in turn, led to the writing of many important books, read throughout England and Europe, and over 600 hymns, some of which are sung throughout the world to this day.

Perhaps his greatest love was that of theology and had been from his youth. Imagine a youth of today using his name to form an acrostic in order to explain Christian doctrine, which young Isaac did at age seven.

I — I am a vile, polluted lump of earth
S — So I've continued ever since my birth
A — Although Jehovah, grace doth daily give me
A — As sure this monster, Satan, will deceive me
C — Come therefore, Lord, from Satan's claws
relieve me.

W — Wash me in thy blood, O Christ
A — And grace divine impart
T — Then search and try the corners of my heart
T — That I in all things may be fit to do
S — Service to thee, and thy praise, too.

The church of his day sang only the psalms in a most dull way. When he complained, his father challenged the young upstart to write something better. The result? A revolution in church music.

Still, Isaac Watts respected the traditional psalms. In 1719 he published a hymnal entitled *Psalms of David Imitated in the Language of the New testament,* in which he used 138 of the psalms as a basis for hymns containing New Testament truth. "Joy to the World" is his paraphrase of the last half of Psalm 98.

Children love music, especially memorable tunes. Children who grow up in church have "Jesus Loves Me" indelibly imprinted on their brains. As parents, that's our goal — to have the things of the Lord so much a part of our children that they can never fully leave.

Some of my very first childhood memories are of playing "church." My older sister would be the preacher and I would be the song leader. I would stand up on a box and wave my arms and sing and sing. I've noticed that "Joy to the World" is one of those songs that stick with kids. Perhaps this was one of my repertoire even then.

Although this song is usually sung at Christmas time, it covers much more. In fact, Isaac Watts' original title for the work was, "The Messiah's Coming and Kingdom." As you'll see, this title fits the song's message. ✄

Joy to the World

And the angel said unto them. . . . For unto you is born this day in the city of David a Savior, which is Christ the Lord" (Luke 2:10–11).

At Christmas time we celebrate the birth of Christ, an occasion of "great joy," for it marked the beginning of the redemptive work of our "Savior, which is Christ the Lord." No other hymn is more enjoyed at this season than "Joy to the World." As we use its words to direct our thoughts, we may be surprised by its theme.

Joy to the world, the Lord is come!
Let earth receive her king;
Let every heart prepare Him room,
And heaven and nature sing.

The presence of the Lord brings joy to those who follow Him, and it did so even before His birth (Luke 1:44). When Mary was carrying Him in her womb, she exclaimed, "My soul doth magnify the Lord, And my spirit hath rejoiced in God my Savior" (Luke 1:46–47). When he came, "there was no room for them [Him] in the inn" (Luke 2:7), but "if thou shalt confess with thy mouth the Lord Jesus, and shalt believe in thine heart that God hath raised him from the dead, thou shalt be saved" (Rom. 10:9). Truly, we can make room for Him in our hearts.

But was He welcomed as King? No, He was "despised and rejected of men; a man of sorrows, and acquainted with grief" (Isa. 53:3), and in just a few short years was crucified for claiming to be King. It has been many times prophesied that "the Lord shall be king over all the earth" (Zech. 14:9), and that all creation shall rejoice. "Sing, O ye heavens shout . . . ye lower parts of the earth . . . ye mountains" (Isa. 44:23).

Thus, we see that this favorite Christmas hymn is not looking back to His first coming, but forward to His second coming (Titus 2:13). When the Lord is come, it will indeed mean "Joy to the World."

The Savior Reigns

But rejoice, inasmuch as ye are partakers of Christ's sufferings; that, when his glory shall be revealed, ye may be glad also with exceeding joy (1 Pet. 4:13).

Our Savior Jesus Christ has finished His work of redemption. Verse two of the Christmas hymn, "Joy to the World," describes results of His victory.

Joy to the earth! the Savior reigns!
Let men their songs employ;
While fields and floods, rocks, hills, and plains
Repeat the sounding joy.

"By him were all things created" (Col. 1:16) and "by him all things consist" (v. 17). But His creation in Adam had rejected His reign and come under the penalty of that wrong choice. Thus, the entire creation "was made subject to vanity" and is under "the bondage of corruption." Indeed, "the whole creation groaneth and travaileth in pain" (Rom. 8:20–22) and does not yet experience its full "joy."

In Genesis 3 we read of the universal penalty for sin. Plants were cursed with "thorns also and thistles" (v. 18). The animals were cursed with the serpent. "Cursed above all cattle, and above every beast of the field" (v. 14). Eve was cursed with sorrow and difficulty in childbirth (v. 16). Adam was cursed with expulsion from Eden and a life of sorrow and toil (v. 17, 19, 23). Even the very "ground" was cursed for his sake (v. 17). Everything is in an irreversible cycle of deterioration and death.

Yet the prophet Isaiah tells us of a time when: "The wilderness and the solitary place shall be glad for them; and the desert shall rejoice, and blossom as the rose. It shall blossom abundantly, and rejoice even with joy and singing" (Isa. 35:1–2).

Christ's first advent gained this victory, but it has not yet been fully realized. This speaks of His second (still future) advent. Then there will be "Joy to the World."

No More Sin and Sorrow

For ye shall go out with joy, and be led forth with peace: the mountains and the hills shall break forth before you into singing, and all the trees of the field shall clap their hands. Instead of the thorn shall come up the fir tree, and instead of the brier shall come up the myrtle tree (Isa. 55:12–13).

The well-loved hymn, "Joy to the World," is not about Christmas, Christ's first coming, at all. Rather it is about His yet future second coming as "King over all the earth" (Zech. 14:9). This theme is obvious in the third verse.

No more let sins and sorrows grow,
Nor thorns infest the ground;
He comes to make His blessings flow
Far as the curse is found.

Today we live in a world dominated by sin and its consequences — pain, sorrow, disease, and death. But when He returns and claims His full victory, He "shall wipe away all tears from their eyes; and there shall be no more death, neither sorrow, nor crying, neither shall there be any more pain: for the former things are passed away" (Rev. 21:4). Even the earth and its flora will rejoice, as we see in our text.

Our home on this "new earth" (Rev. 21:1) will be "the holy city, new Jerusalem" (v. 2). Our food will be "the tree of life" (Rev. 22:2), and our drink "a pure river of water of life" (Rev. 22:1). He promises that He will come to make "the places round about my hill a blessing" (Ezek. 34:26).

The contrast between that world of blessing and our world is great. "The earth also is defiled under the inhabitants thereof. . . . Therefore hath the curse devoured the earth, and they that dwell therein are desolate" (Isa. 24:5–6).

But when He comes, all the consequences of man's rebellion will be removed, "and there shall be no more curse" (Rev. 22:3). Only then will there be "Joy to the World."

He Rules the World

The kingdoms of this world are become the kingdoms of our Lord, and of his Christ; and he shall reign for ever and ever (Rev. 11:15).

Isaac Watts was known for saturating his lyrics with Scripture and biblical doctrines. The final verse deals with our Lord's eternal reign over the earth following His return to earth the second time.

He rules the world with truth and grace,
And makes the nations prove
The glories of His righteousness,
And wonders of His love.

The apostle John, who wrote much about Jesus Christ's glorious second coming, knew Him and loved Him at His first coming. "The Word was made flesh, and dwelt among us (and we beheld his glory, the glory as of the only begotten of the Father), full of grace and truth" (John 1:14).

His reign over the earth will be received with joy by those who remain. "O let the nations be glad and sing for joy: for thou shalt judge the people righteously, and govern the nations upon earth" (Ps. 67:4). God the Father has ordained this righteous reign of Christ. "Unto the Son he saith, Thy throne, O God, is for ever and ever: a scepter of righteousness is the scepter of thy kingdom" (Heb. 1:8).

This present world with all its reminders of sin and death is not acceptable for such a kingdom. It "shall be dissolved, and the elements shall melt with fervent heat. Nevertheless we, according to his promise, look for new heavens and a new earth, wherein dwelleth righteousness" (2 Pet. 3:12–13).

All that has gone on before gives us confidence that what He has promised will surely come to pass. When? We don't know, but, "be ye also patient; stablish your hearts: for the coming of the Lord draweth nigh" (James 5:8). And then, finally, there will be true "Joy in the World."

All My Sins Have Been Forgiven

Philip F. Hiller
Trans. by Esther Bergen

Jean J. Rousseau

1. All my sins have been for-giv - en; God is mer - ci - ful to me;
2. My ac - count is closed for - ev - er; Je - sus Christ has paid it all;
3. How my count-less sins de-pressed me, Gave me sor-row, shame and tears
4. Now my soul shall live for - ev - er; No more can the foe con - demn;

Faith has claimed the Sav-ior's prom - ise, Grace and par - don, full and free;
Shed His blood my sin to cov - er, Paid the price to save my soul;
How His wrath and an - ger crushed me, Filled my heart with doubts and fears.
Noth - ing from God's love can sev - er, Peace and joy are found in Him

O my soul, be ev - er prais - ing, For the great Re - deem-er's love;
There is now no con-dem-na - tion, I am ful - ly rec - on-ciled;
But my soul cried out in an - guish, Called for mer - cy and for grace,
Thus I jour-ney on to heav - en, Cross death's por-tals joy-ful - ly;

Joy - ous songs to Him be rais - ing, Un - to God in heaven a - bove.
What a won - der - ful sal - va - tion, For a sin - ner so de - filed!
Je - sus heard my sup - pli - ca - tion, grant-ed par - don, and re - lease.
All my sins have been for-giv - en, God is mer - ci - ful to me.

23

All My Sins
Have Been Forgiven

Our time in Oklahoma was a true blessing to our family. As a newly married couple with young children, we richly benefited from the fellowship and teaching there. And since it was a small church, there were many opportunities to serve, including occasional preaching and, most importantly, leading the singing!

But in 1984 that chapter in our lives was about to close. My research and speaking on creationist topics in addition to the search for Noah's ark had begun to absorb much of my time, so after much prayer and consultation, I decided to leave my faculty position at the university and join my father at the Institute for Creation Research. Of course, this also meant moving our church home. A going-away party was scheduled for the Sunday evening prior to our departure.

On the Sunday prior to the "goodbye" party, the pastor wanted me to preach a farewell message to those dear friends. Since it would be awkward for one person to lead singing and preach, I relinquished the singing to a good friend (who could read music). He even selected the songs for that morning, including one I had never heard. At the last minute, however, after the bulletins had been printed, he took sick and turned the duty back over to me.

"Don't worry about that new song," he said, "you'll love it, and the tune is easy to pick up. It sounds just like the kid's song 'Go Tell Aunt Rhody.' " Sure enough, it did, and I did.

Over the next week, the song wouldn't leave. "All my sins have been forgiven, God is merciful to me." I sang it day and night. I have been forgiven much and tasted God's mercy. That song became my song.

That next Sunday morning, the congregation was told we would sing my entire list of "top 10" songs at the going-away party that evening. All I had to do was list them. Try as I might, I couldn't get the list below 30, and the new song, "All My Sins Have Been Forgiven," was on it. Believe it or not, that evening my friend led in singing all 30 as I sat weeping in the front row.

Many people rose and publicly said their goodbyes to our family. (The regret at losing my wife seemed more real than *my* leaving.) Those who said something about me had a common theme to their comments — how, through my enthusiasm for good hymns, they had come to love them, too, and to more completely love the God of whom and to whom they sang. The warmth of that evening has stayed with me through the years.

It really stayed with me through the next week. I photocopied those 30-some hymns and carried them with me as I drove across the country, alone in the car loaded with household goods — a car whose radio didn't work. I must have sung those songs at the top of my voice for 1,000 miles and arrived in San Diego with no voice at all.

Of this hymn's history and authors, I know nothing. I do know its words go deep into the precious doctrine of salvation. I also know it's in all-too-few modern hymn books. I've had to use that tattered photocopy to teach it in my new church. I pray that its inclusion in this devotional book will help spread it around. ✄

All My Sins Have Been Forgiven

For thou, Lord, art good, and ready to forgive;
and plenteous in mercy unto all them that call upon
thee (Ps. 86:5).

The doctrine that sets Christianity apart from all other
religions and cults is that of a basis for forgiveness of sins
which is still in keeping with God's holy and just nature.
Each of us sins and offends God's holy nature. His justice
demands that sin's penalty be paid, either by the sinner himself or a sinless substitute. In Christianity, this was accomplished as God the Son, the sinless Lamb of God, died to pay
our penalty, making forgiveness and restoration possible. No
work of our own can be involved, it must be simply believed
and claimed by faith. Such a theme dominates this old hymn,
and we shall use its verses to remind us of these truths.

All my sins have been forgiven;
God is merciful to me;
Faith has claimed the Savior's promise,
Grace and pardon, full and free;
O my soul, be ever praising,
For the great Redeemer's love;
Joyous songs to Him be raising,
Unto God in heaven above.

Our Savior has promised, "I will be merciful to their
unrighteousness, and their sins and their iniquities will I
remember no more" (Heb. 8:12). The promised mercy is desperately needed, for "the Scripture hath concluded all under
sin," thankfully, "the promise by faith of Jesus Christ might
be given to them that believe" (Gal. 3:22). This pardon is
absolutely complete. "As far as the east is from the west, so
far hath he removed our transgressions from us" (Ps. 103:12).
This removal of our sin exceeds forgiveness, it is full "redemption through his blood" (Eph. 1:7). It is also absolutely
free, for "by the righteousness of one the free gift came upon
all men unto justification of life" (Rom. 5:18). Throughout
eternity we will sing "a new song . . . for thou wast slain, and
hast redeemed us to God by thy blood" (Rev. 5:9).

My Account Is Closed Forever

> For all have sinned, and come short of the glory of God; Being justified freely by his grace through the redemption that is in Christ Jesus (Rom. 3:23–24).

Our Redeemer has identified himself thus: "I, even I, am he that blotteth out thy transgression for mine own sake, and will not remember thy sins" (Isa. 43:25). His death fully paid the penalty for our sin. "Blotting out the handwriting of ordinances [i.e., the lengthy list of our sins] that was against us, which was contrary to us, and took it out of the way, nailing it to his cross" (Col. 2:14).

The second verse of the hymn expresses this.

> *My account is closed forever;*
> *Jesus Christ has paid it all;*
> *Shed His blood my sin to cover,*
> *Paid the price to save my soul;*
> *There is now no condemnation,*
> *I am fully reconciled;*
> *What a wonderful salvation,*
> *For a sinner so defiled!*

Surely Jesus Christ has paid our full account. "By his own blood he . . . obtained eternal redemption for us" (Heb. 9:12). As we see in our text, all of us had an account to be paid. In God's just economy, the penalty must be paid, and "the wages of sin is death;" thankfully, however, "the gift of God is eternal life through Jesus Christ our Lord" (Rom. 6:23).

Because the account is closed, "There is therefore now no condemnation to them which are in Christ Jesus" (Rom. 8:1). It was the eternal plan of God the Father who "was in Christ, reconciling the world unto himself, not imputing their trespasses unto them" (2 Cor. 5:19). At the time of His sacrifice, we were "alienated [from Him] and enemies . . . yet now hath he reconciled In the body of his flesh through death, to present you holy and unblameable and unreproveable in his sight" (Col. 1:21–22). Truly this is a wonderful salvation. To defiled sinners He says, "Though your sins be as scarlet, they shall be as white as snow" (Isa. 1:18).

A Pardon Granted

Wash me throughly from mine iniquity, and cleanse me from my sin. For I acknowledge my transgressions: and my sin is ever before me. Against thee, thee only, have I sinned, and done this evil in thy sight (Ps. 51:2–4).

David had developed a sensitive heart toward sin. He experienced the misery of separation from God (Ps. 32:3–4), which drove him to repentance and confession, as we see in our text, and "thou forgavest the iniquity of my sin" (v. 5). The third verse reminds us of David's (and our) inner turmoil.

How my countless sins depressed me,
Gave me sorrow, shame and tears
How His wrath and anger crushed me,
Filled my heart with doubts and fears.
But my soul cried out in anguish,
Called for mercy and for grace,
Jesus heard my supplication,
Granted pardon, and release.

The Creator placed within each person a conscience (Rom. 2:15). Unless this is seared and made ineffective by the constant practice of willful sin, it convicts, and "godly sorrow worketh repentance to salvation" (2 Cor. 7:10). Our sin places us at "enmity against God" (Rom. 8:7), and even if we only "offend in one point, [we are] guilty of all" (James 2:10). Sin exposes our lack of "holiness, without which no man shall see the Lord" (Heb. 12:14).

The estranged son, who after rejecting what he knew was right, returned and said, "Father, I have sinned against heaven, and in thy sight, and am no more worthy to be called thy son" (Luke 15:21). He deserved nothing, but was granted his father's restored favor. "How much more shall your Father which is in heaven give good things to them that ask him?" (Matt. 7:11) including forgiveness and restoration.

As with the forgiven David we can respond in thankfulness: "Blessed is he whose transgression is forgiven . . . the man unto whom the Lord imputeth not iniquity" (Ps. 32:1–2).

God Is Merciful to Me

> But now being made free from sin, and become
> servants to God, ye have your fruit unto holiness, and
> the end everlasting life (Rom. 6:22).

Forgiveness of sin brings cleansing, a secure relationship with God, and makes possible a life of fruitful holiness. It also brings eternal life, which starts at salvation and becomes fully realized when we pass into the life to come. The final verse speaks of this ultimate victory, when "the accuser . . . is cast down" (Rev. 12:10).

> *Now my soul shall live forever;*
> *No more can the foe condemn;*
> *Nothing from God's love can sever,*
> *Peace and joy are found in Him.*
> *Thus I journey on to heaven,*
> *Cross death's portals joyfully;*
> *All my sins have been forgiven,*
> *God is merciful to me.*

Jesus said of those that follow Him, "I give unto them eternal life . . . neither shall any man pluck them out of my hand. My Father, which gave them me, is greater than all; and no man is able to pluck them out of my Father's hand" (John 10:28–29). We are kept by the hands of "Him that is able to keep you from falling, and to present you faultless before the presence of his glory with exceeding joy" (Jude 24).

Secure in Him, we can face death joyfully as citizens of heaven, for we are only "strangers and pilgrims on the earth" (Heb. 11:13). As Paul said, "For to me to live is Christ, and to die is gain" (Phil. 1:21), for, "to be absent from the body, and [is] to be present with the Lord" (2 Cor. 5:8). "Death is swallowed up in victory" (1 Cor. 15:54).

God is so merciful to us. Even though we were "dead in your [our] sins . . . [yet] hath he quickened [i.e., made us alive] together with him, having forgiven you [us] all trespasses" (Col. 2:13). Thus, each of us can say, "Surely goodness and mercy shall follow me all the days of my life: and I will dwell in the house of the Lord for ever" (Ps. 23:6).

Complete in Thee

Aaron R. Wolfe
Refrain, James M. Gray

Talmadge J. Bittikofer

1. Com-plete in Thee! no work of mine May take, dear Lord, the place of Thine;
2. Com-plete in Thee! no more shall sin, Thy grace hath conquered, reign with-in;
3. Com-plete in Thee-each want sup-plied, And no good thing to me de - nied;
4. Dear Sav-ior! when be - fore Thy bar All tribes and tongues as-sem-bled are,

Thy blood hath par-don bought for me, And I am now com-plete in Thee.
Thy voice shall bid the tempt - er flee, And I shall stand com-plete in Thee.
Since Thou my por - tion, Lord wilt be, I ask no more, com-plete in Thee.
A - mong Thy cho-sen will I be, At Thy right hand, com-plete in Thee.

Yes, jus - ti - fied! O bless - ed thought! And sanc-ti - fied! Sal-va-tion wrought!

Thy blood hath par-don bought for me, And glo - ri - fied, I too, shall be!

24

Complete in Thee

Writing devotionals has been good for me. Every preacher will tell you that he learned more in preparation for the sermon than anyone could have learned listening to it. That's true also in the classroom, and it's true in writing.

By far the greater number of my devotionals have dealt with scriptural passages, not with hymns. Topics for these devotionals seem to run in spurts, coming from my own personal study times. Starting with my first devotional on Hebrews 13:5 (mentioned in the earlier discussion on "How Firm a Foundation"), I seemed to encounter, at every turn, Scriptures dealing with the believer's security in Christ. Many of these scriptural encounters developed into careful study and then into devotionals. Once an outline for the devotional can be decided upon, the cross references can be found and the writing begun.

Even now, I love to read my earlier devotionals. They bring back good memories of my preparation time, meditating on a passage, searching for cross references, and praying for God's wisdom in writing. God has taught me so much through this process. I even get to edit and compile. It's one of my favorite tasks, keeping me in the Word to a depth which might be neglected without this discipline.

Another stream of thought which has woven itself into

many of my devotionals is that of the definitions of the terms justification, sanctification, and glorification, all related to the salvation and maturation of believers. "Complete in Thee" — one of my "top ten" songs — deals with these concepts and does so in a wonderful, singable, memorable way. It serves to teach as well as uplift, and that's how it should be.

This song can be found in various hymnals, but I never ran across it until recently. It was introduced to me by Harold (the retired Navy mechanic), my personal expert on obscure hymns. This song is his very favorite.

How could this hymn have slipped into relative obscurity? It's such a beautiful song — so full of doctrinal nuggets. It's a teaching testimony in song. What church wouldn't want their people to know that our works are ineffectual in gaining salvation? Christ has done all that was necessary, and we stand complete in Him, declared righteous before our Holy God! This song ought to be sung often and the truths contained therein made certain.

Unfortunately, I've not been able to find out anything about the history of this hymn or its author. Actually, there are two authors. It seems Aaron Wolfe wrote the verses and James Gray added the chorus later when the music was written in 1905.

Even if it has no known history, this song deserves a future — and a present. ✀

Complete in Thee

Moreover whom he did predestinate, them he also called: and whom he called, them he also justified: and whom he justified, them he also glorified (Rom. 8:30).

When a believer ponders all that God has done for him through Christ's perfect work on the cross, it drives him to his knees in thankfulness. This moving hymn expresses these thoughts well.

Yes justified! O blessed thought!
And sanctified! Salvation wrought!
Thy blood hath pardon bought for me,
And glorified, I too shall be!

The term "justified" may be understood as a forensic term, the declaration a judge would make when a defendant is declared to be fully righteous, not because he himself is righteous, but because Christ's righteousness is imputed to him. "Being justified freely by his grace through the redemption that is in Christ Jesus" (Rom. 3:24).

To be sanctified is to be set apart for holiness. It includes a progressive aspect and has to do with holy character, which cannot be imputed but must be built up through obedience to the word of God. This sanctification comes at a price, for "we are sanctified through the offering of the body of Jesus Christ once for all" (Heb. 10:10).

Pardoned is the same word as "forgiven," a remission of the punishment for sin. "We have redemption through his blood, even the forgiveness of sins" (Col. 1:14).

"Glorified" looks to the future, when He "shall change our vile body, that it may be fashioned like unto his glorious body" (Phil. 3:21) when we achieve complete Christlikeness. As we see in our text, all of this is His doing.

In Him we are complete.

No Work of Mine

Not by works of righteousness which we have done, but according to his mercy he saved us. . . . He shed on us abundantly through Jesus Christ our Savior (Titus 3:5–6).

The first verse of the stirring hymn, "Complete in Thee" amplifies the concept of justification solely as a work of God.

Complete in Thee! no work of mine
May take, dear Lord, the place of Thine;
Thy blood hath pardon bought for me,
And I am now complete in Thee.

As our text reveals, this work comes through His mercy and grace and not by works of righteousness which we have done, "for by the works of the law shall no flesh be justified" (Gal. 2:16), "That no flesh should glory in his presence" (1 Cor. 1:29).

The key to it all is tied up in the phrase "thy blood hath pardon bought for me," and this transaction cannot be overstated. Consider our state without it, "for all have sinned, and come short of the glory of God" (Rom. 3:23), and "the wages of sin is death" (Rom. 6:23). "But God commendeth his love toward us, in that, while we were yet sinners, Christ died for us. . . . being now justified by his blood, we shall be saved from wrath through him" (Rom. 5:8–9).

We could not have been redeemed by our own actions, or the sacrifice of "corruptible things," but only "with the precious blood of Christ, as of a lamb without blemish and without spot" (1 Pet. 1:18–19). Only through "the blood of his cross" can we be "reconciled" to the Father (Col. 1:20), our broken relationship with Him healed.

There will come a time around the throne of the Lamb when we will sing, "Thou art worthy . . . for thou wast slain, and hast redeemed us to God by thy blood out of every kindred, and tongue, and people, and nation" (Rev. 5:9).

In Him and through His blood, we are complete.

Sin Reigns No More

That as sin hath reigned unto death, even so might grace reign through righteousness unto eternal life by Jesus Christ our Lord (Rom. 5:21).

As we observe the words of the beautiful hymn, "Complete in Thee," we notice that verse two deals with the believer's deepening walk in Christ, the setting aside of sinful practices by resisting the tempter, i.e., progressive sanctification.

Complete in Thee! no more shall sin,
Thy grace hath conquered, reign within;
Thy voice shall bid the tempter flee,
And I shall stand complete in Thee.

Contemplate what it means to be complete in Him. "In him dwelleth all the fullness of the Godhead bodily. And ye are complete in him, which is the head of all principality and power" (Col. 2:9–10). This is made possible because we are "buried with him in baptism" (v. 12), "quickened together with him" (v. 13), thus "dead with Christ" to worldly things (v. 20). "If ye then be risen with Christ, seek those things which are above" (Col. 3:1).

Jesus Christ, in His humanity, was tempted to sin (Luke 4:1–13), but He resisted by quoting the word of God (v. 4, 8, 12). Complete in Him, we have the same source of power and victory. "Submit yourselves therefore to God. Resist the devil, and he will flee from you" (James 4:7). "Wherefore take unto you the whole armor of God, that ye may be able to withstand in the evil day, and having done all, to stand" (Eph. 6:13).

Our text sums up this concept well. Sin had reigned in our lives, but now grace reigns. This standing comes only through the work of Jesus Christ. His grace will encourage righteous decisions and habits — victory over sin!

Our goal is that we "may stand perfect and complete in all the will of God" (Col. 4:12).

Thou Art My Portion

My flesh and my heart faileth: but God is the strength of my heart, and my portion for ever (Ps. 73:26).

As we have seen, God's free gift of salvation is based on the work of Christ, "In whom we have redemption through his blood, the forgiveness of sins, according to the riches of his grace" (Eph. 1:7). Indeed, "God shall supply all your need according to his riches in glory by Christ Jesus" (Phil. 4:19), as the third verse of our study hymn reminds us.

> *Complete in Thee — each want supplied,*
> *and no good thing to me denied;*
> *Since Thou my portion, Lord, wilt be,*
> *I ask no more, complete in Thee.*

Consider the fact that He is our Father, that we are the children of God. "If ye then, being evil, know how to give good gifts unto your children, how much more shall your Father which is in heaven give good things to them that ask him?" (Matt. 7:11). Note the recurrence of superlatives in these verses describing His provision. "God is able to make all grace abound toward you; that ye, always having all sufficiency in all things, may abound to every good work . . . Being enriched in every thing to all bountifulness, which causeth through us thanksgiving to God" (2 Cor. 9:8–11).

Our real home is in heaven, as "children of God: And if children, then heirs; heirs of God, and joint-heirs with Christ . . . he that spared not his own Son, but delivered him up for us all, how shall he not with him also freely give us all things?" (Rom. 8:16–32).

King David wrote: "Bless the Lord, O my soul, and forget not all his benefits: Who forgiveth all thine iniquities . . . who crowneth thee with lovingkindness and tender mercies; Who satisfieth thy mouth with good things" (Ps. 103:2–5).

We can ask for nothing beyond completeness in Him.

Before Thy Bar

> For we must all appear before the judgment seat
> of Christ; that every one may receive the things done
> in his body, according to that he hath done, whether
> it be good or bad (2 Cor. 5:10).

Our study of the themes expressed in the doctrinally
rich hymn "Complete in Thee" has noted justification, sanctification, and God's provision — all because Christ's blood
had bought pardon for us. Verse four deals with our ultimate glorification.

> *Dear Savior! When before Thy bar*
> *All tribes and tongues assembled are,*
> *Among Thy chosen will I be,*
> *At Thy right hand, complete in Thee.*

Many things may be uncertain in life, but one thing is
certain. "We shall all stand before the judgment seat of
Christ" (Rom. 14:10), for "it is appointed unto men once to
die, but after this the judgment" (Heb. 9:27). On what legal
basis would the Holy God allow a sinner entrance?

One day there will be "a great multitude, which no man
could number, of all nations, and kindreds, and people, and
tongues, [standing] . . . before the throne, and before the
Lamb . . . [having] washed their robes, and made them white
in the blood of the Lamb" (Rev. 7:9–14). The Judge doesn't
see their guilt, He sees only Christ's righteousness imputed
to them. Sin's penalty has already been paid, for "Christ
died for our sins" (1 Cor. 15:3) and made us fit to "stand
perfect and complete in all the will of God" (Col. 4:12).

But even that's not all! For, "when Christ, who is our
life, shall appear, then shall ye also appear with him in glory"
(Col. 3:4).

How very complete we are in Him.

A Child of the King

Hattie E. Buell

Rev. John B. Sumner

1. My Fa-ther is rich in hous-es and lands, He hold-eth the
2. My Fa-ther's own Son, the Sav-ior of men, Once wan-dered the
3. I once was an out-cast stran-ger on earth, A sin-ner by
4. A tent or a cot-tage, why should I care? They're build-ing a

wealth of the worlds in His hands! Of ru-bies and dia-monds, of
earth as the poor-est of them; But now He is plead-ing our
choice and an al-ien by birth; But I've been a-dopt-ed, my
pal-ace for me o-ver there; Though ex-iled from home, yet,

sil-ver and gold, His cof-fers are full, He has rich-es un-told.
par-don on high, That we may be His when He comes by and by.
name's writ-ten down, An heir to a man-sion, a robe, and a crown.
still I may sing! All glo-ry to God, I'm a child of the King.

I'm a child of the King, A child of the King

With Je-sus my Sav-ior, I'm a child of the King.

25

A Child of the King

In my many travels in Turkey, I have seen about everything. Much of my time has been spent in the frontier near Mount Ararat, where many people live in extremely primitive conditions.

The towns near the base of the mountain have improved somewhat since my first trip in 1971, but the poorest of the poor here in the States would have a difficult time with the standard of living accepted as normal there. Few homes have electricity. Indoor plumbing means you have to carry the pot outside every now and then. Water buffalo roam the streets, and little girls catch the falling buffalo dung to make fuel to cook supper. At supper time, the aroma is unforgettable.

In the villages life is even more sparse. Nearly every waking moment of every member of the family is spent just trying to survive that day. Wheat must be ground. Sheep must be sheared. Thread must be made from the wool to weave garments. The goats and the water buffalo must be milked. Yogurt and cheese must be made from the milk. The herd of sheep must be pastured in the summer, but they must spend the winter inside the mud home with the family. In the "zonas," or shepherd's summer encampments on the mountain—well, at least the air is fresh.

I've also spent much time in the capital cities negotiating with leaders of the country and accepting the hospitality of some of the richest and most powerful families in the country. With servants and cooks and carpets and the best of everything, living is easy and attention can be paid to other matters.

It would be difficult to tell which group is happiest, but I suspect it wouldn't be hard to select which lifestyle you'd prefer, all other things being equal.

The analogy is imperfect, but let it remind you what it means to be a Christian. Our father is the King! We have been adopted into His family. In this life we have true joy and the privilege of serving Him who sacrificed all for us. He who owns everything promises to supply our every material need. We have forgiveness for our sin and freedom from its guilt. He gives us His love to share with others. In the life to come we have an eternal inheritance fit for a child of the King.

In 1876, Hattie Buell attended a Methodist camp meeting in beautiful upstate New York. The hymns and testimonies thrilled her soul and the speaker that morning expounded the blessings given to a sinner through faith in Jesus Christ's finished work on the cross. Children of the King — our Heavenly Father is King — we have a mansion awaiting us when our pilgrimage here is over, he repeated.

As she walked back to her cottage, the words to the heart-warming hymn began to come. "With Jesus my Savior, I'm a child of the King." ✄

A Child of the King

The Spirit itself beareth witness with our spirit,
that we are the children of God: And if children, then
heirs; heirs of God, and joint-heirs with Christ (Rom.
8:16–17).

From time to time it behooves us to step back and take
a broad look at salvation. It helps us to remember our present
standing in Christ, all stemming from His work of redemption. Indeed, we "are all the children of God by faith in Christ
Jesus" (Gal. 3:26). This theme dominates the favorite old
hymn, "A Child of the King," and we can use its chorus and
four verses to remind us.

I'm a child of the King, A child of the King
With Jesus my Savior, I'm a child of the King.

In the eternal counsels of the Trinity, God the Son chose
to be our Savior. Creation had been "very good" (Gen. 1:31)
in the beginning, free from sin and its penalty, death. But
creation, in the person of Adam and Eve, rebelled against
the Creator's authority, opting for sin and the resulting separation from God and His holiness. Sin's penalty must be paid,
either by the sinner (with eternal estrangement from God
ensuing), or the penalty could be paid by an acceptable,
sinless substitute. Such was the penalty paid by Jesus our
Savior, for "when we were enemies, we were reconciled to
God by the death of his Son" (Rom. 5:10). This work of redemption was solely His work. "God sent forth his Son. . . .
To redeem them that were under the law, that we might
receive the adoption of sons" (Gal. 4:4–5).

Think of it — separated from God by our own sinful,
rebellious choices. We were God's enemies under penalty of
death. But "Christ died for our sins" (1 Cor. 15:3). Now an
intimate Father-child relationship envelops us. "Behold, what
manner of love the Father hath bestowed upon us, that we
should be called the sons of God" (1 John 3:1).

And remember, our Father is the King.

My Father Is Rich

O Lord, how manifold are thy works! in wisdom
hast thou made them all: the earth is full of thy riches
(Ps. 104:24).

The words of this rich old hymn remind us throughout
of who we are as royal children. The first verse sets the stage
by reminding us of just who the King, our Father, really is.
He is rich!

> *My Father is rich in houses and lands,*
> *He holdeth the wealth of the worlds in His hands!*
> *Of rubies and diamonds, of silver and gold,*
> *His coffers are full, He has riches untold.*

Our Father, the King, has great natural wealth, especially when using human wealth as an analogy. He says that
"every beast of the forest is mine, and the cattle upon a thousand hills" (Ps. 50:10). And why not? He is the Creator of
all.

In the original created earth, He placed much gold and
precious stones (Gen. 2:12). But He says, "My fruit is better
than gold, yea, than fine gold; and my revenue than choice
silver" (Prov. 8:19).

Our Father's riches are far greater than natural riches,
however, for He "is rich in mercy . . . his great love wherewith he loved us" (Eph. 2:4). "O the depth of the riches both
of the wisdom and knowledge of God!" (Rom. 11:33). Indeed,
"My God shall supply all your need according to his riches in
glory by Christ Jesus" (Phil. 4:19).

Our Father's riches, however, didn't impede His love
for us (as they many times do among men), for "though he
was rich, yet for your sakes he became poor, that ye through
his poverty might be rich" (2 Cor. 8:9), and "that he might
make known [unto us] the riches of his glory" (Rom. 9:23).
As children of the King, His unimaginable wealth is our inheritance.

From Rags to Riches

But made himself of no reputation, and took upon him the form of a servant, and was made in the likeness of men: And being found in fashion as a man, he humbled himself, and became obedient unto death, even the death of the cross (Phil. 2:7–8).

Our text comprises the heart of that glorious passage expounding Christ's gracious choice to leave heaven to become a man and die a sacrificial death on our behalf. While on earth, "The Son of man hath not where to lay his head" (Matt. 8:20). The passage continues this "riches to rags to riches" story, as does verse two of our study hymn, "A Child of the King." "Wherefore God also hath highly exalted him, and given him a name which is above every name: That at the name of Jesus every knee should bow, of things in heaven, and things in earth, and things under the earth; And that every tongue should confess that Jesus Christ is Lord" (Phil. 2:9–11).

My Father's own Son, the Savior of men,
Once wandered the earth as the poorest of them;
But now He is pleading our pardon on high,
That we may be His when He comes by and by.

What is He doing since His return to God's presence? The Bible says He is our defense attorney, pleading our case on just grounds before God the Father. Because "it behoved him to be made like unto his brethren, that he might be a merciful and faithful high priest in things pertaining to God, to make reconciliation for the sins of the people" (Heb. 2:17). Thus, "If any man sin, we have an advocate with the Father" (1 John 2:1). "Wherefore he is able also to save them to the uttermost that come unto God by him, seeing he ever liveth to make intercession for them" (Heb. 7:25).

"Fear not, little flock; for it is your Father's good pleasure to give you the kingdom" (Luke 12:32). Truly, a glorious future awaits the children of the King.

An Adopted Outcast

Now therefore ye are no more strangers and foreigners, but fellow citizens with the saints, and of the household of God (Eph. 2:19).

Consider our former state, how that we "were without Christ, being aliens . . . and strangers from the covenants of promise, having no hope, and without God in the world" versus our present state, "Now in Christ Jesus ye who sometimes were far off are made nigh by the blood of Christ" (Eph. 2:12–13). This theme dominates verse three of the wonderful hymn "A Child of the King."

> *I once was an outcast stranger on earth,*
> *A sinner by choice and an alien by birth;*
> *But I've been adopted, my name's written down,*
> *An heir to a mansion, a robe, and a crown.*

All of us chose sin. "If we say that we have no sin, we deceive ourselves" (1 John 1:8). This rebellious choice has "separated between you and your God, and your sins have hid his face from you" (Isa. 59:2). Furthermore, we are born into sin as Adam's descendants. "By one man sin entered into the world, and death by sin; and so death passed upon all men" (Rom. 5:12). Thankfully, as our text relates, our alien status has been altered to that of "fellow citizens," we've been adopted into "the household of God." "Wherefore thou art no more a servant, but a son; and if a son, then an heir of God through Christ" (Gal. 4:7).

Our inheritance befits children of the King. In our "Father's house are many mansions . . . I go to prepare a place for you" (John 14:2). We will be arrayed in fitting garments, garments once soiled by sin. We will have "washed their [our] robes, and made them white in the blood of the Lamb" (Rev. 7:14). On our heads will be "a crown of righteousness, which the Lord, the righteous judge, shall give" (2 Tim. 4:8) to all His royal children.

Over There

And hath raised us up together, and made us sit together in heavenly places in Christ Jesus: That in the ages to come he might show the exceeding riches of his grace in his kindness toward us through Christ Jesus (Eph. 2:6–7).

We have utilized the words of the encouraging hymn "A Child of the King" to call to mind the benefits of sonship in God's family. These benefits transcend our present experience, and the hymn's final verse points toward our life "over there."

> *A tent or a cottage, why should I care?*
> *They're building a palace for me over there;*
> *Though exiled from home, yet still I may sing!*
> *All glory to God, I'm a child of the King.*

Knowing of the blessings to follow helps us to "be content with such things as ye [we] have: for he hath said, I will never leave thee, nor forsake thee" (Heb. 13:5). "Seek ye first the kingdom of God, and his righteousness; and all these things shall be added unto you" (Matt. 6:33).

The greatest of all blessings is the gift of His Son and the forgiveness we have through Him. "He that spared not his own Son, but delivered him up for us all, how shall he not with him also freely give us all things?" (Rom. 8:32).

In a real sense, we have been living in exile in this life, our true citizenship is in "the city of the living God, the heavenly Jerusalem" (Heb. 12:22). The affairs of this life are not of paramount importance, for we "shall receive the reward of the inheritance: for ye [we] serve the Lord Christ" (Col. 3:24). But we must never lose sight of the truth that our adoption into the King's family has been accomplished by the sacrificial blood of our "older brother" Jesus Christ, "wherein he hath made us accepted in the beloved. In whom we have redemption through his blood, the forgiveness of sins, according to the riches of his grace" (Eph. 1:6–7).

The Church's One Foundation

Samuel J. Stone

Samuel S. Wesley

1. The church's one foun-da-tion Is Je-sus Christ her Lord;
2. E - lect from ev-ery na-tion, Yet one o'er all the earth,
3. Though with a scorn-ful won-der, Men see her sore op-pressed,
4. Mid toil and trib-u-la-tion, And tu-mult of her war,
5. Yet she on Earth hath un-ion, With God the Three in One,

She is His new cre-a-tion, By wa-ter and the word:
Her char-ter of sal-va-tion, One Lord, one faith, one birth;
By schisms rent a-sun-der, By her-e-sies dis-tressed,
She waits the con-sum-ma-tion, Of peace for ev-er-more;
And mys-tic sweet com-mun-ion, With those whose rest is won.

From heaven He came and sought her, To be His ho-ly bride;
One ho-ly name she bless-es, Par-takes one ho-ly food,
Yet saints their watch are keep-ing; Their cry goes up_ "How long?"
Till with the vi-sion glo-rious, Her long-ing eyes are blest,
Oh, hap-py ones and ho-ly! Lord, give us grace that we,

With His own blood He bought her, And for her life He died.
And to one hope she press-es, With ev-ery grace en-dued.
But soon the night of weep-ing, Shall be the morn of song.
And the great church vic-to-rious Shall be the church at rest.
Like them the meek and low-ly, On high may dwell with thee.

26

The Church's One Foundation

The 19th century stands out as a watershed century in the long war against God. It began with Charles Lyell denying the historicity of Genesis, especially the doctrine of the young earth and the great flood of Noah's day. It continued in 1859 with the publication of Charles Darwin's denial of the creation doctrine, in *The Origin of Species*. It ended with Thomas Huxley and Robert Ingersol championing the cause of atheism, deftly turning western education away from God.

Where was the Church through all this? In retreat, and in many cases, aiding those who lead the attack against the faith.

When I first moved from Oklahoma to accept the position at the Institute for Creation Research, ICR was located on the campus of Christian Heritage College. Both organizations had grown and space was of a premium. A new building was being built, but until it was finished a desk for me was set up in an overflow room in the library. An elderly pastor had donated thousands of old Christian books, many from the early 1800s. I'm sorry to admit it, but I spent many hours reading those old books when I should have been doing something more productive.

But actually, I learned some things, especially the state of the Church and the thinking of its leaders in those important days. Much to my surprise, church leaders had already given up the doctrines of young earth and global flood. They had capitulated to the intimidation of Lyell and had even accepted some form of evolution, even before Darwin! Inability to answer simple questions such as "How could all the animals get on board the ark?" and "Where did enough water for the flood come from?" led them to abandon the doctrine of the inerrancy of Scripture. Leaders of the Anglican church were promoting old earth, local flood, and theistic evolution, while those in the church of Scotland promoted the Gap Theory. Scientists opposed these ideas on scientific grounds, but theologians paved the way for the Darwinian world view of naturalism to gain popularity in the late 1800s. But these questions do have answers. The biblical way of thinking will always have the answer if we're willing to study and believe.

One influential leader in the Anglican church who joined enemy forces was Bishop John William Colenso. In 1866 he wrote an influential book attacking the historicity of the Pentateuch, especially Genesis, and nearly wrenched the entire denomination apart.

But the Church has always had a remnant, those who stood firm, defending Scripture. One such man was Pastor Samuel Stone, an energetic warrior for the conservative faith. He spoke out against liberalism, including the accommodation of any form of evolution into Genesis.

His defense of the faith took an interesting turn. He cited 12 integral articles identified in "The Apostle's Creed" and wrote a collection of 12 hymns defending them, one by one. His tactic was effective and helped stem the onrushing tide of higher criticism.

Only one of these 12 hymns is in use today, "The Church's One Foundation," defending the headship and Lordship of Christ over the Church. Its stately music and somber words challenge us all to stand firm against all opposition.

Originally this song had seven verses. Its last two have been combined into the fifth verse. Since using the song I discovered the third, entirely neglected verse, which reads:

The church shall never perish!
Her dear Lord to defend,
To guide, sustain, and cherish,
Is with her to the end;
Though there be those that hate her,
And false sons in her pale
Against the foe or traitor
She ever shall prevail.

We must see this battle clearly if we are to survive it. Our goal is to defend Scripture against all attacks, particularly as it relates to the front-line doctrine of creation. Many, even within the Church, still deny Genesis, but Scripture presents Christ in the multi-faceted role of Creator (Col. 1:16), sustainer (v. 17), head of the Church (v. 18), Redeemer and coming King (v. 20), encompassing the entire work of Jesus Christ from eternity past to eternity future. This is the Good News, and to preach a lesser Christ is to preach a different Christ. Today's compromising offspring of yesterday's compromisers must return to those foundational truths if the Church is ever to regain its fruitfulness, for "If the foundations be destroyed, what can the righteous do?" (Ps. 11:3).

The Church's One Foundation

> For other foundation can no man lay than that
> is laid, which is Jesus Christ (1 Cor. 3:11).

Paul, who had planted the fledgling church in Corinth, had seen them begin to slip away, incorporating other doctrines and practices. Paul wrote to remind them that their local church and the Church at large was founded on none other than Jesus Christ. His admonition in our text is mirrored in this much-loved song and is just as crucial to the modern Church as it was to the Early Church. Its words contain much Scripture which bring important truths to mind.

> *The church's one foundation,*
> *Is Jesus Christ her Lord;*
> *She is His new creation,*
> *By water and the word;*
> *From heaven He came and sought her,*
> *To be His holy bride;*
> *With His own blood He bought her,*
> *And for her life He died.*

The "church" referred to is not an individual local church but the "universal" Church comprised of all true believers. A charismatic leader may enthuse a crowd, but only Christ Jesus could make the ultimate sacrifice necessary, for "Christ . . . loved the Church, and gave himself for it; That he might sanctify and cleanse it with the washing of water by the word" (Eph. 5:25–26). "Therefore if any man be in Christ, he is a new creature [creation]" (2 Cor. 5:17).

There will come a time when the Church gathers around His throne, singing, "Thou art worthy . . . for thou wast slain, and hast redeemed us to God by thy blood out of every kindred, and tongue, and people, and nation" (Rev. 5:9).

He had long ago left that throne to seek, as it were, a pure bride. Finding no such pure bride, "Christ died for the ungodly. . . . Commendeth [commending] his love toward us, in that, while we were yet sinners, Christ died for us" (Rom. 5:6–8). "Let us be glad and rejoice, and give honor to him: for the marriage of the Lamb is come" (Rev. 19:7).

Unity in Diversity

For by one Spirit are we all baptized into one body, whether we be Jews or Gentiles, whether we be bond or free; and have been all made to drink into one Spirit (1 Cor. 12:13).

The true Church of God comes from all backgrounds, yet in Christ we have unity. We may have different gifts and ministries, yet as we see in our text, through the Spirit we are on common ground. Verse two reflects this ideal.

Elect from every nation,
Yet one o'er all the earth,
Her charter of salvation,
One Lord, one faith, one birth;
One holy name she blesses,
Partakes one holy food,
And to one hope she presses,
With every grace endued.

This marvelous unity is strangely fragile and must be guarded: "Endeavoring to keep the unity of the Spirit in the bond of peace. There is one body, and one Spirit, even as ye are called in one hope of your calling; One Lord, one faith, one baptism, One God and Father of all, who is above all, and through all, and in you all" (Eph. 4:3–6).

To be a unified Church, Jesus Christ must be Lord and scriptural truth must be paramount. Any foundation other than this will prove to be shifting sand.

The hymn mentions "holy food," as did Christ himself. "I am the living bread which came down from heaven: if any man eat of this bread, he shall live for ever: and the bread that I will give is my flesh, which I will give for the life of the world" (John 6:51). Eating of this bread gives entrance into the Church.

The hymn also mentions a unified hope, the Christian's "blessed hope, and the glorious appearing of the great God and our Savior Jesus Christ" (Titus 2:13). This hope is a sure hope. "That being justified by his grace, we should be made heirs according to the hope of eternal life" (Titus 3:7).

233

Heretical Divisions

For I am persuaded, that neither death, nor life, nor angels, nor principalities, nor powers, nor things present, nor things to come, Nor height, nor depth, nor any other creature, shall be able to separate us from the love of God, which is in Christ Jesus our Lord (Rom. 8:38–39).

Verse two speaks of a wonderful unity among believers. Unfortunately, such unity is seldom realized. Denominational pedigree and national traditions join with outright false teaching to divide the Church. Verse three bemoans this fact.

Though with a scornful wonder,
Men see her sore oppressed,
By schisms rent asunder,
By heresies distressed,
Yet saints their watch are keeping;
Their cry goes up "How long?"
But soon the night of weeping,
Shall be the morn of song.

"If a kingdom be divided against itself, that kingdom cannot stand" (Mark 3:24). In just the same way, the Church is hindered in her work by disunity.

Worse yet, the Church has been infiltrated by those teaching contrary to sound doctrine on primary issues. "There shall be false teachers among you, who privily shall bring in damnable heresies, even denying the Lord that bought them" (2 Pet. 2:1). "Beloved, believe not every spirit, but try the spirits whether they are of God: because many false prophets are gone out into the world" (1 John 4:1).

What can be done? "Let us not sleep, as do others; but let us watch and be sober" (1 Thess. 5:6). Vigilant oversight by spiritually minded Christians can prevent heretical inroads, but we must be prepared.

Christ, the foundation of the Church, promised His followers: "Blessed are ye that weep now: for ye shall laugh" (Luke 6:21), and that He will lead the singing. "In the midst of the church will I sing praise unto thee" (Heb. 2:12).

Toil and Tribulation

These things I have spoken unto you, that in me ye might have peace. In the world ye shall have tribulation: but be of good cheer; I have overcome the world (John 16:33).

The Church of Jesus Christ must undergo opposition from without as well as "debates, envyings, wraths, strifes, backbitings, whisperings, swellings" from within (2 Cor. 12:20). In many ways the external tribulation makes more sense and is more bearable, and victory over it is sweeter.

> *Mid toil and tribulation,*
> *And tumult of her war,*
> *She waits the consummation,*
> *Of peace for ever more;*
> *Till with the vision glorious,*
> *Her longing eyes are blest,*
> *And the great church victorious,*
> *Shall be the church at rest.*

On a missionary trip to Lystra, the apostle Paul was stoned and left for dead (Acts 14:19). He recovered, but his burden for the new Christians was so great he "returned again to Lystra. . . . Confirming the souls of the disciples, and exhorting them to continue in the faith, and that we must through much tribulation enter into the kingdom of God" (v. 21–22). To Paul, suffering was something to be expected, and even desired. "That I may know him, and the power of his resurrection, and the fellowship of his sufferings, being made conformable unto his death" (Phil. 3:10).

But the Church must look beyond the suffering to the consummation of God's plan for the ages. "We look not at the things which are seen, but at the things which are not seen: for the things which are seen are temporal; but the things which are not seen are eternal" (2 Cor. 4:18).

Peace and rest come as we recognize that our Lord "made peace through the blood of his cross" (Col. 1:20), assuring us of eternal life; "Which hope we have as an anchor of the soul, both sure and stedfast" (Heb. 6:19).

One with God

That they all may be one; as thou, Father, art in me, and I in thee, that they also may be one in us: that the world may believe that thou hast sent me (John 17:21).

Our study hymn has exalted Jesus Christ as "The Church's One Foundation." Verse one explained how the foundations were laid in His blood, verse two with our privileged position. Verse three spoke of opposition from within and verse four of opposition without. Verse five assures us that in spite of all the difficulties, the Church can maintain an intimate walk with her Savior.

Yet she on Earth hath union,
With God the Three in One,
And mystic sweet communion,
With those whose rest is won.
Oh, happy ones and holy!
Lord, give us grace that we,
Like them the meek and lowly,
On high may dwell with Thee.

Nowhere is our fellowship with the Father and Son more clearly stated than in Christ's prayer for His followers shortly before His crucifixion. "Now I am no more in the world, but these are in the world, and I come to thee. Holy Father, keep through thine own name those whom thou hast given me, that they may be one, as we are. . . . Neither pray I for these alone, but for them also which shall believe on me through their word" (John 17:11–20).

Soon Jesus would pray, "Abba, Father" (Mark 14:36), an intimate term of deep affection. Now "because ye are sons, God hath sent forth the Spirit of his Son into your hearts, crying, Abba, Father" (Gal. 4:6). We are privileged to enter into this sweet communion with Father and Son.

The disciple, John, who enjoyed a special measure of Christ's love, wrote of these things to the church, "that ye also may have fellowship with us: and truly our fellowship is with the Father, and with his Son Jesus Christ" (1 John 1:3–4).

Christ the Lord is Risen Today!

Charles Wesley

From Lyra Davidica

1. Christ the Lord is risen to-day, Al - le - lu - ia!
2. Lives a - gain our glo - rious King, Al - le - lu - ia!
3. Love's re - deem - ing work is done, Al - le - lu - ia!
4. Soar we now where Christ hath led, Al - le - lu - ia!

Sons of men and an - gels say, Al - le - lu - ia!
Where, O death, is now thy sting? Al - le - lu - ia!
Fought the fight the bat - tle's won, Al - le - lu - ia!
Fol - lowing our ex - alt - ed Head, Al - le - lu - ia!

Raise your joys and tri - umphs high, Al - le - lu - ia!
Dy - ing once He all doth save, Al - le - lu - ia!
Death in vain for - bids Him rise, Al - le - lu - ia!
Made like Him, like Him we rise, Al - le - lu - ia!

Sing ye heavens and earth re - ply. Al - le - lu - ia!
Where thy vic - to - ry, O grave? Al - le - lu - ia!
Christ hath o - pened Par - a - dise, Al - le - lu - ia!
Ours the cross, the grave the skies, Al - le - lu - ia!

Christ the Lord Is Risen Today

My busy schedule keeps me in airplanes and airports quite a bit. Let's just say my frequent flyer accounts are healthy. While I never enjoy being away from home, I've found I can get a lot more writing done on an airplane than I can in the office. I've never even gotten one phone call on the plane, for instance. Actually, many of my hymn devotionals were written at 30,000 feet. Obviously, I can't take all my study books on the plane, but there is a way to do it if you plan ahead.

Most of my initial study is done on my home computer which contains several of the wonderful Bible study tools available. I type out the main words of each hymn stanza, find scriptural support for each phrase or thought, and eventually print out all the references. There must have been 20 pages of Scripture printed out supporting Charles Wesley's Easter hymn, "Christ the Lord Is Risen Today."

It was a night flight across the country, and all the lights were out except mine and the schoolteacher sitting next to me. We had had a friendly exchange of small talk, but no witnessing opportunity had opened up. She had a book to read, so I was writing.

I got through stanzas one and two, and by this time she

was moderately interested. We talked about ICR and *Days of Praise* and this marvelous hymn. She remembered the hymn from her youth and from Easter-related events in her small town.

Suddenly, I had a problem; I hadn't written all the words to the hymn on the printout, and the last two stanzas were mixed up in my memory. Since she vaguely remembered the hymn, I asked for her help. Reading the Scripture verses in sections, we tried to reconstruct the hymn. We went over and over the Scripture verses, trying to think of rhyming words which would fit. I see the problem now. The last two lines of each of the last two stanzas all rhyme. No wonder I was confused. But aren't you glad that God doesn't get confused. He had arranged this meeting at 30,000 feet; I was just along for the ride.

That night a lost schoolteacher spent two hours pouring over scores of verses dealing with the Resurrection and the believer's destiny. We talked about salvation and eternal life, forgiveness of sin and the believer's victory. It's all there in the hymn, and it was all there in my printout. We have the promise that God's Word doesn't return void even if it's printed on computer paper.

It occurs to me that our God is not only Creator, He's also creative. He can and does use innovative methods to reach the lost. We just need to be available.

Are you aware that when Wesley wrote the original poem, it didn't include the "Alleluia!" after each line? This was added later by the printer, who had extra space on his printer's plate. It's probably a good thing, for without the "Alleluias" the hymn would likely not have gained such lasting popularity. ✼

Christit the Lord Is Risen Today

For to this end Christ both died, and rose, and revived, that he might be Lord both of the dead and living (Rom. 14:9).

Undoubtedly the song sung more than any other at Easter time is Charles Wesley's triumphant hymn, "Christ the Lord Is Risen Today." Each of its four verses is laced with scriptural content, containing thrilling and timeless truths. They will lead us to join in similar praise.

Christ the Lord is risen today, Alleluia.
Sons of men and angels say, Alleluia.
Raise your joys and triumphs high, Alleluia.
Sing ye heavens and earth reply. Alleluia.

"Blessed be the God and Father of our Lord Jesus Christ, which according to his abundant mercy hath begotten us again unto a lively hope by the resurrection of Jesus Christ from the dead" (1 Pet. 1:3). Acknowledging and understanding the benefits that Christ's resurrection brings us and the great standing we have before God the Father because of His work should elicit a response of great praise from all men. Even the angels "Praise . . . him" (Ps. 148:2).

Furthermore, "Let the heavens rejoice, and let the earth be glad; let the sea roar, and the fullness thereof" (Ps. 96:11), for by His return from the dead, He "spoiled principalities and powers, [and thus] he made a shew of them openly, triumphing over them in it" (Col. 2:15).

The term "alleluia" (or "Hallelujah") follows each line of the song. This interesting word is a combination of the Hebrew word, *Hallel,* meaning praise and the shortened word for God or Lord, *Jah.* Thus "alleluia" means, "Praise the Lord!" "Alleluia; Salvation, and glory, and honor, and power, unto the Lord our God: For true and righteous are his judgments. . . . I heard as it were the voice of a great multitude . . . saying, Alleluia: for the Lord God omnipotent reigneth" (Rev. 19:1–6).

Our Glorious King

The blessed and only Potentate, the King of kings, and Lord of lords; Who only hath immortality, dwelling in the light which no man can approach unto; whom no man hath seen, nor can see: to whom be honor and power everlasting. Amen (1 Tim. 6:15–16).

Our King, the Almighty sovereign Creator of all things, willingly became "sin for us, who [himself] knew no sin; that we might be made the righteousness of God in him" (2 Cor. 5:21). He was "put to death in the flesh, but quickened [i.e., risen from the dead] by the Spirit," having "once suffered for sins, the just for the unjust, that he might bring us to God" (1 Pet. 3:18). The second verse of "Christ the Lord Is Risen Today" speaks of such majestic truths. Of a surety, He is a glorious King.

> *Lives again our glorious King, Alleluia!*
> *Where, O death, is now thy sting? Alleluia!*
> *Dying once He all doth save, Alleluia!*
> *Where thy victory, O grave? Alleluia!*

In that great chapter proclaiming victory over death and the grave, the apostle Paul explained our eternal triumph over death purchased by Christ's death and resurrection. "Death is swallowed up in victory. O death, where is thy sting? O grave, where is thy victory? . . . thanks be to God, which giveth us the victory through our Lord Jesus Christ" (1 Cor. 15:54–57).

The nation Israel was required to offer blood sacrifices continually, but "it is not possible" that those animal sacrifices could "take away sins" (Heb. 10:4). Thankfully, this humanly hopeless dilemma was solved when "Christ was once offered to bear the sins of many" (Heb. 9:28), thus "having obtained eternal redemption for us" (v. 12).

Our glorious King became our perfect sacrifice and even now "saves them [us] to the uttermost" (Heb. 7:25).

Love's Redeeming Work

But God, who is rich in mercy, for his great love wherewith he loved us, Even when we were dead in sins, hath quickened us together with Christ, (by grace ye are saved;) And hath raised us up together, and made us sit together in heavenly places in Christ Jesus (Eph. 2:4–6).

The redemptive work of Christ was impelled by His great love for us. "For God so loved the world, that he gave his only begotten Son, that whosoever believeth in him should not perish, but have everlasting life" (John 3:16). Best of all, it is fully done; nothing remains to be done on our part. "It is finished," He cried, nailed to the sacrificial tree (John 19:30). This victory cry and the vanquishing of the enemy which it signaled, form the thoughts behind verse three of our study hymn.

Love's redeeming work is done, Alleluia!
Fought the fight the battle's won, Alleluia!
Death in vain forbids Him rise, Alleluia!
Christ hath opened Paradise, Alleluia!

As Charles Wesley wrote this song, he had more in mind than Christ's resurrection day. Christ not only rose from the dead in history, He is risen today! Years later He even appeared unto John and proclaimed: "I am he that liveth, and was dead; and, behold, I am alive for evermore, Amen; and have the keys of hell and of death" (Rev. 1:18). And then He promised, "To him that overcometh will I give to eat of the tree of life, which is in the midst of the paradise of God" (Rev. 2:7).

How can we gain sweet redemption and enter into this paradise? "If thou shalt confess with thy mouth the Lord Jesus, and shalt believe in thine heart that God hath raised him from the dead, thou shalt be saved" (Rom. 10:9). "Thanks be unto God, which always causeth us to triumph in Christ" (2 Cor. 2:14).

Following Our Exalted Head

Looking unto Jesus the author and finisher of our faith; who for the joy that was set before him endured the cross, despising the shame, and is set down at the right hand of the throne of God (Heb. 12:2).

Shortly before his death, resurrection, and return to heaven, Jesus comforted His disciples with these words: "In my Father's house are many mansions . . . I go to prepare a place for you. And if I go and prepare a place for you, I will come again, and receive you unto myself; that where I am, there ye may be also" (John 14:2–3). Later He prayed, "Father, I will that they also, whom thou hast given me, be with me where I am; that they may behold my glory" (John 17:24). Verse four of "Christ the Lord Is Risen Today" expresses our sure prospect.

> *Soar we now where Christ hath led, Alleluia!*
> *Following our exalted Head, Alleluia!*
> *Made like Him, like Him we rise, Alleluia!*
> *Ours the cross, the grave the skies, Alleluia!*

God has given us the privilege and blessing of total identification with His Son. We are "dead with Christ" (Col. 2:20), "buried with him" (v. 12), "raised with him" (v. 12), and "quickened together with him" (v. 13). "I am crucified with Christ: nevertheless I live; yet not I, but Christ liveth in me: and the life which I now live in the flesh I live by the faith of the Son of God, who loved me, and gave himself for me" (Gal. 2:20).

This identification with Christ necessitates an ongoing responsibility. "If ye then be risen with Christ, seek those things which are above, where Christ sitteth on the right hand of God" (Col. 3:1). His resurrection ensures forgiveness in this life and paradise in the life to come. "I may know him, and the power of his resurrection, and the fellowship of his sufferings, being made conformable unto his death" (Phil. 3:10).

Once for All!

Philip P. Bliss

Philip P. Bliss

1. Free from the law, O hap-py con - di - tion, Je - sus hath bled,
2. Now we are free-there's no con-dem - na - tion, Je - sus pro - vides
3. Chil - dren of God, O glo - ri - ous call-ing, Sure - ly His grace

and there is re - mis - sion; Cursed by the law and bruised by the fall,
a per - fect sal - va - tion; "Come un - to me," O hear His sweet call,
will keep us from fall-ing; Pass-ing from death to life at His call,

Grace hath re - deemed us once for all.
Come, and He saves us once for all. Once for all O sin - ner, re -
Bless - ed sal - va - tion once for all.

ceive it; Once for all O broth-er, be - lieve it; Cling to the

cross, the bur-den will fall, Christ hath re - deemed us once for all.

Once for All!

We've noticed in discussing the song "No Blood, No Altar Now" by Horatius Bonar, that many English and Scottish churches in the 1800s allowed only psalms to be sung, and even they were sung without accompaniment. The song which, more than any other, broke through that barrier is the doctrinally pure "Once for All!" by Philip P. Bliss. It occupies an important place in western hymnody.

D.L. Moody had been mightily used of God in Chicago and elsewhere. His evangelistic messages had seen tens of thousands commit their lives to Christ. The music of his crusades had energized the American church. But now he was in Scotland, a land whose churches prided themselves on doctrinal purity and boring music. Moody's colleague and crusade song leader, Ira Sankey, was with him.

Sankey was a central figure in the American church's adoption of gospel songs, and he longed to introduce the songs to Great Britain. He had seen how they could teach biblical truths and thaw cold hearts. The psalms had a place, but necessarily neglected the New Testament stories of Crucifixion, Resurrection, and new life in Christ. He did not desire to bring in modern, "new-fangled" music for its own sake. He did desire to see true worship and Christian growth rise from the ashes of dead orthodoxy. What to do? How to do it?

That evening in 1873, Ira Sankey strode to the platform to sing a gospel song with fear and trembling. His concern grew as he saw the eminent pastor, Horatius Bonar, in the audience. Bonar himself was a fine hymnwriter, but even his church refrained from using anything but the psalms. What would happen?

Impressed with the solemnity of the occasion, and wishing to offend no one, Sankey asked the congregation to pray with him before he sang. In his prayer, he asked God to bless the presentation of the truth as contained in the song to follow. Since Presbyterians fiercely and rigidly hold to doctrine, including the doctrine of prayer, this totally disarmed those who came to find fault.

The doctrinally mature Scottish congregation bristled but remained hushed as Sankey sang. How could they object to such a clear presentation of the grace of God? The song touches on every doctrine surrounding salvation and does so in such a winsome way.

Immediately following the service, Dr. Bonar strode up to Sankey with a broad smile on his face. "Mr. Sankey, you sang the gospel tonight," he said. Soon all over the British Isles Christians were singing "Once for All!" and other gospel hymns. Even Dr. Bonar's "proper" church began to allow his own songs to be sung in church services.

The song, "Once for All," was written by a prolific hymn writer, Philip P. Bliss, who, in his short life, wrote many important hymns (both lyrics and score), including the music for "It Is Well with My Soul," and "Hallelujah! What a Savior!" discussed earlier in this book. He also wrote "Wonderful Words of Life," "Jesus Loves Even Me," and "I Will Sing of My Redeemer," to name a few.

Unfortunately, Bliss died as a young man in a tragic train accident in 1876, when a railroad bridge collapsed, plunging the train in which he was riding down an embankment. Over one hundred passengers died in the fiery wreck, but Bliss was able to squeeze out through a window. Unable to lift his wife out behind him, he returned to the wreckage only to perish with his wife. His rich legacy continues, cherished on at least two continents. ✑

Free from the Law

By the deeds of the law there shall no flesh be justified in his sight: for by the law is the knowledge of sin. For all have sinned, and come short of the glory of God (Rom. 3:20–23).

Among the most precious doctrines in all of the Bible is that "No man is justified by the law in the sight of God. . . . [Yet] Christ hath redeemed us from the curse of the law" (Gal. 3:11–13). Likewise, among the most precious hymns is Philip P. Bliss' "Once for All!" Its thrilling words help us focus on the biblical truth.

Free from the law, O happy condition,
Jesus hath bled, and there is remission;
Cursed by the law and bruised by the fall,
Grace hath redeemed us once for all.

The law served a necessary function. As we see in our text, its unreachable standard fully exposed our sinfulness and need for a Savior, Christ Jesus, "In whom we have redemption through his blood, the forgiveness of sins, according to the riches of his grace" (Eph. 1:7).

God's holiness allows no sin in His presence, "But God commendeth his love for us, in that, while we were yet sinners, Christ died for us" (Rom. 5:8). Once accomplished, this undeserved death could be applied to the deserved penalty of sinners. "God hath set forth [Christ's death] to be a propitiation through faith in his blood, to declare his righteousness for the remission of [our] sins" (Rom. 3:25).

Under the law we were cursed, for "Cursed is every one that continueth not in all things which are written in the book of the law to do them" (Gal. 3:10). Only when dressed in His righteousness can we be admitted into His presence.

Best of all, this work of Christ on our behalf is permanent. Neither we nor He need be punished again. "We are sanctified through the offering of the body of Jesus Christ once for all" (Heb. 10:10).

Once for All

But now once in the end of the world hath he appeared to put away sin by the sacrifice of himself. . . . Christ was once offered to bear the sins of many (Heb. 9:26–28).

How often we know something intellectually and yet refuse to act rightly on this knowledge. "To him that knoweth to do good, and doeth it not, to him it is sin" (James 4:17). It is likewise true in the realm of saving faith. "Believe on the Lord Jesus Christ, and thou shalt be saved" (Acts 16:31), for "without faith it is impossible to please him" (Heb. 11:6). The chorus of the powerful hymn, "Once for All!" begs us to act in faith on this life-saving truth.

> *Once for all — O sinner, receive it;*
> *Once for all — O brother, believe it;*
> *Cling to the cross, the burden will fall,*
> *Christ hath redeemed us once for all.*

To the sinner, we remind him that God the Son came to earth "made under the law, To redeem them that were under the law, that we might receive the adoption of sons" (Gal. 4:4–5), for "whosoever believeth in him shall receive remission of sins" (Acts 10:43). He should not delay.

To the Christian, we remind him that "Christ is the end of the law for righteousness to every one that believeth" (Rom. 10:4). There is no reason to continue in an attempt to live up to the law. We must live an obedient life pleasing to Him, yes, but there is no saving power in the law.

"Stand fast therefore in the liberty wherewith Christ hath made us free, and be not entangled again with the yoke of bondage" for, if we put ourselves back under the law, "Christ shall profit you [us] nothing" (Gal. 5:1–2).

Yet as we "cling to the cross" we will know "the riches of the glory of his inheritance in the saints, And what is the exceeding greatness of his power us-ward who believe" (Eph. 1:18–19).

Now We Are Free

If the Son therefore shall make you free, ye shall be free indeed (John 8:36).

We have been using the words of this rich old hymn to aid our study, basking in the mighty doctrine it unveils, as contained in its title. We have seen the higher calling and standing of the Christian through the work of the Cross, no longer under the law's bondage. Verse two reveals the means by which we have "become dead to the law by the body of Christ" (Rom. 7:4) and free from its condemning penalty.

Now we are free — there's no condemnation,
Jesus provides a perfect salvation;
"Come unto Me," O hear His sweet call,
Come, and He saves us once for all.

"There is therefore now no condemnation to them which are in Christ Jesus. . . . For the law of the Spirit of life in Christ Jesus hath made me free from the law of sin and death" (Rom. 8:1–2). Jesus said, "He that heareth my word, and believeth on him that sent me, hath everlasting life, and shall not come into condemnation; but is passed from death unto life" (John 5:24).

A sense of salvation's completeness and perfection can be gleaned from the discussion of the absolute sufficiency of Christ's atoning sacrifice throughout the Book of Hebrews. "Wherefore he is able also to save them to the uttermost that come unto God by him, seeing he ever liveth to make intercession for them" (Heb. 7:25). Nothing was left undone that needed to be done to offer salvation to each of us. "How shall we escape, if we neglect so great salvation" (Heb. 2:3).

And now the invitation rings out, "Come. And let him that is athirst come. And whosoever will, let him take the water of life freely" (Rev. 22:17).

A Glorious Calling

> This one thing I do, forgetting those things which are behind, and reaching forth unto those things which are before, I press toward the mark for the prize of the high calling of God in Christ Jesus (Phil. 3:13–14).

The salvation which we have in Christ not only frees us from the unbearable burden of the law, but supplies us with "an holy calling, not according to our works, but according to his own purpose and grace" (2 Tim. 1:9). Furthermore, to "as many as received him, to them gave he power to become the sons of God" (John 1:12). Thus begins the final verse of our study hymn, "Once for All!"

> *Children of God, O glorious calling,*
> *Surely His grace will keep us from falling;*
> *Passing from death to life at His call,*
> *Blessed salvation once for all.*

The Book of Galatians was written to a church tempted to step back under the law, not appropriating their full freedom. Paul's salutation in his letter reminded them of God's grace, and the blessed deliverance that they had experienced through it. "Grace be to you and peace from God the Father, and from our Lord Jesus Christ, who gave himself for our sins, that he might deliver us from this present evil world, according to the will of God and our Father" (Gal. 1:3–4). This deliverance emanates from the Father. It is His will that we be saved. Jesus promised that "no man is able to pluck them out of my Father's hand" (John 10:29).

There are two aspects to passing from "death to life." One, as we have discussed, occurs at salvation, passing from spiritual death to a new life in Christ; the second, as we leave this physical body and pass into our eternal home. "The hour is coming, and now is, when the dead shall hear the voice of the Son of God: and they that hear shall live" (John 5:25). Blessed salvation, once for all!

The Young Earth
by John Morris

Scientifically and biblically, the evidence is overwhelming that our planet is not billions of years old. Read why the issue of an old earth has been devastating for the Church, and why compromise on this issue has rendered much of Bible teaching ineffective. Covers a wide range of topics, from geology to theology. Heavily illustrated.

ISBN: 0-89051-174-8 • 192 pages
8-1/2 x 11 • $14.95

Available at Christian bookstores nationwide

D0000645

Patricia Smith's
DOLL VALUES
Antique to Modern
Ninth Edition

COLLECTOR BOOKS
A Division of Schroeder Publishing Co., Inc.

The current values in this book should be used only as a guide. They are not intended to set prices, which vary from one section of the country to another. Auction prices as well as dealer prices vary greatly and are affected by condition and demand. Neither the Author nor the Publisher assumes responsibility for any losses which might be incurred as a result of consulting this guide.

Searching For A Publisher?

We are always looking for knowledgeable people considered experts within their fields. If you feel that there is a real need for a book on your collectible subject and have a large comprehensive collection, contact us.

COLLECTOR BOOKS
P.O. Box 3009
Paducah, Kentucky 42002-3009

Additional copies of this book may be ordered from:

COLLECTOR BOOKS
P.O. Box 3009
Paducah, KY 42002-3009

@ $12.95 add $2.00 for postage and handling.

1 2 3 4 5 6 7 8 9 0

CREDITS

Thanks to the following for helping to make this a much better book!

Gloria Anderson, Frances Anicello, Sandy Johnson-Barts, Shirley Bertrand (Shirley's Doll House, P.O. Box 99, Wheeling, IL), Sally Bethscheider, Marge-June Blessinger, Irma Branduer, Stan Buler, Barbara Earnshaw-Cain (P.O. Box 14381, Lenexa, KS 66215), Bessie Carson, Sandra Cummins, Ellen Dodge, Durham Arts (36429 Row Ridge Rd., Cottage Grove, OR), Marie Ernst, Frasher Doll Auctions (Rt. 1, Box 72, Oak Grove, MO 64075), Maureen Fukushima, Green Museum (Chatsworth, GA), Susan Giradot, Amanda Hash (photo by Patsy Moyer), Phyllis Houston, Cecil Kates, Janie Koopman, Kris Lundquist, Margaret Mandel, Patty Martin, Jeanie Mauldin, Ellyn McCorkell, Sharon McDowell, Marla McKesh, Peggy Millhouse, June Murkins, Christine Perisho, Barbara Spears, Charmaine Shields, Ricki Small, Paul Spencer (1414 Cloverleaf, Waco, TX 76705), Karen Stephenson, David Spurgeon, Bette Todd, Mary Lu Trowbridge, Turn of Century Antiques (1421 Broadway, Denver, CO), Carol Turpin, Kathy & Don Tvrdik, Sherry Vandermeer, Flip Wilson, Glorya Woods, Patricia Woods.

COVER PHOTO CREDIT

22" "Gibson Bride" with bisque shoulder head and limbs on cloth body. Painted features. Marked "Franklin Heirloom Doll 1987." $400.00.

16" boy doll on jointed toddler body, marked "J.D.K. 220." Has sleep eyes, open mouth with two upper teeth, and modeled tongue. Rare character mold number. Shown with German bear from the 1930's and a Steiff "Wotan sheep" from the 1960's. Boy - $6,350.00; bear - $150.00; sheep - $175.00. *Courtesy Frasher Doll Auctions.*

Large 32" girl on French jointed body, marked "1248 Germany/Simon & Halbig/Santa 16." Has sleep eyes, lashes, open mouth, and is of extremely fine bisque. $2,400.00. *Courtesy Frasher Doll Auctions.*

PRICES

This book is divided into "Antique" and "Modern" sections, with the older dolls in the first section and the newer dolls in the second section. To make a quick reference, each section alphabetically lists the dollmaker, type of material or name of doll. (Example: Bye-lo or Kewpie.) An index is provided for locating a specific doll.

In modern dolls, the condition of the doll is the uppermost concern in pricing. An all original modern doll in excellent condition will bring a much higher price than listed in this price guide. A doll that is damaged, without original clothes, soiled and dirty, will bring far less than the top price listed. The cost of doll repairs and cleanup has soared, so it is wise to judge the damage and estimate the cost of repairs before you attempt to sell or buy a damaged doll.

In antique dolls, the uppermost concern is the conditions of the head and body. It is also important for the body to be correct to the doll. An antique doll must be clean, nicely dressed and ready to place into a collection. It must have no need of any repair for it to bring book price. An all original doll with original clothes, marked shoes and original wig will bring a lot more than list price. Boxes are very rare and also will bring a higher price for the doll.

For insurance reasons, it is very important to show the "retail" price of dolls in a price guide and to try to be as accurate as possible. The "retail" price can be referred to as "replacement cost" so that insurance companies or postal services can appraise a damaged or stolen doll for the insured, and the collectors can judge their own collections and purchase adequate amounts of insurance.

No one knows your collection better than yourself and in the end, when you consider a purchase, you must ask yourself if the doll is affordable to you and whether you want it enough to pay the price. You will buy the doll, or pass it up — it is as simple as that!

Prices shown are for dolls that are clean, undamaged, well-dressed and in overall excellent condition. Many prices are also listed for soiled, dirty, and redressed dolls.

ANTIQUE AND OLDER DOLLS

Back row: 31" closed mouth Jumeau, 29" opened mouth
Jumeau marked "1907," and 29" closed mouth Kestner.
Center row: 15" mechanical waltzing Steiner with open
mouth (unusual), 15½" Kammer & Reinhardt mold number
114 "Gretchen," 17" closed mouth Kestners – one on
jointed body; the other on kid body. In trunk: 7½" Kestner
on body with straight arms, jointed at knees. *Courtesy Frasher
Doll Auctions.*

This 22" Henri Alexandre doll was made from 1889 to 1891 only and is marked "10/H ⚔ A." She has a closed mouth with a white space between the lips, fat cheeks, and an early French body with straight wrists. (Also see under "Phenix" section.) She holds a 5½" wooden peg mother and baby that is all original. 18" – $6,500.00; 22" – $7,300.00; 25" – $7,600.00. Wooden peg doll: $800.00 up. *Courtesy Frasher Doll Auctions.*

French all bisque dolls are jointed at the necks, shoulders and hips. They have slender arms and legs, glass eyes and most have kid-lined joints. Most of the heads have sliced pates with tiny cork inserts. French all-bisque dolls have finely painted features with outlined lips, well-tinted bisque, and feathered eyebrows. They can have molded-on shoes, high-top boots with painted toes, high-top buttoned boots with four or more painted straps. They can also be barefooted or just have stockings painted on the legs. Any French bisque should be in very good condition, not have any chips, breaks, or hairline cracks to bring the following prices. Allow more for original clothes.

Swivel Neck: (Socket head) Molded shoes or boots. 5-6" - $1,400.00; 7-8" - $2,300.00.

Bare Feet: 5-6" - $1,100.00; 8-9" - $1,800.00; 11" - $2,700.00.

With Jointed Elbows: 5½-6" - $2,500.00; 9-10" - $3,500.00.

With Jointed Elbows and Knees: 6-7" - $3,500.00; 8-9" - $4,400.00.

S.F.B.J., UNIS: Or other late French all bisques. Painted eyes. 5-6" - $600.00; 7" - $800.00.

Marked E.D., F.G.: Or other French makers. Glass eyes, bare feet: 6-7" - $2,600.00-3,000.00.

5½" French all bisque with socket swivel head, glass eyes, closed smiling mouth. Has painted-on shoes and long socks, original wig and clothes. Shown with rare and unusual 18" Heinrich Handwerck doll that is marked with mold number 89. White space between uncut lips; fully jointed body. 5½" all bisque - $1,400.00; 18" Heinrich Handwerck - $2,450.00.

ALL BISQUE – GERMAN

German-made all bisque dolls run from excellent to moderate quality. Prices are for excellent quality and condition with no chips, cracks, breaks or hairlines. Dolls should be nicely dressed and can have molded hair or wig. They generally have painted-on shoes and socks. Ca. 1880s-1930s.

French Types: Slender dolls, one piece body and head. Usually peg or wire jointed hips and shoulders, glass eyes, closed mouth. Molded boots or shoes; 1880s on. 3-4" - $200.00-285.00; 5-6" - $300.00-365.00.

Swivel Neck, Glass Eyes: 1880-1910. Open or closed mouth, good wig, nicely dressed, painted-on shoes and socks. Allow more for unusual boot

13" rare German all bisque with one-piece body and head, painted features with closed mouth. Excellent detail. Shown with rare 15" Armand Marseille mold #230 "Fany." Modeled hair, closed mouth and on toddler body. 13" - $1,200.00; 15" - $4,000.00 up.
Courtesy Frasher Doll Auctions.

colors (orange, gold or yellow). 3½-4½" - $365.00–425.00; 5" - $465.00; 6" - $550.00; 8" - $800.00; 10" - $1,250.00 up. **Jointed knees or elbows:** 6" - $2,000.00; 8" - $3,000.00. **Swivel waist:** 6" - $1,900.00.

Swivel Neck, Painted Eyes: Open or closed mouth, one-strap shoes and painted socks. Nice clothes and wig. 2" - $145.00; 4" - $250.00; 6" - $350.00; 8" - $500.00; 10" - $800.00 up.

One-Piece Body and Head (sometimes also legs), Glass Eyes: 1880-1913. Excellent bisque, open or closed mouth with good wig and nicely dressed. Allow $35.00-45.00 more for unusual footwear such as yellow boots, multi-strap boots. 3" - $265.00; 4-5" - $275.00-295.00; 7" - $500.00; 8-9" -

$550.00-650.00; 10" - $975.00. **Bent at knees:** 6" - $275.00.

One-Piece Body and Head (sometimes also legs), Painted Eyes: 1880-1913; 1921-1932. Open or closed mouth with good wig or molded hair and nicely dressed. 1½-2½" - $70.00-90.00; 5" - $185.00; 6" - $225.00; 8" - $325.00; 10" - $825.00.

Marked: 155, 156, 158, 162: Smiling, closed or open/closed mouth, glass eyes and swivel head. 5½" - $650.00; 7" - $850.00. Same, with one-piece body and head: 6" - $425.00; 7" - $525.00.

Molded-on Clothes or Underwear: Ca. 1890's. Jointed at shoulders only or at shoulders and hips. Molded hair, painted eyes, molded shoes or bare feet. Excellent artist workmanship. No cracks, chips or breaks. 3½-4½" - $165.00; 6-7" - $365.00. (See photo in Series 5, pg. 11.) **Glass eyes:** 5" - $365.00; 7" - $525.00. Medium to poor quality: 3" - $85.00; 4-5" - $100.00; 6-7" - $150.00. **Molded Bonnet:** See listing in this section.

Marked: 100, 125, 161, 225: (Made by Alt, Beck and Gottschalck.) Closed mouth or open/closed, sleep or inset glass eyes, chubby body and limbs and molded-on one-strap shoes with painted socks. No chips, cracks or breaks. Has one-piece body and head: 5" - $245.00; 6½" - $325.00; 8" - $475.00; 10" - $700.00.

Marked 130, 150, 257, 602: (Made by Kestner or Bonn.) One-piece body and head, painted-on one strap shoes with painted socks. Glass eyes, not damaged and nicely dressed. 4" - $285.00; 6" - $385.00; 7" - $425.00; 8" - $550.00; 9" - $750.00; 10" - $950.00; 11" - $1,000.00; 12" - $1,250.00.

Marked 130, 150, 160, 208, 602: Kestner, with painted eyes. Jointed shoulders and hips. Open mouth, wigged, painted blue or pink stockings, black strap shoes. No dam-

age and very good quality. 4½-5" - $265.00; 6" - $325.00; 7" - $385.00; 8" - $475.00; 9" - $685.00; 10-11" - $965.00; 12" - $1,200.00.

Marked 130, 150, 160, 208, 602: With swivel neck and glass eyes. 4" - $375.00; 6" - $475.00; 8" - $650.00; 10" - $1,100.00.

Marked 184: Kestner, swivel neck, sweet face, glass eyes. Outlined, solid colored boots. 4-5" - $425.00; 7-8" - $625.00.

Molded Hair: One-piece body and head, painted eyes, painted-on shoes and socks. Excellent quality bisque and artist workmanship. No chips, cracks, and nicely dressed: 4½-5½" - $185.00 up; 7" - $365.00 up.

Marked: 881, 886, 890: (Simon and Halbig or any all bisque marked S&H. Swivel neck, painted-on high-top boots with four or five straps. No damage and nicely dressed. 6-7" - $1,200.00; 8-9" - $1,550.00. **With painted to above knee stockings:** 5½" - $685.00; 6½-7½" - $800.00; 8½" - $975.00 up.

Black or Brown All Bisque: See Black Section.

Molded-on Hat or Bonnet: All in perfect condition. 5-6½" - $450.00 up; 8-9" - $600.00 up. **Stone (Porous) Bisque:** 4-5" - $175.00; 6-7" - $195.00.

With Long Stockings: To above the knees. Glass eyes, open or closed mouth. Jointed at neck. Stockings will be black, blue or green. Perfect condition. 4-5½" - $465.00; 6½-7" - $600.00.

Hertel, Schwab: See that section.

Flapper: One-piece body and head, wig, painted eyes, painted-on long stockings and has thin limbs, fired-in tinted bisque, one-strap painted shoes. 6" - $365.00; 8" - $485.00. **Same, with molded hair:** 6" - $325.00; 8" - $425.00. **Medium quality bisque and artist workmanship:** 5" - $150.00; 7-8" - $250.00.

Marked With Maker: (S&H, JDK, A.B.G., etc.) Closed mouth, early fine quality face. 7-8" - $1,450.00; 9½-11" - $1,750.00 up. **Same, with open mouth:** Later quality bisque: 6" - $700.00; 8" - $1,000.00; 10" - $1,400.00. **K*B:** 8" - $1,500.00 up.

Pink Bisque: 1920s and 1930s. Jointed shoulders and hips with painted features, can have molded hair or wig. All in excellent condition: 2-3" - $45.00; 4-5½" - $65.00. **Loop in hair for bow:** 3" - $50.00; 7" - $85.00.

6" all bisque character, very much like the "Wrestler." Round face, two strap boots, delicate modeling, original mohair wig. One-piece body and head; legs modeled apart. 6" - $565.00. *Courtesy Turn of Century Antiques.*

Bathing Dolls: See that section. **Mold 415:** Aviator with molded-on goggles and cap. 3½" - $250.00; 5" - $300.00; 7" - $425.00. **Figurines:** Called "Immobilies" (no joints). **Child:** 3" - $50.00 up. **Adults:** 5" - $80.00 up. **Bride & groom cake top:** 6" - $365.00. **Santa:** 3½" - $135.00. **Child with animal on string:** 3½" - $100.00. **Wrestler:** So called; considered French. Fat thighs, bent arm at elbow, open mouth (can have two rows of teeth) or closed mouth, stocky body. Glass eyes, socket head, individual fingers or molded fists. **Painted boots:** (Multi-strapped, various colors) 6" - $1,000.00 up; 8" - $1,300.00 up; 9½" - $1,800.00. **Bare feet:** 5-6" - $1,500.00; 8½" - $2,300.00; 11" - $3,200.00. **Long painted stockings:** Above knees. 6-7" - $1,600.00; 8-9½" - $1,900.00. **Jointed elbows and/or knees:** 6" - $1,750.00; 8" - $2,600.00 up.

ALL BISQUE – BABIES

All bisque babies were made in both Germany and Japan, and dolls from either country can be excellent quality or poor quality. Prices are for excellent painting and quality of bisque. There should be no chips, cracks, or breaks. Dressed or nude - 1900; bent limbs - after 1906.

Germany (Jointed Necks, Shoulders and Hips): Wigs or painted hair. **Glass eyes:** 4" - $200.00; 5" - $250.00; 7" - $450.00; 9" - $600.00. **Painted eyes:** 3½" - $165.00; 5" - $195.00; 6½" - $385.00; 8½" - $525.00.

Germany (Jointed at Shoulders and Hips Only): Well-painted features, free-formed thumbs and many have molded bottle in hand. Some have molded-on clothes. 3½" - $95.00; 5-5½" - $150.00.

Germany (Character Baby): Jointed shoulders and hips, molded hair, painted eyes with character face. 4" - $185.00; 6" - $285.00. **Glass eyes:** 4" - $450.00; 6" - $550.00. **Mold #830, 833, and others:** 8" - $700.00 up; 11" - $1,100.00 up. **Swivel neck, glass eyes:** 6" - $650.00; 10" - $1,000.00 up.

Germany (Toddler): Jointed neck, glass eyes, perfect condition. 7" - $725.00; 9" - $1,000.00; 11" - $1,400.00 up.

8" laughing all bisque chunky toddler. Rare character with open/closed laughing mouth, one lower tooth and glass eyes. Jointed shoulders and hips. Incised "369" and resembles a Gebruder Heubach doll. 8" - $1,100.00.
Courtesy Turn of Century Antiques.

"Candy Babies": (Can be either German or Japanese.) Ca. 1920's. Generally poorly painted with high bisque color. Were given away at candy counter with purchase. 4" - $40.00; 6" - $55.00.

Pink Bisque Baby: Ca. 1920's. Jointed at shoulders and hips, painted features and hair, bent baby legs. 2" - $35.00; 4" - $50.00; 8" - $125.00. **Mold #231:** (A.M.) Toddler. Open mouth, glass eyes. 9" - $1,300.00 up.

ALL BISQUE CHARACTERS

All bisque dolls with character faces or stances were made both in Germany and Japan. The German dolls have finer bisque and workmanship of the painted features. Most all bisque character dolls have jointed shoulders only, with some having joints at the hips and a very few have swivel heads. They can have molded-on shoes or be barefooted. Prices are for dolls with no chips, cracks, hairlines or breaks.

Annie Rooney, Little: 3" - $300.00; 6" - $425.00.
Baby Bo Kaye: Made by Alt, Beck & Gottschalck. Marked with mold number **1394**. 4½" - $1,300.00; 6½" - $1,700.00.
Baby Bud: Glass eyes, wig: 6-7" - $700.00 up.
Baby Darling: Mold #497; Kestner #178. (Allow more for toddler body.) **Swivel neck, glass eyes:** 6" - $550.00; 8" - $850.00. **One-piece body, painted eyes:** 6" - $450.00; 8" - $650.00; 10" - $950.00 up.
Baby Peggy Montgomery: Made by Louis Amberg and marked with paper label. 3½-4" - $385.00; 6-7" - $585.00.
Bonnie Babe: Made by Georgene Averill. Has paper label. 5" - $750.00; 7" - $1,000.00. **Molded-on clothes:** 6" - $1,300.00.
Bye-Lo. Made by J.D. Kestner. Has paper label. Jointed neck, glass eyes, solid dome. 4" - $525.00; 6" - $700.00. **Jointed neck, wig, glass eyes:** 5" -

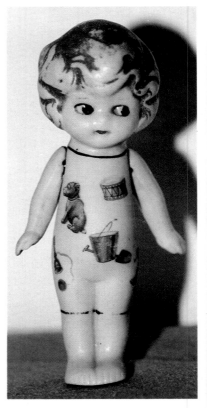

5" German all bisque with painted features and extremely unusual decal body decoration. Jointed shoulders only. These type dolls were made from stone bisque in Japan and will be marked "Japan" or "Nippon." German models made of all bisque will be marked "Germany." 5" - $185.00 up. *Courtesy Barbara Spears.*

11

$700.00; 7-8" - $1,200.00. **Painted eyes, molded hair and one-piece body and head:** 5" - $385.00; 7-8" - $650.00. **Immobilies:** "Salt" and "Pepper" on back or stomach. 3-3½" - $400.00. **One piece:** Various poses. 3-3½" - $400.00. **Campbell Kids:** Molded-on clothes, "Dutch" hairstyle. 5" - $250.00.

Chi Chi: Made by Orsini. 5-6" - $1,400.00. **Painted eyes:** $950.00.

Chin-Chin: Made by Heubach. 4½" - $325.00. **Poor quality:** 4½" - $175.00.

Didi: Made by Orsini. 5-6" - $1,400.00. **Painted eyes:** $950.00.

Fefe: Orsini. 5-6" - $1,400.00. **Painted eyes:** $950.00.

Googly: 1911-on. **Glass eyes:** 4½" - $465.00, 5½" - $650.00. **Painted eyes:** 4" - $325.00; 6" - $500.00. **Glass eyes, swivel neck:** 5-6" - $700.00; 8" - $1,200.00. **Jointed elbow and/or knees:** 5-6" - $2,000.00; 7-7½" -$2,700.00. **Marked with maker (example K*R):** 6½-7" - $2,600.00 up.

Grumpy Boy: Marked "Germany." 4" - $150.00. Marked "Japan": 4" - $65.00.

Happifats: Boy or girl. 5" - $365.00 each and up.

Hebee or Shebee: 4½" - $450.00-$475.00. (See photo in Series 5, pg. 11; Series 7, pg. 9.)

Heubach: Molded hair, side glance eyes. Molded ribbon or bows: 7" - $825.00; 9" - $1,000.00. Wigged: 7" - $925.00.

Bunny Boy or Girl figurine: By Heubach. 5" - $450.00; 8½" - $600.00.

Little Imp: Has hooved feet. 6½" - $650.00.

Kestner: Marked mold number **257, 262,** etc. **Baby:** Glass eyes, swivel head. 9-10" - $985.00. **One piece body and head:** 5½"-6½" - $265.00.

Max and Moritz: Kestner. 6" - $2,450.00 up each. (See photo in Series 7, pg. 12.)

Medic: One piece, molded-on uniform, carries case. 3½-4" - $265.00. (See photo in Series 7, pg. 9.)

Mibs: Made by Louis Amberg. May be marked "1921" on back and have paper label with name. 3½" - $250.00; 5" - $400.00.

Mimi: Made by Orsini. 6" - $1,400.00. Painted eyes: $950.00.

Orsini: Head tilted to side, made in one piece and hands hold out dress. 2½-3" - $475.00; 6" - $700.00.

6" all bisque "Veve" made by Orsini. Glass eyes, open/closed mouth, upper and lower teeth, and painted-on shoes and socks. Costume may be original. 6" - **$1,400.00** up. *Courtesy Ellen Dodge.*

Our Fairy: Molded hair and painted eyes. 9-10" - $1,700.00. **Wig and glass eyes:** 9-10" - $2,000.00.

Our Mary: Has paper label. 4½" - $475.00.

Peek-a-boo: By Drayton. 5" - $350.00.

Peterkin: 9" - $475.00.

Peterkin, Tommy: Horsman. 4" - $275.00.

Prize Baby (Mildred) #880: 7" - $1,850.00; 8½" - $2,250.00.

Queue San Baby: Various poses. **Germany:** 4½-5½" - $265.00. **Japan:** 4" - $70.00-90.00.

Scootles: Made by Cameo. 5-6" - $850.00 up.

Sonny: One piece body and head; made by Averill. 5" - $850.00 up. **Glass eyes, swivel neck:** 6-7" - $2,000.00.

Teenie Weenie: Made by Donahey. Painted one-piece eyebrows and features. 4½" - $265.00.

Tynie Baby: Made by Horsman. **Glass eyes:** 6" - $1,000.00; 9" - $1,700.00. **Painted eyes:** 6" - $565.00.

Wide Awake Doll: Germany: 7½" - $425.00. **Japan:** 7½" - $145.00.

Veve: Made by Orsini. 6" - $1,400.00. **Painted eyes:** $950.00.

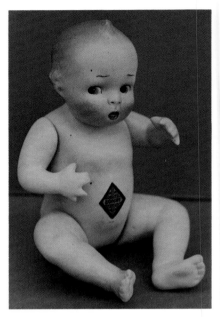

All bisque 6¾" "Sonny" with bent baby legs. "Sonny" in red, white and blue label on torso. Has ink stamp on crotch marked "Nippon." Purchased at a Kansas State Wheat Show in 1915 for 25¢. Painted features, open/closed mouth, and one-piece body and head. 6¾" - $900.00 up. *Courtesy Janie Koopman.*

ALL BISQUE – NODDERS

"Knotters" are called "Nodders" since when their heads are touched, they "nod." The reason they should correctly be called "knotters" is due to the method of stringing. The string passed through a hole in the head and knotted. They can also be made with cutouts on the bodies to take a tiny rod that comes out of the side of the neck. Both styles were made in Germany and Japan. Ca. 1920's.

Santa Claus or Indian: 6" - $175.00–200.00

Teddy Bear: 6" - $185.00.

Other Animals: (Rabbit, dog, cat, etc.) 3½-5" - $40.00-85.00. **Molded-on clothes:** 4-4½" - $145.00 up.

Comic Characters: 3½-5" - $85.00-145.00 up.

Children/Adults: Made in Germany. 4½-5½" - $65.00-165.00.

Japan/Nippon: 3½" - $25.00; 4½" - $40.00.

Sitting Position: 6" - $185.00 up; 8" - $265.00.

All bisque dolls from Japan vary a great deal in quality. They are jointed at shoulders and may have other joints. Good quality bisque is well painted with no chips or breaks. (Also see all bisque characters and nodder sections.) **Marked Nippon:** The mark "Nippon" ceased in 1923. 4" - $45.00; 6" - $75.00.

"Betty Boop": Style with bobbed hair, large painted eyes to side and one-piece body and head. 4" - $20.00; 6-7" - $35.00.

Child: With molded clothes. 3½-4½" - $35.00-40.00; 6-7" - $55.00-60.00.

Child: 1920's and 1930's. Pink or painted bisque, jointed shoulders and hips, painted features. Molded hair or wig. Excellent condition. 3" - $25.00; 4-5" - $37.50; 7" - $60.00. **Loop in hair**

for bow: 4" - $35.00; 7" - $75.00.

Comic Characters: See "All bisque – Comic Characters" section.

Occupied Japan: 3½" - $25.00; 5" - $35.00; 7" - $45.00.

Figurines: Called "Immobilies" (no joints). **Bride & groom cake top:** 6-6½" - $110.00. **Children:** 3-4" - $10.00-20.00, 6-7" - $25.00-45.00. **Teddy Bears:** 3" - $65.00. **Indians, Dutch, etc:** 2½" - $30.00. **Santa Claus:** 3½" - $95.00. **Adults:** 5" - $75.00. **Child with animal on string:** 3½" - $95.00.

Bent Leg Baby: May or may not be jointed at hips and shoulders. Very nice quality: 3½-5" - $25.00-60.00.

Bye-Lo Copy: (See photo in Series 6, pg. 12.) 3½" - $95.00, 5" - $145.00. **Medium to poor quality:** 3½-5" - $6.00-45.00.

This is an exceptional example of a fully jointed and painted bisque little girl made in Japan. She is 6½" tall, has hole so hair bows can be tied, and original clothes in better than average condition. 6½" doll only - $75.00; Doll and wardrobe - $125.00. *Courtesy Carol Turpen.*

4½" and 3" Dutch children that are made in Japan. Molded-on clothes. The two tall ones are jointed at shoulders and hips; the small one is one piece. Girl has oversized googly eyes. 3" - $60.00 up; 4½" - $85.00 up. *Courtesy Patty Martin.*

ALL BISQUE - COMIC CHARACTERS

Annie Rooney, Little: Made in Germany. 4" - $350.00; 7" - $475.00.

Betty Boop: With musical instrument. Made in Japan. 3½" - $70.00 up.

Betty Boop: Fleisher Studios. Made in Japan. 3½" - $45.00 up.

Dick Tracy: Made in Germany. 5" - $225.00.

Gasoline Alley: Uncle Walt, Auntie Blossom (black), Corky, Rachel. 2-3½", each - $90.00 up.

Made in Japan: Paint washes off easily. 3-4½" - $35.00 up.

Jackie Coogan: Japan. 6½" - $165.00.

Johnny: "Call for Phillip Morris." Made in Germany. 5" - $135.00.

Katzenjammer: Mama: 4" - $50.00; 8" - $100.00. **Uncle Ben:** 4" - $60.00, 8" - $125.00. **Kids:** 4" - $60.00 each ; 6" - $145.00 each. **Papa:** 4" - $65.00; 8" - $165.00.

Max or Moritz (K*R): 5-5½", each - $2,450.00 up.

Mickey Mouse: Walt Disney. 5", each - $250.00 up.

Mickey Mouse: With musical instrument. $250.00 up.

Minnie Mouse: Walt Disney. $250.00 up.

Moon Mullins and Kayo: Mushmouth (black), Uncle Willie, Aunt Mamie, Little Egypt, Emmy, and Lord Plushbottom. 4" - $80.00 up.

Orphan Annie: 3½" - $60.00. Nodder - $70.00 up.

Mr. Peanut: Made in Japan. 4" - $45.00.

Our Gang: Boys: 3½" - $60.00. Girls: 3½" - $70.00.

Popeye: 3" - $125.00 up.

Seven Dwarfs: Walt Disney. 3½", each - $95.00 up.

Skeezix: 3½" - $70.00.

Skippy: 5" - $125.00 up. (See photo in Series 6, pg. 13.)

Snow White: Japan. 5½" - $100.00. **In box with Dwarfs:** $550.00 up. (See photo in Series 6, pg. 13.) **Germany:** $800.00.

Three Bears/Goldilocks: Japan, boxed set: $300.00 up. **Germany:** $600.00.

Winnie Winkle: Mr. Bibb, Pa & Ma Winkle, Perry Winkle, Patsy. **Germany:** 3-4½", each - $95.00 up.

15

Painted bisque has a layer of paint over the bisque which has not been fired. These dolls have molded hair, painted features, painted-on shoes and socks, and are jointed at shoulder and hips. All should be in good condition with no paint chips.

Boy or Girl: 3" - $30.00; 4½-5" - $55.00-60.00.

Baby: 3½" - $45.00; 5" - $60.00.

ALT, BECK & GOTTSCHALCK

Alt, Beck & Gottschalck was located at Nauendorf, Germany, near Ohrdruf, as a porcelain factory from 1854. It is not known when they started making dolls. The firm was the maker of both the **"Bye-lo"** baby and **"Bonnie Babe"** for the distributor, George Borgfeldt. The leading authorities in Germany, and now the United States, have assigned nearly all the turned-head dolls as being made by Alt, Beck & Gottschalck, with the bodies being made by **Wagner & Zetzsche.** It is claimed that this firm produced dolls with tinted bisque and molded hair (see that section of this book), as well as wigged turned head and shoulder head dolls and also dolls made of china. There is a vast variation to the eyebrows among these dolls. Prices are given for just one eyebrow style. (Also see All Bisque section.)

Marks:

A B₊C

698✕ 9

1235 # №̷ 10.

Babies: After 1909. Open mouth, some have pierced nostrils, bent leg baby body and are wigged. Prices will be higher if on toddler body or has flirty eyes. Allow more for toddler body. Clean, nicely dressed and with no cracks, chips or hairlines. 12-13" - $425.00; 17" - $650.00; 21" - $850.00; 25" - $1,600.00.

Child, #1361, 1362, 1367, etc.: Socket head on jointed composition body, sleep or set eyes. No crack, chips or hairlines. Clean and nicely dressed. 12" - $400.00; 14" - $450.00; 17" - $525.00; 21" - $600.00; 25" - $750.00; 31" - $1,100.00; 36" - $1,600.00; 40-42" - $2,600.00.

Character Child or Baby: Ca. 1910 on. Socket head on jointed composition body, sleep or set eyes, open mouth. Nicely dressed with good wig or molded hair with no hairlines, cracks or chips. **#630:** 24" - $2,600.00. **#911:** Closed mouth. 19" - $2,650.00. **#1322:** 15" - $525.00; 19" - $700.00. **#1352:** 12" - $425.00; 16" - $550.00; 21" - $800.00. **#1357:** 14" - $650.00; 18" - $900.00. **#1358, 1359:** 14" - $2,000.00; 18" - $3,300.00. **#1361:** 12" - $395.00; 16" - $525.00; 21" - $775.00. **#1367:** 16" - $500.00; 20" - $750.00.

Turned Shoulder Head: 1880's. Bald head or plaster pate, closed mouth, glass eyes, kid body with bisque lower arms. All in good condition with no chips, hairline and nicely dressed. Dolls marked "DEP" or "Germany" date after 1888. Some have the

Wagner & Zetzsche mark on head or paper label inside top of body. Some mold numbers include: **639, 698, 870, 890, 911, 912, 916, 990, 1000, 1008, 1028, 1032, 1044, 1064, 1123, 1127, 1142, 1234, 1235, 1254, 1288, 1304.** Glass eyes: 13½" - $575.00; 15" - $750.00; 17" - $825.00; 21" - $1,000.00; 24" - $1,450.00. (Allow more for molded bonnet or elaborate hairdo.)

Turned Shoulder Head: Same as above, but with open mouth. 16" - $550.00; 20" - $650.00; 24" - $750.00.

Bisque Shoulder Head: 1880's. Molded hair, glass or painted eyes, closed mouth. Cloth or kid body, bisque lower limbs. No damage and nicely dressed. **Painted eyes:** 14" - $325.00; 17" - $465.00; 21" - $550.00. **Glass eyes:** 13" - $475.00; 16" - $600.00; 20" - $875.00.

China Shoulder Head: 1880's. Blonde or black hair, china limbs (or leather), cloth body and nicely dressed with no damage. **Mold #784, 786, 1000, 1003, 1008, 1028, 1032, 1046, 1142, 1144, 1210.** May also have mark ✗ or ✗ß. 14-16" - $325.00-375.00; 18-20" - $385.00-425.00; 22-25" - $450.00-625.00.

17" turned head lady doll with kid body and bisque lower arms. Attributed to Alt, Beck & Gottschalck. Glass eyes and closed mouth, excellent quality bisque. 17" - $825.00. *Courtesy Frasher Doll Auctions.*

AMBERG, LOUIS & SONS

Louis Amberg & Sons were in business from 1878 to 1930 in New York City and Cincinnati, Ohio.

Prices are for dolls in perfect condition, with no cracks, chips or breaks, clean and nicely dressed. (Allow more for original clothes and wig.)

Baby Peggy (Montgomery): 1923 and 1924. Closed mouth, socket head. **Mold # 973 or 972:** 19" - $2,700.00; 23" - $2,950.00.

Marks:

L.A. & S. 1926

ᴬᴹBERᴳ
DOLLS
THE WORLD
STANDARD
MADE
IN
U.S.A.

AMBERG
L.A. & S. 1928

Baby Peggy: Shoulder head. **Mold #983 or 982:** 18" - $2,900.00; 22" - $3,150.00. **Baby Peggy:** All bisque. See "All Bisque" section.

Baby Peggy: Composition head and limbs with cloth body, painted eyes, closed mouth, molded brown short bobbed hairdo. 1923. 13" - $350.00; 17" - $525.00; 20" - $725.00. **Baby, Mold #88678:** Cloth body. 18" - $1,350.00; 23" - $1,700.00.

Charlie Chaplin: Marked "Amberg. Essamay Film Co." 1915-1920's. Portrait head of composition with painted features, composition hands, cloth body and legs. Black suit and white shirt. Cloth tag on sleeve or inside seam of coat. 13-14" - $500.00; 20" - $765.00.

Newborn Babe: Bisque head with cloth body and can have celluloid, composition or rubber hands. Lightly painted hair, sleep eyes, closed mouth with protruding upper lip. 1914 and reissued in 1924. Marks: "L.A.&S. 1914/**G45520** Germany." Some will be marked "L. Amberg and Son/**886**" and some will be marked "Copyright by Louis Amberg." (See photo in Series 7, pg. 15.) 8-9" - $365.00; 13" - $550.00; 17" - $1,200.00.

Newborn Babe: Open mouth version. Marked "L.A.&S. **371.**" 9-10" - $375.00; 15" - $650.00.

Mibs: Marked "L.A.&S. 1921/ Germany" and can have two different paper labels with one "Amberg Dolls/ Please Love Me/I'm Mibs," and some

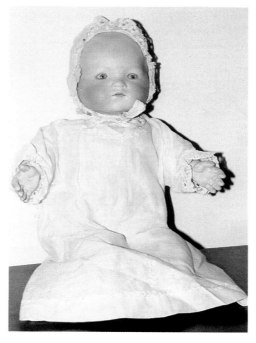

13" "Newborn Babe" with cloth body and composition gauntlet hands. Marked "L.A. & S. 1914. G45520 Germany." 13" - $550.00.
Courtesy Gloria Anderson.

with the same label, but does not carry the name of Amberg. Molded hair with long strand down center of forehead. Composition head and limbs with cloth body, painted eyes. All in good condition. (See photo in Series 6, pg. 17.) 10-11" - $500.00; 15-16" - $865.00.

Mibs: All bisque. See All Bisque section.

Sue (or Edwina): All composition with painted features, molded hair and with a waist that swivels on a large ball attached to the torso. Jointed shoulders, neck and hips. Molded hair has side part and swirl bangs across forehead. Marked "Amberg/Pat. Pen./ L.A.&S." 1928. (See photo in Series 6, pg. 17.) 13-14" - $465.00

Twist 1928. All c̲ made from Boy or gir painted fea clothes: "An . Pat. Pend. #8

Vanta ἰ Baby-Amberg _., Composition head and limbs with fat legs. Cloth body, spring strung, sleep eyes, open/ closed mouth with two teeth. Made to advertise Vanta baby garments. 1927. 20" - $285.00; 24" - $400.00.

Vanta Baby: Same as above, but with bisque head. (See photo in Series 6, pg. 17.) Glass eyes, open mouth. 20" - $1,000.00; 24-25" - $1,600.00. **Glass eyes, closed mouth:** 20" - $1,250.00; 25" - $1,850.00.

ARMAND MARSEILLE

Prices are for perfect dolls with no chips, cracks, breaks or hairline cracks. Dolls need to be clean and nicely dressed.

Armand Marseille made the majority of their dolls after the 1880s and into the 1920s, so they are some of the most often found dolls today. The factory was at Koppelsdorf, Germany. A.M. marked dolls can be of excellent to very poor quality. The finer the bisque and artist workmanship, the higher the price. This company also made a great many heads for other companies, such as George Borgfeldt, Amberg (Baby Peggy,) Hitz, Jacobs & Kassler, Otto Gans, Cuno & Otto Dressel, etc. They were marked with "A.M." or full name "Armand Marseille."

Mold #370, 326, 309, 273, 270, 375, 376, 920, 957: Kid or kidaleen bodies, open mouths. 12" - $185.00; 15" - $250.00; 21" - $350.00; 24" - $425.00; 26" - $500.00.

Mold #390, 266, 300, 310, (not "Googly"), 384, 390N, 391, 395: Socket head, jointed body and open mouth. 6" (closed mouth) - $265.00; 10" (crude 5-piece body) - $175.00; 10" (good quality jointed body) - $285.00; 14" - $285.00; 16" - $350.00; 18" - $385.00; 22" - $450.00; 24" - $525.00; 26" - $600.00; 28" - $700.00; 32" - $975.00; 36" - $1,300.00; 42" - $2,000.00.

Large Sizes Marked Just A.M.: Jointed bodies, socket head and open mouths. 36"- $1,400.00; 38" - $1,650.00; 42" - $2,100.00.

Mold Number 1776, 1890, 1892, 1893, 1894, 1896, 1897 (which can be a shoulder head or have a socket head); **1898, 1899, 1901, 1902, 1903, 1908, 1909, 3200:** Kid or kidaleen body, open mouth. (See below for prices if on composition bodies.) 10" - $165.00; 14" - $245.00; 19" - $465.00; 23" - $500.00; 27" - $700.00.

19" marked "1894 AM 4 DEP." Sleep eyes, open mouth and on fully jointed body. 19" - $600.00. *Courtesy Frasher Doll Auctions.*

Same as previously listed, on composition jointed bodies: 10" - $365.00; 14" - $400.00; 19" - $600.00; 23" - $750.00; 28" - $875.00; 31" - $925.00; 35" - $1,250.00; 39" - $1,500.00.

Alma, Floradora, Mabel, Lily, Darling, My Playmate, Sunshine, Dutchess, #2000, 3700, 14008: 1890s. Kid or kidaleen body. 10" - $165.00; 14" $225.00; 17" - $325.00; 21" - $385.00; 24" - $450.00; 29" - $850.00.

Same as above, on composition body: 15" - $350.00; 19" - $465.00; 23" - $525.00; 27" - $700.00; 30" - $950.00.

Queen Louise, Beauty, Columbia, Jubilee, Majestic, Princess, Rosebud: Kid or kidaleen body. 13" - $235.00; 16" - $285.00; 22" - $385.00; 24" - $475.00; 27" - $650.00; 30" - $900.00.

Same as last listing, on composition body: 12" - $345.00; 15" -

$350.00; 19" - $450.00; 23" - $500.00; 25" - $575.00; 28" - $800.00; 32" - $950.00; 36" - $1,100.00.

Babies (infant style): Some from 1910; others from 1924. Can be on composition bodies, or have cloth bodies with curved or straight cloth legs. (Add $100.00-150.00 more for toddler babies.)

Mold #340, 341: With closed mouth (**My Dream Baby,** also called **Rock-A-Bye Baby.**) Made for the Arranbee Doll Co. **Composition body:** 6-7" - $265.00; 9" - $250.00; 12" - $365.00; 14" - $575.00; 16" - $650.00; 20" - $775.00; 24" - $1,100.00; 28" - $1,500.00. **Toddler:** 20" - $750.00; 25" - $1,000.00.

Mold #345, 351: With open mouth. Same as above, but some will also be marked **"Kiddiejoy"** or **"Our Pet."** 7-8" - $195.00; 10" - $265.00; 14" - $575.00; 20" - $750.00; 28" - $1,400.00.

Mold #340, 341 or 345, 347, 351: Twin puppets in basket - $850.00 up. Hand puppet, single doll - $550.00.

Mold #341, 345, 351 ("Kiddiejoy" or **"Our Pet"):** With fired-on black or brown color. See Black section.

Babies: 1910 on. (Add $100.00-150.00 for toddler bodies.) **Mold #256, 259, 326, 327, 328, 329, 360, 750, 790, 900, 927, 971, 975, 980, 984, 985, 990, 991, 992, 995, 996, 1321, 1330, 1330A, 1333:** 10" - $325.00; 12" - $350.00; 15" - $450.00; 20" - $600.00; 22" - $675.00; 25" - $875.00. **Same mold numbers as above, but painted bisque:** 13" - $225.00; 17" - $350.00; 20" - $450.00; 25" - $600.00

Character Babies: 1910 on. (Add $100.00-150.00 for toddler body.) Composition jointed body. Can have open mouth or open/closed mouth.

Mold #233: 10" - $285.00; 14" - $550.00; 17" - $685.00; 20" - $775.00.

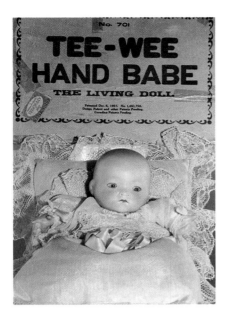

Bisque head, celluloid hands, attached to cloth pillow that has place for hand in back to make doll a puppet. Marked "Germany/KiddieJoy (Made by Armand Marseille)." Box: "Tee-Wee Hand Bebe. Patented Dec. 6, 1927. No. 1,65,738." Side of box: "Manufactured by S&H Novelty Co. Atlantic City, NJ." (This is *not* Simon & Halbig of Germany.) **$550.00.** *Courtesy Gloyra Woods.*

Mold #248: Open/closed mouth: 16" - $1,700.00. **Open mouth:** 16" - $900.00.

Mold #251: With open/closed mouth. 15" - $1,600.00; 17" - $1,800.00. With open mouth, 16" - $900.00.

Mold #327, 328: 10" - $275.00; 14" - $425.00; 18" - $585.00; 22" - $765.00.

Mold #346: 16" - $600.00; 21" - $725.00; 26" - $900.00.

Mold #347: 15" - $500.00.

Mold #352: (See photo in Series 7, pg. 18.) 9" - $250.00; 13" - $375.00; 17" - $575.00; 24" - $900.00.

Mold #355: A. Eller/3K. Closed mouth, sweet face. 13" - $785.00; 18" - $975.00.

Mold #362: 10" - $245.00; 15" - $550.00; 18" - $750.00.

Mold #410: Two rows of teeth, some are retractable. 14" - $950.00; 16" - $1,300.00; 25" - $975.00.

Mold #518: 16" - $575.00; 22" - $700.00.

Mold #506A, 560A: 12" - $525.00; 14" - $585.00; 19" - $800.00.

Mold #570: Open/closed mouth. 17" - $1,700.00; 21" - $2,000.00.

Mold #550, 580: Has open/closed mouth. 12-13" - $1,300.00; 18" - $1,700.00; 22" - $2,000.00.

Mold #590: Has open/closed mouth. (See photo in Series 7, pg. 19.) 17" - $1,700.00; 23" - $2,200.00. Open mouth: 12-13" - $600.00; 16" - $950.00.

23" marked "Armand Marseille. Germany 390/A. 7½ M." Fully jointed body, open mouth with four teeth, sleep eyes. Excellent quality bisque. **23"** - **$500.00.** *Courtesy Frasher Doll Auctions.*

12" character marked "Armand Marseille 400 Germany 3/0." Closed mouth, jointed body, glass eyes. 12" - $1,800.00. *Courtesy Frasher Doll Auctions.*

Mold #920: Cloth body, shoulder head. 20" - $925.00.

Mold #970: 17" - $550.00; 21" - $800.00; 25" - $950.00.

Baby Gloria: Mold #240: (See photo in Series 5, pg. 18.) 10" - $400.00; 14" - $600.00; 18" - $1,000.00; 24" - $1,400.00.

Baby Phyllis: Heads by Armand Marseille. Painted hair, closed mouth. 12" - $450.00; 16" - $650.00; 20" - $1,100.00.

Baby Florence: 13" - $525.00; 18" - $1,200.00.

Baby Betty: 1890s. Jointed composition child body, but few heads found on bent limb baby body. 14-15" - $500.00; 18" - $650.00; 22" - $775.00. **Kid body:** 15" - $285.00; 18" - $450.00.

Fany Baby: Mold #231 along with incised "Fany." Can be baby, toddler or child. With wig: 15" - $4,400.00; 19" - $7,000.00.

Fany Baby: Mold #230 along with incised "Fany." Molded hair. 15" - $4,600.00; 19" - $7,600.00; 25" - $8,400.00.

Just Me: Mold #310. See Googly section.

Melitta: (See photo in Series 8, pg. 20.) Baby: 15" - $525.00; 19" - $750.00. Toddler: 19" - $950.00; 24" - $1,200.00.

Character Child: 1910 on. May have wig, molded hair, glass or intaglio painted eyes and some will have fully closed mouths while others have open/closed mouth. For these prices, doll must be in excellent condition and have no damage.

Mold #250: 14-15" - $800.00; 18" - $1,250.00.

Mold #340: 14" - $2,700.00.

Mold #345: (See photo in Series 5, pg. 17.) 10" - $1,000.00; 18" - $2,000.00.

Mold #350: Socket head, glass eyes, closed mouth. 9" - $1,200.00; 15" - $2,200.00; 22" - $3,800.00.

Mold #360: 13" - $425.00; 17" - $800.00.

Mold #372 "Kiddiejoy": Kid body, molded hair, glass eyes. (See photo in Series 5, pg. 18.) 14" - $650.00; 19" - $1,000.00; 23" - $1,500.00.

Mold #400: Glass eyes, socket head and closed mouth. 12" - $1,800.00; 15" - $2,400.00; 18" - $3,000.00.

Mold #449: Painted eyes, socket head and closed mouth. 10" - $450.00; 18" - $1,200.00; 20" - $1,550.00.

Mold #450: Socket head, glass eyes and closed mouth. 22" - $2,100.00 up.

Mold #500, 520: Molded hair, intaglio eyes, open/closed mouth. 9" - $450.00; 16" - $1,100.00; 23" - $1,700.00.

Mold #500, 520, 620, 640: Wigged, glass eyes and open/closed mouth. **Composition, jointed body:** 9" - $675.00; 17" - $1,300.00; 22" -

$2,100.00. **Same, with kid body:** 16" - $1,000.00; 20" - $1,600.00.

Mold #550, 600, 640: (See photo in Series 7, pg. 19.) **Molded hair, painted eyes:** 10" - $1,000.00; 15" - $1,800.00. **Glass eyes:** 12" - $1,750.00; 17" - $3,400.00; 22" $4,000.00. **Closed mouth, dimples:** 14" - $1,500.00.

Mold #570, 590: Open mouth: 10" - $500.00; 15" - $875.00. Open/ closed mouth: 17" - $1,800.00.

Mold #700: (See photo in Series 8, pg. 21.) **Glass eyes:** 12" - $2,000.00; 14-15" - $3,000.00; 18" - $3,600.00. **Painted eyes:** 13-14" - $2,200.00.

Mold #701, 709, 711: Glass eyes, closed mouth, sweet expression. 10" - $1,200.00; 18" - $2,900.00.

Mold #800, 820: Glass eyes, open/closed mouth. (See photo in Series 6, pg. 21.) 18" - $2,200.00; 22" - $2,900.00.

Mold #950: Painted hair and eyes, open mouth. 10" - $400.00; 15" - $900.00.

Character with Closed Mouth Marked only "A.M.": Intaglio, 16" - $4,600.00. Glass eyes, 18" - $5,200.00.

Googly: See Googly section.

Black or Brown Dolls: See that section.

Adult Lady Dolls: 1910-1920s. Adult face with long, thin jointed limbs. Knee joint is above knee area.

Mold #300: 10" - $1,000.00.

Mold #400, 401: Closed mouth. 10" - $1,400.00; 13" - $1,900.00; 16" - $2,400.00.

Mold #400, 401: Open mouth. 10" - $700.00; 13" - $1,000.00; 16" - $1,300.00.

Painted Bisque: Mold #400, 401: 15" - $750.00; 17" - $965.00.

Painted Bisque: Mold #242, 244, 246, etc. 16" - $400.00; 20" - $650.00; 28" - $850.00.

Biscoloid: Like painted bisque but material under paint more plastic type.

Mold #378, 966, etc. 15" - $450.00; 17" - $700.00.

On the left is a glass eyes model of AM mold #700. Sleep eyes, closed pouty mouth and on fully jointed body. On the right is a painted eye version of same mold number that is 13" tall and has very pouty expression. Fully jointed body. Glass eyes - $2,800.00; Painted eyes - $2,200.00. *Courtesy Frasher Doll Auctions.*

A. **Thuillier** made dolls in Paris from 1875 to 1893 and may be the maker of the dolls marked with "A.T." A.T. marked dolls can be found on wooden, jointed composition or kid bodies and can range in sizes from 14" to 30". The dolls can have closed mouths or open mouths with two rows of teeth. The following prices are for marked A.T. dolls on correct body, clean, beautiful face, dressed nicely and with no damage, such as a hairline cracks, chips or breaks. (See photos in Series 7, pgs. 21-22.)

Closed Mouth: (See photo in Series 8, pg. 23.) Jointed composition body. 13-14" - $49,000.00; 16" - $52,000.00; 18" - $58,000.00; 22" - $63,000.00; 25" - $70,000.00.

Marks:

A.T. N°3
A N°6 T
A. 8 T.

Open Mouth: Jointed composition body. 14" - $19,000.00; 17" - $23,000.00; 20" - $26,000.00; 24" - $30,000.00.

13" marked "A. 4 T." Open mouth with lips barely parted and two rows of teeth. On original A.T. jointed body. 13" - $19,000.00. *Courtesy Frasher Doll Auctions.*

Georgene Averill used the business names of Madame Georgene Dolls, Averill Mfg. Co., Georgene Novelties and Madame Hendron. Averill began making dolls in 1913 and designed a great many for George Borgfeldt.

First prices are for extra clean dolls. Second prices for dolls with chips, craze lines, dirt, or missing some or all of the original clothes.

Baby Georgene or Baby Hendron: 1918 on. Composition/cloth and marked with name on head. Add $50.00 more if mint, original with tag. 15" - $195.00, $80.00; 21" - $285.00, $95.00; 25" - $385.00, $125.00.

Baby Yawn: Composition with closed eyes and yawn mouth. 14" - $485.00, $165.00; 17" - $565.00, $225.00.

Body Twist Dolls: 1927. Composition with large ball joint at waist, painted hair and features. 13-14" - $365.00, $90.00.

Bonnie Babe: Mold #1368-140 or 1402. 1926. Bisque head, cloth body, open mouth/two lower teeth, molded hair and composition arms/or hands. 14" - $900.00; 16" - $1,100.00; 22" - $1,600.00 up. **Celluloid head:** 15-16" - $675.00 up. **Composition body, bisque head:** 8-9" - $1,300.00.

Bonnie Babe: All bisque. See "All Bisque" section.

Right: 21" **Georgene Doll with composition head and hands, mint condition red flannel clothes. Middle right:** 17" **"Mary Jane,"** 1953, **by Kathryn Kay Toy Kreations. All hard plastic walker with sleep eyes and long molded lashes. In original case with clothes is a** 15" **all composition "Nancy" by Arranbee. Left: All original** 13" **"Scooties" by Cameo.** 21" - $350.00; 17" - $265.00; 15" in case - $600.00; 13" - $475.00. *Courtesy Frasher Doll Auctions.*

Cloth Dolls: 1930s. Mask face with painted features, yarn hair, cloth body. First price for clean dolls; second for soiled dolls. **Characters:** Such as Becassine, etc. 1950s. Must be mint. (See photo in Series 7, pg. 24.) 13-14" - $400.00. **International:** 12" - $95.00, $20.00; 15" - $165.00, $60.00. **Children:** 12" - $95.00; $35.00; 16" - $165.00, $50.00; 20" - $225.00, $60.00; 25" - $300.00, $100.00. **Musical:** 15" - $225.00, $70.00. **Brownies:** 15" - $200.00, $70.00. **Scout:** $250.00, $80.00.

Tear Drop Baby: One tear painted on cheek. 16" - $300.00, $65.00.

Right: 16" Drayton design for Georgene Averill. Composition shoulder head with molded hair and painted features, cloth body and legs with composition arms. Original. Left: 25" character by Kestner marked "K½ Made in Germany 14½/ 143." Open mouth, plaster pate and early body with straight wrists. 16" - $485.00; 25" - $1,900.00. *Courtesy Frasher Doll Auctions.*

Animals: 1930s on. Must be mint. B'rer Rabbit, Fuzzy Wuzzy, Nurse Jane, Uncle Wiggley, etc. (See photos in Series 7, pg. 25; Series 8, pg. 25.) 18" - $500.00. **Children:** Composition, cloth body. Perfect and original. 13" - $285.00, 17" - $425.00; less than mint - $165.00. **Scout, Pirate, Brownie, Storybook:** 13" - $350.00, $100.00; 18" - $600.00, $225.00. **Patsy type:** 14" - $245.00, $95.00.

Comic Characters: 1944-1951. All cloth with mask faces and painted features. Includes **Little Lulu, Nancy, Sluggo, Tubby Tom.** 12-13" - $465.00.

Dolly Dingle (for Grace Drayton): All cloth. 12" - $450.00, $125.00.

Dolly Record: 1922. Composition with record player in back. 26" - $565.00, $250.00.

Googly: Composition/cloth. 12" - $250.00, $70.00; 15" - $325.00, $100.00; 17" - $465.00, $150.00.

Indian, Cowboy, Sailor, Soldier, Scout, Pirate: Composition/cloth, molded hair or wig, sometimes yarn hair, painted features. 14" - $400.00, $125.00.

Krazy Kat: Felt, unjointed, 1916. (See photo in Series 6, pg. 27.) 14" - $350.00, $85.00. 18" - $500.00, $125.00.

Snookums: 1927. Composition/cloth. Smile face, character from George McManus's "The Newlyweds." 14" - $385.00, $150.00.

Vinyl Head, Laughing Child: With oil cloth body. 28" - $185.00, $70.00.

Whistling Dan: Sailor, cowboy, policeman, child, etc. 1925-1929. (See photo in Series 6, pg. 26.) 14" - $250.00, $85.00; 16" - $300.00, $100.00.

Whistling Rufus: Black doll. 14" - $425.00, $125.00.

Whistling Dolly Dingle: 14" - $425.00, $125.00.

Babies, Infant Types: 1920s. Composition/cloth, painted hair, sleep eyes. 16" - $185.00, $70.00; 21" - $285.00, $100.00.

19" "Uncle Wiggley" and "Nurse Jane." He has long ears while she has short felt ones. Made of all cloth. Shown with rare "Uncle Wiggley" book with original dust jacket, 1942. "Uncle Wiggley" - $850.00 up; "Nurse Jane" - $700.00. Book with jacket - $55.00; without jacket - $45.00. *Courtesy Ellen Dodge.*

26" large "Dutch Children" by Georgene Averill. Have original tags. Mask faces with real eyelashes. Both are original. 26" - $365.00 each. *Courtesy Ellen Dodge.*

27

BABY BO-KAYE

Bisque heads for Baby Bo-Kaye were made by Alt, Beck & Gottschalck in 1925. Celluloid heads were made in Germany, and composition heads were made in the U.S. by Cameo Doll Company. Designer of the doll was Joseph L. Kallus, owner of Cameo Doll Co. (See photo in Series 8, pg. 26.)

Bisque Head: Molded hair, open mouth, glass eyes, cloth body, composition limbs. **Mold #1307-124, 1394-30.** In overall good condition with no damage. 16" - $2,550.00; 19-21" - $3,100.00.

Celluloid Head: Same as "Bisque Head" description. 12" - $375.00; 15" - $685.00.

Composition Head: Same as above description. 14" - $550.00. Light craze: 14" - $425.00. Cracks and/or chips: 14" - $125.00.

All Bisque: 4½" - $1,300.00; 6½" - $1,700.00.

16" "Baby Bo-Kaye" marked "Cop-r. by J.L. Kallus Germany 1394/30." Molded hair, sleep eyes, flange neck on cloth body with composition arms. Shown with 11" Googly "Uncle Sam" marked "Dep Elite." Fully jointed body. 16" - $2,550.00; 11" - $2,600.00.
Courtesy Frasher Doll Auctions.

BAHR & PROSCHILD

Bahr & Proschild operated at Ohrdruf, Germany from 1871 into late 1920s. They also made celluloid dolls (1910).

Marks:

Character Baby: 1909 on. Bent limbs, sleep eyes, wigged and open mouths. Allow $100.00-150.00 more for toddler body. Clean, nicely dressed and no damage.

Mold #592: Baby: 10-12" - $700.00. **Toddler:** 10-12" - $1,050.00.

Mold #585, 586, 587, 604, 620, 624, 630, 678, 619, 641: 13" - $485.00; 16" - $625.00; 19" - $785.00; 25" - $985.00. **Toddler:** 9-10" - $650.00; 15" - $800.00.

Mold #169: 12" - $500.00; 16" - $750.00; 20" - $850.00.

Character Child: Can be on fully jointed composition body or toddler body. Ca 1910. Nicely dressed, clean and no damage. Can have molded hair or be wigged.

Mold #526, 2072, or marked B.P: 1910. Open/closed mouth. 16" - $3,200.00; 20" - $4,400.00.

Mold # in 200 and 300 Series: Now attributed to Bahr & Proschild. Can be on French bodies. Open mouth, jointed composition bodies. Ca. 1880s. Prior to recent findings, these dolls were attributed to Kestner.

Mold #204, 224, 239, 246, 273, 274, 275, 277, 281, 286, 289, 293, 297, 309, 325, 332, 340, 379, 394, etc.: 1880s. As described above. 8", five-piece body - $375.00; 10" - $525.00; 14" - $625.00; 17" - $745.00; 21" - $850.00; 24" - $1,000.00.

Same as above, on kid bodies: Open mouth. 16" - $450.00; 19" - $500.00; 23" - $600.00.

Same as above, closed mouth: Dome head or "Belton type," socket head on composition or kid body with bisque shoulder plate. 12" - $1,650.00; 15" - $1,950.00; 20" - $2,450.00; 23" - $3,150.00.

Mold #2025: Painted eyes, closed mouth: 16" - $1,700.00. **Glass eyes:** 20" - $4,300.00.

Mold #2072: Closed mouth, glass eyes. 18" - $3,600.00. **Toddler:** 22" - $4,350.00.

12" baby marked "B & P 0 Harmus Germany 630-3." Has open/closed mouth with two upper teeth, sleep eyes, and on bent limb baby body. Musical cradle that is all wood; 9" long, 16" high. Shown with 20" shoulder head doll marked "DEP 154." Made by Kestner. Kid body with bisque lower arms. 12" - $425.00; Cradle - $95.00; 20" - $750.00. *Courtesy Frasher Doll Auctions.*

Bathing dolls of the 1920s can be in any position, including standing on a base. They are all bisque and will have painted-on bathing costumes or be nude. They were made in Germany and some in the United States. Prices are for dolls with no damage, chips or breaks. Must be clean.

Excellent quality bisque and artist workmanship, painted eyes: 3" - $275.00; 5-6" - $485.00; 8-9" - $625.00

up. **With animal:** 5½" - $1,650.00 up. **Two modeled together:** 4½-5½" - $1,350.00 up. **Glass eyes:** 4½" - $450.00; 6" - $650.00. **Swivel neck:** 5" - $675.00; 6" - $725.00.

Fair quality of bisque and workmanship or marked Japan: 3" - $95.00; 5-6" - $145.00; 9" - $225.00.

Ederle, Gertrude: In diving pose. (See photo in Series 7, pg. 26.) 8" - $700.00; 13" - $1,450.00; 18" - $1,850.00.

Bathing dolls from 1920's of all bisque with painted-on clothes and features. Left: Marked "Germany 3689." Center: 3" standing doll marked "Germany 5722." Right: Marked "Germany 6399." Note fin-like feet. 3" - $275.00; 5" - $485.00.
Courtesy Frasher Doll Auctions.

12" long beautiful quality bathing beauty with excellent detail, molded hair with cloth headband and string style sandals. $900.00. *Courtesy Ellen Dodge.*

"Belton-type" dolls are not marked or will just have a number on the head. They have a concave top to a solid uncut head with one to three holes for stringing and/or plugging in wig. The German dome heads have a full round solid uncut head, but some of these may even have one or two holes in them. (See photo in Series 7, pg. 28.) This style doll was made from 1875 on, and most likely a vast amount of these dolls were actually German made, although they must be on a French body to qualify as a "Belton-type." Since these dolls are found on French bodies, it can be assumed the German heads were made for French firms.

Prices are for nicely dressed dolls with excellent quality bisque with closed or open/closed mouths. Bodies are French with straight wrists and no damage.

French Style Face: 8" on five-piece body - $825.00; 8" on jointed body - $1,250.00; 10" - $1,650.00; 12" - $1,800.00; 15" - $2,500.00; 18" - $3,000.00; 20" - $3,300.00; 23" - $3,600.00; 26" - $4,100.00.

Bru Look: 16" - $2,850.00; 20" - $3,100.00. (*See Bahr & Proschild #200 series for open mouth dolls.)

German Style Face: 10" - $1,250.00; 12" - $1,350.00; 14" - $1,550.00; 16" - $1,750.00; 21" - $2,100.00; 25" - $2,450.00.

25" very early and pale Belton-type with concave dome and two string holes. Open/closed mouth with white space between lips. On French body with straight wrists. 25" - $4,100.00. *Courtesy Frasher Doll Auctions.*

22" Belton-type marked "14" on head. Concave dome with two holes, open/closed mouth with white space between lips. On French jointed body with straight wrists. 17" large "Stuart Baby" with molded-on bonnet, cloth body, and bisque lower arms. Made by Heubach. 22" - $3,200.00; Baby - $2,200.00. *Courtesy Frasher Doll Auctions.*

BERGMANN, C.M.

Charles M. Bergmann made dolls from 1889 at both Waltershausen and Friedrichroda, Germany. Many of the Bergmann heads were made for him by other companies, such as Simon & Halbig, Kestner, Armand Marseille and others.

Marks:

C.M. BERGMANN

S. & H
C.M. BERGMANN
Waltershausen
Germany

Child: 1880s into early 1900s. On fully jointed composition bodies and open mouth. (Add $100.00 more for heads by Simon & Halbig.) 10" - $425.00; 18" - $475.00; 24" - $750.00; 27" - $865.00; 30" - $1,000.00; 40-42" - $2,200.00.

Character Baby: 1909 and after. Socket head on five-piece bent limb baby body. Open mouth. 10" - $365.00; 15" - $485.00; 17" - $550.00; 20" - $685.00.

Mold #612 Baby: Open/closed mouth. 15" - $1,300.00; 19" - $1,900.00.

Lady Doll: Adult-style body with long thin arms and legs. "Flapper-style" doll. 13" - $685.00; 16" - $875.00; 20"- $1,650.00.

31" marked "C.M. Bergmann. Simon
& Halbig 14½"." Open mouth and on
fully jointed body. 31" - $1,000.00.

B.F.

The French dolls marked "B.F." were made by Ferte (Bébé Ferte), and some collectors refer to them as Bébé Française by Jumeau. They are now being attributed to Danel & Cie who also used the Bébé Française trademark. They have closed mouths and are on jointed French bodies with most having straight wrists.

Child: 12" - $2,400.00; 14" - $2,600.00; 16" - $3,900.00; 18" - $4,500.00; 24" - $5,500.00; 27" - $5,900.00.

Marks:

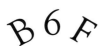

Dolls marked "B.L." are referred to as "Bébé Louvre," but they most likely were made by Alexandre Lefebvre, who made dolls from 1890 and by 1922 was part of S.F.B.J. (See photo in Series 7, pg. 30; Series 8, pg. 31.) 18" - $4,000.00; 21" - $4,300.00; 25" - $4,800.00; 27" - $5,200.00.

20" "Bebe Louvre" marked "B 9 L." Closed mouth with white space between lips and on French jointed body. 20" - $4,200.00. *Courtesy Frasher Doll Auctions.*

BLACK OR BROWN DOLLS

Black or brown dolls can have fired-in color or be painted bisque, composition, cloth, papier maché and other materials. They can range from very black to a light tan and also be a "dolly" face or have Negroid features. The quality of these dolls varies greatly and prices are based on this quality.

Both the French and Germans made these dolls. Prices are for undamaged, nicely dressed and clean dolls.

Alabama: See Cloth Doll section.

All Bisque: Glass eyes, one-piece body and head. 4-5" - $450.00.

All Bisque: Glass eyes, swivel head. 5-6" - $750.00.

All Bisque: Painted eyes, one-piece body and head. 5" - $250.00. Swivel head: 5" - $450.00. **French type:** 4" - $385.00. **All Bisque marked with maker:** (S&H, JDK, etc.): 6½-7" - $1,400.00.

A.M. 341 or 351: 10-11" - $400.00; 14" - $600.00; 17" - $865.00; 21" - $1,200.00.

A.M. 362: 14-15" - $700.00.

A.M. 390: (See photo in Series 6, pg. 39.) 15" - $550.00, 18" - $775.00; 23" - $925.00.

A.M. 390n: 15" - $600.00; 23" - $975.00.

A.M. 518, 362, 396, 513: 16"- $725.00; 20" - $975.00.

A.M. 451, 458 (Indians): 9" - $325.00; 12" - $475.00.

A.M. 971, 992, 995 Baby or Toddler: 9" - $285.00; 13" - $575.00; 18" - $975.00.

A.M 1894, 1897, 1912, 1914: 10" - $385.00; 12" - $485.00.

Baby Grumpy: Made by Effanbee. 12" - $265.00; 17" - $475.00. Craze, dirty: 12" - $95.00; 17" - $125.00.

Bahr & Proschild #277: Open mouth. 12" - $675.00; 15" - $1,600.00.

Bruckner: See Cloth Section.

Bru Jne: 19" - $32,000.00 up; 25" - $46,000.00 up.

Bru, Circle Dot or Brevette: 14" - $20,000.00 up; 17" - $29,000.00 up.

Bubbles: Made by Effanbee. 16" - $425.00; 20" - $650.00. Craze, dirty: 16" - $100.00; 20" - $200.00.

Bye-Lo: 14-15" - $2,700.00 up.

Candy Kid: 12" - $325.00. Craze, dirty: 12" - $145.00.

Celluloid: All celluloid (more for glass eyes.) 16" - $325.00; 19" - $600.00. Celluloid shoulder head, kid body (more for glass eyes): 16" - $300.00; 19" - $425.00.

Chase: 23" - $7,800.00; 27" - $9,000.00.

Cloth: See cloth section.

15" wonderful character by unknown maker. Marked "N.I." Fired-in bisque shoulder head with glass eyes, open/closed mouth, modeled tongue and teeth, original wig and clothes. (Beads not original.) Cloth body, bisque lower arms, and composition lower legs. 15" - **$7,500.00.** *Courtesy Frasher Doll Auctions.*

Composition: Made in Germany. Glass eyes, sometimes flirty. 15" - $550.00; 19" - $725.00; 24" - $950.00.

E.D.: Open mouth: 17" - $2,300.00; 23" - $2,900.00.

F.G.: Open/closed mouth. 17-18" - $3,700.00. **Fashion:** Kid body, swivel neck. 17" - $3,600.00.

Fashion: Swivel neck. **Original:** 17" - $14,600.00. **Redressed:** 17" - $9,200.00. **Shoulder Head: Original:** 17" - $6,000.00. **Redressed:** 17" - $4,200.00.

French, Unmarked or Marked "DEP": Closed mouth, bisque head: 15" - $3,200.00; 19" - $4,300.00. Painted bisque: 15" - $975.00; 19" - $1,200.00.

Beautiful quality little 7" black girl with glass set eyes and closed mouth. Five-piece composition body. May be of French origin. 4" black all bisque with glass eyes and jointed at shoulders and hips. 7" - $800.00; 4" - $625.00.
Courtesy Shirley Bertrand.

French, Unmarked or Marked "DEP": Open mouth, bisque head: 10" - $500.00; 15" - $1,200.00; 22" - $1,900.00. Painted bisque: 15" - $500.00; 20" - $800.00. With Negroid features: 18" - $4,400.00 up.

French marked "SNF": Celluloid. 14" - $200.00; 18" - $365.00.

Frozen Charlotte or Charlie: 3" - $165.00; 6" - $285.00; 8" - $365.00. Jointed shoulder: 3" - $200.00; 6" - $350.00.

German, Unmarked: Closed mouth, bisque head: 10" - $565.00; 14" - $850.00; 16" - $1,000.00. Painted bisque: 14" - $350.00; 20" - $600.00.

German, Unmarked: Open mouth, bisque head. 10-11"-$325.00; 13"-$425.00; 16" - $575.00; 20" - $850.00. **Painted bisque:** 15" - $375.00; 18" - $550.00.

Heinrich Handwerck: Open mouth. 18" - $900.00; 22" - $1,000.00; 26" - $1,500.00.

Hanna: Made by Schoenau & Hoffmeister. 8" - $325.00; 10" - $485.00; 13" - $685.00.

Heubach, Gebruder Mold #7657, 7658, 7668, 7671: 9" - $1,400.00; 12-13" - $1,950.00.

Heubach, Gebruder: (Sunburst mark) Boy, eyes to side. 12" - $2,100.00.

Heubach, Gebruder Mold #7661, 7686: 10" - $1,300.00; 13" - $2,700.00; 16" - $3,900.00.

Heubach Koppelsdorf Mold #320, 339 350: 10" - $425.00; 13" - $585.00; 18" - $800.00; 21" - $1,000.00.

Heubach Koppelsdorf Mold #399: Allow more for toddler. 8-9" - $425.00; 12-13" - $625.00; 16" - $800.00. **Celluloid:** 14" - $325.00; 17" - $625.00.

Heubach Koppelsdorf Mold #414: 15" - $800.00; 18" - $1,400.00.

Heubach Koppelsdorf Mold #418: (Grin) 10" - $675.00; 13" - $900.00.

Heubach Koppelsdorf Mold #463: 12" - $600.00; 16" - $950.00.

Heubach Koppelsdorf Mold #444, 451: 9-10" - $425.00; 13-14" - $725.00.

Heubach Koppelsdorf Mold #452: 12" - $500.00; 15" - $675.00.

Heubach Koppelsdorf Mold #458: 10" - $450.00; 15" - $700.00.

Heubach Koppelsdorf Mold #1900: 15" - $500.00; 18" - $700.00.

Kestner #134: 10-11" - $675.00; 13-14" - $975.00.

Kestner #245, 237: Hilda. 13-14" - $3,450.00; 17" - $5,800.00; 20" - $7,200.00.

Kestner: Child, no mold number. 12" - $500.00; 16" - $700.00. **Five-piece body:** 12" - $350.00.

Jumeau (Tete): Open mouth. 14" - $2,800.00; 17" - $2,700.00; 22" - $3,200.00.

Jumeau (Tete): Closed mouth. 14" - $4,800.00; 16" - $5,000.00; 21" - $6,000.00.

Jumeau Type: Unmarked/number only. (See photo in Series 7, pg. 33.) 12" - $2,600.00; 15" - $3,200.00; 19" - $4,000.00.

Jumeau: Marked "E.J." 15" - $7,200.00; 19" - $8,600.00.

K Star R: Child, no mold number. 14" - $675.00.

K Star R #100: (See photo in Series 6, pg. 38.) 15" - $1,100.00; 17" - $1,500.00; 19" - $1,800.00.

K Star R #101: 15", painted eyes: $2,100.00. **Glass eyes:** 17" - $4,900.00.

K Star R #114: (See photo in Series 7, pg. 35.) 14" - $3,200.00

K Star R #116, 116a: 15" - $3,000.00; 19" - $3,500.00.

K Star R #126: (See photo in Series 5, pg. 28.) Baby. 10" - $750.00; 17" - $1,300.00.

Kewpie: "Hottentot," bisque. 4" - $400.00; 5" - $500.00; 9" - $900.00. **Papier maché:** 8" - $185.00.

Kewpie: Composition. 12" - $350.00. **Toddler:** 12" - $550.00; 16" - $700.00.

KW/G (Konig & Wernicke) 18" - $750.00.

Papier Maché: Negroid features: 10" - $300.00; 14" - $675.00; 18-19" - $825.00. **Others:** 14" - $300.00; 24" - $800.00.

Paris Bébé: 15" - $4,400.00; 18" - $5,500.00.

Parson-Jackson: Baby: 13-14" - $485.00. **Toddler:** 13-14" - $565.00.

Recknagel: Marked "R.A." May have mold **#138.** 15" - $950.00; 21" - $1,900.00.

Schoenau & Hoffmeister #1909: (See photo in Series 5, pg. 29.) 15-16" - $585.00; 18" - $745.00.

Scowling Indian: (See photo in Series 6, pg. 41.) 10" - $375.00; 13" - $500.00.

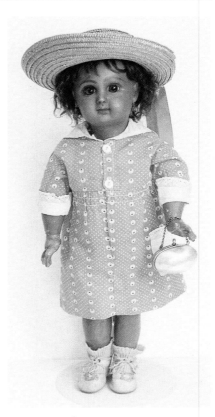

16" brown Tete Jumeau with original wig, paperweight eyes and closed mouth. Ears are pierced. 16" - $5,000.00. *Courtesy Ellen Dodge.*

Scootles: Composition: 15" - $725.00 up. Vinyl: 14" - $250.00; 19" - $425.00; 27" - $585.00.

Simon & Halbig #729: Open mouth and smiling. 16-18" - $3,800.00-4,000.00

Simon & Halbig #739: (See photo in Series 6, pg. 38.) Closed mouth: 17" - $2,850.00; 22" - $3,850.00.

Simon & Halbig #939: Closed mouth: 18" - $3,500.00; 21" - $4,500.00. **Open mouth:** (See photo in Series 7, pg. 34.): 16" - $1,450.00; 20" - $1,900.00.

Simon & Halbig #949: Closed mouth: 18" - $3,000.00; 21" - $3,700.00. **Open mouth:** 18" - $1,400.00.

Simon & Halbig #969: Open mouth, puffed cheeks. 17" - $1,200.00.

Simon & Halbig #1039, 1079: (See photo in Series 8, pg. 35.) **Open mouth:** 16" - $1,400.00; 19" - $1,700.00. **Pull string, sleep eyes:** 19" - $2,400.00.

Simon & Halbig #1248: Open mouth. 14" - $750.00; 17" - $1,000.00.

Simon & Halbig #1302: Closed mouth, glass eyes, very character face. **Black:** 18" - $6,600.00. **Indian:** 18" - $7,500.00.

Simon & Halbig #1303 Indian: 16" - $5,800.00; 21" - $7,200.00.

Simon & Halbig #1339, 1358: 16" - $5,800.00; 20" - $7,200.00.

Simon & Halbig #1368: (See photo in Series 6, pg. 37.) 14" - $5,500.00; 17" - $6,200.00.

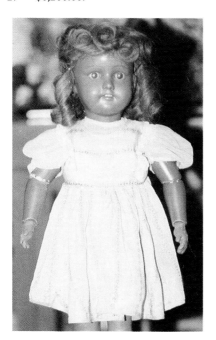

19" composition and wood, open mouth with teeth, original human hair wig. Marked "TREGO" in circle. "Made in U.S.A." 19" - **$725.00.** *Courtesy Sandra Cummins.*

21" marked "34-29 by S.F.B.J." Open mouth, glass eyes, and on French jointed body. 21" - **$5,200.00.** *Courtesy Frasher Doll Auctions.*

S.F.B.J. #301 or 60: Open mouth. 10" - $450.00; 14" - $625.00.

S.F.B.J. #235: Open/closed mouth. 15" - $2,600.00; 17" - $2,900.00.

S.F.B.J. 34-29: Open mouth. 17" - $4,600.00 up; 23" - $5,400.00.

Sarg, Tony: Mammy Doll. Composition/cloth. (See photo in Series 8, pg. 36.) 18" - $575.00.

S.P. mark: Toddler, glass eyes, open mouth: 16" - $650.00.

Steiner, Jules: Open mouth. "A" series: 15" - $4,400.00; 18" - $5,100.00.

Steiner, Jules: Closed mouth. "A" series: 17" - $5,600.00; 21" - $6,300.00. "C" series: 17" - $5,200.00; 19" - $6,000.00.

Stockinette: Oil painted features. 16-17" - $2,350.00; 22" - $2,700.00.

S & Q #251: 9" - $600.00; 16" - $2,100.00. **#252:** 14" - $1,700.00.

Unis #301 or 60: Open mouth. 13" - $385.00; 16" - $625.00.

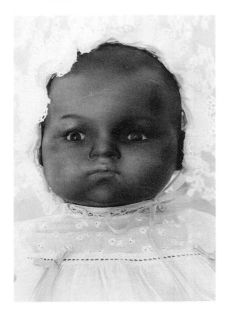

16" with 13" head circumference "Dream Baby," mold #341 with closed mouth. Sleep eyes, cloth body. 16" - $785.00. *Courtesy Turn of Century Antiques.*

Black marionette marked "Lucifer Austin Effanbee." Painted features. Shown with 6" black all bisque with molded kinky hair, painted features and clothes. Marionette - $300.00; 6" - $475.00. *Courtesy Turn of Century Antiques.*

Early black pair of papier maché dolls with cloth bodies, large glass eyes. Original wigs and clothes. $300.00 pair. *Courtesy Turn of Century Antiques.*

Bonnet Dolls date from the 1880's to the 1920's. They can be all bisque or have cloth or kid bodies. The lower limbs can be china, leather, or stone bisque. Most were made in Germany, but some were made in Japan. Also see under Goebel, Googly, and Recknagel sections.

All Bisque: One-piece body and head, painted or glass eyes. Germany. 4-5" - $95.00; 6½" - $135.00; 8" - $175.00; 12" - $225.00.

7" excellent quality hatted bisque with modeled shirt top, red cloth body with bisque lower limbs. Painted features. **7" - $285.00.** *Courtesy Turn of Century Antiques.*

All Bisque: Swivel neck, glass eyes. Germany. 4½-5" - $375.00; 7" - $500.00 up.

Bisque Head: Excellent bisque. Glass eyes, hat or bonnet, molded hair. Five-piece papier maché, kid, or cloth body. 7" - $185.00; 9" - $300.00; 12" - $425.00; 16" - $650.00; 22" - $1,000.00; 25" - $1,250.00.

Bisque Head: Excellent bisque. Glass eyes, hat or bonnet, molded hair. Fully jointed composition or kid body with bisque lower arms. 7" - $225.00; 9" - $365.00; 12" - $485.00; 16" - $725.00; 22" - $1,200.00; 25" - $1,450.00.

Stone Bisque: 8-9" - $175.00; 12" - $235.00; 15" - $400.00; 18" - $675.00; 21" - $865.00.

Stone Bisque with molded bonnet or hat: 4-5" - $175.00; 6-7" - $195.00.

Googly: See that section.

Japan: 8-9" - $95.00; 12" - $135.00.

7" molded bonnet doll of exceptional quality bisque and painting. Long molded hair would make this doll difficult to dress. Made in Germany. Good hand detail and pin jointed. 7" - $185.00. *Courtesy Barbara Spears.*

The "Bonnie Babe" was designed by Georgene Averill in 1926 with the bisque heads being made by Alt, Beck & Gottschalck and the cloth bodies made by the K & K Toy Co. (NY). The dolls were distributed by George Borgfeldt. The doll can have cloth body and legs or composition arms and legs with cloth body.

Marks: "Copr. by Georgene Averill/Germany/1005/3652" and sometimes "1368."

All Bisque: See the All Bisque section.

Bisque head, crooked smile, open mouth: 9-10" - $465.00; 14" - $800.00; 15-16" - $950.00; 23" - $1,400.00; 25" - $1,700.00.

Celluloid head: 10" - $425.00; 16" - $725.00.

Composition Body: Socket head. 8-9" - $1,100.00-1,300.00.

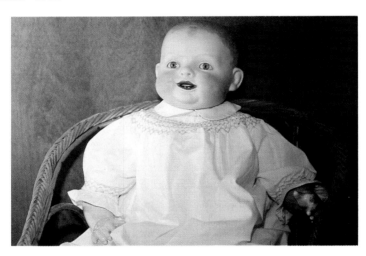

22" large "Bonnie Babe" with bisque head, cloth body and composition limbs. Sleep eyes and open mouth with two lower teeth and molded tongue. Marked "Georgene Averill/Germany." 22" - $1,400.00. *Courtesy Jeannie Mauldin.*

BORGFELDT, GEORGE

George Borgfeldt imported, distributed and assembled dolls in New York. The dolls that he carried or had made ranged from bisque to composition. Many dolls were made for him in Germany. Many heads were made for this firm by Armand Marseille.

Marks:

G.B.

Child: Mold #325, 327, 329, or marked "G.B.": 1910-1922. Fully jointed composition body, open mouth. No damage and nicely dressed. 10" - $275.00; 13" - $265.00; 16" - $345.00; 19" - $485.00; 21" - $575.00; 23" - $650.00; 27" - $800.00.

Baby: 1910. Five-piece bent limb baby body, open mouth. 10" - $300.00; 15" - $565.00; 18" - $675.00; 23" - $925.00; 29" - $1,600.00 up.

23" marked "Germany/G.B." Made for George Borgfeldt. Sleep eyes, open mouth and on fully jointed body. $650.00. *Courtesy Kathy Tvrdik.*

BOUDOIR DOLLS

Boudoir dolls are also called "Flapper" dolls and were most popular during the 1920's and early 1930's, although they were made through the 1940's. Very rarely is one of these dolls marked with the maker or country of origin, but the majority were made in the United States, France and Italy.

The most desirable Boudoir dolls are the ones from France and Italy (Lenci, especially. See that section.) These dolls will have a silk or cloth painted face mask, an elaborate costume, and be of excellent quality.

The least expensive ones have a full or half-composition head, some with glass eyes, and the clothes will be stapled or glued to the body.

Boudoir Dolls: Finely painted features and excellent clothes. **Excellent quality:** 16" - $265.00 up; 28" - $400.00 up; 32" - $465.00 up. **Average quality:** 16" - $100.00; 28" - $175.00; 32" - $225.00. **Undressed:** 16" - $45.00; 28-32" - $85.00.

Boudoir Dolls: With composition head, stapled or glued-on clothes. No damage, and original clothes. 15" - $95.00; 28" - $150.00; 32" - $175.00.

Lenci: See that section.

Smoking Doll: Cloth: 16-17" - $275.00 up; 25" - $450.00 up. **Composition:** 25" - $225.00 up; 28" - $350.00 up.

Velvet face mask boudoir doll with mohair wig, original clothes and painted features. Cloth body with long thin limbs. 28" - $400.00. *Courtesy Marla McKesh.*

Original 29" boudoir doll with composition head and painted features. Mohair braids in circles over ears. Composition lower arms and legs, cloth body. Marked "WKS, Inc." on shoulder. $175.00. *Courtesy Kathy Tvrdik.*

BRU

Bru dolls will be marked with the name Bru or Bru Jne, Bru Jne R. Some will have a circle and dot ($\odot$) or a half circle and dot ($\cup$). Some have paper labels – see marks. Prices are for dolls with no damage at all, very clean, and beautifully dressed. Add $2,000.00 up for all original clothes and marked shoes.

Marks:

BEBE BRU BTE SGDG

BEBE
BREVEE SDGD
PARIS

Closed Mouth Dolls: All kid body. Bisque lower arms. 16" - $10,500.00; 18" - $13,500.00; 21" - $24,000.00; 26" - $29,500.00.

Bru Jne: Ca. 1880's. Kid over wood, wood legs, bisque lower arms. 12-13" - $23,000.00; 14" - $19,000.00; 16" - $24,500.00; 20" - $27,500.00; 22" - $32,000.00; 25" - $39,000.00; 28" - $42,000.00.

Bru Jne: All wood body. 16" - $16,000.00; 20" - $22,000.00.

Circle Dot or Half Circle: Ca. 1870's. 16" - $23,000.00; 19" - $26,000.00; 23" - $29,000.00; 26" - $33,000.00; 30" - $37,000.00.

Brevette: Ca. 1870's. 14" - $16,000.00; 17" - $19,500.00; 20" - $26,000.00.

Bru Jne R., Closed Mouth: 18" - $8,500.00; 22" - $9,200.00.

Bru Jne R., Open Mouth: 1890's. Jointed composition body. First price for excellent quality bisque and second for poor quality bisque. 14" - $6,500.00, $4,000.00; 17" - $7,400.00, $5,200.00; 22" - $8,300.00, $6,400.00; 25" - $10,000.00, $7,600.00.

Walker Body, Throws Kiss: 18" - $7,600.00; 22" - $8,300.00; 26" - $9,400.00.

Nursing Bru: 1878-1899. Operates by turning key in back of head. **Early, excellent quality:** 12" - $5,400.00 up; 15" - $8,200.00; 18" - $9,800.00. **Not as good quality:** 15" - $5,400.00; 18" - $6,200.00. **High color, late S.F.B.J. type:** 12" - $2,600.00; 15" - $3,200.00.

Breathing, Crying, Kissing: (See photo in Series 7, pg. 41.) 19" - $16,000.00; 23-24" - $18,500.00.

Early Bru Brevette style doll with bisque shoulder plate, closed mouth, almond-shaped glass eyes. Original cloth lady's body with leather arms, original fur wig. 14" - **$16,000.00.** *Courtesy Frasher Doll Auctions.*

14" marked "Bru Jne 3" on head and shoulder, gusset-jointed kid body with bisque lower arms. 8" parasol and antique hat/wig. 14" - **$19,000.00. Parasol - $1,000.00 up. Hat - $250.00 up.** *Courtesy Frasher Doll Auctions.*

16" marked "Bru Jne 6" on head and shoulder plate. Original Bru paper label on torso. Open mouth, kid body with kid over wood upper arms and wooden lower legs. Bisque lower arms. Nurser with ball in head and wing screw in back of head that activates it. Origin of costume unknown. 16" - $9,000.00.
Courtesy Frasher Doll Auctions.

16" "Brevette Bru." Early pale bisque, kid body and bisque lower hands. May be original. Shoes are marked "Bru." 16" - $16,000.00. *Courtesy Ellen Dodge.*

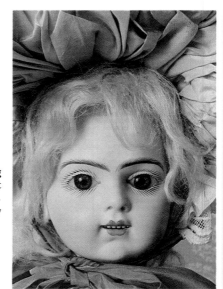

21½" incised "Bru Jne 9." Pull string talker, blows kiss. Open mouth, excellent quality bisque and artist workmanship. 21½" - $8,300.00. *Courtesy Turn of Century Antiques.*

The Bye-Lo baby was designed by Grace Storey Putnam, distributed by George Borgfeldt, and the cloth bodies were made by K & K Toy Co. of NY. The bisque heads were made by Kestner, Alt, Beck & Gottschalck and others. The all bisque dolls were made by Kestner. The dolls date from 1922. Most dolls have celluloid or composition hands. Prices are for undamaged, clean and nicely dressed dolls.

Marks:

1923 by
Grace S. Putnam
Made in Germany
7372145

Copy. By
Grace S. Putnam

Bye-Lo Baby
Pat. Appl'd For

Bisque Head: 8" - $495.00; 10" - $525.00; 12"- $625.00; 15" - $1,000.00; 17-18" - $1,600.00. **Black:** 14-15" - $2,700.00 up.

Mold #1415, Smiling Mouth: Bisque – very rare, painted eyes. 14-15" - $4,900.00 up. **Composition head:** 14-15" - $900.00 up.

Socket Head: Bisque head on five-piece bent limb baby body. 14-15" - $1,700.00; 17" - $2,200.00.

Composition Head: 1924. 10-11" - $325.00; 13-14" - $400.00; 16-17" - $600.00.

Painted Bisque: With cloth body, composition hands. 10" - $275.00; 13" - $400.00; 15" - $575.00.

Schoenhut, wood: 1925. Cloth body, wooden hands. 14-15" - $1,700.00.

All Celluloid: 6" - $200.00. **Celluloid head/cloth body:** 10-11" - $350.00; 13-14" - $465.00.

All Bisque: See All Bisque section, Characters.

Vinyl Heads: Early 1950's. Cloth/stuffed limbs. Marked "Grace Storey Putnam" on head. 15" - $285.00.

Honey Child: Bye-lo look-a-like made by Bayless Bros. & Co. in 1926. 15" - $325.00; 21" - $485.00.

Wax Bye-lo: Cloth or sateen body. 15-16" - $3,700.00 up.

Basket with blanket and extra clothes: Five babies in basket, bisque heads: 12" - $4,400.00 up. Composition heads: 12" - $2,700.00 up.

Mold #1418, Fly-Lo Baby (Baby Aero): Bisque head, cloth body, celluloid hands, glass eyes. Closed mouth, deeply molded hair. Very rare. 10" - $3,200.00; 14" - $4,400.00; 16" - $5,000.00.

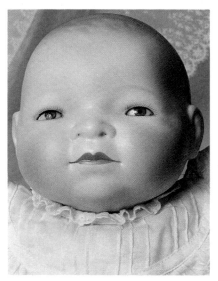

Larger than life size "Bye-lo" with 15" head circumference. Blue sleep eyes, cloth body and celluloid hands. Marked "Copy. Grace Storey Putnam." 17" - $1,600.00.
Courtesy Turn of Century Antiques.

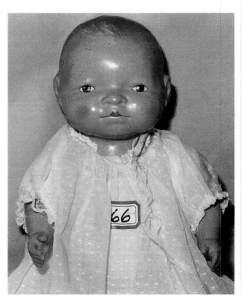

All composition "Bye-Lo" copy incised "Honey Child" and made in 1926 by Bayless Bros. & Co. Painted features. 15" - $325.00. *Courtesy Frasher Doll Auctions.*

CATTERFELDER PUPPENFABRIK

Catterfelder Puppenfabrik of Germany made dolls from 1902 until the late 1930's. The heads for their dolls were made by various German firms, including Kestner.

Marks:

$$C \underset{5}{\overset{P}{\underset{219}{}}} \quad C \underset{}{\overset{P}{}} \atop 201/40 \\ Deponiert$$

Catterfelder
Puppenfabrik
45

Child: Ca. 1900's. Composition jointed body. Open mouth. **Mold #264:** Or marked "C.P." 17" - $700.00; 23" - $875.00.

Character Child: 1910 or after. Composition jointed body, closed mouth and can be boy or girl, with character face. **Mold #207:** 15-16" - $5,800.00. **Mold #215:** 16" - $4,600.00; 20" - $4,800.00 **Mold #219:** 16" - $3,850.00; 20" - $4,600.00.

Babies: 1909 or after. Wig or molded hair, five-piece bent limb baby body, glass or painted eyes.

Mold #262, 263, 264: 10-11" - $375.00; 15" - $525.00; 21" - $775.00; 25" - $1,000.00.

Mold #200, 201: 16" - $625.00.

Mold #207, 208, 209, etc.: 14" - $500.00; 18" - $700.00; 22" - $925.00; 26" - $1,100.00.

CATTERFELDER PUPPENFABRIK

Very rare mold number 207 by Catterfelder Puppenfabrik, ca. 1902. 16" tall and all original in unplayed with condition. Closed mouth, painted eyes with modeled eyelids, jointed body. 16" - $5,800.00.
Courtesy Frasher Doll Auctions.

CELLULOID DOLLS

Celluloid dolls date from the 1880's into the 1940's when they were made illegal in the United States because they burned or exploded if placed near an open flame or heat. Some of the makers were:

United States: Marks Bros., Irwin, Horsman, Averill, Parsons-Jackson, Celluloid Novelty Co.

France: Societe Industrielle de Celluloid (Sisoine), Petitcolin (eagle symbol), Societe Nobel Francaise (SNF in diamond), Jumeau/Unis (1950's), Neumann & Marx (dragon symbol).

Germany: Rheinische Gummi and Celluloid Fabrik Co. (turtle mark), Minerva (Buschow & Beck) (helmet symbol), E. Maar & Sohn (3 M's mark), Adelheid Nogler Innsbruck Doll Co. (animal with spread wings and a fish tail, in square), Cellba (mermaid symbol).

Poland: P.R. Zask ("ASK" in triangle).

England: Cascelloid Ltd. (Palitoy).

Prices for perfect, undamaged dolls.

All Celluloid Baby: 1910 on. Painted eyes: 7" - $85.00; 10" - $125.00; 14" - $185.00; 16" - $200.00; 19" - $300.00; 22" - $400.00; 26" - $500.00. **Glass inset eyes:** 14" - $200.00; 16" - $265.00; 19" - $425.00; 22" - $485.00.

Bye-Lo: See that section.

All Celluloid Child Dolls: (Germany) Jointed at neck, shoulders and hips. **Painted eyes:** 6" - $65.00; 9" - $95.00; 13" - $145.00; 16" - $200.00; 19" - $385.00. **Jointed at neck and shoulders only:** 5" - $30.00; 7" - $45.00; 9" - $65.00.

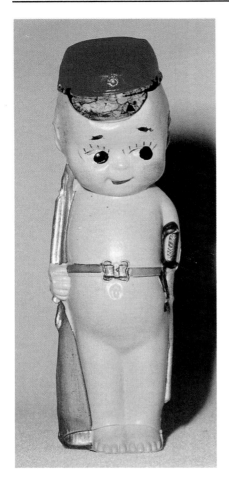

4" celluloid Kewpie soldier. There is a triangle mark on back with some kind of symbol in it along with "Made in Japan." 4" - $100.00. *Courtesy Patty Martin.*

All Celluloid Child Dolls: Same as previous listing but with glass eyes: 13" - $200.00; 15" - $300.00; 17-18" - $465.00. **Jointed at neck and shoulders only:** 12" - $150.00; 16" - $225.00.

All Celluloid Child Dolls: Same as above, but marked "France": 8" - $165.00; 10" - $225.00; 16" - $325.00; 19" - $500.00.

All Celluloid, Molded on Clothes: Jointed at shoulders only. 4" - $55.00; 6" - $75.00; 8" - $125.00. **Immobilies:** No joints. 4" - $25.00; 6" - $40.00.

All Celluloid Black Dolls: See Black Doll section.

Celluloid Shoulder Head: 1900-1912. Germany. Molded hair or wigged, painted eyes, open or closed mouth, kid, kidaleen, or cloth bodies. Can have any material for arms. 13" - $165.00; 16" - $200.00; 19" - $300.00.

Celluloid Shoulder Head: Same as above, but with glass eyes: 13" - $200.00; 16" - $265.00; 19" - $385.00; 23" - $450.00.

Celluloid Socket Heads: (Germany.) Glass eyes (allow more for flirty eyes). Ball-jointed body or five-piece bodies. Open or closed mouths. 14" - $265.00; 17" - $385.00; 20" - $475.00;

6½" all celluloid "Betty Boop" type with molded-on short top. Star-like "Kewpie" hands, painted features. 6½" - $80.00. *Courtesy Phyllis Houston.*

25" - $625.00.

Bye-Lo: 4-4½" - $135.00; 6" - $200.00.
Jumeau: Marked on head, jointed body. 13" - $425.00; 16" - $575.00.
Heubach Koppelsdorf Mold #399: Brown or Black. See Black section.
Kruse, Käthe: All original. 14" - $500.00; 17" - $800.00.
Kammer & Reinhardt: (K star R) Mold #406, 700: Child or baby. 13"- $385.00. **Mold #701:** 14" - $750.00. **Mold #714 or 715:** 15" - $750.00. **Mold #717:** 16" - $465.00; 20" - $800.00. **Mold #728, 828:** 15" - $525.00; 19" -

$775.00. **Mold #826, 828, 406, 321, 255, 225: Baby:** 12" - $225.00; 14" - $465.00; 17" - $575.00; 20" - $700.00. **Child:** 14" - $385.00; 16" - $585.00; 20" - $725.00; 23" - $875.00.
Kewpie: See that section.
Konig & Wernicke (K&W): Toddler: 15" - $450.00; 19" - $625.00.
Japan: 4" - $25.00; 7" - $40.00; 10" - $65.00; 14" - $125.00; 17" - $225.00; 19" - $300.00; 22" - $375.00.
Parsons-Jackson: Baby: 13-14" - $285.00. **Toddler:** 14-15" - $385.00. **Black:** 13-14" - $485.00.

Girl and boy celluloid with molded-on and painted clothes. These molds are also found in stone bisque and can be nodders. Both are marked "Japan." 6" - $75.00 up. *Courtesy Patty Martin.*

4½" all celluloid body and limbed baby with unusual metal head. Painted hair and features. Has eagle mark and made by Petitcolin of France. 4½" - $125.00. *Courtesy Kathy Tvrdik.*

3" all celluloid "Charlie Chaplin" with cane through hand, jointed at shoulders only. Pull string in back raises hat off head. 3" - $100.00. *Courtesy Kathy Tvrdik.*

18" unknown character, "W.C. Fields" type, that may have been made in Germany. Winter clothes, tuft of mohair wig, painted features. Celluloid and plush with felt scarf. 18" - $265.00 up. *Courtesy Carol Turpen.*

CENTURY DOLL CO.

Right: 15½" tall doll marked "Century Doll Co. Kestner Germany 279/3." Shoulder head with molded hair, glass eyes, open mouth, cloth body and composition limbs. **Left:** 23" marked "S&H 1488." Lovely closed mouth character by Simon & Halbig. 15½" - $1,000.00; 23" - $5,600.00.
Courtesy Frasher Doll Auctions.

CHAD VALLEY

Chad Valley dolls usually will have a felt face and all velvet body that is jointed at the neck, shoulders and hips. They can have painted or glass eyes and will have a mohair wig. First prices are for those in mint condition. Second prices are for dolls that are dirty, worn or soiled and/or do not have original clothes.

Marks: "Hygienic Toys/Made in England by/Chad Valley Co. Ltd."

"The Chad Valley Hygienic Textile/Toys/Made in England."

Child With Painted Eyes: 9" - $150.00, $45.00; 12" - $350.00, $100.00; 16" - $550.00, $200.00; 18" - $675.00, $300.00.

Child With Glass Eyes: 14" - $600.00, $150.00; 16" - $750.00, $225.00; 18" - $850.00, $350.00.

Child Representing Royal Family: Four in set: Princess Elizabeth, Princess Margaret Rose, Prince Edward, Princess Alexandria. All four have glass eyes. (See photos in Series 5, pgs. 39-40.) **Prince Edward as Duke of**

Kent: 15" - $1,700.00, $600.00; 18" - $1,900.00, $700.00. **As Duke of Windsor:** 15" - $1,700.00, $600.00; 18" - $1,900.00, $700.00. **Others:** 15" - $1,200.00 up, $500.00; 18" - $1,400.00 up, $500.00.

Long John Silver, Captain Bly, Policeman, Train Conductor, Pirates, Fisherman, etc.: (See photo in Series 6, pg. 56.) 18" - $950.00 up, $325.00; 20" - $975.00 up.
Ghandi/India: 13" - $675.00 up, $200.00.
Animals: Cat: 12" plush - $135.00 up; 6" cloth - $95.00 up. **Dog:** 12" plush - $185.00 up. **Bonzo:** Cloth dog with painted eyes almost closed and smile. 4" - $225.00; 13" - $500.00. Eyes open: 5½" - $250.00; 14" - $550.00.

"Rahma-Jah" made by Chad Valley, imported by Louis Wolf in 1923-1924. Some sold to Progressive Mercantile Co. for Calvin Coolidge election campaign. Banner: "Prosperity Pal - Out of Adversity Springeth Prosperity." Coincided with King Tutankhamen Tomb display in United States. Represents Ethiopian slave. All velvet, stitched fingers and pressed face. Felt and beads used for features. 26" - **$850.00.** *Courtesy Margie-June Blessinger.*

CHASE, MARTHA

Martha Jenks Chase of Pawtucket, Rhode Island began making dolls in 1893, and they are still being made by members of the family. They all have oil painted features and are made of stockinette and cloth. They will be marked "Chase Stockinette" on left leg or under the left arm. There is a paper label (often gone) on the backs with a drawn head, shown here. The words "Stockinette Doll" may also appear on brim of hat.

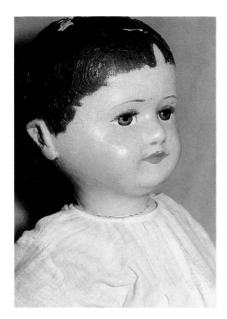

31" Chase stockinette, oil-painted child. Ca. 1920. 31" - $2,500.00 up. *Courtesy Frasher Doll Auctions.*

The older Chase dolls are jointed at the shoulders, hips, knees and elbows; the newer dolls are jointed at the shoulders and hips with straight arms and legs. Prices are for very clean dolls with only minor wear.

OLDER DOLLS:

Babies: 15" - $685.00; 18" - $825.00; 23" - $950.00. **Hospital used:** 23" - $500.00; 28" - $785.00.

Child: Molded bobbed hair. 12-13" - $1,250.00; 15" - $1,500.00; 23" - $2,400.00.

Lady: 15" - $2,600.00; 18" - $2,900.00; 22" - $3,000.00. **Life size, hospital used:** $2,200.00.

Man: 16" - $2,900.00; 23" - $3,000.00. **Life size:** $2,400.00.

Black: 23" - $7,800.00; 27" - $9,000.00.

Alice In Wonderland: 16" - $1,800.00.

Frog Footman: 16" - $2,000.00 up.
Mad Hatter: 16" - $2,100.00 up.
Dutchess: 16" - $1,900.00 up.
Tweedledum: 16" - $2,200.00 up.
George Washington: 25" - $2,700.00 up.

NEWER DOLLS:

Babies: 14" - $185.00; 16" - $250.00; 20" - $400.00.

Child, boy or girl: 14" - $250.00; 16" - $350.00.

Chase Type: Child. 14" - $1,300.00; 19" - $1,700.00.

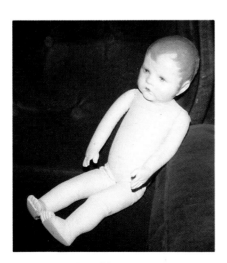

Pouty Martha Chase boy with oil-painted head and shoulders. Stitched fingers with free standing thumbs. Unusual "accordion" jointed hips. *Courtesy Irma Branduer.*

Almost all china heads were made in Germany between 1840 and the 1900's. Most have black hair, but blondes became popular by the 1880's and by 1900, one out of every three was blonde. China dolls can be on a cloth or kid body with leather or china limbs. Generally, these heads are unmarked, but a few will have a number and/or "Germany" on the back shoulder plate. Prices are for clean dolls with no cracks, chips, or repairs on a nice body and nicely dressed. Also see Huret/Rohmer under "Fashions" and Alt, Beck & Gottschalck.

Alice In Wonderland: Snood, head band: 18" - $650.00; 22" - $950.00. **With flange neck:** Motschman style body. 9" - $1,800.00; 12" - $2,600.00.

Alice In Wonderland

Adelina Patti: 1860's. Center part, roll curl from forehead to back on each side of head and "spit" curls at temples and above exposed ears. 14" - $300.00; 18" - $450.00; 22" - $525.00.

Adelina Patti

Bald Head/Biedermeir: Ca. 1840. Has bald head, some with top of head glazed black, takes wigs. **Excellent quality:** 12" - $675.00; 14" - $925.00; 20" - $1,400.00. **Medium quality:** 10-12" - $300.00; 14" - $450.00; 20" - $765.00. **Glass eyes:** 16" - $1,600.00; 21" - $2,500.00.

Bald Head/Biedermeir

Bangs: Full across forehead, 1870's. **Black hair:** 14" - $250.00; 18" - $425.00; 22" - $525.00. **Blondes:** 15" - $275.00; 22" - $550.00; 27" - $665.00.

Brown eyes: (See photo in Series 8, pg. 51.) Painted eyes, can be any hairstyle and date, but usually has short, "flat top" Civil War hairdo. 15" - $650.00; 18" - $1,100.00; 22" - $1,350.00.

Brown hair: Early hairdo with flat top or long sausage curls around head. Center part and smooth around face. 16" - $3,200.00; 20" - $4,000.00. **With bun:** 16-17" - $3,650.00 up.

Bun: China with bun, braided or rolled and pulled to back of head. Usually has pink luster tint. 1830's & 1840's. Cloth body, nicely dressed and undamaged. Prices depend upon rarity of hairdo and can run from $700.00 - 3,800.00.

Bun Hairdo

Early Hairdo: Also see "Wood Body." 7" - $1,300.00 up; 14" - $1,700.00 up; 17" - $2,400.00 up; 23" - $3,200.00 up.

Common Hairdo: Called "Lowbrow" or "Butterfly." Made from 1890, with most being made after 1900. Black or blonde hair. Wavy hairdo, center part with hair that comes down low on forehead. Also see "Pet Names." 8" - $80.00; 12" - $145.00; 14" - $165.00; 17" - $200.00; 21" - $265.00; 25" - $345.00. **Jewel Necklace:** 14" - $225.00; 20" - $325.00. **Molded-on Poke Bonnet:** 8" - $165.00; 13" - $225.00.

Common Hairdo

Child: Swivel neck, china shoulder plate and may have lower torso and limbs made of china. 12" - $2,600.00.

Child or Boy: Short black or blonde hairdo, curly with partly exposed ears. 14" - $285.00; 20" - $450.00.

Currier & Ives: 14" - $475.00; 19" - $685.00.

Currier & Ives

Covered Wagon: 1840's. Hair parted in middle with flat hairstyle and has sausage-shaped curls around head. 8" - $185.00; 12" - $285.00; 15" - $525.00; 18" - $625.00; 22" - $800.00; 35-36" - $975.00 up.

Covered Wagon

Countess Dagmar: Pierced ears. 16" - $650.00; 19" - $965.00.

Countess Dagmar

Curly Top: 1845-1860's. Ringlet curls that are loose and over entire head. 16" - $550.00; 20" - $725.00.

Curly Top

Dolly Madison: 1870-1880's. Loose curly hairdo with modeled ribbon and bow in center of the top of the head. Few curls on forehead. 14" - $325.00; 18" - $525.00; 21" - $600.00; 24" - $685.00; 28" - $765.00.

Dolly Madison

Early Marked China (Nurenburg, Rudustat, etc.): 16" - $2,800.00; 18" - $3,600.00 up.

Fancy Hairstyles: Flared sides, rolls of hair over top of head, long hair cascading down back, ringlet curls around face and full exposed ears. 14" - $500.00 up; 17" - $600.00 up; 21" - $750.00 up.

Flat Top, Civil War: Also called **"High Brow."** 1850-1870's. Black hair parted in middle, smooth on top with short curls around head. 12" - $165.00; 14" - $265.00; 17" - $350.00; 20" - $400.00; 24" - $450.00; 26" - $500.00; 35" - $950.00. **Swivel neck:** 14" - $800.00 up; 21" - $1,500.00 up.

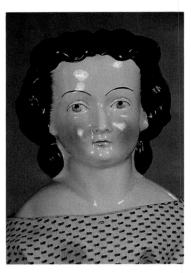

29" lady china doll with fancy hairdo and brush strokes around forehead, modeled comb at nape of neck, molded eyelinds. Cloth body with leather arms. **29" - $1,800.00.** *Courtesy Frasher Doll Auctions.*

Glass eyes: Can have a variety of hairdos. 1840-1870's. 14" - $1,200.00; 18" - $1,650.00; 23" - $2,000.00.

Hat or Bonnet: Molded on. 13" - $3,500.00; 16" - $4,200.00.

Highbrow: Like Covered Wagon, but has very high forehead, smooth on top with a center part, curls over ears and around base of neck, and has a very round face. 1860-1870's. 14" - $465.00; 20" - $700.00; 24" - $825.00.

Highland Mary: 16" - $500.00; 19" - $685.00; 23" - $785.00.

Flat Top, Civil War

French: China shoulder head, painted eyes, cut pate with cork, wigged, fashion kid body. (See Fashions, Huret type.) 16" - $3,500.00; 19" - $4,400.00.

Highland Mary

Japanese: 1910 - 1920's. Can be marked or unmarked. Black or blonde and can have a "common" hairdo, or have much more adult face and hairdo. 12" - $125.00; 14" - $185.00.

Jenny Lind: Hair pulled back in bun. 16" - $1,000.00.

Kling: Number and bell. 13" - $350.00; 16" - $450.00; 20" - $750.00.

Man or Boy: Excellent quality, early date, side part hairdo. Brown hair. 14" - $1,900.00; 17" - $2,400.00; 21" - $3,100.00 up.

Man hairdo with side part

Jenny Lind

Man or Boy: Glass eyes. 15" - $2,300.00; 17" - $3000.00; 21" - $3,800.00.

Man: Coiled, graduated size curl hairdo. 16" - $1,500.00; 20" - $2,000.00.

Man hairdo with curls

Mary Todd Lincoln: Has snood. 15" - $600.00- 19" - $800.00.

8" china boy with pink luster skin tones to head and shoulders, brush strokes around face, cloth body with china limbs. May be original clothes. 8" - **$650.00 up.** *Courtesy Ellen Dodge.*

Mary Todd Lincoln

Open Mouth: Common hairdo. 14" - $450.00; 18" - $800.00.

Pet Names: 1905, same as "Common" hairdo with molded shirtwaist with the name on front: **Agnes, Bertha, Daisy, Dorothy, Edith, Esther, Ethel, Florence, Helen, Mabel, Marion, Pauline.** 8-9" - $135.00; 14" - $200.00; 16" - $245.00; 19" - $285.00; 22" - $325.00; 25" - $465.00.

Pierced Ears: Can have a variety of hairstyles (ordinary hairstyle, flat top, curly, covered wagon, etc.) 14" - $465.00 up; 18" - $700.00 up.

Pierced Ears: Rare hairstyles. 14" - $1,200.00 up; 18" - $1,800.00 up.

Snood, Combs: Applied hair decoration. 14" - $650.00; 17" - $800.00.

Grapes in hairdo: 18" - $1,850.00 up.

Sophia Smith: Straight sausage curls ending in a ridge around head rather than curved to head. 14" - $2,300.00; 18" - $3,200.00.

Sophia Smith

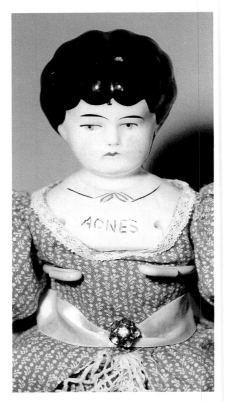

12" pet name china "Agnes" with modeled-on shirtwaist and lowbrow hairdo. 1900's on. 12" - $145.00.
Courtesy Kathy Tvrdik.

Spill Curls: With or without headband. Many individual curls across forehead and over shoulders. Forehead curls continued to above ears. 14" - $475.00; 18" - $825.00; 27" - $950.00.

Spill Curls

Swivel Flange Neck: 8-9" - $1,800.00 up; 12" - $2,600.00 up.

Whistle: Has whistle holes in head. 14" - $575.00; 18" - $750.00.

Young Queen Victoria: 16" - $1,600.00; 21" - $2,000.00; 25" - $3,200.00.

Wood Body: Articulated with slim hips, china lower arms. 1840-1850's. Hair pulled back in bun or coiled braids. 6" - $1,200.00; 8" - $1,400.00; 12" - $1,500.00 up; 15" - $1,800.00 up; 18" - $3,600.00 up. **Same with Covered Wagon hairdo:** 8" - $775.00; 12" - $985.00; 16" - $1,400.00.

Alabama Indestructible Doll: All cloth with head molded and painted in oils, painted hair, shoes and stockings. Marked on torso or leg "Pat. Nov. 9, 1912. Ella Smith Doll Co." or "Mrs. S.S. Smith/Manufacturer and dealer/ The Alabama Indestructible Doll/ Roanoke, Ala./Patented Sept. 26, 1905 (or 1907)." Prices are for clean dolls with only minor scuffs or soil. Allow more for mint dolls. **Child:** 16" - $2,000.00; 22" - $2,700.00. **Baby:** 14" - $1,850.00; 21" - $2,450.00. **Black Child:** 18" - $6,500.00; 23" - $7,000.00. **Black Baby:** 20" - $6,600.00.

Art Fabric Mills: See Printed Cloth Dolls.

Babyland: Made by E.I. Horsman from 1904 to 1920. Marked on torso or bottom of foot. Oil painted features, photographic features or printed features. With or without wig. All cloth, jointed at shoulders and hips. First price for extra clean, original dolls; second price for dolls in fair condition that show wear and have slight soil. Allow more for mint dolls. **Oil Painted Features:** 13" - $765.00, $325.00; 15" - $875.00, $400.00; 18" - $1,000.00, $500.00; 22" - $1,450.00, $650.00; 28" - $1,950.00, $900.00. **Black Oil Painted Features:** 14" - $975.00, $450.00; 17" - $1,200.00, $550.00; 26" - $2,000.00, $950.00; 29" - $2,400.00; $1,000.00.

Back: 27" black Martha Chase stockinette doll with oil-painted features and kinky wig. Right: 13½" "Alabama" cloth baby with mask face and painted curly hair. Lower limbs are oil painted; painted-on boots. May be original. Left: 14: laughing bisque head marked "Heubach Koppelsdorf 418." 27" - $9,000.00 up; 13½" - $4,500.00; 14" - $900.00. *Courtesy Frasher Doll Auctions.*

Photographic Face: 14-15" - $465.00, $200.00; 19" - $875.00, $400.00. **Black Photographic Face:** 14-15" - $650.00, $275.00; 19" - $1,000.00; $450.00. **Printed:** 16" - $285.00, $95.00; 20" - $575.00, $125.00; 23" - $785.00, $250.00. **Black printed:** 16" - $400.00, $150.00; 20" - $700.00, $200.00; 23" - $925.00, $325.00.

Beecher: 1893–1910. Stuffed stockinette, painted eyes, needle sculptured features. Originated by Julia Jones Beecher of Elmira, N.Y., wife of Congregational Church pastor. Dolls made by sewing circle of church and all proceeds used for missionary work, so dolls can also be referred to as **"Missionary Babies."** Have looped wool hair. Extra clean: 16" - $3,000.00; 23" - $6,600.00. Slight soil and wear:

All original, painted hair Bing boy with painted cloth head and stuffed cloth body. Unusual and attractive features. Ca. 1920's. 14" - $685.00. *Courtesy Ricki Small.*

16" - $1,500.00; 23" - $2,500.00. **Black:** Extra clean: 15" - $3,300.00; 21" - $7,000.00 up. Soil and wear: 16" - $1,500.00; 23" - $3,500.00.

Bing Art: By Bing Werke; Germany, 1921–1932. All cloth, all felt, or composition head with cloth body. Molded face mask, oil painted feature, wig or painted hair, can have pin joints on cloth body, seams down front of legs, mitt hands with free formed thumbs. **Painted hair, cloth or felt:** Unmarked or "Bing" on sole of foot. 10" - $625.00; 15" - $785.00. **Wig:** 10" - $300.00; 15" - $500.00. **Composition head:** 7-8" - $100.00; 12" - $145.00; 15" - $185.00.

Left: 21½" black "Babyland" cloth with painted features and stitched joints. Right: 28" "Columbian" doll by Emma Adams. Oil-painted features, unusual size. 21½" - $1,400.00; 28" - $7,000.00. *Courtesy Frasher Doll Auctions.*

Bruckner: Made for Horsman, 1901 on. Marked on shoulder "Pat'd July 8, 1901." Cloth with mask face stiffened and printed. Clean: 13-15" - $265.00 up. Soil and wear: 13-15" - $100.00. **Black:** Clean: 13-15" - $375.00 up. Soil and wear: 13-15" - $165.00.

Columbian Doll: Ca. 1890's. Sizes 15-29". Stamped "Columbian Doll/Manufactured by/Emma E. Adams/Oswego Centre/N.Y." After 1905–1906, the mark was "The Columbian Doll/ Manufactured by/ Marietta Adams Ruttan/Oswego, NY." All cloth with painted features and flesh-painted hands and feet. Stitched fingers and toes. Extra clean: 15" - $4,600.00; 23" - $7,000.00. Fair, with slight scuffs or soil: 15" - $3,800.00; 23" - $6,800.00. **Columbian type:** 16" - $1,500.00 up; 22" - $2,900.00 up.

Comic Characters: Extra clean: 16" - $625.00. Soil and wear: 16" - $200.00.

Deans Rag Book Dolls: Golliwogs (black): (See photo in Series 6, pg. 65.) 12" - $245.00; 14" - $325.00. **Child:** 10" - $300.00; 16" - $625.00; 18" - $825.00. **Printed face:** 10" - $100.00; 16" - $165.00; 18" - $225.00.

Drayton, Grace: Dolly Dingle. 1923 by Averill Mfg. Co. Cloth with printed features, marked on torso. 11" - $425.00; 15" - $600.00. **Chocolate Drop:** 1923 by Averill. Brown cloth with printed features and three tufts of

Beautiful 19" "Columbian Doll" by Emma Adams. Oil-painted features, stitched fingers and toes. May be original. Shown with 17" Izannah Walker all cloth doll with oil-painted pressed head. Vertical curls in front of detailed ears. Painted-on high top shoes. Original. 19" - $6,500.00; 17" - $14,000.00. Fair condition - $8,000.00. *Courtesy Frasher Doll Auctions.*

yarn hair. 11" - $400.00; 16" - $625.00. **Hug Me Tight:** By Colonial Toy Mfg. Co. in 1916. One-piece printed cloth with boy standing behind girl: 12" - $275.00; 16" - $450.00. **Peek-A-Boo:** Made by Horsman in 1913–1915. All cloth with printed features. 10" - $175.00; 12" - $265.00. **Embroidered Features (Primitive):** Home made, all cloth, yarn, lamb's wool or painted hair. **White:** 16" - $265.00 up; 20" - $485.00 up. **Black:** 15" - $365.00 up; 19" - $825.00 up. **Fangel, Maud Toursey:** 1938 on. All cloth, printed features. Can have printed cloth body or plain without "undies." Mitt-style hands with freeformed thumbs. **Child:** Must be near mint condition. 9" - $425.00; 12" - $650.00; 15" - $775.00; 18" - $865.00. **Baby:** 14" - $600.00; 17" - $875.00.

Farnell's Alpha Toys: Marked with label on foot "Farnell's Alpha Toys/Made in England." (See photo in Series 6, pg. 58.) **Child:** 14" - $465.00; 16" - $575.00. **Baby:** 14" - $500.00; 17" - $550.00. **King George VI:** 16" - $1,200.00. **Palace Guard/Beefeater:** 16" - $750.00.

Georgene Novelties: See Averill, Georgene section.

Kamkins: Made by Louise Kampes. 1928–1934. Marked on head or foot, also has paper heart-shaped label on chest. All cloth with molded face mask and painted features, wigs, boy or girl. Extra clean: 20" - $1,800.00; 25" - $2,600.00. Slight wear/soil: 20" - $850.00; 25" - $1,000.00.

Kewpie Cuddles: See Kewpie section.

Krueger, Richard: New York, 1917 on. All cloth, oil-painted mask face, yarn or mohair wig, oil cloth body. Clean and original. Marked with tag "Krueger, N.Y. Reg. U.S. Pat. Off. Made in USA. **Child:** 13" - $100.00; 16" - $145.00; 20" - $185.00. **Character:** Such as Pinocchio. 15-16" - $300.00 up.

Kruse, Käthe: See that section. **Lenci:** See Lenci section. **Liberty of London Royal Dolls:** Marked with cloth or paper tag. Flesh-colored cloth faces with stitched and painted features. All cloth bodies. 1939 Royal Portrait dolls are 10" and include Queen Mary, King George VI, Queen Victoria and Princess Elizabeth. (See photo in Series 7, pg. 53) Extra clean: 10" - $200.00. Slight wear/soil: 10" - $95.00. **Other Historical or Coronation figures:** Extra clean: 10" - $200.00. Slight wear/soil: 10" - $95.00.

Madame Hendron: See Averill section.

Mammy Style Black Dolls: All cloth with painted or sewn features. **Ca. 1910–1920's:** 14" - $225.00; 17" - $365.00. **Ca. 1930's:** 15" - $165.00 up.

Missionary Babies: See Beecher in this section.

Mollye: See Mollye in Modern section.

Mother's Congress Doll: Patented Nov. 1900. All cloth, printed features and hair. Mitt-style hands without formed thumbs. Designed and made by Madge Mead. Marked with cloth label "Mother's Congress Doll/Children's Favorite/Philadelphia, Pa./Pat. Nov. 6, 1900." Extra clean: 17" - $900.00 up; 25" - $1,100.00 up. Slight soil: 17" - $400.00; 22" - $500.00. **Oil painted faces and hair:** Unidentified, cloth body and limbs. 22" - $700.00; 27" - $950.00.

Old Cottage Doll: England, 1948 on. Cloth and English composition. Later versions have hard plastic heads. Hand painted features. 8" - $145.00 up; 12" - $185.00 up.

Philadelphia Baby: Also called **"Sheppard Doll."** Made by J.B. Sheppard in late 1890's to early 1900's. Stockinette covered body with painted cloth arms and legs. Modeled cloth head is painted. Extra clean: 22" - $4,000.00. Slight soil and wear: 22" - $2,200.00. Very worn: 22" - $1,200.00.

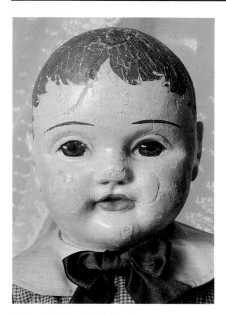

21" "Philadelphia Boy" by J.B. Sheppard & Co., ca. 1900. All cloth with treated, oil-painted shoulder-type head with ears, lower arms, and legs. 21" - **$4,000.00.** *Courtesy Turn of Century Antiques.*

Petzold, Dora: Germany, 1920's. Pressed paper head, painted old features, wig, stockinette body filled with sawdust, short torso. Soft stuffed arms, free formed thumbs, stitched fingers. Legs have formed calves. (See photo in Series 7, pg. 139.) 18" - $650.00; 22" - $825.00; 25" - $975.00.

Poir, Eugenie: 1920's, made in New York and France. All cloth body with felt face and limbs or can be all felt. Painted features, majority of eyes are painted to the side, mohair wig. Stitched four fingers together with free-standing thumb. Unmarked except for paper label. Extra clean: 17" - $725.00; 23" - $950.00. Slight soil and wear: 17" - $400.00; 23" - $500.00. **Photographic faces:** (Also see Babyland in this section) Extra clean: 16" - $750.00. Slight soil and wear: 16" - $350.00.

Printed Cloth Dolls: 1903 on. All cloth with features and/or underwear/clothes printed. These dolls are cut and sew types. **Rastus, Cream of Wheat:** 18" - $145.00. **Aunt Jemima:** Set of four dolls. $100.00 each; **Printed-on underwear (Dolly Dear, Merry Marie, etc.)** Cut: 7" - $95.00; 16" - $200.00; 19" - $265.00. Uncut: 7" - $125.00; 16" - $225.00; 19" - $300.00. **Boys and girls with printed outer clothes:** Cut: 9-10" - $125.00; 14" - $225.00; 19" - $300.00. Uncut: 9" - $145.00; 14" - $250.00; 19" - $325.00. **Black boy or girl:** 17" - $450.00; 21" - $625.00. **Brownies:** By Palmer Cox, 1892. 8" - $100.00; 14" - $200.00. **George and Martha Washington:** 1901 by Art Fabric - Cut: $450.00, set of four; Uncut: $850.00, set of four. **St. Nicholas/Santa Claus:** Marked "Pat. Dec. 28, 1886. Made by E.S. Peck, NY." One arm stuffed with toys and other arm holds American flag. Cut: 15" - $350.00. Uncut: 15" - $695.00

Raynal: Made in France by Edouard Raynal. 1920's. Cloth body and limbs (sometimes has celluloid hands), felt mask face with painted features. Eyes painted to side. Marked on soles of shoes or will have necklace imprinted "Raynal." Original clothes generally are felt, but can have combination felt/organdy or just organdy. Extra clean: 16" - $600.00; 21" - $875.00. Slight soil and wear: 16" - $250.00; 21" - $400.00.

Rollinson Dolls: Molded cloth with painted features, head and limbs. Molded hair or wig. Designed by Gertrude F. Rollinson, made by Utley Doll Co. Marked with a stamp of doll in a diamond and printed around border "Rollinson Doll Holyoke, Ma." Molded hair, extra clean: 21" - $1,300.00 up. Molded hair, slight soil and wear: 21" - $550.00. **Wigged by Rollinson:** Extra clean: 20" - $2,000.00 up, 26" -

$2,800.00. Wigged, slight soil and wear: 20" - $950.00; 26" - $1,200.00. **Toddler with wig:** 18" - $1,900.00.

Smith, Mrs. S.S.: See Alabama in this section.

Soviet Union: 1920–1930's. (See photo in Series 8, pg. 57.) All cloth with stockinette hands and head. Molded face mask with painted features. Dressed in regional costumes. Marked "Made in Soviet Union." Extra clean: 10" - $100.00, 14" - $185.00. Slight soil and wear: 10" - $40.00; 14" - $85.00. **Tea Cozies:** (See photo Series 8, pg. 57.) Doll from waist up and has full skirt that is hollow to be placed over pot to keep contents warm. 17" - $175.00; 22" - $265.00; 28" - $350.00.

Steiff: See Steiff section.

Walker, Izannah: Made in 1870's and 1880's. Modeled head with oil painted features, applied ears, cloth body and limbs, painted-on boots. Brushstroke or corkscrew curls around face over ears. Hands and feet are stitched. Marked "Patented Nov. 4, 1873." Very good condition: 17" - $21,000.00; 20" - $24,000.00. Fair condition: 17" - $9,600.00; 20" - $12,000.00. Poor condition: 17" - $2,500.00; 20" - $3,400.00. **Two vertical curls in front of ears:** Very good condition: 20" - $23,000.00 up; 26" - $28,000.00 up. Fair condition: 20" - $14,000.00; 26" - $18,000.00.

Wellings, Norah: See Wellings section.

Wellington: 1883 on. Label on back: "Pat. Jan. 8, 1883." All stockinette, oil painted features, lower limbs. Features are needle-sculpted. Hair is painted. Has distinctive buttocks; rounded. Excellent condition: 22-23" - $14,500.00 up. Fair to poor condition: 22-23" - $4,200.00 up.

COMPOSITION DOLLS – GERMANY

Most German manufacturers made composition-headed dolls as well as dolls of bisque and other materials. Composition dolls were made in Germany before World War I, but the majority were made in the 1920's and 1930's. They can be all composition or have a composition head with cloth body and limbs. Prices are for excellent quality and condition.

Child Doll: All composition with wig, sleep/flirty eyes, open or closed mouth and jointed composition body. Unmarked or just have numbers. 14" - $185.00; 18" - $285.00; 21" - $400.00; 24" - $525.00.

Child: Same as above, but with name of company (or initials): 14" - $300.00; 18" - $475.00; 25" - $600.00; 28" - $750.00.

Baby: All composition, open mouth. 14" - $185.00; 16" - $225.00; 19" - $325.00. **Toddler:** 18" - $400.00; 22" - $585.00.

Baby: Composition head and limbs with cloth body, open mouth, sleep eyes. 16" - $165.00; 22" - $285.00; 27" - $450.00.

Painted Eyes: Child: 14" - $145.00; 18" - $225.00. **Baby:** 14" - $165.00; 18" - $300.00.

Shoulder Head: Composition shoulder head, glass eyes, wig, open or closed mouth, cloth or kidaleen body with composition arms (full arms or lower arms only with cloth upper arms), and lower legs. May have bare feet or modeled boots. Prices for dolls in extra clean condition and nicely dressed. Unmarked. (Also see Wax Section.) **Excellent Quality:** Extremely fine modeling. 16" - $450.00; 21" -

$565.00; 24" - $700.00; 29" - $875.00.
Average Quality: May resemble a china head doll. 12" - $165.00; 14" - $200.00; 17" - $250.00; 22" - $325.00; 25" - $365.00; 29" - $500.00.

Painted Hair: 10" - $185.00; 15" - $265.00; 19" - $425.00.

Swivel Neck: On composition shoulder plate. 14" - $425.00; 17" - $550.00; 23" - $700.00.

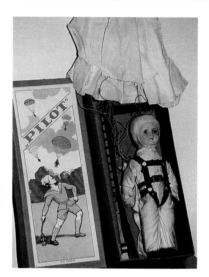

Mint 19" "Pilot" in box with composition head and cloth body and limbs. Made in Germany, ca. 1930's. $450.00 in box.
Courtesy Carol Turpen.

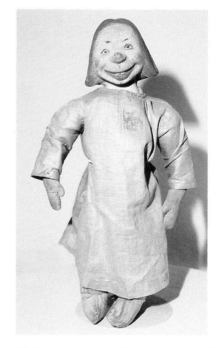

All composition baby with sleep eyes and open mouth. Head is marked "40 Germany." Made in 1920's or earlier. 19" - $345.00. *Courtesy Carol Turpen.*

12" German composition head on all cloth body. Has painted features. May represent "Max" from the "Max & Moritz" comics. Original top with pants missing. Had paper label on chest. Fair condition - $150.00. *Courtesy Carol Turpen.*

Many French and German dolls bear the mark "DEP" as part of their mold marks, but the dolls referred to here are marked *only with the* DEP *and a size number.* They are on French bodies with some bearing a Jumeau sticker. The early 1880's DEP dolls have fine quality bisque and artist workmanship, and the later dolls of the 1890's and into the 1900's generally have fine bisque, but the color will be higher, and they will have painted lashes below the eyes with most having hair eyelashes over the eyes. The early dolls will have outlined lips but the later ones will not. Prices are for clean, undamaged and nicely dressed dolls.

Marks:

Open Mouth: 12" - $675.00; 14" - $750.00; 18" - $1,100.00; 21" - $1,400.00; 25" - $1,800.00; 30" - $2,500.00. **Open mouth, very Jumeau looking, red check marks:** 18" - $1,500.00; 23" - $1,900.00; 30" - $2,800.00.

Closed Mouth: 14" - $2,400.00; 18" - $2,900.00; 25" - $3,800.00; 28" - $3,300.00.

Walking, Kissing, Open Mouth: 16" - $1,300.00; 19" - $1,700.00; 22" - $1,900.00; 26" - $2,500.00.

26" marked "DEP 11." Closed mouth with thin white space between lips, on French jointed body. 12½" Jules Steiner doll with fired-in brown bisque and open mouth. Marked "A-5 Paris" on head; "Bebe La Petit Parisien" on body. 26" - $3,800.00; 12½" - $2,600.00.
Courtesy Frasher Doll Auctions.

16½" doll marked "DEP 6." Has sleep eyes, open mouth with four teeth, and original wig. On French jointed body. 16½" - $800.00. *Courtesy Frasher Doll Auctions.*

DOLL HOUSE DOLLS

Doll House Man or Woman: With molded hair/wig and painted eyes. 6-7" - $185.00-250.00.

Children: All bisque: 3½" - $95.00, 5½" - $145.00. **Bisque/cloth:** 3½" - $100.00; 5½" - $165.00.

Man or Woman with Glass Eyes/Wigs: 6-7" - $350.00-465.00.

Man or Woman with Molded Hair, Glass Eyes: 6-7" - $400.00.

Man with Mustache: 5½-6½" - $185.00-245.00.

Grandparents, Old People, or Molded-on Hats: 6-7" - $300.00.

Military Men: Have mustaches. Original. (See photo in Series 8, pg. 128.) 6-7" - $650.00 up.

Black Man or Woman: Molded hair, all original. 6-7" - $465.00.

Swivel Neck: Wig or molded hair. 6-7" - $800.00 up.

China Glaze with early hairdos: 4-5" - $300.00-385.00; **Low brow/common hairdo:** 1900's and after. $95.00-165.00.

Beautiful 18" example of Kestner "Bru-type" with swivel head on bisque shoulder plate, sleep eyes, open/closed mouth, and molded teeth. Kid body with bisque lower arms. Factory costume which may be original. Holds 4" all bisque doll house military officer with molded helmet and 2½" all bisque doll house child with swivel neck that is all original. 4" - **$650.00; 2½" - $400.00; 18" - $5,400.00.** *Courtesy Frasher Doll Auctions.*

DOOR OF HOPE DOLLS

Door of Hope dolls were created at the Door of Hope Mission in China from 1901 into 1910. They have cloth bodies; head and limbs are carved of wood by carvers who came from Ning-Po Province. They usually are between 8-13" tall, and if marked, will have label "Made in China." (Many of the dolls listed here are shown in Series 8, pgs. 63-65.)

Manchu: Mandarin man or woman - $775.00 up.

Mother and Baby: $725.00.

Adult: 9" - $625.00; 11" - $750.00.

Child: 6" - $485.00; 8" - $565.00.

Bride: $825.00.

Carved flowers in hair: $800.00 up.

Priest: $900.00.

Widow: $900.00.

Mourner: $850.00.

Groom: $785.00

Bridesmaid: $825.00.

Grandfather: $785.00.

Amah (Governess): $765.00.

21" in red hat, marked "S & H 1129." Almond-shaped sleep eyes, open mouth. 16" in blue is marked "1199 DEP." Sleep eyes, open mouth. 8" and 9" Door of Hope carved wooden dolls with cloth stuffed bodies, original. 21" - $3,500.00; 16" - $2,800.00; 8-9" - $625.00 each. *Courtesy Frasher Doll Auctions.*

DRESSEL, CUNO & OTTO

Cuno & Otto Dressel operated in Sonneberg, Thuringia, Germany and were sons of the founder. Although the firm was in business in 1700, they are not listed as dollmakers until 1873. They produced dolls with bisque heads or composition over wax heads, which can be on cloth, kid, or jointed composition bodies. Some of their heads were made for them by other German firms, such as Simon & Halbig, Heubach, etc. They registered the trademark for "Jutta" in 1906 and by 1911 were also making celluloid dolls. Prices are for undamaged, clean and nicely dressed dolls.

Marks:

C.O.D.

C.O.D 49 D.E.P.

Made in Germany

Babies: 1910 on. Marked "C.O.D." but without the word "Jutta." Allow more for toddler body. 12" - $325.00. 15" - $425.00; 18" - $525.00; 24" - $765.00.

Child: 1893 on. Jointed composition body, with open mouth. 15" - $325.00; 18" - $425.00; 23" - $550.00;

25" - $600.00; 30" - $875.00; 35" - $1,400.00.

Child: On kid, jointed body, open mouth. 14" - $250.00; 18" - $375.00; 24" - $475.00.

Jutta: 1910–1922. **Baby:** Open mouth and five-piece bent limb body. 12" - $500.00; 14" - $565.00; 17" - $650.00; 20" - $950.00; 24" - $1,450.00; 27" - $1,800.00.

Toddler Body: 8" - $585.00; 14" - $865.00; 17" - $1,000.00; 20" - $1,300.00; 24" - $1,600.00; 26" - $1,900.00.

Child: Marked with **"Jutta"** or with S&H **#1914, #1348, #1349,** etc.: 13" - $585.00; 15" - $650.00; 19" - $700.00; 23" - $850.00; 25" - $950.00; 30" - $1,400.00; 38-39" - $2,900.00-3,200.00.

Lady Doll: 1920's with adult face, closed mouth and on five-piece composition body with thin limbs and high heel feet. Original clothes. Marked **#1469**. 14" - $3,800.00; 16" - $4,200.00. **Redressed or Nude:** 14" - $2,100.00; 16" - $2,500.00.

12" doll in 22" x 15" original box with wardrobe. Doll by Cuno & Otto Dressel. Has red "Holz-Masse" stamp on back of jointed body's torso. 12" in case - $1,500.00; 12" doll only - $265.00.
Courtesy Frasher Doll Auctions.

Character Dolls: 1909 and after. Closed mouth, painted eyes, molded hair or wig. May be glazed inside head. 12" - $1,700.00; 14" - $2,200.00; 17" - $2,600.00; 22" - $2,900.00.

Character Dolls: Same as above, but with glass eyes. 14" - $2,400.00; 17" - $2,900.00; 22" - $3,200.00; 24" - $3,500.00.

Character Dolls: Marked with letter and number, such as **B/4** or **A/2.** Jointed child or toddler body, painted eyes, closed mouth. No damage and ready to display. 12" - $1,200.00; 15-16" - $2,200.00; 18" - $2,600.00.

Composition: Shoulder head of 1870's, glass or painted eyes, molded hair or wig and on cloth body with composition limbs with molded-on boots. Will be marked with Holz-Masse:

With wig: Glass eyes. 14" - $275.00; 12" - $350.00; 24" - $550.00. **Molded hair:** 17" - $400.00; 24" - $565.00.

Portrait Dolls: 1896. Such as **Uncle Sam, Farmer, Admiral Dewey, Admiral Byrd, Old Rip, Witch, etc.** Portrait bisque head, glass eyes, composition body. Some will be marked with a **"D"** or **"S."** Heads made for Dressel by Simon & Halbig. Prices for clean, undamaged and origi-

nally dressed. **Military dolls:** (See photo in Series 6, pg. 72) 9" - $900.00; 13" - $1,800.00; 16" - $2,500.00. **Old Rip or Witch:** 9" - $750.00; 13" - $1,600.00; 16" - $1,900.00. **Uncle Sam:** 9" - $825.00; 13" - $1,675.00; 16" - $2,250.00.

Fur covered: Glued on body/limbs. 8-9" - $185.00; 12" - $265.00.

Center: 14" C.O.D. character marked "B/4." Intaglio eyes and jointed body. Rear: 18" Armand Marseille mold 351 "Kiddiejoy." Left: 15" sleep eye Schoenhut; right: 16" Franz Schmidt mold #1295 flirty eye toddler with open mouth. Front: Nurenberg kitchen. 14" C.O.D. - $1,100.00; 18" - $575.00; 15" - $1,350.00; 16" - $600.00; Kitchen - $450.00.

E.D.

E. Denamur of Paris made dolls from 1885 to 1898. The E.D. marked dolls seem to be accepted as being made by Denamur, but they could have been made by E. Dumont, Paris. Composition and wood jointed bodies. Prices are for excellent quality bisque, no damage and nicely dressed.

Marks:

E 6 D

E 5 D
DEPOSE

Closed or Open/Closed Mouth: 15" - $2,700.00; 17" - $3,200.00; 22" - $3,700.00; 25" - $3,900.00.
Open Mouth: 16" - $1,700.00; 18" - $1,900.00; 22" - $2,400.00; 25" - $2,950.00.
Black: Open mouth. 18" - $2,400.00; 24" - $3,000.00.

21" marked "E 9 D" with closed mouth, of excellent bisque, on jointed French body with straight wrists. 21" - **$3,600.00.** *Courtesy Frasher Doll Auctions.*

EDEN BÉBÉ

Fleischmann & Bloedel of Fürth, Bavaria; Sonneberg, Thuringia; and Paris, France was founded in 1873 and making dolls in Paris by 1890. The company became a part of S.F.B.J. in 1899. Dolls have composition jointed bodies and can have open or closed mouths. Prices are for dolls with excellent color and quality bisque, no damage and nicely dressed.

Marks:

EDEN BÉBÉ PARIS

Closed or Open/Closed Mouth: Pale bisque. 15" - $2,500.00; 18" - $2,800.00; 22" - $3,100.00; 26" - $3,900.00.
Closed Mouth: High color bisque. 15" - $1,700.00; 18" - $2,200.00; 22" - $2,400.00; 26" - $2,700.00.
Open Mouth: 15" - $1,300.00; 18" - $2,100.00; 22" - $2,500.00; 26" - $3,000.00.

Walking Kissing Doll: Jointed body with walker mechanism, head turns and one arm throws a kiss. Heads by Simon & Halbig using mold **#1039** (and others). Bodies assembled by Fleischmann & Bloedel. Price for perfect, working doll. 21" - $1,250.00 up.

20" marked "Eden Bébé 1." Closed mouth and large paperweight eyes. Original wig and on French jointed body. 20" - $3,000.00; Poor bisque - $2,200.00. *Courtesy Frasher Doll Auctions.*

ELLIS, JOEL

Joel Ellis made dolls in Springfield, Vermont, in 1873 and 1874 under the name Co-operative Manufacturing Co. All wood jointed body has tenon and mortise joints, arms are jointed in same manner. The hands and feet are made of pewter. Has molded hair and painted features.

Springfield Wooden Doll: It must be noted that dolls similar to the Joel Ellis ones were made in Springfield, Vt. also by Joint Doll Co. and D.M. Smith & Co. They are very much like the Joel Ellis except when standing the knee joint will be flush with the method of jointing not showing. The hips are cut out with the leg tops cut to fit the opening, and the detail of the hands is not as well done.

Doll in fair condition: Does not need to be dressed. 12" - $500.00. Excellent condition: 12" - $900.00 up; 15" - $1,100.00 up; 18" - $1,800.00 up.

Large 15" Joel Ellis wooden doll with pewter hands and feet. Fully jointed with extra joints at elbows and knees. Molded hair. 15" - $700.00. *Courtesy Ellen Dodge.*

These "adult" style dolls were made by a number of French firms from about 1860 into 1930's. Many will be marked only with a number or have a stamp on the body, although some of the stamps/labels may be the store from where they were sold and not the maker. The most available fashion doll seems to be marked F.G. dolls. Prices are for dolls in perfect condition with no cracks, chips, or repairs and in beautiful old or newer clothes made of appropriate age materials.

Articulated Wood: Marked or unmarked. Or blown kid bodies and limbs. Some have bisque lower arms. 16" - $6,500.00 up; 20" - $8,400.00 up.

Articulated: Marked or unmarked. With bisque lower legs and arms with excellent modeling detail. 15" - $8,500.00 up; 21" - $9,500.00 up.

Marked "Bru": (Also see Smiling Mona Lisa in this section.) 1860's. Round face, swivel neck, glass eyes:

Left: 15¼" "smiling" fashion doll on all wood articulated body. Jointed waist with rounded wooden torso. Right: 17" on gusset jointed all kid body. Both have swivel necks on shoulder plates. 15¼" - $6,200.00; 17" - $5,500.00. *Courtesy Frasher Doll Auctions.*

14" extremely pretty French Fashion with excellent bisque, wood articulated arms, and kid body. Original wig, old clothes. 14" - $3,900.00. *Courtesy Turn of Century Antiques.*

(See photo in Series 6, pg. 79.) 14" - $3,300.00; 17" - $5,000.00; 20" - $5,700.00 up. **Wood body:** 14" - $4,800.00.

Marked "Huret": Bisque or china glazed shoulder head, kid body with bisque lower arms. **Painted eyes:** 16" - $5,600.00; 19" - $6,800.00. **Glass eyes:** 16" - $6,200.00. **Wood body:** 16" - $8,700.00 up; 19" - $10,000.00 up. **Gutta Percha body:** 16" - $9,400.00 up; 19" - $11,000.00 up.

Huret Type: China shoulder head, painted eyes, cut pate with cork, wigged, kid fashion body, curved china lower arms. 16" - $3,600.00; 21" - $4,600.00. **Painted Black Hair:** Kid body. 16" - $1,600.00. **Flat Glass eyes:** Wire controlled to sleep. 26-27" - $12,400.00.

Huret Child: 16" - $26,000.00; 20" - $32,000.00.

Marked "Rohmer": (See photo in Series 7, pg. 65 and Series 8, pg.

71.) Bisque or china glazed shoulder head (can be jointed). Kid body with bisque lower arms (or china). **Glass eyes:** 16" - $7,500.00; 19" - $13,500.00; **Painted eyes:** 16" - $6,500.00; 19" - $12,000.00. **Wood body:** 16" - $8,000.00; 19" - $14,000.00.

Unmarked Rohmer or Huret Type: Painted eyes. 16" - $3,500.00; 20" - $4,600.00; 26" - $6,200.00. **Wire controlled sleep eyes:** 27" - $12,000.00.

Marked "Jumeau": (See photo in Series 7, pg. 79.) Will have number on head and stamped body. **Portrait-style head:** 15" - $3,900.00; 18" - $6,000.00; 21" - $6,900.00; 24" - $7,500.00. 29-30" - $10,000.00 **Wood body:** 15" - $6,500.00; 18" - $9,500.00 up; 24" - $14,000.00 up; 27" - $17,500.00.

Marked "Jumeau": Swivel head. 13-14" - $2,600.00; 17" - $3,000.00; 21" - $3,500.00. **Wood body:** Bisque limbs. 17" - $4,800.00; 21" - $5,600.00. **Very large eyes:** 11-12" - $2,100.00; 15-16" - $2,600.00.

Marked "F.G.": 1860 on. All kid body, one-piece shoulder and head, glass eyes. 11" - $975.00; 13" - $1,200.00; 16" - $1,700.00. **Painted eyes:** 11" - $800.00; 13" - $1,000.00; 16" - $1,500.00.

Marked "F.G.": 1860 on. All kid body (or bisque lower arms), swivel head on bisque shoulder plate. Glass eyes. 10-12" - $1,650.00; 14-15" - $2,500.00; 17-18" - $2,900.00; 21-22" - $3,300.00; 25-26" - $4,200.00. **Black:** 13" - $2,400.00; 17" - $3,600.00.

Marked "F.G.": Early face, Gesland cloth-covered body with bisque lower arms and legs. 15" - $5,000.00; 18" - $6,200.00; 23" - $6,600.00; 26" - $7,000.00.

Marked "F.G.": Gesland cloth-covered body with composition or papier maché lower arms and legs. 15" - $3,500.00; 18" - $4,200.00; 23" - $4,600.00; 26" - $5,200.00.

15" very large-eyed Jumeau Fashion, marked "2" on head. Blue Jumeau stamp on all kid body. Swivel head on bisque shoulder plate. 15" - $3,200.00.
Courtesy Frasher Doll Auctions.

Smiling "Mona Lisa": After 1866. Now being referred to as made by Bru. Kid body with leather lower arms, stitched fingers or bisque lower arms. Swivel head on bisque shoulder plate. Marked with letter (example: E, B, D, etc.) 12-13" - $2,800.00; 15" - $3,900.00; 18" - $5,500.00; 22" - $6,000.00; 26" - $7,200.00; 29" - $13,000.00. (Allow more for wood body or arms.)

Unmarked with Numbers Only: With one-piece head and shoulder. Extremely fine quality bisque, undamaged. **Glass eyes:** 12" - $1,500.00; 14" - $1,700.00; 22" - $2,400.00; 18" - $2,800.00. **Painted eyes:** 14" - $900.00; 17" - $1,500.00; 22" - $1,700.00.

Unmarked with Numbers Only: Swivel neck with bisque shoulder plate. Extremely fine quality bisque and undamaged. 12" - $2,000.00; 14" - $2,600.00;

16" - $3,000.00; 18" - $3,600.00. **Black:** 14" - $3,000.00 up.

Unmarked: Swivel neck, glass eyes, fully jointed wood body. 14" - $3,900.00 up; 17" - $4,500.00 up.

Unmarked: Medium to fair quality. **One-piece head and shoulder:** 11" - $650.00; 15" - $850.00-1,000.00. **Swivel Head:** On bisque shoulder plate. 15" - $1,000.00; 19" - $1,700.00 up.

Marked E.B. (E. Barrois): 1854–1877. (See photo in Series 7, pg. 67.) **Glass eyes:** 16" - $3,400.00; 20" - $4,900.00. **Painted eyes:** 17" - $3,200.00; 21" - $3,900.00. (Allow more for bisque or wood arms.)

Marked Simone: Glass eyes: 20" - $5,500.00; 24" - $6,500.00.

Factory Original Fashion Clothes: Dress: $600.00 up. **Wig:** $250.00 up. **Boots:** $250.00 up. **Cape:** $300.00 up.

17" Fashion marked "L Depose D" on shoulder plate. Swivel neck, kid body and wooden arms, jointed at shoulders, elbows and wrists. Excellent quality. **17" - $7,300.00.** *Courtesy Frasher Doll Auctions.*

17½" swivel head on bisque shoulder plate. Kid body with mortise and tenon joints at shoulders, delicately detailed lower arms. 10" Belton-type with closed mouth on French jointed body with straight wrists. Also shown is original parasol in original box and leather trunk with accessories. **17½" - $5,600.00; 10" - $1,600.00; Parasol/box - $900.00 up; Trunk - $2,000.00.** *Courtesy Frasher Doll Auctions.*

F. Gaultier (earlier spelled Gauthier) is the accepted maker of the F.G. marked dolls. These dolls are often found on the cloth-covered or all composition bodies that are marked "Gesland." The Gesland firm was operated by two brothers. One of them had the initial "F" (1887–1900).

Marks:

(1887–1900)

F. 8 G.
(1879–1887 Block Letter Mark)

Child with Closed Mouth: Scroll mark. Excellent quality bisque, no damage and nicely dressed. 7-8" - $800.00; 12" - $1,450.00; 14" - $2,800.00; 17" - $3,200.00; 20" - $3,600.00; 23" - $3,900.00; 25" - $4,700.00; 30" - $5,200.00.
Child with Closed Mouth: Same as above, but with high face color, no damage and nicely dressed. 14" - $1,700.00; 16" - $1,900.00; 19" - $2,100.00; 22" - $2,500.00; 25" - $3,100.00.
Child with Open Mouth: Scroll mark. Excellent quality bisque, no damage and nicely dressed. 10-12" - $650.00; 15" - $1,750.00; 17" - $2,000.00; 20" - $2,600.00; 23" - $3,000.00; 27" - $3,400.00.
Child with Open Mouth: Scroll mark. With high face color, very dark lips, no damage and nicely dressed. 15" - $800.00; 17" - $1,000.00; 20" - $1,300.00; 23" - $1,800.00; 27" - $2,300.00.
Marked "F.G. Fashion": See Fashion section.

22" marked with block letters "F 9 G." Has large paperweight eyes, closed mouth, and jointed body. 22" - $5,200.00. *Courtesy Frasher Doll Auctions.*

Child on Marked Gesland Body: (See photo is Series 6, pg. 80.) Bisque head on stockinette over wire frame body with composition limbs. **Closed mouth:** 16" - $4,800.00; 19" - $5,300.00; 25" - $6,200.00. **Open mouth:** 17" - $2,800.00; 21" - $3,200.00; 26" - $4,200.00.
Block Letter (so called) F.G. Child: 1879–1887. Closed mouth, chunky composition body, excellent quality and condition. 12-13" - $3,900.00; 16-17" - $4,650.00; 19-21" - $5,000.00; 23-24" - $5,400.00; 26-27" - $5,900.00.
Block Letter (so called) F.G. Child: Closed mouth, bisque swivel head on bisque shoulder plate with gusseted kid body and bisque lower arms. 17" - $4,900.00; 21" - $5,200.00; 26" - $6,000.00.

A variety of French doll makers produced unmarked dolls from the 1880's into the 1920's. These dolls may only have a head size number or be marked "Paris" or "France." Many of the accepted French dolls that have a number are now being attributed to German makers and it will be questionable for some time.

Unmarked French Bébé: Closed or open/closed mouth, paperweight eyes, excellent quality bisque and artist painting on a French body. Prices are for clean, undamaged and nicely dressed dolls.

Early Desirable, Very French-style Face: Marks such as "J.D.," "J.M. Paris," numbers only. 15" - $16,000.00; 19" - $23,000.00 up; 23" - $27,000.00 up; 26" - $30,000.00 up.

Jumeau Style Face: May be marked "R.R." 14" - $3,000.00; 17" - $3,400.00; 23" - $4,800.00; 27" - $5,600.00.

Excellent Quality: Unusual face. 14" - $4,400.00; 16" - $4,800.00; 21" - $6,000.00; 27" - $8,000.00.

Medium Quality: May have poor painting and/or blotches to skin tones: 16" - $1,600.00; 21" - $2,100.00; 26" - $2,600.00.

Open Mouth: 1890's and later. Will be on French body. Excellent quality: 15" - $1,800.00; 18" - $2,300.00; 22" - $2,500.00; 25" - $3,200.00.

Open Mouth: 1920's with high face color and may have five-piece papier maché body. 16" - $750.00; 20" - $900.00; 24" - $1,100.00.

16" marked "136." Closed mouth with space between lips. Cut pate with original mohair wig. Many "136" marked dolls are Belton types. French jointed body. Factory original dress. 16" - $2,900.00. *Courtesy Frasher Doll Auctions.*

Left: 15½" French doll only marked "5." Very Jumeau-style face. Bisque swivel head on bisque shoulder plate. Early 1870's. French kid body with bisque lower arms. Right: 13" Belton type with three holes on top of head and marked "5." Closed mouth and fully jointed body. 15½" - $3,000.00; 13" - $2,650.00. *Courtesy Frasher Doll Auctions.*

27" marked only "17." Very much like a Bebe Mothereau. Large paperweight eyes, closed mouth and on French jointed body with straight wrists. 27" - $7,500.00. *Courtesy Frasher Doll Auctions.*

Right: 28" unknown maker doll marked "137" on head. Set glass eyes, open/closed mouth with space between lips. On fully jointed body. Left: 15½" doll marked "S & H 949" with open mouth and on fully jointed body. 28" - $3,500.00; 15½" - $1,000.00. *Courtesy Frasher Doll Auctions.*

Freundlich Novelty Company operated in New York from 1923. Most of their dolls have a cardboard tag and will be unmarked or may have name on the head, but no maker's name. **Baby Sandy:** (See photo in Series 6, pg. 85) 1939–1942. All composition with molded hair, sleep or painted eyes. Marked "Baby Sandy" on head. **Excellent condition:** No cracks, craze or chips. Original or appropriate clothes. 8" - $165.00; 12" - $225.00; 16" - $325.00; 19" - $500.00. **With light crazing:** Clean; may be redressed: 8" - $85.00; 12" - $100.00; 16" - $125.00; 19" - $200.00. **General Douglas MacArthur:** (See photo in Series 6, pg. 85) Ca. 1942. Portrait doll of all composition, painted features and molded hat. Jointed shoulders and hips. **Excellent condition:** Original. 16" - $285.00; 18" - $325.00. **Light craze:** Clothes dirty. 16" - $100.00; 18" - $125.00. **Military Dolls:** (See photo in Series 5, pg. 65; Series 6, pg. 85) Ca. 1942 and on. All composition with painted features, molded-on hats and can be a woman or man (W.A.V.E, W.A.A.C., sailor, Marine, etc.) **Excellent condition:** Original and no crazing. 16" - $200.00. **Light craze:** Clothes in fair condition: 16" - $95.00. **Ventriloquist Doll:** (See photo in Series 7, pg. 73.) **Dummy Dan:** Looks like Charlie McCarthy. 21" - $300.00 up.

FROZEN CHARLOTTE

Frozen Charlotte and Charlie figures can be china, partly china (such as hair and boots), stone bisque or fine porcelain bisque. They can have molded hair, have painted bald heads or take wigs. The majority have no joints, with hands extended and legs separate (some are together). They generally come without clothes and they can have painted-on boots, shoes and socks or be barefooted.

It must be noted that in 1976 a large amount of the 15½-16" "Charlie" figures were reproduced in Germany and their quality is excellent. It is almost impossible to tell that these are reproductions.

Prices are for doll figures without any damage. More must be allowed for any with unusual hairdos, an early face or molded eyelids or molded-on clothes.

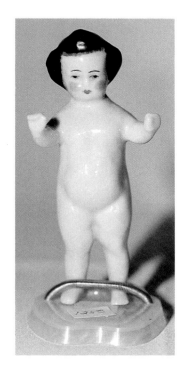

5" unjointed "Frozen Charlotte" with legs spread and china glaze finish. Side puffed hairdo. 5" - $150.00.

All China: Glazed with black or blonde hair, excellent quality of painting and unjointed. 2" - $55.00; 5" - $110.00; 7" - $150.00; 9" - $235.00; 10" - $250.00. **Bald head with wig:** 6" - $165.00; 8" - $195.00; 10" - $275.00. **Charlie:** Molded black hair, flesh tones to neck and head. 14" - $425.00; 17" - $575.00. **Blonde:** 14-15" - $500.00. **Untinted Bisque (Parian):** Molded hair, unjointed. 4" - $150.00; 7" - $185.00. **Untinted Bisque:** 1860's. Molded hair, jointed at shoulders. 4" - $160.00; 7" - $250.00. **Stone Bisque:** Unjointed, molded hair, medium to excellent quality of painting. 4" - $55.00; 8" - $75.00. **Black Charlotte or Charlie:** Unjointed, no damage. 3" - $200.00; 5" - $365.00; 7" - $400.00. **Jointed at shoulders:** 4" - $225.00; 7" - $425.00.

Molded Head Band or Bow: Excellent quality: 5" - $250.00; 8" - $385.00. **Medium quality:** 5" - $125.00; 8" - $175.00. **Molded-on Clothes or Bonnet:** Unjointed, no damage and medium to excellent quality. 6" - $450.00; 8" - $550.00. **Dressed:** In original clothes. Unjointed Charlotte or Charlie. No damage and in overall excellent condition. 5" - $135.00; 7" - $185.00. **Jointed at Shoulder:** Original clothes and no damage. 6" - $175.00; 8" - $285.00. **Molded-on, Painted Boots:** Unjointed, no damage. 5" - $185.00; 7" - $265.00. **Jointed at shoulders:** 5" - $225.00; 7" - $350.00.

Fulper Pottery Co. of Flemington, N.J. made dolls from 1918-1921. They made children and babies and used composition and kid bodies.

Marks:

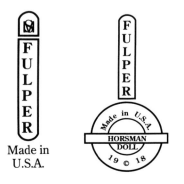

Made in U.S.A.

Child: Fair to medium quality bisque head painting. No damage, nicely dressed. **Composition body, open mouth:** 14" - $365.00; 16" - $500.00; 20" - $625.00. **Kid body, open mouth:** 15" - $365.00; 17" - $425.00; 21" - $550.00.

Child: Poor quality (white chalky look, may have crooked mouth and be poorly painted.) **Composition body:** 16" - $265.00; 21" - $375.00. **Kid body:** 16" - $185.00; 21" - $350.00.

Baby: Bent limb body. Fair to medium quality bisque, open mouth, no damage and dressed well. Good artist work on features. 14-15" - $525.00; 18" - $625.00; 25" - $900.00.

Toddler: Same as baby but has toddler jointed or straight leg body. 18" - $725.00; 26" - $1,000.00.

Baby: Poor quality bisque and painting. 16" - $200.00; 25" - $500.00.

Toddler: Poor quality bisque and painting. 18" - $375.00; 26" - $750.00.

FULPER

21" marked "Fulper/Made in USA."
Five-piece bent limb baby body, open
mouth. Grey mohair bear, ca. 1920.
21" - $750.00; Bear - $600.00 up.
Courtesy Frasher Doll Auctions.

GANS & SEYFARTH

Dolls with the "G.S." or "G & S"
were made by Gans & Seyfarth of
Germany who made dolls from 1909
into the 1930's. Some dolls will be
marked with the full name.

Child: Open mouth, composition
body. Good quality bisque, no damage
and nicely dressed. 15" - $275.00; 18" -
$350.00; 20" - $450.00; 25" - $775.00.

Baby: Bent limb baby body, in
perfect condition and nicely dressed.
15" - $350.00; 18" - $525.00; 22" -
$650.00; 25" - $725.00. (Add more for
toddler body.)

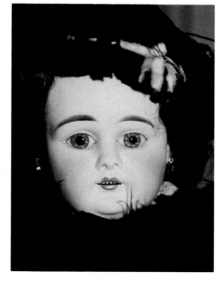

21½" marked "G & S Germany." Made by
Gans and Seyfarth. Open mouth with six
teeth. Unusual threaded eyes. On fully
jointed body. 21½" - $485.00. *Courtesy
Frasher Doll Auctions.*

Some of these unmarked dolls will have a mold number and/or a head size number and some may have the mark "Germany."

Closed Mouth Child: Excellent bisque. 1880-1890's. Composition jointed body, no damage and nicely dressed. 12" - $1,200.00; 16" - $1,800.00; 21" - $2,700.00; 25" - $3,200.00.

Closed Mouth Child: On kid body (or cloth). May have slightly turned head, bisque lower arms. 12" - $625.00; 15" - $850.00; 20" - $1,200.00; 24" - $1,400.00; 26" - $1,600.00.

Open Mouth Child: Late 1880's to 1900. Excellent pale bisque, jointed composition body. Glass eyes, no damage and nicely dressed. 12" - $385.00; 15" - $475.00; 20" - $625.00; 23" - $725.00; 26" - $875.00; 30" - $1,300.00.

16" early closed mouth German bisque with no marks. Solid dome head, one-piece head and shoulder plate. Kid body with bisque lower arms. 16" - $1,300.00. *Courtesy Frasher Doll Auctions.*

Open Mouth Child: Same as above, but on kid body with excellent quality bisque and bisque lower arms. 12" - $185.00; 15" - $325.00; 20" - $485.00; 23" - $575.00; 26" - $675.00.

Open Mouth Child: 1888-1920's. With very "dolly" type face. Overall excellent condition, composition jointed body. 12" - $325.00; 15" - $485.00; 18" - $565.00; 22" - $675.00; 25" - $765.00; 28" - $985.00; 32" - $1,100.00.

Open Mouth Child: Same as above, but with kid body and bisque lower arms. 12" - $200.00; 15" - $325.00; 18" - $425.00; 22" - $525.00.

Belton Type: May have **mold #132, 136, 137, etc.** Composition jointed body. Glass eyes. 12" - $1,400.00; 15" - $1,800.00; 20" - $2,600.00; 24" - $2,900.00.

Glass Eyes, Closed Mouth: May have **mold #132, 136, 137, etc.**

Foreground: Beautiful 15" unmarked German child with bisque shoulder head, glass eyes, closed mouth, kid body with bisque lower arms. Background: 19" marked "Tete Jumeau" with open/closed mouth and white space between lips. On marked Jumeau body. 15" - $1,200.00; 19" - $4,600.00; Set/Fan - $225.00. *Courtesy Frasher Doll Auctions.*

Composition jointed body. Excellent overall quality. 16" - $2,200.00; 19" - $2,600.00; 23" - $3,000.00.

All Bisque: See "All Bisque – German" section.

Molded Hair: See that section.

Infants: Bisque head, molded/painted hair, cloth body with composition or celluloid hands, glass eyes. No damage. 10-12" - $365.00; 15" - $550.00; 18" - $700.00.

Babies: Solid dome or wigged, glass eyes, five-piece baby body, open mouth, nicely dressed and no damage. (Allow more for closed or open/closed mouth or very unusual face and toddler doll.) 8-9" - $285.00; 14" - $500.00; 17" - $600.00; 22" - $765.00. **Toddler:** 14" - $650.00; 17" - $750.00.

Babies: Same as above, but with painted eyes. 8-9" - $185.00; 14" - $365.00; 17" - $450.00; 22" - $600.00.

Both dolls are 21" tall and unmarked. Both have excellent bisque, glass eyes and open mouths. Both are on fully jointed German bodies. Each - $700.00.
Courtesy Frasher Doll Auctions.

8½" marked "Germany DEP." Original felt jacket. Owner made pants and hat and handcrafted wooden sailboat. Glass eyes, open mouth, fully jointed body. 8½" - $300.00. *Courtesy June Murkins.*

Bonnet or Hat: See "Bonnet Doll" section.

Tiny Unmarked Doll: Head is bisque of good quality on five-piece papier maché or composition body, glass eyes, open mouth. No damage. 6" - $245.00; 9" - $325.00; 12" - $425.00.

Tiny Doll: Same as above, but on full jointed composition body. 6" - $350.00; 9" - $450.00; 12" - $525.00.

Tiny Doll: Closed mouth, jointed body. 6" - $350.00; 9" - $500.00; 12" - $650.00. **Five-piece body:** 6" - $250.00; 9" - $350.00; 12" - $425.00.

Character Child: Unidentified, closed mouth, very character face, may have wig or solid dome, glass eyes, closed or open/closed mouth. Excellent quality bisque, no damage and nicely dressed. 16" - $4,800.00; 20" - $5,600.00.

Character: Closed mouth, glass eyes. **Mold #128, 134,** and others of this quality. 16" - $7,500.00 up; 22" - $10,000.00 up. **Painted eyes:** 16" - $6,000.00 up; 22" - $8,500.00 up. **Mold #111:** (See photo in Series 8, pg. 82.) **Glass eyes:** 22" - $24,000.00 up. **Painted eyes:** 21" - $15,000.00 up. **Mold #163:** 16" - $950.00.

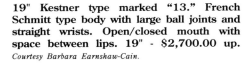

19" Kestner type marked "13." French Schmitt type body with large ball joints and straight wrists. Open/closed mouth with space between lips. 19" - **$2,700.00 up.**
Courtesy Barbara Earnshaw-Cain.

40" German child marked "47 S/19." Maker unknown. Set eyes with hair lashes, open mouth, fully jointed body. 40" - $2,600.00.
Courtesy Frasher Doll Auctions.

GLADDIE

Gladdie was designed by Helen Jensen in 1929. The German-made doll was distributed by George Borgfeldt. The cloth body has composition limbs, and the head has glass eyes. (See photos in Series 5, pg. 69; Series 6, pg. 92; Series 7, pg. 79.)

Ceramic Style Head or Biscaloid: 16-17" - $975.00; 19-20" - $1,200.00 up. **Bisque Head: Mold #1410.** 16-17" - $4,200.00; 19-20" - $5,300.00; 25-26" - $6,700.00.

In box is 19" all original "Gladdie" with ceramic style head, open/closed smile mouth, and five-piece composition body. Shown with 18" all felt Santa made by R. John Wright. In center row is an all original 16½" cloth doll in peach by Krueger. The 15½" boy doll has a felt face and is made by Dean's Rag Book Dolls. The 16" Schoenhut girl is all original. On front row is an all composition 9" "Swiss" by Madame Alexander and an original 9" Bing type pair. "Gladdie" - $1,200.00; Santa - $1,700.00; Krueger - $300.00; Dean's - $500.00; Schoenhut - $1,400.00; Madame Alexander - $175.00; Bing $375.00.

GOEBEL

The Goebel factory has been operating since 1879 and is located in Oeslau, Germany. The interwoven W.G. mark has been used since 1879. William Goebel inherited the factory from his father, Franz Detlev Goebel. About 1900, the factory only made dolls, dolls heads and porcelain figures. They worked in both bisque and china glazed items.

Marks:

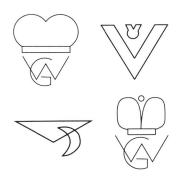

Child: 1895 and later. Open mouth, composition body, sleep or set eyes with head in perfect condition, dressed and ready to display. 5-6" - $175.00; 14" - $465.00; 18"- $600.00; 22" - $725.00.

Child: Open/closed mouth, wig, molded teeth, shoulder plate, kid body, bisque hands. 17" - $825.00; 20" - $950.00.

Child: Deeply molded hair; may have molded bows. Intaglio eyes, open/closed mouth, smile, jointed body. (See photo in Series 7, pg. 80.) Rare. 12" - $1,800.00; 15" - $3,200.00; 17" - $3,800.00.

Character: After 1910. Molded hair that can be in various styles, with or without molded flowers or ribbons, painted features and on five-piece papier maché body. No damage and nicely dressed. 7" - $365.00; 9" - $465.00; 12" - $575.00.

Character Baby: After 1909. Open mouth, sleep eyes and on five-piece bent limb baby body. No damage and nicely dressed. 13" - $450.00; 16" - $600.00; 19" - $800.00; 24" - $925.00. **Toddler:** 14" - $600.00; 17" - $775.00; 22" - $900.00.

Molded-on Bonnet: Closed mouth, five-piece papier maché body, painted features and may have various molded-on hats or bonnets and painted hair. 7" - $350.00; 9" - $475.00; 12" - $565.00.

21" toddler body in five pieces, bisque head with Goebel mark of crown woven over "G-B5-11." Sleep eyes and open mouth. Steiff monkey is mohair with felt ears and glass eyes, ca. 1930. 21" - **$900.00.** *Courtesy Frasher Doll Auction.s*

Bisque head with glass or set eyes to the side, closed smiling mouth, impish or watermelon-style mouth, original composition or papier maché body. Molded hair or wigged. 1911 and after. Not damaged in any way and nicely dressed.
All Bisque: See All Bisque section.
Armand Marseille: #200: (See photo in Series 8, pg. 21.) 8" - $1,600.00; 12" - $2,600.00. **#210:** 8" - $2,200.00; 12" - $3,200.00. **#223:** 7" - $900.00; 10" - $1,200.00. **#240, 241:** 10-11" - $2,450.00; 13" - $2,900.00. **#248:** 9" - $1,100.00. **#252:** 8" - $1,000.00. **#253, 353:** 7" - $800.00; 9" - $1,000.00; 12" - $1,400.00. **#254:** 10" - $1,050.00. **#255- #310:** (Just Me) 8-9" - $1,200.00; 11" - $1,600.00; 13-13½" - $1,850.00. **#310** with painted bisque: 8" - $775.00; 12"- $1,000.00. **#320:** 9" - $1,300.00. **Glass eyes:** $1,100.00. **Painted eyes:** 6" - $750.00; 8" - $900.00. **#323:** Fired-in color. 7" - $600.00; 10" - $925.00; 14" - $1,400.00. **On baby body:** 14" - $1,000.00. **Painted bisque:**

5½" all bisque googly toddler with extra joints at knees and elbows. Sleep eyes, painted-on shoes and socks. Expressive hands. Marked "112." 5½" - $2,000.00.
Courtesy Turn of Century Antiques.

9" - $550.00; 14" - $800.00. **#325:** 7" - $700.00; 12" - $975.00.
B.P. (Bahr & Proschild) #686: 12" - $2,500.00; 14" - $2,900.00 Baby: 12" - $1,500.00.
Demalcol: (See photo in Series 7, pg. 82) 10" - $650.00; 14" - $850.00.
Elite: See end of this section.
Hansi: "Gretel." (See photo in Series 8, pg. 87.) Molded hair, shoes and socks. Made of composition/ celluloid-type material "prialytine." 12" - $3,500.00.
Hertel Schwab: See that section.
Heubach Einco: 9-10" - $4,800.00; 15" - $7,500.00; 17" - $8,200.00.
Heubach (marked in square): 9" - $1,000.00; 13" - $1,900.00. **#8556:**

9" Armand Marseille mold #253 googly with sleep eyes, on five-piece toddler body. 9" - **$1,000.00.** *Courtesy Turn of Century Antiques.*

15-16" - $9,000.00 up. **#8676:** 7" - $750.00; 12" - $1,200.00. **#9573:** 7" - $800.00; 9" - $1,200.00; 12" - $2,200.00. **#9578, 11173:** Called "Tiss Me." 8" - $1,500.00; 12" - $1,800.00. **Heubach Koppelsdorf:** (See photo in Series 6, pg. 96) **#260, 261, 263, 264:** 7" - $400.00; 10" - $500.00. **#318:** 9" - $1,300.00; 14" - $2,100.00. **#319:** 7" - $675.00; 11" - $1,300.00. **#417:** 7" - $500.00; 13" - $1,250.00. **Kestner: #111.** Jointed body. (See photo in Series 8, pg. 8.) 10" - $2,900.00; 14" - $3,400.00.

Kestner: #163, 165: (This number now attributed to Hertel & Schwab): 13" - $4,500.00; 15" - $5,200.00. **#172-173** (Attributed to Hertel & Schwab): 11" - $3,000.00; 14" - $4,100.00. **#217, 221:** 6" - $1,300.00; 10" - $3,500.00; 12-13" - $4,600.00; 14" - $5,100.00; 16" - $5,700.00; 17" - $5,850.00.

Kammer & Reinhardt (K star R): 9" on five-piece body: $2,700.00. **#131:** 10" - $5,400.00; 14" - $7,300.00.

Kley & Hahn (K&H): Mold #180. 15" - $2,900.00; 17" - $3,400.00.

Oscar Hitt: 13" - $6,000.00; 16" - $8,000.00.

Our Fairy: See All Bisque section.

P.M. (Otto Reinecke): #950: 6" - $1,100.00; 8" - $1,350.00; 12-13" - $1,500.00; 15-16" - $2,000.00 up.

S.F.B.J.: #245: (See photo in Series 6, pg. 96) **Five-piece body:** 8" - $1,400.00. **Fully jointed body:** 12" - $2,600.00; 15" - $4,800.00 up.

Steiner, Herm: 9" - $950.00; 12" - $1,200.00.

Composition Face: Very round composition face mask or all composition head with wig, glass eyes to side and closed impish watermelon-style mouth. Body is stuffed felt. In original clothes. **Excellent condition:** 8" - $475.00; 12" - $600.00; 14" - $925.00; 16" - $1,200.00; 20" - $1,700.00. **Fair condition:** Cracks or crazing, nicely

8" sweet character googly called "Tiss Me" is marked with Gebruder Heubach mold #11173. Original wig and romper. **8" - $1,500.00 up.** *Courtesy Ellen Dodge.*

redressed. 7" - $165.00; 11" - $300.00; 13" - $450.00; 15" - $525.00; 19" - $750.00.

Painted Eyes: Composition or papier maché body with painted-on shoes and socks. Bisque head with eyes painted to side, closed smile mouth and molded hair. Not damaged and nicely dressed. **A.M. 320, Goebel, R.A., etc.:** 6" - $365.00; 8" - $525.00; 10" - $645.00; 12" - $725.00. **Heubach, Gebruder:** 7-8" - $475.00 up.

Disc Eyes: Bisque socket head or shoulder head with molded hair (can have molded hat/cap), closed mouth and inset celluloid discs in large googly eyes. (See photo in Series 8, pg. 85.) 10" - $1,100.00; 14" - $1,400.00; 17" - $1,700.00; 21" - $2,100.00.

10" cute googly that is marked with "Heubach" in square. Molded painted hair, side glace painted eyes. Body is five-piece and made of papier maché with painted-on shoes and socks. 10" - $1,500.00.
Courtesy Frasher Doll Auctions.

GREINER

Ludwig Greiner of Philadelphia, PA, made dolls from 1858 into the late 1800's. The heads are made of papier maché, and they can be found on various bodies. Some can be all cloth; many are homemade. Many have leather arms or can be found on Lacmann bodies that have stitched joints at the hips and the knees and are very wide at the hip line. The Lacmann bodies will be marked "J. Lacmann's Patent March 24th, 1874" in an oval. The Greiner heads will be marked "Greiner's Patent Doll Heads/ Pat. Mar. 30, '58." Also "Greiner's/ Improved/Patent Heads/Pat. Mar. 30, '58." The later heads are marked "Greiner's Patent Doll Heads/Pat. Mar. 30, '58. Ext. '72."

Greiner Doll: Can have black or blonde molded hair, blue or brown painted eyes and be on a nice homemade cloth body with cloth arms or a commerical cloth body with leather arms. Dressed for the period and clean, with head in near perfect condition with no paint chips and not repainted.
With '58 Label: 18" - $950.00; 24" - $1,250.00; 27" - $1,450.00; 30" - $1,700.00; 35" - $1,950.00; 38" - $2,350.00. **With chips/flakes or repainted:** 17" - $500.00; 23" - $700.00; 26" - $825.00; 29" - $925.00; 34" - $1,000.00; 37" - $1,400.00.
With '72 Label: 19" - $500.00; 22" - $600.00; 27" - $800.00; 32" - $1,200.00. **With chips/flakes or repainted:** 19" - $250.00; 22" - $350.00; 27" - $450.00; 32" - $525.00.

Glass Eyes: 22" - $2,200.00; 27" - $2,700.00. With chips and flakes or repainted: 22" - $975.00; 27" - $1,200.00. **Unmarked:** So called "Pre-Greiner," ca. 1850. Papier maché shoulder head, cloth body can be home-made. Leather, wood or cloth limbs. Painted hair, black eyes with no pupils. Glass eyes, old or original clothes. **Good condition:** 19" - $1,000.00; 27" - $1,400.00; 32" - $1,800.00. **Fair condition:** 19" - $500.00; 27" - $700.00; 32" - $900.00.

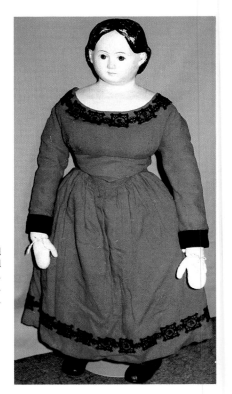

31" Greiner papier maché shoulder head marked "Pat. Mar. 30, '58." Painted features and hair. Cloth body and limbs. Hands covered by mittens look large. May be original dress. **31" - $1,700.00.**
Courtesy Frasher Doll Auctions.

HALF DOLLS (PINCUSHIONS)

Half dolls can be made of any material including bisque, papier maché and composition. Not all half dolls were used as pin cushions. They were also used for powder box tops, brushes, tea cozies, etc. Most date from 1900 into the 1930's. The majority were made in Germany, but many were made in Japan. Generally, they will be marked with "Germany" or "Japan." Some have numbers; others may have the marks of companies such as William Goebel ⚲ or Dressel, Kister & Co. *⌇*).

The most desirable are the large figures, or any size for that matter,

that have both arms molded away from the body or are jointed at the shoulder. (Allow more if marked by maker.)

Arms and hands extended: Prices can be higher depending on detail and rarity of figure. Marked; china or bisque. 3" - $135.00 up; 5" - $215.00 up; 8" - $600.00 up; 12" - $1,000.00 up.

Arms extended: But hands attached to figure. **China or bisque:** 3" - $85.00; 5" - $125.00; 8" - $175.00. **Papier maché or composition:** 5" - $40.00; 7" - $95.00.

Bald head, arms away: 4" - $165.00 up. **Arms attached:** 4" - $85.00 up.

Common Figures: Arms and hands attached. **China:** 3" - $30.00; 5" - $40.00; 8" - $55.00. **Papier maché or composition:** 3" - $20.00; 5" - $30.00; 8" - $40.00.

Jointed Shoulders: China or bisque: 5" - $100.00; 8" - $125.00; 10" - $165.00. Papier maché: 4" - $35.00; 7" - $75.00. Wax over papier maché: 4" - $40.00; 7" - $100.00.

Children or Men: 3" - $50.00; 5" - $85.00; 7" - $100.00. **Jointed shoulders:** 3" - $65.00; 5" - $95.00; 7" - $165.00.

Japan marked: 3" - $20.00; 5" - $35.00; 7" - $55.00.

4" tall half doll with both arms away. Has rose in hand, rare modeled-on hat with ribbon, and brown hair. $700.00 *Courtesy Ellen Dodge.*

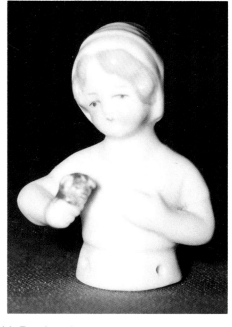

German made half dolls. Left: 2½" doll with Dutch style bonnet. Both arms attached to body; holds flower. Right: 2½" child half doll with molded-on bonnet. One arm away from figure holding flower. Dutch - $40.00; Child - $65.00. *Courtesy Stan Buler.*

Beautiful 5" half doll by Dressel & Kister. Much modeling, applied porcelain flowers in hair and hand. Both arms away from figure. 5" - $450.00.

2¾" stamped in red "Made in Japan" on back and incised "Japan" on rim. Both arms attached to figure. Dress underglaze washed over onto arm. 2¾" - $20.00. *Courtesy Patty Martin.*

Half doll with cushion stamped "Made in Japan" in black. Overall dimension is 4½". $35.00. *Courtesy Patty Martin.*

Heinrich Handwerck began making dolls and doll bodies in 1876 at Gotha, Germany. The majority of their heads were made by Simon & Halbig. In 1897 they patented, in Germany, a ball jointed body #100297 and some of their bodies will be marked with this number.

Mold numbers include: **12x, 19, 23, 69, 79, 89, 99, 100, 109, 118, 119, 124, 125, 139, 152, 189, 199, 1001, 1200, 1290.**

Sample mold marks:

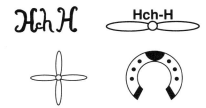

37" large doll marked "Heinrich Handwerck/Simon & Halbig." Sleep eyes, open mouth and on fully jointed body. 37" - $1,900.00. *Courtesy Frasher Doll Auctions.*

Child: No mold number. After 1885. Open mouth, sleep or set eyes, on ball jointed body. Bisque head with no cracks, chips or hairlines, good wig and nicely dressed. 14" - $400.00; 16" - $485.00; 19" - $575.00; 23" - $695.00; 25" - $1,000.00; 32" - $1,400.00; 36" - $1,650.00; 41-42" - $2,750.00.

Child: Same as above but with mold marks. 12" - $525.00; 14" - $575.00; 17" - $625.00; 21" - $735.00; 24" - $825.00; 28" - $1,100.00; 32" - $1,600.00; 35-36" - $2,100.00; 42" - $3,600.00.

Kid Body: Bisque shoulder head, open mouth. All in good condition and nicely dressed. 16" - $350.00; 19" - $475.00; 25" - $600.00; 27" - $875.00.

Mold #79, 89: With closed mouth. 14" - $1,600.00; 17" - $1,950.00; 21" - $2,300.00.

Mold #189: With open mouth. 14" - $465.00; 17" - $825.00; 21" - $975.00.

14" bisque head marked "Ruthie" by Heinrich Handwerck. Silver mohair teddy bear body. Owner has original box. 14" - $650.00. *Courtesy Ellen Dodge.*

Max Handwerck started making dolls in 1900 and his factory was located at Waltershausen, Germany. In 1901, he registered "Bébé Elite" with the heads made by William Goebel. The dolls from this firm are marked with the full name, but a few are marked with "M.H."

Child: Bisque head, open mouth, sleep or set eyes, on fully jointed composition body, no damage and nicely dressed. **Mold #283, 287, 291, etc.:** 16" - $365.00; 20" - $485.00; 24" -

$575.00; 28" - $825.00; 32" - $1,100.00; 40" - $2,200.00.

Bébé Elite: (See photo in Series 7, pg. 88.) Bisque heads with no cracks or chips, sleep or set eyes, open mouth. Can have a flange neck on cloth body with composition limbs or be on a bent leg composition baby body. Upper teeth and smile: 15" - $425.00; 21" - $700.00. **Toddler:** 17" - $650.00; 22" - $850.00; 26" - $1,300.00. **Socket head on fully jointed body:** 17" - $625.00; 21" - $850.00.

Hertel, Schwab & Co. has been recognized by the German authors Jurgen and Marianne Cieslik as the maker of many dolls that were attributed to other companies all these years. There does not seem to be a "common denominator" to the Hertel, Schwab doll lines and any style can be included.

Babies: Bisque head, molded hair or wig, open or open/closed mouth, sleep or painted eyes, bent limb baby body. Good condition with no damage.

Mold #125, 127 ("Patsy"): 12-13" - $925.00; 16" - $1,150.00.

Mold #126 ("Skippy"): 11" - $975.00; 14-15" - $1,200.00.

Mold numbers: 130, 136, 142, 150, 151, 152, 153, 154: 9" - $325.00; 11" - $435.00; 15" - $525.00; 17" - $600.00; 22" - $825.00.

Child: Bisque head, painted or sleep eyes, closed mouth, jointed composition body, no damage and nicely dressed.

#119, 134, 141, 149: 16" - $4,800.00; 18" - $5,900.00.

#154, closed mouth: 16" - $2,300.00; 22" - $2,650.00. **Open mouth:** 18" - $1,200.00; 22" - $1,600.00.

#169, closed mouth: 18" -

$3,200.00; **Toddler:** 22" - $4,200.00; 26" - $5,400.00. **Baby:** Open mouth. 21", $1,200.00; 24" - $1,600.00.

All Bisque: One-piece body and head, glass eyes, closed or open mouth. All in perfect condition.

Prize Baby (mold #208): 6" - $325.00; 8" - $565.00.

Swivel Neck: 6" - $485.00; 8" - $750.00; 10" - $875.00. (See #222 below.)

Googly: Wig or molded hair. Large, side glance sleep or set eyes. Closed mouth, no damage and nicely dressed.

#163: 11" - $3,000.00; 15" - $5,400.00.

#165: 11" - $3,000.00; 15" - $5,600.00;

#172: 14-15" - $6,300.00.

#173: 11" - $3,000.00; 14" - $4,100.00.

#222 (Our Fairy): Painted eyes, molded hair. 9-10" - $1,700.00; 12" - $2,250.00 up. **Wig and glass eyes:** 9-10" - $2,000.00; 12" - $2,500.00 up.

HERTEL, SCHWAB & CO.

24" character baby marked "152/13.
Sleep eyes, open mouth, cheek dimples,
and on five-piece bent leg baby body.
24" - $945.00. *Courtesy Marcia Picwicz.*

HEUBACH, GEBRUDER

The Heubach Brothers (Gebruder) made dolls from 1863 into the 1930's at Lichte, Thuringia, Germany. They started producing character dolls in 1910. Heubach dolls can reflect almost every mood and are often found on rather crude, poor quality bodies, and many are small dolls.

Marks:

Character Dolls: Bisque head, open/closed or closed mouth, painted eyes (allow more for glass eyes), on kid, papier maché or jointed composition bodies. Molded hair or wig. No damage and nicely dressed.

#1017: Baby faced toddler with open mouth. 18" - $1,400.00; 22" - $1,700.00; 28" - $2,150.00.

#2850, 8058: Open/closed mouth, two rows teeth. Molded braided hair, blue ribbon bow. 17" - $9,600.00 up; 21" - $12,000.00 up.

#5636: Laughing child, two lower teeth, intaglio painted eyes. 9" - $900.00; 12" - $1,200.00. **Glass eyes:** 12" - $1,500.00; 16" - $2,300.00.

#5689: Open mouth, smiling. Glass eyes. 16" - $1,800.00; 18" - $2,200.00; 23" - $2,500.00.

#5730 (Santa): 14" - $1,600.00; 17" - $2,500.00; 24" - $2,800.00.

Right: 13" "Dolly Dimples," Heubach mold #7307. Sleep eyes, open/closed mouth with modeled teeth, dimples. On fully jointed body with two pull strings and cryer box in body. Left: 11½" Belton type with closed mouth, jointed body with straight wrists. May be original wig and clothes. 13" - $2,500.00; 11½" - $1,600.00. *Courtesy Frasher Doll Auctions.*

#5777, 7307, 9355 (Dolly Dimples): Ball jointed body. 12-13" - $2,500.00; 16" - $2,800.00; 22" - $3,500.00; 24" - $3,700.00.

#6692: Shoulder head, smiling, intaglio eyes. 15" - $875.00.

#6736, 6894: Laughing, wide open/closed mouth, molded lower teeth. 10" - $850.00; 16" - $1,700.00.

#6894, 6898: Baby, closed mouth, pouty. 5" - $235.00; 6½" - $265.00; 9½" - $400.00; 12-13" - $525.00.

#6896: Pouty, jointed body. 15" - $850.00; 18" - $1,000.00.

#6969, 6970, 7246, 7347, 7407, 8017, 8420: Pouty boy or girl, jointed body, painted eyes. 10" - $950.00; 12" - $1,100.00; 16" - $1,700.00; 20" - $2,200.00. **Toddler:** 21" - $2,600.00; 25" - $3,200.00. **Glass eyes:** 14" - $2,500.00; 17" - $3,100.00; 20" - $3,600.00. **Toddler, glass eyes:** 20" - $3,900.00; 24" - $4,500.00.

#7172, 7550: 14" - $1,500.00.

#7448: Open/closed mouth, eyes half shut. 14" - $2,700.00.

#7602: Painted eyes and hair, long face pouty, closed mouth. 16" - $2,000.00; 20" - $2,700.00 up. **Glass eyes:** 16" - $2,600.00; 20" - $3,200.00.

#7604: Laughing, jointed body, intaglio eyes. 10" - $525.00; 12" - $650.00. **Baby:** 14" - $775.00.

#7616: Open/closed mouth with molded tongue. Socket or shoulder head. Glass eyes. 12" - $1,400.00; 15" - $1,900.00.

11" glass eyed Gebruder Heubach mold number 6970. On fully jointed body. Excellent face modeling details for such a small doll. 11" - $1,700.00. *Courtesy Turn of Century Antiques.*

15" Heubach marked "7602 Germany" with "Heubach" in square. Intaglio eyes, closed mouth, and on jointed body. Shown with 8" googly marked "R46A 11/0." Molded hair, intaglio eyes, and on five-piece toddler body. Made by Recknagel. 15" - $2,000.00; 8" - $525.00.00. *Courtesy Frasher Doll Auctions.*

#7622, 76262: Molded hair, intaglio eyes, closed mouth and light cheek dimples. 14" - $1,900.00; 16" - $2,400.00. **Pouty:** 14" - $965.00; 17" - $1,200.00.

#7623: Molded hair, intaglio eyes, open/closed mouth, molded tongue, on bent limb baby body. 12" - $850.00; 16" - $1,300.00. **Jointed body:** 15" - $1,500.00; 21" - $2,000.00.

#7634: Crying, squinting eyes. 14" - $1,000.00; 16" - $1,400.00.

#7636: 10" - $800.00; 13" - $1,000.00.

#7644: Laughing, socket or shoulder head, intaglio eyes. 14" - $850.00; 17" - $1,150.00.

#7665: Smile. 14" - $1,200.00.

#7666: Squinting eyes, crooked smile. 16" - $3,500.00.

#7661, 7686: Wide open/closed mouth, deeply molded hair. 14" - $2,300.00; 17" - $3,700.00.

#7669, 7679: Open/closed mouth, laughing, glass eyes. Walker. 14" - $1,750.00; 17" - $2,300.00.

7668, 7671: See Black or Brown Doll section.

#7679: Whistler, socket head. 14" - $1,200.00; 16" - $1,500.00.

#7684: Screamer. Molded tongue, painted eyes. 12" - $875.00; 16" - $1,400.00

#7701: Pouty, intaglio eyes. 14" - $1,400.00; 18" - $1,800.00.

#7711: Open mouth, jointed body. 12" - $465.00; 15" - $875.00; 22" - $900.00.

30" character marked "Heubach." Glass sleep eyes, open/closed mouth with space between lips, deep dimples, and on fully jointed body. 30" - $7,800.00. *Courtesy Frasher Doll Auctions.*

#7745, 7746: Wide open/closed mouth, two painted lower teeth, molded hair. Baby or toddler: 16" - $2,100.00.

#7751: Squinting eyes, open/closed mouth modeled as yawn. Molded hair, jointed body. 16" - $3,400.00; 19" - $4,200.00.

#7759: Closed mouth pouty baby. 5" - $235.00; 7" - $265.00; 10" - $400.00; 13" - $525.00.

#7763: Same description as #7768, 7788.

#7764: Wide open/closed mouth, intaglio eyes to side, deeply sculptured hair, large molded bow. 5-piece body or toddler body. 14" - $1,200.00 up; 17" - $1,900.00 up.

#7768, #7788 ("Coquette"): Tilted head, molded hair and can have ribbon modeled into hairdo. 8½" - $565.00; 11" - $865.00; 15" - $1,000.00. **Swivel neck:** 8" - $550.00; 10" - $875.00.

#7849: Closed mouth, intaglio eyes. 14" - $800.00.

#7851: Same description as #7764. Cloth body, composition limbs. 12" - $1,200.00.

#7852, 7862, 119: (See photo in Series 8, pg. 96.) Braids coiled around ear (molded), intaglio eyes. 16" - $2,800.00 up; 18" - $3,300.00 up.

#7911: Grin. 14-15" - $1,300.00.

#7925, 7926 (Adult): Painted eyes: 15" - $3,400.00 up. **Glass eyes:** 17" - $4,200.00.

#7958: Deeply modeled hair and bangs. Dimples, open/closed mouth, intaglio eyes. 16" - $3,800.00.

#7959: Intaglio eyes, molded-on bonnet, deeply molded hair, open/closed mouth. 17" - $3,500.00; 21" - $4,600.00 up.

#7975 (Stuart Baby): Glass eyes, removable porcelain bonnet. 11-12" - $1,500.00.

#7977, #7877 (Stuart Baby): Molded baby bonnet, painted eyes. 10" - $1,100.00; 12" - $1,450.00; 14" - $1,800.00; 16" - $2,200.00. **Glass eyes:**

12" - $2,150.00, 14" - $2,400.00; 16" - $2,650.00.

#8035: Boy, molded hair, painted eyes, jointed body, long cheeks, short chin, full lips (closed mouth). 16-17" - $9,000.00.

#8050: Lightly modeled hair, intaglio eyes, open/closed laugh mouth with two rows of teeth. 16" - $2,400.00.

#8053: Round cheeks, closed mouth, painted eyes to side, large ears. 19" - $3,500.00.

#8058: Laughing, open/closed mouth, two rows teeth, painted eyes, molded hair with ribbon around head. 16-17" - $9,000.00.

#8145: Toddler with closed smile mouth, painted eyes to side, painted hair. 16" - $1,500.00 up; 20" - $1,900.00 up.

#8191: Smiling openly, jointed body. 12" - $1,000.00; 14" - $1,200.00; 17" - $1,500.00.

13" marked "8420" with "Heubach" in a square. Sleep eyes, closed mouth. Shown with Steiff llama, ca. 1957. 13" - $1,300.00; Llama - $300.00.
Courtesy Frasher Doll Auctions.

18" Gebruder Heubach mold number 76262. Modeled, painted hair, molded eyelids, intaglio eyes, and closed mouth. On fully jointed body. 18" - $2,900.00.
Courtesy Frasher Doll Auctions.

#8192: Open/closed smiling mouth with tongue molded between teeth. 8" - $400.00; 11" - $700.00; 15" - $1,100.00; 21" - $1,800.00. **Open mouth:** 14" - $700.00; 17" - $950.00.

#8197: Deeply molded curls, molded loop for bow, pretty face, closed mouth, full lips. Shoulder head, kid body, bisque lower arms, composition legs. 16-17" - $8,700.00 up.

#8316: Open/closed mouth, molded teeth, smile, glass eyes, wig. 15" - $3,500.00 up; 18" - $4,700.00 up. **Painted eyes:** 13" - $1,000.00 up.

#8381: Closed mouth, pensive expression, painted eyes, molded hair, ribbon around head with bow, exposed ears. 17-18" - $3,500.00 up.

#8420: Pouty, painted eyes. 14" - $700.00; 17" - $825.00. **Glass eyes:** 14" - $1,300.00; 16" - $1,600.00; 19" - $2,800.00.

#8459, 8469: Wide open/closed laughing mouth, two lower teeth, glass eyes. 12" - $2,700.00; 15" - $3,300.00.

#8555: Shoulder head, painted bulging eyes. (See photo in Series 8, pg. 97.) 14" - $4,800.00.

#8590: Closed mouth, puckered lips. 15" - $1,500.00; 18" - $2,000.00. **Baby:** 15" - $1,400.00; 17" - $1,700.00.

#8596: Smile, intaglio eyes. 14" - $725.00; 16" - $950.00.

#8648: Extremely pouty closed mouth, intaglio eyes to side. 20" - $2,800.00; 24" - $3,600.00.

#8774 ("Whistling Jim"): Eyes to side and mouth modeled as if whistling. 12" - $750.00; 14" - $950.00; 17" - $1,350.00.

#8868: Molded hair, glass eyes, closed mouth, very short chin. 16" - $2,000.00; 20" - $2,600.00.

#8991: Molded hair, painted eyes to side, open/closed mouth with molded tongue, protruding ears. **Toddler body:** 15" - $2,900.00. **Kid Body:** 12-13" - $1,250.00.

#9141: Winking. Glass eyes: 9" - $1,500.00. Painted eyes: 7-8" - $950.00.

#9189: Same description as #7764 but no bun in molded hair. Cloth body, composition limbs. 11-12" - $1,250.00.

#9355: Shoulder head. 16" - $925.00; 22" - $1,650.00.

#9457 (Indian): 16-17" - $4,600.00.

#9891: Molded-on cap, intaglio eyes. **Aviator:** 12-13" - $1,200.00. **Sailor:** 12-13" - $1,100.00. **Farmer:** 12-13" - $950.00.

#10532: Open mouth, jointed body. 10" - $425.00; 14" - $675.00; 17" - $900.00; 20" - $1,300.00.

#10586, #10633: Child with open mouth, jointed body. 16" - $625.00; 19" - $765.00; 23" - $965.00.

#11173: Glass eyes, five-piece body, pursed closed mouth with large indented cheeks. Called **"Tiss-Me."** 8" - $1,500.00 up; 12" - $1,800.00.

Child with Dolly-type Face (non-character): Open mouth, glass sleep or set eyes, jointed body, bisque head with no damage and nicely dressed. 14" - $475.00; 16" - $550.00; 19" - $750.00; 24" - $950.00; 27" $1,100.00.

Googly: See that section.

Indian Portrait, #8467: Man or woman. 14" - $3,900.00 up.

Babies or Infants: Bisque head, wig or molded hair, sleep or intaglio eyes, open/closed pouty-type mouths.

#6894, #6898, #7602: 6" - $250.00; 8" - $350.00; 12" - $450.00; 15" - $575.00; 17" - $800.00; 22" - $985.00; 25" - $1,400.00; 27" - $1,650.00

#7604: Laughing. 12-13" - $675.00.

#7745, 7746: Laughing. 15-16" - $4,400.00.

Molded Bonnet, #7959: Deep modeling to pink or blue bonnet. Molded hair to front and sides of face. 11-12" - $2,000.00.

HEUBACH (ERNST) KOPPELSDORF

Ernst Heubach began making dolls in 1887 in Koppelsdorf, Germany. Marks of this firm can be the initials "E.H." or the dolls can be found marked with the full name, Heubach Koppelsdorf, or:

Some mold numbers from this company: **27X, 87, 99, 230, 235, 236, 237, 238, 242, 250, 251, 262, 271, 273, 275, 277, 283, 300, 302, 312, 317, 320, 321, 330, 335, 338, 339, 340, 342, 349, 350, 367, 399, 407, 410, 417, 438, 444, 450, 452, 458, 616, 1310, 1342, 1900, 1901, 1906, 1909, 2504, 2671, 2757, 3027, 3412, 3423, 3427, 7118, 32144.**

Child: #250, 275, 302 etc.: After 1888. Jointed body, open mouth, sleep or set eyes. No damage and nicely dressed. 8" - $200.00; 10" - $225.00; 14" - $275.00; 18" - $400.00; 22" - $485.00; 26" - $600.00; 30" - $825.00; 38" - $1,200.00.

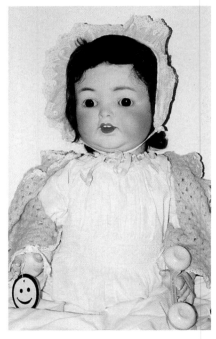

22" marked "Heubach Koppelsdorf 342.7. Germany." Sleep eyes, open mouth with two upper teeth, and on five-piece bent limb baby body. 22" - $650.00. *Courtesy Gloria Anderson.*

Child: On kid body with bisque lower arms, bisque shoulder head, some turned head, open mouth. No damage and nicely dressed. 14" - $225.00; 20" - $365.00; 24" - $425.00; 30" - $800.00.
Child: Painted bisque. 8" - $125.00; 12" - $150.00.
Babies: #300, 320, 342, etc. 1910 and after. On five-piece bent limb baby body, open mouth with some having wobbly tongue and pierced nostrils. Sleep eyes. No damage and nicely dressed. 6" - $265.00; 9" - $325.00; 15" - $450.00; 17" - $485.00; 20" - $545.00; 24" - $800.00.
#300, 320: Fully jointed body. 18" - $465.00; 23" - $625.00.
Baby on Toddler Body: Same as above, but on a toddler body. 9-10" - $365.00; 15" - $575.00; 18" - $650.00; 22" - $875.00; 25" - $975.00.
Baby, Painted Bisque: 10" - $165.00; 16" - $275.00. **Toddler:** 15" - $385.00.

Infant: 1925 and after. Molded or painted hair, sleep eyes, closed mouth, flange neck bisque head on cloth body with composition or celluloid hands. No damage and nicely dressed.
#338, #340: 13" - $675.00; 15" - $925.00.
#339, #349, #350: 14" - $675.00; 16" - $825.00.
#399: White only. (See Black doll in Black or Brown Dolls section.) 14" - $465.00.
Infant: 1925. Cloth body, celluloid or composition hands. Painted hair, sleep eyes, closed mouth. No damage, nicely dressed.
#339, 349, 350: 9½" - $425.00; 12" - $550.00.
#338, 340: 14" - $700.00; 16" - $800.00.
#320, 335, 339, 340, 349, 350, 399: See Black or Brown Doll section.
Character Child: 1910 on. Molded hair, painted eyes and open/closed mouth. No damage. **#262, #330 and others:** 12" - $500.00; 16" - $875.00.

18" marked "Heubach Koppelsdorf/300-4." Open mouth, cheek dimples, moving tongue and on five-piece baby body. Shown with 8½" doll marked "15/)S(/ Germany/240." Sleep eyes, solid dome, cloth body with composition hands. Made by Herm Steiner. 18" - $625.00; 8½" - $265.00. *Courtesy Gloyra Woods.*

Jullien marked dolls were made in Paris, France from 1875 to 1904. The heads will be marked Jullien and a size number. In 1892, Jullien advertised "L'Universal" and the label can be found on some of his doll bodies. (See photo in Series 7, pg. 96.)

Child: Closed mouth, paperweight eyes, French jointed body of composition, papier maché with some having wooden parts. Undamaged bisque head and all in excellent condition. 17" - $3,800.00; 20" - $4,300.00; 22" - $4,650.00; 24" - $4,900.00; 26" - $5,300.00.

Child: Same as above, but with open mouth. 15" - $1,450.00; 17" - $1,950.00; 20" - $2,200.00; 22" - $2,400.00; 25" - $2,800.00. **Poor quality, high color:** 15" - $1,100.00; 20" - $1,750.00; 22" - $1,950.00; 25" - $2,300.00.

29" marked "Jullien." Long cheeks, unusual modeled chin with dimple, open mouth, and on fully jointed French body. 29" - $3,400.00. *Courtesy Turn of Century Antiques.*

JUMEAU

Known Jumeau Sizes: 0 – 8-9"; 1 – 10"; 2 – 11"; 3 – 12"; 4 – 13"; 5 – 14-15"; 6 – 16"; 7 – 17"; 8 – 19"; 9 – 20"; 10 – 21-22"; 11 – 24-25"; 12 – 26-27"; 13 – 29-30".

Tete Jumeau: 1879–1899 and later. Marked with red stamp on head and oval sticker on body. Closed mouth, paperweight eyes, jointed body with full joints or jointed with straight wrists. Pierced ears with larger sizes having applied ears. No damage at all to bisque head, undamaged French body, dressed and ready to place into collection. 9-10" - $4,900.00 up; 12" - $3,600.00; 14" - $3,900.00; 16" - $4,400.00; 18" - $4,600.00; 20" - $4,900.00; 22" - $5,400.00; 24" - $5,700.00; 28" - $6,600.00; 30" - $7,400.00.

Tete Jumeau on Adult Body: Open mouth. (See photo in Series 5, pg. 87.) 19-20" - $6,800.00; 25" - $7,500.00.

10½" Size 1 Jumeau with large paperweight eyes, rare open mouth with upper teeth in the petite size. Fully jointed Jumeau body. 10½" - $4,900.00. *Courtesy Frasher Doll Auctions.*

30" beautiful marked Tete Jumeau. Applied ears, open/closed mouth with space between lips. Jumeau body with straight wrists. 30" $7,400.00. *Courtesy Frasher Doll Auctions.*

25" adult figured Jumeau marked "Depose Tete Jumeau/B SGDG 10." Open/closed mouth with space between lips. Wood and composition lady body with molded bosom, narrow waist and full hips. 25" - $7,500.00. *Courtesy Frasher Doll Auctions.*

Tete Jumeau on Adult Body:

Same as previous listing but with closed mouth. 14" - $2,300.00; 16" - $2,500.00; 19" - $2,800.00; 20" - $2,900.00; 22" - $3,100.00; 24" - $3,400.00; 28" - $3,900.00; 30" - $4,100.00; 34" - $4,600.00.

1907 Jumeau: Incised "1907," sometimes has the Tete Jumeau stamp. Sleep or set eyes, open mouth, jointed French body. No damage, nicely dressed. 14" - $1,700.00; 16" - $2,350.00; 19" - $2,600.00; 22" - $2,900.00; 25" - $3,300.00; 29" - $3,700.00; 34" - $4,300.00.

E.J. Child: Ca. early 1880's. Head incised "Depose/E. 6 J." Paperweight eyes, closed mouth, jointed body with straight wrist (unjointed at wrist). Larger dolls will have applied ears. No damage to head or body and nicely dressed in excellent quality clothes. 10" - $5,600.00 up; 15" - $6,000.00; 16" - $6,600.00; 19" - $7,000.00; 24" - $8,400.00; 27" - $10,000.00.

E.J. Child: Mark with number over the E.J. (Example: E.^{6}J.) 17-18" - $11,000.00; 22-23" - $18,000.00.

E.J./A Child: 19" - $15,000.00; 22" - $20,000.00; 26" - $25,000.00 up.

Depose Jumeau: (Incised) 1880. Head will be incised "Depose Jumeau" and body should have Jumeau sticker. Closed mouth, paperweight eyes and on jointed body with straight wrists, although a few may have jointed wrists. No damage at all and nicely dressed. 15" - $5,700.00; 18" - $6,600.00; 22" - $7,400.00; 25" - $8,500.00.

Long Face (Triste Jumeau): 1870's. Closed mouth, applied ears, paperweight eyes and straight wrists on Jumeau marked body. Head is generally marked with a size number. No damage to head or body, nicely dressed. 20-21" - $24,000.00 up; 25-26"- $26,000.00 up; 29-30" - $30,000.00 up; 33-34" - $36,000.00.

19" marked "Depose Tete Jumeau" on marked jointed Jumeau body. Open/ closed mouth. 19" - $4,900.00 up. *Courtesy Turn of Century Antiques.*

30" Jumeau marked "X 13" on head. Open mouth and on Jumeau fully jointed body. 30" - $4,100.00. *Courtesy Frasher Doll Auctions.*

Portrait Jumeau: 1870's. Closed mouth, usually large almond-shaped eyes and jointed Jumeau body. Head marked with size number only and body has the Jumeau sticker or stamp. 10" - $6,000.00; 12" - $6,900.00; 15" - $7,400.00; 21" - $10,000.00; 25" - $16,000.00; 28" - $18,000.00. **Very almond-shaped eyes:** 12" - $6,600.00; 15-16" - $10,000.00; 19" - $16,500.00; 24" - $24,000.00.

Phonograph Jumeau: Bisque head with open mouth. Phonograph in body. No damage, working and nicely dressed. 20" - $8,500.00; 25" - $13,000.00 up.

Wire Eye (Flirty) Jumeau: Lever in back of head operates eyes. Open mouth, jointed body, straight wrists. 18" - $6,800.00; 21" - $8,200.00; 26" - $9,600.00.

Walker: Open mouth: 20" - $2,600.00; 24" - $2,900.00. **Throws kisses:** 20" - $2,800.00; 24" - $3,200.00.

13" marked "Depose E. 5 J." on head. Open/closed mouth with white space between lips and on marked Jumeau body with straight wrists. Shown with French doll accessories. 13" - $5,400.00; Accessories - $475.00.
Courtesy Frasher Doll Auctions.

Celluloid Head: Incised Jumeau. 14" - $675.00 up.

Mold #200 Series: Examples: **201, 203, 205, 208, 211, 214, 223.** (See photo in Series 7, pg. 100.) *Very character faces* and marked Jumeau. Closed mouth. No damage to bisque or body. 22" - $78,000.00 up.

Mold #230 Series: Ca. 1906. Open mouth. 14" - $1,300.00; 16-17" - $1,600.00; 20" - $1,900.00 up.

S.F.B.J. or Unis: Marked along with Jumeau. Open mouth, no damage to head and on French body. 16" - $1,400.00; 20" - $1,800.00. Closed mouth: 16" - $2,400.00; 20" - $3,000.00.

Two-Faced Jumeau: Has two different faces on same head, one crying and one smiling. Open/closed mouths,

17½" very almond-eyed Portrait Jumeau with closed mouth and on jointed body with straight wrists. 17½" - **$15,000.00.**
Courtesy Frasher Doll Auctions.

jointed body. No damage and nicely dressed. 14" - $13,000.00 up.

Fashion: See Fashion section.

Mold #221: Ca. 1930's. Small dolls (10") will have a paper label "Jumeau." Adult style bisque head on five-piece body with painted-on shoes. Closed mouth and set glass eyes. Dressed in original ornate gown. No damage and clean. 10-11" - $725.00.

Mold #306: Jumeau made after formation of Unis and mark will be "Unis/France" in oval and "71" on one side and "149" on other, followed by "306/Jumeau/1939/Paris." Called "Princess Elizabeth." Closed mouth, flirty or paperweight eyes. Jointed French body. No damage and nicely dressed. 20" - $2,400.00; 30" - $3,800.00.

Marked Shoes: #5 and up - $500.00 up.

25" twin dolls on typical Jumeau marked bodies. Both have open mouths and are pull string talkers. Each - **$3,500.00.** *Courtesy Frasher Doll Auctions.*

KAMMER & REINHARDT

Kammer and Reinhardt dolls generally have the Simon and Halbig name or initials incised along with their own name or mark, as Simon & Halbig made most of their heads. They were located in Thuringia, Germany, at Waltershausen and began in 1895, although their first models were not on the market until 1896. The trademark for this company was registered in 1895. In 1909, a character line of fourteen molds (#100–#114) was exhibited at the Leipzig Toy Fair.

Marks:

Character Boy or Girl: Closed or open/closed mouth, on jointed body or five-piece body. No damage and nicely dressed.

#101: Boy "Peter"; girl "Marie." **Five-piece body:** 9" - $1,700.00; 11" - $2,300.00. **Fully jointed body:** 9"- $1,800.00; 11" - $2,400.00. 14" - $3,000.00; 16" - $3,600.00; 18" - $4,800.00; 22" - $6,300.00. **Glass eyes:** 14" - $7,200.00; 17" - $9,200.00; 21" - $12,000.00.

#102: Boy "Karl," extremely rare. 12" - $28,000.00 up; 15" - $34,000.00. **Glass eyes:** 17" - $38,000.00 up.

#103: Closed mouth, sweet expression, painted eyes **or #104:** Open/closed mouth, dimples, mischievous expression, painted eyes, extremely rare. 19" - $58,000.00 up.

#105: Extremely rare. Open/closed mouth; much modeling around intaglio eyes. 20" - $90,000.00 up.

#106: Extremely rare. Full round face, pursed closed full lips, intaglio eyes to side and much chin modeling. 23" - $60,000.00 up.

#107: Pursed, pouty mouth, intaglio eyes. 13" - $17,000.00 up; 21" - $38,000.00 up. **Glass eyes:** 17" - $38,000.00.

#109: "Elise." Very rare. (See photo in Series 8, pg. 105.) 14" - $16,000.00; 20" - $25,000.00. **Glass eyes:** 20" - $30,000.00.

#112, #112X, #112A: (See photo in Series 5, pg. 91.) Very rare. 15" - $9,800.00; 18" - $19,000.00; 23" - $26,000.00. **Glass eyes:** 18" - $22,000.00; 24" - $30,000.00.

#114: Girl "Gretchen"; boy "Hans." 8" - $1,850.00; 10" - $3,000.00; 15" - $4,300.00; 19" - $5,600.00; 23" - $8,400.00.

16" "Gretchen," mold #114. Rare version with glass eyes. Excellent facial modeling. Very pouty, expressed not only with mouth but also eyebrows. 16" - **$7,000.00.** *Courtesy Frasher Doll Auctions.*

Glass eyes: 18" - $8,800.00; 24" - $14,500.00.

#117: Closed mouth. 14" - $4,100.00; 17" - $4,900.00; 22" - $6,400.00; 25" - $7,400.00; 28" - $8,300.00.

#117A: Closed mouth. 15" - $4,500.00; 18" - $5,400.00; 22" - $6,700.00; 25" - $7,700.00; 28" - $8,450.00.

#117n: Open mouth, flirty eyes. (Subtract $200.00 for sleep eyes only.) 16" - $1,400.00; 20" - $1,800.00; 23" - $2,000.00; 28" - $2,600.00; 32" - $2,900.00.

#123, #124 (Max & Moritz): (See photo in Series 8, pg. 107.) 17" - $25,000.00 up each.

#127: Molded hair, open/closed mouth. Toddler or jointed body: 17" - $2,000.00; 21" - $2,600.00; 25" - $3,300.00.

Character Babies: Open/closed mouth or closed mouth on five-piece bent limb baby body, solid dome or wigged. No damage and nicely dressed.

#100: Called "Kaiser Baby." Intaglio eyes, open/closed mouth. 12" - $565.00; 15" - $700.00; 18" - $965.00; 21" - $1,250.00. **Glass eyes:** 14" - $1,900.00; 19" - $2,500.00. **Black:** 15" - $1,100.00; 17" - $1,800.00.

#115, #115a "Phillip": 15" - $4,550.00; 18" - $4,900.00; 24" - $5,500.00; 26" - $5,900.00. **Toddler:** 16" - $4,850.00; 18" - $5,300.00; 24" - $5,900.00.

#116, #116a: 15" - $3,000.00; 18" - $3,500.00; 25" - $4,300.00. **Toddler:** 16" - $4,400.00; 21" - $4,800.00; 25" - $5,200.00. **Open Mouth:** 16" - $1,400.00; 18" - $2,300.00. **Toddler:** 20" - $2,600.00.

#127: 12" - $875.00; 16" - $1,300.00; 21" - $1,650.00; 24" - $2,000.00. **Toddler:** 15" - $1,400.00; 20" - $1,900.00; 26" - $2,500.00. **Child:** 14" - $1,450.00; 17" - $2,000.00; 22" - $2,500.00; 25" - $3,300.00.

Babies with Open Mouth: Sleep eyes on five-piece bent limb baby body. Wigs, may have tremble tongues or "mama" cryer in body. No damage

and nicely dressed. Allow more for flirty eyes.

#118a: 15" - $1,400.00; 18" - $2,000.00. 20" - $2,200.00.

#119: 16" - $4,000.00; 20" - $4,900.00.

#121: 12" - $600.00; 15" - $700.00; 18" - $800.00; 23-24" - $1,200.00. **Toddler:** 14"- $1,100.00; 21" - $1,500.00; 25" - $1,800.00.

#122, #128: 12" - $585.00; 15" - $765.00; 18" - $1,200.00; 22" - $1,400.00. **Toddler:** 14" - $1,200.00; 18" - $1,450.00; 24" - $1,850.00.

#126: 11" - $465.00; 15" - $585.00; 18"- $700.00; 22" - $950.00; 26" - $1,350.00. **Toddler:** 6½-7" - $625.00; 9" - $700.00; 15" - $875.00; 23" - $1,400.00; 25" - $1,700.00; 29" - $2,200.00. **Child Body:** 22" - $900.00; 34" - $1,800.00.

#135: 15" - $1,400.00; 21" - $2,300.00.

14¼" and 15" marked "K*R 116/A 32." Sleep eyes, open/closed mouths with molded tongues and upper teeth. Both are on toddler bodies. Doll on left is all original; the other possibly has original middy top. Each - $4,400.00.
Courtesy Frasher Doll Auctions.

#172: Ca. 1925. Five-piece baby body. (Allow more for flirty eyes.) 16" - $3,000.00; 20" - $3,500.00.

Child Dolls: 1895–1930's. Open mouth, sleep or set eyes and on fully jointed body. No damage and nicely dressed. Most often found mold numbers are: **#109, 191, 290, 400, 403:** (Add more for flirty eyes. Add 50% for all original clothes.) 8" - $485.00; 12" - $565.00; 15" - $695.00; 18" - $785.00; 21" - $875.00; 24" - $1,150.00; 29" - $1,350.00; 34" - $1,800.00; 39" - $3,000.00; 42" - $3,500.00.

#192: Closed mouth, sleep eyes, fully jointed body. No damage. 6-7" - $585.00; 16" - $2,300.00; 22"- $2,650.00; 25" - $3,200.00. **Open mouth:** 7-8" - $450.00; 14" - $700.00; 20" - $1,100.00; 25" - $1,400.00.

Large 19" "Kaiser Baby" mold #100. Molded eyelids, intaglio eyes, and open/closed mouth. Painted hair and on bent limb five-piece baby body. 19" - **$1,200.00.** *Courtesy Turn of Century Antiques.*

25" marked "K*R Simon & Halbig 121." Sleep eyes, open mouth with two upper teeth. On jointed toddler body. Right: 22" with molded hair marked "Simon & Halbig/K*R 127N 50." Sleep eyes, open mouth with two upper teeth. On jointed toddler body. Also shown is a 7" all original Armand Marseille googly marked "323 A 11/0 M." German Jack-in-the-box and ca. 1910 iron horse and coach. 25" - $2,500.00; 22" - $2,800.00; 7" - $600.00; Jack-in-box - $55.00; Horse/coach - $475.00. *Courtesy Frasher Doll Auctions.*

Very large 24" Kammer & Reinhardt mold # 126 baby with open mouth and tremble tongue, sleep eyes and "fly away" eyebrows. On five-piece bent limb baby body. 24" - $1,100.00. *Courtesy Turn of Century Antiques.*

Right: 21" marked "K*R 192 B." Sleep eyes, open mouth, and on fully jointed body. Left: 21" marked "7." Maker unknown. Set glass eyes, open mouth, and on fully jointed German body. 21" - $1,100.00; 21", unknown maker - $600.00. *Courtesy Frasher Doll Auctions*

Small Child Dolls: Open mouth, sleep eyes (some set) and on five-piece bodies. No damage. 6" - $385.00; 8" - $525.00. Jointed body: 8" - $550.00; 10" - $650.00.

Small Child Doll: Open mouth, flapper style, painted bisque. 8" - $475.00.

Small Child Doll: Closed mouth: 6" - $575.00; 8" - $650.00.

Googly: See Googly section.

Celluloid: See Celluloid section.

Infant: 1924 on. Molded hair and glass eyes, open mouth and cloth body with composition hands. 15-16" - $3,200.00 up.

Open mouth doll with four teeth, marked "K*R No. 43." On fully jointed body. 18" - $785.00. *Courtesy Gloria Anderson.*

KESTNER, J.D.

Johannes Daniel Kestner's firm was founded in 1802, and his name was carried through the 1920's. The Kestner Company was one of the few that made entire dolls, both bodies and heads. In 1895, Kestner started using the trademark of the crown and streamers. (Also see German - All Bisque.)

Sample marks:

**B MADE IN 6
GERMANY
J.D.K.
126**

F GERMANY 11

**J.D.K.
208
GERMANY**

Child Doll, Closed mouth: Ca. 1880. Some appear to be pouties. Sleep or set eyes, jointed body with straight wrist. No damage and nicely dressed. **#X, XII, XV:** 14" - $3,400.00; 19" - $4,000.00; 24" - $4,400.00; 27" - $4,600.00.
#XI, 103: Very pouty. (See photo in Series 7, pg. 106.) Price will be less for kid body. 11-12" - $2,950.00; 15" - $3,350.00; 19" - $3,985.00; 23" - $4,300.00; 26" - $4,400.00.
#128 Pouty, #169, or unmarked Pouty: On five-piece body. 6½-7" - $965.00; 8" - $1,300.00; 10" - $2,000.00; 12" - $2,300.00; 14" - $2,500.00; 18" - $2,700.00; 21" - $3,000.00; 25" - $3,600.00; 29" - $4,000.00.
Turned Shoulder Head: Ca. 1880's. Closed mouth. Set or sleep eyes, on kid body with bisque lower arms. No damage and nicely dressed. (Allow more for swivel neck.) 18" - $1,000.00; 22" - $1,400.00; 26" - $1,800.00. **Open mouth:** 18" - $600.00; 22" - $750.00; 26" - $900.00.

26" pouty by Kestner with mold #128. Sleep eyes, closed mouth and on fully jointed body. 26" - $3,600.00. *Courtesy Frasher Doll Auctions.*

Early Child, Square Cut Porcelain Teeth: Jointed body and marked with number and letter. 10" - $685.00; 14" - $825.00; 17" - $1,000.00; 21" - $1,500.00 up; 25" - $1,900.00.
A.T. Type: (See photo in Series 8, pg. 111.) Composition jointed body with straight wrists. **Closed mouth:** 11" - $12,000.00; 13" - $15,000.00; 15" - $18,000.00; 17" - $21,000.00. **Open Mouth:** 13" - $2,100.00; 15" - $2,900.00; 17" - $3,300.00.
Bru Type: (See photo in Series 7, pg. 107; Series 8, pg. 112.) Open/closed mouth, modeled teeth. **Composition lower arms, kid body:** 16" - $2,500.00; 22" - $3,200.00. **Bisque lower arms:** 17" - $5,200.00; 24" - $6,400.00. **On jointed composition body, straight wrists:** 18" - $4,600.00; 23" - $5,400.00.
Character Child: 1910 and after. Closed mouth or open/closed unless noted. Glass or painted eyes, jointed

27" marked **"16 X."** Nice example of the Kestner X model doll. Closed mouth and on jointed body with straight wrists. **27" - $4,600.00.** *Courtesy Frasher Doll Auctions.*

An adorable 11" A.T. type Kestner with closed mouth and slightly modeled tongue, sleep eyes, and on chubby jointed body with straight wrists. Original clothes. 11" - $12,000.00; With original clothes - $15,000.00. *Courtesy Frasher Doll Auctions.*

16" Bru type Kestner marked "10." Full cheeks, open/closed mouth with modeled upper teeth, paperweight eyes on composition jointed body. 16" - $2,500.00. *Courtesy Frasher Doll Auctions.*

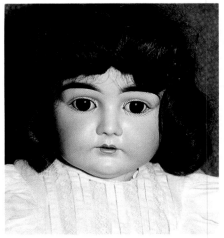

31½" Kestner marked "P Made in Germany." Turned shoulder head, kid body, bisque lower arms and open mouth. 31½" - $1,600.00. *Courtesy Frasher Doll Auctions.*

body and no damage and nicely dressed. **#175, 176, 177, 178, 179, 180, 181, 182, 183, 184, 185, 187, 188, 189, 190:** These mold numbers can be found on the boxed set doll that has one body and interchangable four heads. (See photos in Series 5, pg. 96; Series 6, pg. 124.) **Boxed set with four heads:** 11-12" - $9,000.00 up. **Larger size with painted eyes, closed or open/closed mouth:** 12" - $3,000.00; 15" - $3,500.00; 17" - $4,000.00. **Same as above but has glass eyes:** 12" - $3,600.00; 15" - $4,100.00; 17" - $5,200.00. **Glass eyes, molded-on bonnet:** 16" - $4,800.00.

#151: 15" - $2,600.00; 18" - $3,500.00.

#155: Five-piece body: 8-9" - $525.00. **Jointed body:** 8-9" - $785.00.

#206: Fat cheeks, closed mouth. (See photo in Series 8, pg. 112.) **Child or toddler:** 16" - $9,600.00; 20" - $16,500.00; 23" - $21,000.00.

12" character Kestner with mold #184. Painted features and on fully jointed body. 12" - $3,000.00. *Courtesy Frasher Doll Auctions.*

#208: Painted eyes: 16" - $5,000.00; 19" - $9,400.00; 26" - $14,000.00. **Glass eyes:** 18" - $11,000.00; 24" - $14,500.00.

#212: 10" - $2,000.00; 15" - $3,600.00.

#239: Child or toddler. (Also see "Babies."): 17" - $3,800.00; 21" - $4,800.00; 26" - $6,400.00.

#241: Open mouth, glass eyes. (See photo in Series 7, pg. 108.) 15" - $4,400.00; 21"- $5,800.00.

#249: 22" - $2,000.00.

#260: Jointed or toddler body: 8" - $650.00; 12" - $850.00; 16" - $1,300.00; 22" - $1,800.00.

Child Doll: Late 1880's to 1930's. Open mouth on fully jointed body, sleep eyes, some set, with no damage and nicely dressed.

#128, 129, 134, 136, 141, 142, 144, 146, 152, 156, 159, 160, 161, 162, 164, 168, 174, 196, 211, 214, 215: 10" - $650.00; 15" - $750.00; 18" - $825.00; 21" - $925.00; 24" - $1,000.00; 27" - $1,300.00; 32" - $1,800.00; 36" - $2,400.00; 40" - $3,200.00.

#143, 189: (See photo in Series 6, pg. 126.) Character face, open mouth. 9" - $765.00; 12" - $885.00; 18" - $1,500.00; 21" - $1,700.00; 25" - $1,900.00.

#192: 15" - $675.00; 18" - $800.00; 21" - $975.00.

Child: Open mouth, square cut teeth part of head (not separate). 10-11" - $685.00; 14" - $825.00; 16-17" - $1,000.00; 20-21" - $1,500.00; 25" - $1,900.00.

Child Doll, Kid Body: "Dolly" face with open mouth, sleep or set eyes, bisque shoulder head with bisque lower arms. No damage and nicely dressed.

#145, 147, 148, 149, 155, 166, 167, 170, 195, etc. (Add more for fur eyebrows): 8" - $285.00; 12" - $325.00; 16" - $485.00; 19" -

$550.00; 22" - $650.00; 25" - $900.00; 29" - $1,200.00.

#142, 144, 146, 154, 164, 167, 168, 171, 196, 214: Jointed body, open mouth. 10" - $685.00; 14" - $650.00; 17" - $725.00; 22" - $865.00; 25" - $950.00; 30" - $1,250.00; 35" - $1,650.00; 42" - $3,400.00 up. **Same mold numbers, with swivel bisque head:** On bisque shoulder head. Open mouth. 17" - $765.00; 21" - $1,000.00; 26" - $1,400.00. **Same mold numbers, kid body:** 17" - $550.00; 21" - $650.00; 26" - $965.000.

#171 ("Daisy"), some #154: Blonde, side part mohair wig, white dress, red hooded cape. 18" only. Original - $965.00; Redressed - $825.00.

Character Babies: 1910 and later. On bent limb baby bodies, sleep or set eyes, open mouth, can be wigged or have solid dome with painted hair. No damage and nicely dressed.

#121, 142, 150, 151, 152, 153, 154: Now attributed to Hertel, Schwab & Co. 10" - $350.00; 14" - $525.00; 17" - $600.00; 20" - $725.00; 24" - $950.00.

#211, 226, 236, 260, 262, 263: 10-11" - $525.00; 15"- $625.00; 18" - $775.00; 20" - $1,000.00; 24" - $1,450.00.

#220: 13" - $5,200.00; 17" - $6,200.00. **Toddler:** 16" - $6,350.00; 23-24" - $7,600.00.

#234, 235, 238: 13" - $650.00; 16" - $750.00; 20" - $925.00; 24" - $1,200.00.

#237, 245, 1070 (Hilda): Wigged or solid dome. 12" - $2,800.00; 16" - $3,600.00; 22" - $5,200.00; 26" - $6,500.00. **Toddler:** 16" - $5,300.00; 21" - $5,600.00; 24" - $6,700.00.

#239: 15" - $2,600.00; 17" - $3,100.00; 23" - $3,600.00.

#247: 12" - $1,300.00; 16" - $1,900.00; 19" - $2,400.00; 22" - $5,100.00.

#249: 16" - $1,600.00; 20" - $2,050.00.

26" marked "Hilda JDK Gesch 1070/ Made in 20 Germany." Solid dome with painted hair, sleep eyes, open mouth and on five-piece bent limb baby body. Shown with all original 12" wax child's candy container with glass eyes and open/closed mouth. Has "mama-papa" pull strings. 10" early Steiff teddy bear, ca. 1910. 26" - $6,500.00; 12" - $650.00; Bear - $650.00. *Courtesy Frasher Doll Auctions.*

#257: 9" - $485.00; 14" - $650.00; 18" - $875.00; 21" - $1,000.00; 25" - $1,600.00. **Toddler:** 22" - $1,450.00; 27" - $2,100.00.

#279, 200 (Century Doll): Molded hair with part, bangs, cloth body, composition hands. 15" - $1,000.00; 18" - $1,500.00.

#281 (Century Doll): Open mouth: 20" - $925.00.

J.D.K. Marked Baby: Called "Sally" or "Sammy." Solid dome, painted eyes and open mouth. 13" - $850.00; 15" - $1,200.00; 20" - $1,850.00.

Adult Doll, #162: Sleep eyes, open mouth, adult jointed body (thin waist and molded breasts) with slen-

der limbs. No damage and very nicely dressed. 14" - $1,400.00; 17" - $1,600.00; 22" - $2,300.00.

Adult #172: 1910, "Gibson Girl." Bisque shoulder head with closed mouth, kid body with bisque lower arms, glass eyes. No damage and beautifully dressed. 10-11" - $1,150.00; 15" - $2,000.00; 18" - $3,600.00; 22" - $4,200.00.

Oriental #243: Olive fired-in color to bisque. Matching color five-piece bent limb baby body (or jointed toddler-style body), wig, sleep or set eyes. No damage and dressed in oriental style. 14" - $5,000.00; 17" - $6,500.00. **Child:** Same as above, but on jointed Kestner olive-toned body. 15" - $5,400.00; 18" - $7,600.00. **Molded hair baby:** 14" - $5,200.00.

Small Dolls: Open mouth, five-piece bodies or jointed bodies, wigs, sleep or set eyes. No damage and nicely dressed. 7" - $525.00; 9" - $700.00.

#133: 8" - $700.00.

#155: Five-piece body: 8-9" - $550.00. **Jointed body:** 8-9" - $825.00.

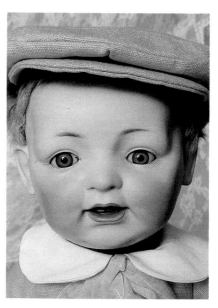

18" "Sammy" mold #211 by Kestner. Sleep eyes, open mouth and has original skin/fur wig. On five-piece bent limb baby body. 18" - $1,000.00. *Courtesy Turn of Century Antiques.*

KEWPIES

Designed by Rose O'Neill and marketed from 1913. All prices are for dolls that have no chips, hairlines or breaks. (See Modern section for composition and vinyl Kewpies.)

Labels:

COPYRIGHT ROSE O'NEILL

KEWPIE REG. U.S. PAT. OFF

KEWPIE GERMANY

All Bisque: One-piece body and head, jointed shoulders only. Blue wings, painted features with eyes to one side. 2½" - $100.00; 4½" - $135.00; 6" - $185.00; 7" - $225.00; 8" - $365.00; 10" - $700.00. **With any article of clothing:** 3" - $225.00; 5" - $250.00; 7" - $345.00; 9" - $600.00 up.

All Bisque: Jointed at hips and shoulders. 4" - $465.00; 9" - $875.00; 12" - $1,500.00. **Painted shoes and socks:** 4-5" - $485.00.

Shoulder Head: Cloth body. 6-7" - $600.00. **Head Only:** 3" -$300.00.

Action Kewpie: Arms folded: 4½" - $550.00. **Confederate Soldier:**

4½" - $700.00. **Cowboy:** Big hat, gun. Made as lamp. (See photo in Series 7, pg. 11.) 10½" - $850.00. **Farmer:** 4" - $485.00. **Gardener:** 4" - $485.00. **Governor:** 4" - $400.00. **Groom with Bride:** 4" - $365.00. **Guitar Player:** 3½" - $365.00. **Holding pen:** 3" - $345.00. **Holding cat:** 3½" - $465.00; **Holding butterfly:** 4" - $525.00. **Hugging:** 3½" - $265.00. **On stomach, called "Blunderboo":** 4" - $425.00. **Soldier:** 4½" - $700.00. **Thinker:** 4" - $300.00; 6" - $450.00. **Traveler (tan or black suitcase):** 3½" - $350.00. **With broom:** 4" - $485.00. **With dog, Doodle:** 3½" - $1,000.00 up. **With helmet:** 6" - $700.00. **With outhouse:** 2½" - $1,200.00. **With pumpkin:** 4" - $365.00; **With rabbit:** 2½" - $325.00. **With rose:** 2" - $350.00. **With shamrock:** 4" - $365.00; **With teddy bear:** 4" - $625.00. **With turkey:** 2" - $365.00. **With umbrella and dog:** 3½" - $1,700.00.

Kewpie Soldier & Nurse: 6" - $2,000.00 up.

Kewpie Tree: (Or mountain) 17 figures. $20,000.00 up.

Kewpie Driving Chariot: $3,000.00 up.

Kewpie on Inkwell: Bisque: 3½" - $650.00. Cast metal: 3½" - $400.00; 6" - $750.00.

Kewpie In Basket With Flowers: 3½" - $650.00.

Kewpie With Drawstring Bag: 4½" - $625.00.

Blunderboo: On stomach, head to side: 4" - $425.00.

Buttonhole Kewpie: $165.00.

Sitting in chair, arms crossed: (See photo Series 8, pg. 96.) 3½" - $525.00.

Kewpie and dog on bench: 4" - $2,600.00 up.

Kewpie Doodle Dog: (See photo in Series 8, pg. 117.) 1½" - $700.00; 3" - $1,600.00.

Three styles of Kewpie. First is a 3½" "Action Kewpie" and is called that because it is doing something. The second is the most often found Kewpie, a 6" standing model that is jointed at shoulders only. The third is a much rarer 4" standing Kewpie that is jointed at the shoulders and also at the hips. "Action" - $465.00; 6" standing - $185.00; 4" standing - $465.00. *Courtesy Shirley Bertrand.*

Hottentot Black Kewpie: 3½" - $400.00; 5" - $500.00; 9" - $900.00.
Kewpie Perfume Bottle: 3½" - $450.00 up.
Pincushion Kewpie: 3" - $325.00.
Celluloid Kewpies: 2" - $40.00; 5" - $85.00; 9" - $165.00. Black: 5" - $145.00. Jointed shoulders: 3" - $70.00; 5" - $110.00; 9" - $175.00; 12" - $250.00; 16" - $600.00 up; 22" - $900.00 up. Soldier or Action: 4" - $100.00 up.
Cloth Body Kewpie: With bisque head, painted eyes. 10" - $1,600.00; 14" - $2,400.00. Glass eyes: 12" - $2,800.00 up; 16" - $5,000.00 up. Composition head and half arms: 13" - $285.00 up.
Glass Eye Kewpie: On chubby toddler body, jointed. Bisque head. Marks: "Ges. Gesch./O'Neill J.D.K." 10" - $4,200.00; 12" - $4,600.00; 16" - $6,500.00; 20" - $8,400.00.

All Cloth: (Made by Kreuger) All one-piece with body forming clothes, mask face. Mint condition: 7-8" - $165.00; 12" - $185.00; 15" - $325.00; 21" - $500.00; 26" - $1,000.00. Fair condition: 12" - $90.00; 15" - $150.00; 21" - $250.00; 26" - $450.00.
All Cloth: Same as above, but with original dress and bonnet. Mint condition: 12" - $265.00; 15" - $400.00; 21"- $650.00; 26" - $1,200.00.
Kewpie, composition, hard plastic, and vinyl: See Modern Section.
Kewpie Tin or Celluloid Talcum Container: Excellent condition: 7-8" - $200.00.
Kewpie Soaps: 4" - $85.00 each. Boxed set of five: $500.00.
Japan: Bisque. 2" - $30.00; 3" - $55.00; 4" - $75.00; 5" - $95.00; 6" - $125.00.

Left: 7" tall calling card holder that is all white enamel over metal. Some flowers are painted red. Kewpie is all pewter and very heavy. Right: 6" heavy metal ink well/pen holder Kewpie painted ivory. Holds real pen with ivory handle. The ink wells are glazed porcelain on the inside. Card holder - $700.00; Ink well - $750.00.

Kley & Hahn operated in Ohrdruf, Germany from 1895 to 1929. They made general dolls as well as babies and fine character dolls.

Marks:

K & H $\;\;\searrow$ K H $\;\nwarrow$

Character Child: Boy or girl. Painted eyes (some with glass eyes), closed or open/closed mouth; on jointed body. No damage and nicely dressed.
#320, 520, 523, 525, 526, 531, 536, 546, 549, 552: 16" - $3,350.00; 20" - $4,250.00; 24" - $5,000.00; 26" - $5,600.00.

Same Mold Numbers on Toddler Bodies: 16" - $1,800.00; 20" - $2,600.00; 24" - $3,000.00.

Same Mold Numbers on Bent Limb Baby Body: 14" - $950.00; 17" - $1,300.00; 21" - $2,100.00; 25" - $2,500.00.

Same Mold Numbers with Glass Eyes: 14" - $3,200.00; 17" - $4,450.00; 21" - $5,400.00; 25" - $5,900.00.

Character Baby: Molded hair or wig, glass sleep eyes or painted eyes. Can have open or open/closed mouth. On bent limb baby body, no damage and nicely dressed. #130, 132, 138, 142, 150, 151, 158, 160, 162, 167, 176, 199, 458, 522, 525, 531, 538, 585, 680: 12" - $485.00;

Front: 21" marked "Walküre/Kley & Hahn 1902." Sleep eyes and open mouth; on fully jointed body. Back: 23½" Heinrich Handwerck with sleep eyes and open mouth. 28" Armand Marseille 390N with sleep eyes and open mouth. 21" - $685.00; 23½" - $695.00; 28" - $700.00. *Courtesy Turn of Century Antiques.*

Left: 33" Kley & Hahn marked "Walküre Germany." Open mouth and fully jointed body. Shown with 31" Kestner marked "16 Made in Germany 171." Open mouth and original. 18" "Princess Elizabeth" marked "306 Jumeau 1938 Paris Unis France 149 71." Closed mouth, glass eyes, and original. 23" Kammer & Reinhardt open mouth toddler, mold #121. 33" - $1,600.00; 31" - $1,500.00; 18" original - $1,650.00; 23" - $1,600.00. *Courtesy Frasher Doll Auctions.*

119

15" - $675.00; 21" - $965.00; 25" - $1,200.00; 28" - $1,550.00.
Same Mold Numbers on Toddler Bodies: 14" - $625.00; 16" - $825.00; 20" - $1,100.00; 24" - $1,450.00; 28" - $1,700.00.
#547: Closed mouth, glass eyes. 18" - $6,400.00.
#538, 548, #568: 16" - $725.00; 18" - $850.00; 21" - $1,000.00. **Toddler:** 20" - $1,300.00; 25" - $1,800.00.
#162 with Talker Mechanism in Head: 17" - $1,400.00; 23" - $2,200.00; 25" - $2,750.00.
#162 with Flirty Eyes and Clockworks in Head: 19" - $2,000.00; 26" - $3,500.00.
#680: 16" - $825.00. **Toddler:** 19" - $1,400.00.
#153, 154, 157, 166, 169: (See photo in Series 7, pg. 114.) Child, closed mouth. 15" - $3,000.00; 20" - $3,900.00. **Open mouth:** 15" - $1,400.00; 20" - $1,800.00.
#159 Two-faced Doll: 12" - $1,900.00; 15" - $2,400.00.
#166: With molded hair and open mouth. 17-18" - $1,700.00. **Closed mouth:** 18" - $2,800.00.
#169: Closed mouth. **Toddler:** 14" - $2,300.00; 18" - $3,600.00. **Open mouth:** 20" - $1,400.00.
#119: Child, glass eyes, closed mouth. 20" - $4,800.00. **Painted eyes:** 20" - $3,300.00. **Toddler:** Glass eyes. 20" - $4,900.00.
Child Dolls, Walküre, and/or #250: Sleep or set eyes, open mouth, jointed body. No damage and nicely dressed. 8" - $345.00; 18" - $525.00; 22" - $685.00; 24" - $745.00; 29" - $1,000.00; 34" - $1,600.00.

KNOCH, GEBRUDER

Gebruder Knoch porcelain factory operated in Neustadt, Germany from 1887 into the 1920's. Most of their dolls have bisque shoulder heads and kid or cloth bodies, but some will be on jointed bodies and/or have kid bodies with composition jointed limbs.

Marks:

Character Doll: No damage and ready to display in collection.
#206: 10" - $900.00; 16" - $1,400.00.
#216: 13" - $1,900.00; 17" - $2,500.00.
#218: 14" - $2,200.00; 17" - $2,800.00.
#246: Winking, has molded cap. 14" - $3,000.00.
#237: Molded decorated bonnet. 10" - $785.00; 14" - $1,250.00.
Child Doll: Perfect, no damage, nicely dressed. Sleep eyes, wig, open mouth, ball-jointed body. 13" - $265.00; 16" - $385.00.

Left: 14" Gebruder Knoch mold #218. Modeled girl's hairdo with protruding ears, painted features, and wide open/closed mouth with molded lower teeth. Shoulder head with kid body and bisque lower arms. Marked "Ges. N. 218 Gesch 15/0." Matching boy is mold #216. Right: Back view. 14" - $2,200.00. *Courtesy Ricki Small.*

KRUSE, KÄTHE

Käthe Kruse began making dolls in 1910. In 1916, she obtained a patent for a wire coil doll, and in 1923 she registered a trademark of a double "K" with the first one reversed, along with the name Käthe Kruse. The first heads were designed after her own children and copies of babies from the Renaissance period. The dolls have molded muslin heads that are handpainted in oils, and jointed cloth bodies. These early dolls will be marked "Käthe Kruse" on the foot and sometimes with a "Germany" and number.

Early Marked Dolls, Model I: 1910. Wide hips, painted hair. In excellent condition and with original clothes. (See photo in Series 7, pg. 116; Series 8, pg. 120.) 16" - $3,000.00; 19" - $3,500.00. **Fair condition:** Not original. 16" - $2,000.00; 19" - $2,400.00. **Ball jointed knees:** 16" - $4,000.00; 19" - $4,400.00.

Model II: 1922 on. Smile, baby. 14" - $2,200.00.

Model III, IV: 1923 on. Serious child. 16" - $1,800.00 up.

Model V, VI: 1925 on. Typical Kruse. 16" - $1,600.00; 19" - $1,900.00.

Baby: Painted open or closed eyes. 20" - $3,400.00 up.

Model VII: 1927 on. (See photo in Series 7, pg. 116.) 15-16" - $1,400.00; 19" - $1,850.00.

Model VIII, IX: 1929 on. 16" - $1,500.00; 21" - $2,300.00. **Good condition:** 21" - $1,500.00.

Model X: 1935 on. 14-15" - $1,300.00.

1920's Dolls: Model IH and others. (See photo in Series 7, pg. 116.) Molded hair or wigged, hips are wide. **Excellent condition:** Original.

16" - $2,350.00; 21" - $3,000.00. **Fair condition:** Not original. 16" - $1,400.00; 21" - $2,000.00.

U.S. Zone: Germany 1945–1951 (Turtle mark.) 14" - $765.00.

Plastic Dolls: 1950's–1975. Glued-on wigs, sleep or painted eyes. Marked with turtle mark and number on head and back "Modell/Käthe Kruse/" and number. 15" - $500.00; 18" - $585.00.

Celluloid: 12" - $235.00; 16" - $425.00.

1975 to date: 9" - $175.00; 13" - $350.00; 17" - $450.00.

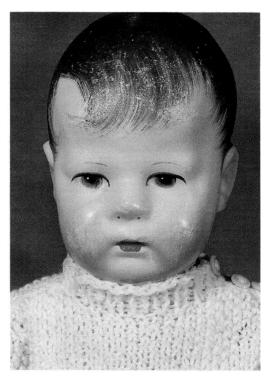

18" early Käthe Kruse in mint condition. Jointed shoulders and hips. 18" - $3,200.00. *Courtesy Turn of Century Antiques.*

Left: 16" Model I early Käthe Kruse all cloth doll with pressed mask face that is oil painted. All original. Right: 14½" body twist mint and original "Dimmie" by Georgene Averill. Painted features, loop molded in hair for bow. 16" - $3,000.00; 14½" - $365.00. *Courtesy Frasher Doll Auctions.*

Left: 20½" Käthe Kruse Model VIII. Cloth with different material used for head, painted features, and all original clothes. Ca. 1940's. Right: 22" marked "B.L.10." with closed mouth, French jointed body. Shown with blue Jasperware Kewpie clock marked "Rose O'Neill Kewpie/Germany/Copyright." 20½" - $1,400.00; 22" - $4,500.00; Clock - $475.00. *Courtesy Frasher Doll Auctions.*

KUHNLENZ, GEBRUDER

Kuhnlenz made dolls from 1884 to 1930 and was located in Kronach, Bavaria. Marks from this company include the "G.K." plus numbers such as 56-38, 44-26, 41-28, 56-18, 44-15, 38-27.

Other marks now attributed to this firm are:

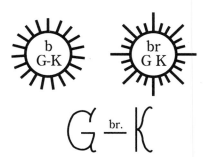

Child with Closed Mouth: Mold #31, 32. Bisque head in perfect condition, jointed body and nicely dressed. 10" - $685.00; 15" - $1,100.00; 19" - $1,600.00; 23" - $1,950.00.

Mold #34: Bru type. 17" - $2,850.00.

Mold #38: Kid body, bisque shoulder head. 15" - $685.00; 22" - $1,000.00.

Child with Open Mouth: Mold #41, 44, 56. Bisque head in perfect condition, jointed body and nicely dressed. 15" - $600.00; 19" - $850.00; 23" - $1,100.00.

Mold #61: Shoulder head, kid body. 20" - $745.00.

Mold #165: Bisque head in perfect condition, jointed body and nicely dressed. 18" - $475.00; 24" - $685.00.

Tiny Dolls, Mold #44, 46 and others: Bisque head in perfect condition, five-piece body with painted-on shoes and socks, open mouth. 8" - $225.00. **Closed mouth:** 8" - $500.00. **Fully jointed body:** 8" - $285.00 up.

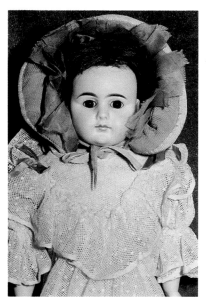

19" marked "38-27." Closed mouth, glass eyes, and slightly turned bald head on shoulder plate. Kid body with bisque lower arms. Made by Gebruder Kuhlenz. Ca. 1890's. 19" - $875.00.
Courtesy Frasher Doll Auctions.

LANTERNIER (LIMOGES)

A. Lanternier & Cie of Limoges, France made dolls from about the 1890's on into the 1930's. Before making dolls, they produced porcelain pieces as early as 1855. Their doll heads will be fully marked and some carry a name such as "LaGeorgienne Favorite, Lorraine, Cherie," etc. They generally are found on papier maché bodies but can be on fully jointed composition bodies. Dolls from this firm may have nearly excellent quality bisque to very poor quality.

Marks:

FABRICATION
FRANCAISE

AL & CIE
LIMOGES

Child: 1915. Open mouth, set eyes on jointed body. No damage and nicely dressed. Good quality bisque with pretty face. 16" - $725.00; 20" - $850.00; 22" - $925.00; 24" - $1,100.00. **Poor quality bisque:** Very high coloring or blotchy color bisque. 16" - $500.00; 20" - $600.00; 24" - $850.00; 27" - $900.00.

"Jumeau" Style Face: Has a striking Jumeau look. Good quality bisque. 19" - $1,200.00; 23" - $1,500.00. **Poor quality bisque:** 19" - $750.00; 23" - $950.00.

Character: 1915. Open/closed mouth with teeth, smiling fat face, glass eyes, on jointed body. No damage and nicely dressed. Marked "Toto." 17" - $950.00; 21" - $1,300.00.

Lady: 1915. Adult-looking face, set eyes, open/closed or closed mouth. Jointed adult body. No damage and nicely dressed. 15" - $975.00; 18" - $1,400.00.

Boy doll is an 18" Lanternier with open/closed smiling mouth with two rows of teeth. Has dimples and on French jointed body. Shown with 19" girl with character face, sleep eyes, and open mouth. Marked with Goebel bee mark. Also, 11" "Belton type" marked "2." Has set eyes, open/closed mouth, and on fully jointed French body. The English handcrafted boat is 18½" long. 18" - $825.00; 19" - $650.00; 11" - $1,300.00, Boat - $350.00. *Courtesy Frasher Doll Auctions.*

30" doll marked "L (anchor) C/C 13." Made by LeConte & Alliot. Has sleep eyes, open mouth, excellent quality bisque, and on jointed French body. Shown with 5½" all bisque with sleep eyes, swivel neck. Came in cylindrical trunk with extra pieces of clothing. 30" - $2,300.00; 5½" with trunk/clothing - $500.00. *Courtesy Frasher Doll Auctions.*

LENCI

Lenci dolls are all felt with a few having cloth torsos. They are jointed at neck, shoulders and hips. The original clothes will be felt or organdy or a combination of both. Features are oil painted and generally eyes are painted to the side. Other characteristics are middle and fourth fingers sewn together, and a seamless steam-molded felt head with sewn-on felt ears. Size can range from 5" to 45". (Mint or rare dolls will bring higher prices.)

Marks: On cloth or paper label: "Lenci Torino Made in Italy." "Lenci" may be written on bottom of foot or underneath one arm.

Children: No moth holes, very little dirt, doll as near mint as possible and all in excellent condition. 14" - $950.00 up; 16" - $1,200.00 up; 18" - $1,400.00 up; 20" - $1,800.00 up. **Dirty, original clothes in poor condition or redressed:** 14" - $400.00; 16" - $600.00; 18" - $750.00; 20" - $950.00.

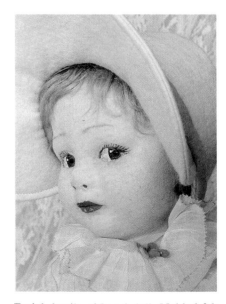

Facial details of Lenci doll. Molded felt face, oil-painted features, mohair wig, original felt and organdy clothes. 16" - **$1,200.00.** *Courtesy Turn of Century Antiques.*

Baby: (See photos in Series 5, pg. 108.) 16" - $1,800.00; 20" - $2,300.00. **Fair condition:** $800.00-1,200.00.

Tiny Dolls (Called Mascottes): (See photos in Series 7, pg. 120.) **Excellent condition:** 5" - $250.00; 8-9" - $365.00. **Dirty, redressed or original clothes in poor condition:** 5" - $95.00; 8-9" - $165.00.

Ladies with Adult Faces: "Flapper" or "Boudoir" style with long limbs. (See photos in Series 5, pg. 107, Series 6, pg. 136.) **Excellent condition:** 24" - $1,800.00 up; 27" - $2,400.00 up. **Dirty or in poor condition:** 24" - $900.00; 28" - $1,000.00.

Clowns: Excellent condition: 18" - $1,600.00; 27" - $2,000.00. **Poor condition:** 18" - $750.00; 27" - $1,000.00.

Indians or Orientals: Excellent condition: 17" - $3,700.00. **Dirty and poor condition:** 17" - $1,300.00.

Golfer: Excellent, perfect condition. 16" - $2,400.00. **Poor condition:** 16" - $950.00.

Pan: Hooved feet. 9½-10" - $2,100.00. **Dirty and fair condition:** 9½-10" - $450.00.

Shirley Temple Type: Excellent condition. 28" - $2,500.00. **Dirty and poor condition:** 28" - $1,000.00.

Bali Dancer: Excellent condition: 21" - $2,200.00. Poor condition: 22" - $750.00.

Smoking Doll: In excellent condition, painted eyes: 25" - $2,100.00 up. **Poor condition:** 25" - $1,000.00.

Glass Eyes: Excellent condition. 17" - $2,600.00; 22" - $3,300.00. **Poor condition:** 17" - $1,000.00; 22" - $1,300.00.

Rare Lenci 9½" "Pan," the mythical Greek figure, with wooden hooves, ca. 1930. Original. Shown with 17½" Kestner mold #183 character girl with painted eyes, open/closed mouth, and molded teeth. On fully jointed body. "Pan" - $2,100.00; 17½" - $4,000.00. *Courtesy Frasher Doll Auctions.*

10¼" "winking" Lenci character boy. Painted facial features with thick curled lashes, open/closed mouth with painted teeth. Ca. mid-1920's. Original. 11" - $2,800.00. *Courtesy Frasher Doll Auctions.*

"Surprise Eyes" Doll: Very round painted eyes and O-shaped mouth. 15" - $1,900.00; 19" - $2,500.00. **Flirty glass eyes:** 15" - $2,500.00; 19" - $3,200.00.

Teenager: Long-legged child. 16-17" - $1,100.00 up.

Boys: Side part hairdo, excellent condition. 18" - $2,200.00 up; 23" - $2,600.00. **Poor condition:** 18" - $850.00; 23" - $975.00. **In Fascist uniform:** 17" - $1,800.00 up.

Lenci Type: Can be made in Italy, Germany, France, Spain, or England. 1920's through 1940's. Felt and cloth.

Child: Felt or cloth, mohair wig, cloth body. Original clothes. 16" - $775.00; 18" - $850.00.

Small Dolls: Dressed as child. 7-8" - $50.00; 12" - $100.00. **In foreign costume:** 7-8" - $35.00.

Front: 20" glass-eyed "Widow Allegra" by Lenci. Felt with oil-painted "surprise" expression, black taffeta costume, felt shoes and decoration. Carries small mohair dog. Back center: 27" Dora Petzold cloth doll (see Series 7, pg. 139) and German-made all cloth man and woman. Marked "Feltscher Puppe 335" on foot. Center seamed face has lithographed features. Ca. 1910. 20" - $3,200.00; 27" - $850.00; German pair - $2,200.00. *Courtesy Frasher Doll Auctions.*

19" all original Lenci. All felt with oil-painted features. Felt and organdy clothes. 19" - $1,800.00.

20" all felt Lenci girl with painted features. Jointed neck, shoulders and hips. All original felt clothes. 20" - $1,800.00. *Courtesy Frasher Doll Auctions.*

Left: All original 21" surprise-eyed character with painted features. 16" "Red Devil" character by Lenci with cloth tag and felt horns. Center: 18" Lenci brown South Seas girl with long slender limbs and pregnant torso, original. 16" Lenci boy in sailor suit with brass emblem "M.N. Vulcania," original. 11" "Bambi" by Lenci with oval paper tag, celluloid eyes with felt eyelids. Butterfly on tail. Upper right: 15½" all original Dean's Rag Book girl with oil-painted cloth face, cloth body and limbs. Original. Lower right: 18" character girl from 1300 series. Plump cheeks, pouty expression, all original. 21" - $2,600.00; 16" - $700.00; 18" islander - $2,800.00; 16" sailor - $1,600.00; Bambi - $475.00; 15½" - $675.00; 18" girl - $1,600.00. *Courtesy Frasher Doll Auctions.*

LIMBACH

These dolls were made mostly from 1893 into the 1920's by Limbach Porzellanfabrik, Limbach, Germany. Allow more for excellent bisque and artist workmanship.

Mark:

MADE IN GERMANY

Child: 1893–1899, 1919 and after. Incised with clover mark. Bisque head, open mouth, glass eyes. Jointed body. No damage and nicely dressed. 15" - $600.00; 17" - $950.00; 20" - $1,100.00; 23" - $1,300.00.

Same as above, with closed mouth: 15" - $1,600.00; 17" - $1,900.00; 20" - $2,200.00; 23" - $2,800.00.

Same as above, with incised name: Ca. 1919. Incised names such as "Norma," "Rita," "Wally," etc. 17" - $550.00; 20" - $625.00; 23" - $725.00.

LORI

The "Lori Baby" is marked "D Lori 4" with green stamp "Geschuz S & Co." and was made by Swaine & Co. It has lightly painted hair, sleep eyes, open/closed mouth, and on five-piece bent limb baby body.

Glass Eyes: (See photo in Series 7, pg. 122.) 14" - $1,400.00; 20" - $2,200.00; 23" - $2,800.00; 26" - $3,300.00.

Intaglio Eyes: (See photo in Series 6, pg. 138.) 20" - $2,000.00; 24" - $2,500.00.

Flocked Hair: 20" - $2,700.00; 25" - $3,400.00.

Far right: 16" "Lori Baby" marked "232/5" with painted hair, sleep eyes, open mouth, holds Victorian baby rattle. Shown with 8" painted bisque, all original, "Just Me," #310-A.M., 16" Kley & Hahn #154-6 on bent limb baby body, open mouth, cotton dress. Far left: 14½" Kammer & Reinhardt #116A with open/closed mouth. "Lori Baby" - $1,500.00; "Just Me" - $775.00; Kley & Hahn - $1,400.00; Kammer & Reinhardt - $2,800.00; Rattle - $350.00. *Courtesy Frasher Doll Auctions.*

Mascotte Dolls were made by May Freres Cie. They operated from 1890 to 1897, then became part of Jules Steiner in 1898. This means the dolls were made from 1890 to about 1902, so the quality of the bisque can vary greatly, as well as the artist painting. Dolls will be marked "BÉBÉ MASCOTTE PARIS" and some will be incised with "M" and a number.

Child: Closed mouth and marked "Mascotte." Excellent condition and no damage. (See photo in Series 8, pg. 128.) 14" - $3,600.00; 17" - $4,600.00; 19" - $4,900.00; 23" - $5,800.00; 27" - $6,300.00.

Child: Same as above, but marked with "M" and a number. 14" - $3,000.00; 17" - $3,500.00; 19" - $4,000.00; 23" - $4,600.00; 27" - $5,200.00.

24" marked "Mascotte" with closed mouth, fully jointed French body. 24" - $5,900.00. *Courtesy Frasher Doll Auctions.*

MECHANICALS

A. Theroude mechanical walker patented in 1840 with papier maché head, bamboo teeth in open mouth and stands on three wheels (two large and one small), tin cart with mechanism attached to legs. 16" - $3,600.00.

Autoperipatetikos: Base is like clockworks and has tin feet and when key wound, the doll walks. Heads can be china, untinted bisque or papier maché. **Early China Head:** 11" - $1,800.00. **Untinted Bisque:** 11" - $1,300.00. **Papier maché:** 11" - $900.00.

Hawkins, George: Walker with pewter hands and feet, wood torso. Hands modeled to push a carriage, which should be a Goodwin, patented in 1867–1868. Carriage has two large wheels and a small one in front. Molded hair and dolls head will be marked "X.L.C.R./Doll head/Pat. Sept. 8, 1868." (China heads may not be marked.) 11" - $2,200.00.

Jumeau: Raises and lowers both arms; head moves. Holds items, such as a hankie and bottle; book and fan, one in each hand. Key wound music box in base. Closed mouth, marked "Jumeau." 15" - $3,900.00 up; 20" - $4,800.00 up. **Same with open mouth:** 15" - $2,500.00 up; 20" - $3,600.00 up.

Jumeau: Marked "Jumeau." Standing or sitting on key wound music box and doll plays an instrument. 14" - $4,000.00 up; 18" - $5,500.00 up.

Jumeau: Marked "Jumeau" walker with one-piece legs, arms jointed at elbows. She raises her arm to an open mouth to throw kisses as head turns. 15" - $2,000.00 up; 22" - $3,000.00 up.

Jumeau: Marked "Jumeau" and stands on three-wheel cart and when cart is pulled, doll's head turns from side to side and arms go up and down. 15" - $3,600.00 up; 18" - $4,600.00 up.

Paris Bébé, R.D., E.D., Eden Bébé: Marked doll standing on key wound music box. Has closed mouth. Holds items in hands and arms move and head nods or moves from side to side. 21" - $5,200.00 up.

Jumeau: 18-20" doll stands at piano built to scale and hands attached to keyboard with rods. Key wound piano. $20,000.00 up.

Steiner, Jules: Bisque head, open mouth with two rows of teeth. Key wound, waltzes in circles, original clothes. Glass eyes, arms move as it dances. 17" - $10,000.00.

Steiner, Jules: Bisque head on composition upper and lower torso-chest, also lower legs and all the arms. Twill-covered sections between parts of body. Key wound, cries, moves head and kicks legs. Open mouth, two rows of teeth. 17" - $2,400.00; 24" - $3,000.00. **Same as above, but bisque torso sections:** 18" - $7,700.00 up.

German Makers: One or two figures on music box, key wound, or pulling cart. Dolls have open mouths. **Marked with name of maker:** $1,600.00 up. **1960's, 1970's:** German-made reproductions of this style dolls. $300.00.

Center: Solid dome baby is rocked in a 12" x 10" reed baby cradle by a bisque head, open mouthed doll. When handle is turned, the cradle rocks and baby cries as music plays. Ca. 1900, Germany. Shown with 19" closed mouth Tete Jumeau doll on left and 29" Tete Jumeau with closed mouth on right. Mechanical - $4,000.00; 19" - $4,800.00; 29" - $6,700.00. *Courtesy Frasher Doll Auctions.*

7½" Gebruder Knoch mechanical clapping boy incised "DRGM Germany." Very character head with intaglio eyes, painted hair. Press stomach and hands clap. 7½" nude - $400.00. *Courtesy Turn of Century Antiques.*

Very unusual "swimmer" doll with cork body, wooden arms with hands modeled in "stroke" position, and wooden jointed legs. Head by Simon & Halbig has glass eyes with eyelashes and original wig. Wears original clothes. Is contained in case with oil-painted ocean background. $1,600.00 up. *Courtesy Ellen Dodge.*

Metal heads made in Germany, 1888-on; United States, 1917-on.

Marks:

(Buschow & Beck)

(Alfred Heller)

JUNO (Karl Standfuss)

Metal Shoulder Head: Cloth or kid body. Molded hair, painted eyes. 14" - $145.00; 17" - $185.00. **Molded hair, glass eyes:** 14" - $185.00; 17" - $250.00. **Wig, glass eyes:** 14" - $250.00; 17" - $300.00; 21" - $385.00.

All Metal Child: Wig or molded hair, fully jointed. Some are also jointed at wrist, elbow, knee, and ankle. Open/closed mouth with painted teeth. Some have metal hands and feet with composition body. 15-16" - $450.00; 19-20" - $550.00.

All Metal Jointed Dolls: Made in Switzerland. Metal ball joints, patented 1921 through 1940. **Man:** 6" - $125.00; 10" - $185.00. **Comic Character:** 6" - $145.00; 10" - $200.00. **Hitler:**

Metal headed baby with painted hair, celluloid over tin sleep eyes, and open mouth. Cloth body with composition limbs. 13" - $185.00. *Courtesy David Spurgeon.*

6" - $200.00; 10" - $250.00. **Chauffeur:** 6" - $145.00; 10" - $185.00. **Animal Head:** 6" - $135.00; 10" 175.00.

Same as above, but with composition heads, hands, and feet: 6" - $100.00 up; 10" - $150.00 up.

Metal Baby: All metal bent baby body. Some are spring jointed. Painted features, wig or molded hair. 13-14" - $125.00. **Glass eyes:** 13-14" - $185.00.

MOLDED HAIR BISQUE

The molded hair bisque dolls are just like any other flesh-toned dolls, but instead of having wigs, they have molded hair, glass set eyes or finely painted and detailed eyes, and generally they will have closed mouths. They almost always are one-piece shoulder heads on kid or cloth bodies with bisque lower arms. Some will have compostion lower legs. These dolls are generally very pretty. Many molded hair dolls are being attributed to A.B.G. (Alt, Beck & Gottschalck) mold **#890, 1000, 1008, 1028, 1064, 1142, 1256, 1288,** etc.

Child: Closed mouth. 6½" - $145.00;
10" - $225.00; 16" - $485.00; 21" -
$775.00; 24" - $1,300.00; 26" - $1,500.00.
   Boy: 17" - $650.00; 20" - $850.00;
23" - $1,200.00.
   Decorated Shoulder Plate: With
elaborate hairdo. 20" - $2,400.00 up.
   Japan: Marked 𝒯𝒴 or ⊕. Bows
on sides of head. Cloth body, long legs,
black silk feet, oilcloth arms. 17" -
$250.00; 20" - $375.00.

15" Kling molded hair bisque. Marked with
number "131-4." Glass set eyes, closed
mouth, and partially exposed ears. 15" -
$485.00. *Courtesy Turn of Century Antiques.*

Beautiful 32" marked "B.6M." by
Mothereau. Closed mouth with
white space between lips. On
jointed French body with straight
wrists. 32" - $32,000.00; 25" -
$27,000.00-24,000.00; 18" -
$16,000.00-18,000.00. *Courtesy
Frasher Doll Auctions.*

Charles Motschmann has always been credited as the manufacturer of a certain style doll, but now his work is only being attributed to the making of the voice boxes in the dolls. Various German makers such as Heinrich Stier and others are being given the credit for making the dolls. They date from 1851 into the 1880's.

The early dolls were babies, children and Orientals. They have glass eyes, closed mouths, heads of papier maché, wax over papier maché or wax over composition. They can have lightly brush stroked painted hair or come with a wig. If the mouth is open, the doll will have bamboo teeth. The larger dolls will have arms and legs jointed at wrists and ankles. The lower torso and lower arms and legs are composition or wood; the upper torso and upper arms and legs are twill cloth. The mid-section will also be cloth. If the doll is marked, it can be found on the upper cloth of the leg and will be stamped:

Baby: Motschmann marked or type. **In extremely fine condition:** 13" - $650.00; 16" - $800.00; 20" - $1,100.00; 25" - $1,500.00. **In fair condition:** 13" - $400.00; 16" - $525.00; 20" - $675.00; 25" - $800.00.

Child: In extremely fine condition: 15" - $900.00; 18" - $1,000.00; 23" - $1,500.00. **In fair condition:** 15" - $425.00; 18" - $685.00; 23" - $825.00.

Child: Bisque with cloth at waist and mid-limbs. 18" - $6,900.00 up.

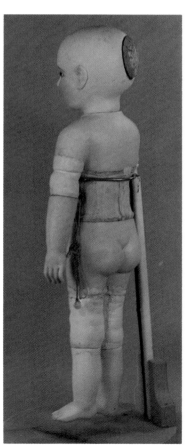

Motschmann style body. Most will have composition/cloth body parts. A rare one, such as this, has bisque body parts. 18" - $6,900.00 up.

Munich Art character dolls were designed by Marion Kaulitz, 1908–1912. Composition, painted features, on fully jointed body. 13-14" - $2,300.00. **Fair condition:** 18-19" - $3,800.00; 13-14" - $1,150.00; 18-19" - $1,650.00.

19" Munich Art girl with wonderful character face. All original. Composition with hand-painted features. 19" - $3,800.00. *Courtesy Shirley Bertrand.*

ORIENTAL DOLLS

Bisque dolls with fired-in Oriental color and on jointed yellowish tinted bodies were made in Germany by various firms. They could be children or babies and most were made after 1900. Must be in excellent condition and in Oriental clothes with no damage to head. **Amusco, Mold #1006:** Bisque head. 14-15" - $1,000.00.

Armand Marseille: Girl or boy marked only "A.M." 6" - $575.00; 8-9" - $725.00. **Painted bisque:** Excellent condition. 8" - $265.00; 12" - $475.00.

#353 Baby: 12" - $1,150.00; 15" - $1,350.00; 17" - $1,600.00. **Painted bisque:** 15" - $650.00.

Bruno Schmidt (BSW) #220: Closed mouth. 16" - $3,850.00.

#500 (BSW): 14" - $2,000.00; 16" - $2,300.00. **All bisque:** 6" - $685.00.

Kestner (J.D.K.) #243: Baby: 14" - $5,000.00; 17" - $6,500.00. **Molded hair baby:** 14" - $5,200.00. **Child:** 15" - $5,400.00; 18" - $7,600.00. **All bisque:** 6" - $1,250.00.

Schoenau & Hoffmeister, #4900: (S, PB in star H) See photo in Series 5, pg. 116.) 16" - $1,800.00; 20" - $2,100.00.

Simon & Halbig (S & H) #164: 16" - $2,300.00; 19" - $2,700.00.

#220: (See photo in Series 6, pg.

21" marked "SH 1129." Almond-cut glass sleep eyes, open mouth and on fully jointed body. 21" - $3,500.00. *Courtesy Frasher Doll Auctions.*

13" baby marked "F Made in Germany 10/243 J.D.K." Glass sleep eyes, open mouth, and on five-piece bent limb baby body. Original costume. 20" marked "S&H 1099 DEP" and red stamp "Wimpern." Slanted glass eyes with hair lashes, open mouth, on French-style jointed body with long slender fingers. 13" original - $4,800.00; 20" - $3,500.00. *Courtesy Frasher Doll Auctions.*

13" marked "AMUSCO/1006" with papier maché shoulder head, inset almond-shaped glass eyes, closed mouth. Mohair wig with queue braid in back. Cloth body with composition limbs. Original silk and elaborate embroidered outfit. 13" - $600.00. *Courtesy Glorya Woods.*

145.) Solid dome or "Belton" type. Closed mouth. 16" - $3,300.00.

#1099, 1129, 1159, 1199: (See photo in Series 7, pg. 129.) 15" - $2,850.00; 19" - $3,500.00.

#1329: (See photo in Series 7, pg. 129.) 13" - $1,900.00; 18" - $2,800.00.

All Bisque: Unmarked. 7-8" - $800.00.

Unmarked: Open mouth. 14" - $1,200.00; 18" - $1,800.00. **Closed mouth:** 14" - $1,800.00; 18" - $2,600.00. **All bisque:** Glass eyes. 6" - $485.00; 10-11" - $885.00 up.

Nippon – Caucasian Dolls Made in Japan: 1918–1922. Most made during World War I. These dolls can be near excellent quality to very poor quality. Morimura Brothers mark is ⊛. Dolls marked 𝓕𝓨 were made by Yamato. Others will just be marked with NIPPON along with other marks such as "J.W."

Nippon Marked Baby: Good to excellent bisque, well painted, nice body and no damage. 10" - $165.00; 12" - $200.00; 15" - $285.00; 21" - $425.00; 24" - $775.00. **Poor quality:** 12" - $125.00; 16" - $175.00; 20" - $265.00; 25" - $365.00. **"Hilda" look-alike:** Excellent quality. 15" - $700.00; 18" - $950.00. Medium quality: 15" - $500.00; 18" - $745.00.

Nippon Child: Good to excellent quality bisque, no damage and nicely dressed. 14" - $265.00; 17" - $325.00; 22" - $650.00. **Poor quality:** 15" - $135.00; 19" - $225.00; 23" - $325.00.

Molded Hair: Molded bows on side, cloth body, oilcloth lower arms, silk feet. Marked 𝓕𝓨 or ⊛. 1920 – 1930's. 14" - $275.00; 17" - $400.00.

Traditional Doll: Made in Japan. Papier maché swivel head on shoulder plate, cloth mid-section and upper arms and legs. Limbs and torso are papier

12" Oriental baby with bisque head and limbs, original. Black pupilless eyes. 12" - **$225.00** up. *Courtesy Turn of Century Antiques.*

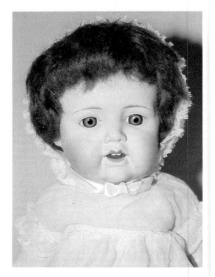

18" marked "FY #76018/Nippon/605." Bisque head with set eyes, open mouth and excellent quality bisque. On five-piece bent limb baby body. 18" - $365.00. *Courtesy Kathy Tvrdik.*

maché, glass eyes, pierced nostrils. The early dolls will have jointed wrists and ankles and will be slightly sexed.

Early fine quality: Original dress, 1890's. 14" - $350.00; 19" - $575.00; 26" - $1,000.00.

Early Boy: With painted hair. 17" - $475.00; 22" - $800.00; 26" - $1,200.00. **1930's or later:** 14" - $145.00; 17" - $265.00. **1940's:** 13" - $85.00.

Lady: All original and excellent quality. 1920's: 12" - $200.00; 16" - $285.00. **Later Lady:** 1940's–1950's. 12" - $85.00; 14" - $100.00.

Emperor or Empress in Sitting Position: 1920's–1930's. 4-5" - $100.00; 8" - $175.00 up; 12" - $300.00 up.

8½" lady with crushed oyster shell paste head and inset pupilless eyes. This is the Seven Hat scene from *Dohjohji*, a famous Japanese drama. 8½" - **$95.00.** *Courtesy Kathy Tvrdik.*

Warrior: 1880's–1890's: 16-18" - $650.00 up. **On horse:** 16" - $1,200.00 up. **Early 1920's:** 12" - $300.00 up. **On horse:** 12" - $800.00 up.

Japanese Baby: With bisque head. Sleep eyes, closed mouth and all white bisque. Papier maché body: Original and in excellent condition. Late 1920's. 8" - $75.00; 12" - $100.00. **Glass eyes:** 8" - $125.00; 12" - $225.00.

Japanese Baby: Head made of crushed oyster shells painted flesh color, papier maché body, glass eyes and original. 8" - $65.00; 12" - $95.00; 16" - $145.00; 19" - $200.00.

Oriental Dolls: All composition, jointed at shoulder and hips. Painted features, painted hair or can have bald head with braid of yarn down back with rest covered by cap, such as "Ling

Large 27" lady with composition/clay head covered with crushed oyster shell paste, and painted eyes. Attached to wooden stand. She is one of the Kakata Ning Yo dolls made after dancers and actors. 27" - **$400.00.** *Courtesy Kathy Tvrdik.*

Ling" or "Ming Ming" made by Quan Quan Co. in 1930's. Painted-on shoes. 10" - $175.00.
Chinese Traditional Dolls: Man or woman. Composition-type material with cloth-wound bodies or can have wooden carved arms and feet. In traditional costume and in excellent condition. 9" - $350.00; 12" - $575.00.
Door of Hope Dolls: (See also Door of Hope section.) Wooden heads, cloth bodies and most have carved hands. Chinese costume. **Adult:** 9" - $625.00. **Child:** 7" - $525.00. **Mother and Baby:** 11" - $725.00. **Man:** 9" - $625.00. **Carved flowers in hair:** 12" - $800.00. **Brides:** 12" - $825.00.

5" traditional Japanese baby made of crushed oyster shell paste and painted. Pupilless eyes and original. 5" - $50.00.
Courtesy Kathy Tvrdik.

P.D.

P.D. marked dolls were made in Paris, France by Petit & DuMontier, 1878–1890. (See Series 8, pg. 77.)

Child: Closed mouth, jointed body, metal hands. No damage, nicely dressed. 16" - $17,000.00; 19" - $19,000.00; 22" - $23,000.00; 24" - $28,000.00; 26" - $30,000.00.

P.G.

Pintel & Godchaux of Montreuil, France made dolls from 1890 to 1899. They held one trademark – "Bébé Charmant." The heads will be marked "P.G."

Child: 16" - $2,400.00; 21" - $2,900.00; 25" - $3,800.00.
Child, Open Mouth: 15" - $1,300.00; 20" - $2,000.00; 23" - $2,500.00.

PAPIER MACHÉ

Papier maché dolls were made in U.S., Germany, England, France and other countries. Paper pulp, wood and rag fibers containing paste, oil or glue are formed into a composition-like moldable material. Flour, clay and/or sand is added for stiffness. The hardness of papier maché depends on the amount of glue that is added.

Many so called papier maché parts were actually laminated paper with several thicknesses of molded paper bonded (glued) together or pressed after being glued.

"Papier maché" means "chewed paper" in French, and as early as 1810, dolls of papier maché were being mass produced by using molds.

Marked "M&S Superior": (Muller & Strassburger) Papier maché shoulder head with blonde or black molded hair, painted blue or brown eyes, old cloth body with kid or leather arms and boots. Nicely dressed and head not repainted, chipped or cracked. 16" - $400.00; 18"- $600.00; 24" - $750.00. **Glass eyes:** 20" - $850.00. **With wig:** 18" - $775.00. **Repainted nicely:** 16" - $275.00; 21" - $450.00. **Chips, scuffs or not repainted well:** 16" - $95.00; 21" - $110.00.

French or French Type: (See photos in Series 5, pg. 151; Series 7, pg. 133.) Painted black hair, some with brush marks, on solid dome. Some have nailed-on wigs. Open mouths have bamboo teeth. Inset glass eyes. In very good condition, nice old clothes. All leather/kid body. 16" - $1,300.00; 19" - $1,700.00; 23" - $2,100.00; 26" - $2,500.00; 30" - $3,300.00. **Wooden jointed body:** 7-8" - $865.00. **Painted eyes:** 7" - $425.00; 15" - $900.00.

23" French papier maché with solid dome shoulder head with painted hair. Open mouth with tiny ivory upper and lower teeth. Kid body and limbs. 23" - **$2,100.00.** *Courtesy Frasher Doll Auctions.*

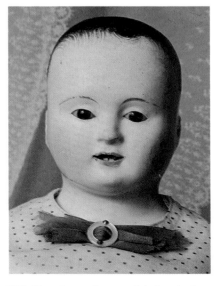

29" French papier maché by Andres Voit, 1816–1860. Glass eyes, brush stroked painted hair, open mouth with two rows of bamboo teeth. Cloth/leather body, individual stitched fingers. 29" - **$3,200.00.** *Courtesy Turn of Century Antiques.*

Early Papier Maché: (See photo in Series 6, pg. 153.) With cloth body and wooden limbs. Early hairdo with top knots, buns, puff curls or braiding. Not restored and in original or very well made clothes. In very good condition but may show a little wear. 12" - $525.00; 14" - $675.00; 18" - $900.00; 21" - $1,200.00; 25" - $1,500.00. **Glass eyes:** 20" - $1,900.00. **Flirty eyes:** 20" - $2,500.00.

Long Curls: 9" - $625.00; 13" - $750.00.

Covered Wagon/Flat Top Hairdo: 7" - $345.00; 11" - $525.00; 14-15" - $685.00.

1820's – 1860's (Milliner's Models): Braided bun, side curls: 9-10" - $785.00; 13-14" - $1,250.00. **Side curls with high top knot:** 12" - $1,000.00; 17" - $1,900.00. **Coiled braids over ears, braided bun:** 19-20" - $2,200.00 up. **Braided bun, coiled braids at ears:** 18" - $1,800.00.

9" papier maché called "Milliner's Model." Leather body with wooden limbs. Original clothes. Modeled long curls around head. 9" - $785.00. *Courtesy Ellen Dodge.*

Marked "Greiner": Dolls of 1858 on: Blonde or black molded hair, brown or blue painted eyes, cloth body with leather arms, nicely dressed and with very little minor scuffs. See Greiner section.

Motschmann Types: With wood and twill bodies. Separate hip section, glass eyes, closed mouth and brush stroke hair on solid domes. Nicely dressed and ready to display. 15" - $725.00; 21" - $975.00; 25" - $1,500.00.

German Papier Maché: 1870–1900's. Various molded hairdos, painted eyes and closed mouth. May be blonde

32" Greiner-type unmarked papier maché shoulder head with painted features and blonde hair. Cloth body with leather arms. 32" - $950.00. *Courtesy Frasher Doll Auctions.*

or black hair. Nicely dressed and not repainted. 14" - $275.00; 17" - $365.00; 19" - $450.00; 23" - $525.00; 25" - $600.00; 30" - $850.00. **Glass eyes:** 14" - $485.00; 17" - $600.00. **Showing wear and scuffs, but not touched up:** 17" - $225.00; 21" - $300.00; 25" - $350.00; 30" - $450.00.

Turned Shoulder Head: Solid dome, glass eyes, closed mouth. Twill cloth body with composition lower arms. In very good condition and nicely dressed. 17" - $700.00; 22" - $950.00.

German Character Heads: (See photo in Series 6, pg. 152.) These heads are molded just like the bisque ones. Glass eyes, closed mouth and on fully jointed body. In excellent condition and nicely dressed. 15" - $1,000.00 up; 21" - $1,500.00 up.

1920's on – Papier Maché: Head usually has bright coloring. Wigged, usually dressed as a child, or in provincial costumes. Stuffed cloth body and limbs or have papier maché arms. In excellent overall condition. 8" - $75.00; 12" - $125.00; 14" - $200.00.

Clowns: Papier maché head with painted clown features. Open or closed mouth, molded hair or wigged and on cloth body with some having composition or papier maché lower arms. In excellent condition. 10" - $250.00; 14" - $485.00.

PARIAN-TYPE (UNTINTED BISQUE)

"Parian-type" dolls were made from the 1850's to the 1880's, with the majority being made during the 1870's and 1880's. There are hundreds of different heads, and all seem to have been made in Germany. If there is a mark, it will be found on the inside of the shoulder plate. It must be noted that the very rare and unique unglazed porcelain dolls are difficult to find and their prices will be high.

"Parian-type" dolls can be found with every imaginable thing applied to the head and shirt tops – flowers, snoods, ruffles, feathers, plumes, etc. Many have inset glass eyes, pierced ears and most are blonde, although some will have from light to medium brown hair, and a few will have glazed black hair.

Various Fancy Hairstyles: (See photo in Series 5, pg. 121.) With molded combs, ribbons, flowers, head bands, or snoods. Cloth body with cloth/Parian-type limbs. Glass eyes. Perfect condition and very nicely

18" rare swivel head Parian with Parian shoulder plate. Brownish sausage curls around head, painted features with blue glass eyes. Cloth body with Parian limbs. Beautiful original costume. 18" - $3,000.00 up. *Courtesy Ellen Dodge.*

dressed. 18" - $1,800.00 up; 22" - $2,300.00 up. **Painted eyes, unpierced ears:** 18" - $1,200.00; 22" - $1,600.00.

Swivel Neck: Glass eyes. 18" - $3,000.00; 22" - $3,600.00.

Molded Necklaces: Jewels or standing ruffles (undamaged). **Glass eyes, pierced ears:** 18" - $1,900.00 up; 22" - $2,500.00 up. **Painted eyes, unpierced ears:** 18" - $1,200.00; 22" - $1,600.00.

Bald Head: Solid dome, takes wigs, full ear detail. 1850's. Perfect condition and nicely dressed. 13" - $775.00; 17" - $995.00; 21" - $1,600.00.

Molded Head Band: (See photo in Series 5, pg. 121; Series 7, pg. 137.)

Called "Alice." 13" - $385.00; 16" - $600.00; 19" - $900.00.

Very Plain Style: With no decoration in hair or on shoulders. No damage and nicely dressed. 10" - $175.00; 15" - $350.00; 20" - $485.00; 24" - $575.00.

Men or Boys: Hairdos with center or side part, cloth body with cloth/ Parian-type limbs. Decorated shirt and tie. 16" - $900.00; 19" - $1,300.00.

Undecorated Shirt Top: 16" - $285.00; 19" - $500.00; 25" - $785.00.

Molded Hat: (See photos in Series 8, pg. 140.) Painted eyes. 15" - $2,200.00; 18" - $2,800.00 up. **Glass eyes:** 14" - $2,600.00; 16" - $3,100.00; 20" - $3,900.00.

Left: 17" Parian with center part, hair pulled back over ribbon. Cloth body, bisque lower arms. Behind her is 20" Parian with hair pulled back into braid with ribbon. Glass eyes, kid body, bisque lower arms. Center: Mold #172 "Gibson Girl" by Kestner that is 20" tall. Right: 23½" slender face bisque with closed mouth on marked Jumeau adult body. 17" - $600.00; 20" Parian - $800.00; 20" "Gibson Girl" - $3,800.00; 23½" - $7,700.00. *Courtesy Frasher Doll Auctions.*

PARIAN-TYPE (UNTINTED BISQUE)

Right: 23" fancy hairdo Parian with glass eyes, pierced ears and leather arms on cloth body. Left: 28" Parian with glass eyes and boy or girl hairdo. 23" - $2,300.00; 28" - $1,900.00.
Courtesy Turn of Century Antiques.

24" "Alice in Wonderland" Parian with white porcelain and painted features. Comb marked molded hair and black head band. Cloth body. 24" - $950.00.
Courtesy Frasher Doll Auctions.

PARIS BÉBÉ

These dolls were made by Danel & Cie in France from 1889 to 1895. The heads will be marked "Paris Bébé" and the body's paper label will be marked with a drawing of the Eiffel Tower and "Paris Bébé/Brevete."

Paris Bébé Child: Closed mouth, no damage and nicely dressed. 17" - $4,600.00; 21" - $5,000.00; 25" - $5,650.00; 27" - $5,800.00. **High color to bisque, closed mouth:** 17" - $3,200.00; 21" - $3,600.00; 25" - $4,000.00; 27" - $4,300.00.

18" "Paris Bébé" with paperweight eyes and closed mouth that is highly colored. On French jointed body. Original clothes. (See full length photo in Series 7, pg. 138.) 18" with high color - $3,700.00.
Courtesy Frasher Doll Auctions.

19" "Paris Bébé" by Danel & Cie. Marked Tete Depose Paris Bebe 8." Closed mouth. Fully jointed body marked "Depose Paris Bébé." 19" - $4,800.00. *Courtesy Frasher Doll Auctions.*

PHÉNIX (ALEXANDRE, HENRI)

Phénix Bébé dolls were made by Henri Alexandre of Paris who made dolls from 1885 to 1901. The company was sold to Tourel in 1892 and Jules Steiner in 1895.

Mark:

(1885–1891)

22" marked with star symbol/93. Closed mouth, eyebrows almost meet, large eyes, jointed French body. 12" and 6" printed cloth pug dog dolls. 22" - $5,400.00; dogs $135.00. *Courtesy Frasher Doll Auctions.*

147

Child, closed mouth: #81: 10" - $1,800.00. **#85:** 14" - $3,200.00. **#88:** 17" - $4,400.00. **#90:** 18" - $4,600.00. **#91:** 19-21" - $4,900.00. **#93:** 22" - $5,400.00. **#94:** 23-24" - $5,500.00. **#95:** 23-25" - $5,600.00.

Child, open mouth: 17" - $2,000.00; 19" - $2,300.00; 23" - $2,700.00; 25" - $3,000.00.

1885–1891: Perfect, early jointed body, beautiful clothes, closed mouth, glass eyes. 15" - $3,600.00; 17½" - $4,800.00. Marked:

PIANO BABIES

Piano babies were made in Germany from the 1880's into the 1930's and one of the finest quality makers was Gebruder Heubach. They were also made by Kestner, Dressel, Limbach, etc. A number of these figures were reproduced in the late 1960's to late 1970's. Painting and skin tones will not be as "soft" as old ones.

Piano Babies: All bisque, unjointed, molded hair and painted features. The clothes are molded on and they come in a great variety of positions.

Excellent Quality: Extremely good artist workmanship and excellent detail to modeling. 4" - $190.00; 8" - $450.00 up; 12" - $750.00 up; 16" - $900.00 up.

Medium Quality: May not have painting finished on back side of figure. 4" - $125.00; 8" - $265.00; 12" - $400.00; 16" - $550.00.

With Animal, Pot, On Chair, With Flowers or Other Items: (See photos in Series 6, pg. 158; Series 7, pg. 141.) Excellent quality. 4" - $250.00; 8" - $450.00; 12" - $825.00 up; 16" - $1,200.00 up.

Black: Excellent quality: 4" - $365.00; 8" - $475.00; 12" - $625.00; 16" - $1,000.00 up. **Medium quality:** 4" - $165.00; 8" - $250.00; 12" - $400.00; 16" - $800.00.

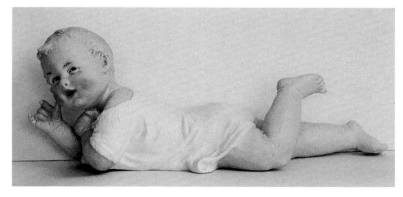

8" beautiful piano baby with excellent modeling and detail to hair. Intaglio eyes and open/closed mouth. Made by Gebruder Heubach. 8" - $450.00. *Courtesy Ellen Dodge.*

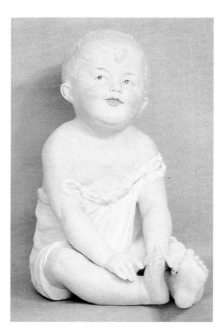

10" piano baby with a great look and excellent detail. Made by Gebruder Heubach (marked). 10" - $600.00. *Courtesy Ellen Dodge.*

6" x 5½" marked Heubach piano baby holding toe to mouth. Excellent quality and modeling. 13½" Kestner baby with mold #247. Original factory clothes. 6" - $650.00; 13½" - $1,600.00. *Courtesy Frasher Doll Auctions.*

8" piano baby with intaglio eyes, modeled-on chemise. Marked "3102" plus a "28" and "23." Also sunburst Gebruder Heubach mark. 8" - $450.00. *Courtesy Ellen Dodge.*

RABERY & DELPHIEU

Rabery & Delphieu began making dolls in 1856. The very first dolls have kid bodies and are extremely rare. Most of their dolls are on French jointed bodies and are marked "R.D." A few may be marked "Bébé de Paris."

Child: With closed mouth, in excellent condition with no chips, breaks or hairlines in bisque. Body in overall good condition and nicely dressed. Pretty face. 12" - $2,600.00; 16" - $3,100.00; 19" - $3,600.00; 22" - $3,900.00; 24" - $4,400.00; 27" - $5,300.00.

Child: With open mouth and same condition as above. 15" - $1,200.00; 19" - $1,900.00; 22" - $2,500.00; 24" - $3,000.00; 28" - $3,300.00.

Child: Lesser quality, high color, poor artist workmanship. **Closed mouth:** 16" - $2,100.00; 19" - $2,600.00; 22" - $2,800.00. **Same, open mouth:** 15" - $675.00; 19" - $900.00; 22" - $1,050.00.

17½" marked "ROD." Heavy feather eyebrows, paperweight glass eyes, and closed mouth. On French jointed body. 17½" - **$3,200.00.** *Courtesy Frasher Doll Auctions.*

RAVCA, BERNARD

Bernard Ravca made dolls in Paris from 1924 to the mid-1930's when he moved to New York. The dolls were stitched stockinette characters and personalities. If made in France, doll will bear a label marked "Original Ravca/ Fabrication Francaise" or a wrist tag "Original Ravca" plus handwritten name of doll. Some of the dolls will be cloth and stockinette, some with cloth body and limbs, and others will be a gesso/ papier maché combination. His dolls can range in size from 7" to 35."

Peasants/Old People: 7" - $85.00; 9" - $95.00; 12" - $125.00; 15" - $200.00 up.

Character from books/poems: 7" - $100.00 up; 9" - $125.00 up; 12" - $165.00 up; 15" - $200.00 up; 17" - $285.00 up.

Gesso/Papier Maché and cloth dolls: Personality figures. 12" - $400.00; 15" - $565.00; 17" - $985.00; 20" - $1,425.00.

Military Figures: Such as Hitler, Mussolini. 17" - $1,000.00; 20" - $1,800.00; 27" - $4,000.00 up.

Above: Three 17" dolls made by Bernard Ravca. Each doll is made of gesso, cloth, and papier maché. Left: "Thomas Dewey." Excellent likeness. Center: "Bob Hope" has original price tag of $49.95 from a department store, "Wolf & Cessauer." Arm tag has Ravca name and name of character. Right "Lauren Bacall" with extremely well detailed hair. Wrist tag has name of Ravca as well as character. Each - $1,000.00. *Courtesy Christine Perisho.*

Right: 14" organ grinder with stockinette hand sculptured features and hands. The rest of the body is cloth. Wooden box that plays music. 14" - $200.00 up. *Courtesy Christine Perisho.*

RECKNAGEL OF ALEXANDRINENTHAL

Dolls marked with "R.A." were made by Recknagel of Alexandrinenthal, Thuringia, Germany. The R.A. dolls date from 1886 to after World War I and can range from very poor to excellent quality bisque and artist workmanship. Prices are for dolls with good artist workmanship, such as the lips and eyebrows painted straight, feathered or at least not off-center. Original or nicely dressed and no damage.

Child: 1890's–1914. Set or sleep eyes, open mouth with small dolls having painted-on shoes and socks. 8" - $165.00; 12" - $225.00; 16" - $325.00; 20" - $425.00; 23" - $625.00.

#1907, 1909, 1914, etc.: 8" - $185.00; 12" - $275.00; 16" - $365.00; 20" - $475.00; 23" - $700.00.

Baby: Ca. 1909–1910 on. Five-piece bent limb baby body or straight leg, curved arm toddler body and with sleep or set eyes. No damage and nicely dressed. 7" - $245.00; 9" - $275.00; 12" - $350.00; 16" - $475.00; 20" - $575.00.

Character: With painted eyes, modeled bonnet and open/closed mouth, some smiling, some with painted-in teeth. No damage and nicely dressed. 8" - $685.00; 12" - $950.00.

Character: Glass eyes, closed mouth, and composition bent limb baby body. 7" - $685.00; 10" - $865.00; 14" - $1,000.00.

9" character girl with molded hair and stand up hair ribbon. Crude five-piece body with painted-on shoes and socks. Open/closed mouth with lower teeth. May have been made by Recknagel about 1909. 9" - $950.00. *Courtesy Jane Walker.*

REINECKE, OTTO

Dolls marked "P.M." were made by Otto Reinecke of Hof-Moschendorf, Bavaria, Germany from 1909 into the 1930's. The mold number found most often is the **#914** baby or toddler. (See photo in Series 7, pg. 144.)

Child: Bisque head with open mouth and on five-piece papier maché body or fully jointed body. Can have sleep or set eyes. No damage and nicely dressed. 10" - $165.00; 14" - $275.00; 17" - $450.00; 21" - $575.00.

Baby: Open mouth, sleep eyes or set eyes. Bisque head on five-piece bent limb baby body. No damage and nicely dressed. 10" - $185.00; 12" - $245.00; 15" - $325.00; 21" - $475.00; 26" - $700.00.

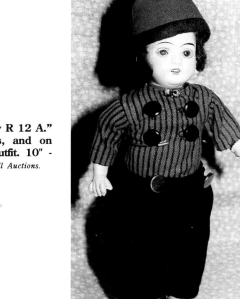

10" marked "21 Germany R 12 A."
Open mouth, sleep eyes, and on
five-piece body. Original outfit. 10" -
$165.00. *Courtesy Frasher Doll Auctions.*

SCHMIDT, BRUNO

Bruno Schmidt's doll factory was located in Waltershausen, Germany and many of the heads used by this firm were made by Bahr & Proschild, Ohrdruf, Germany. They made dolls from 1898 on into the 1930's.

Mark:

2033-6

Child: Bisque head on jointed body, sleep eyes, open mouth, no damage and nicely dressed. 16" - $500.00; 20" - $700.00; 25" - $950.00. **Flirty eyes:** 21" - $900.00; 29" - $1,500.00.

Character Baby, Toddler or Child: Bisque head, glass eyes or painted eyes, jointed body, no damage and nicely dressed.

#2025, 2026: Closed mouth, glass eyes. 20" - $4,300.00. **Painted eyes:** 16" - $1,700.00.

#2069: Closed mouth, glass eyes, sweet face, jointed body. 13" - $4,000.00; 17" - $6,500.00.

#2048, 2094, 2096: Called "Tommy Tucker." (See photo in Series 6, pg. 163.) Molded, painted hair, open mouth. 14" - $1,300.00; 18" - $1,500.00; 23" - $1,750.00; 26" - $1,950.00.

#2048, 2094, 2096: "Tommy Tucker" with closed mouth. Otherwise, same as above. (See photo in Series 8,

17" character girl marked "BSW" in heart and "529." Painted features, closed mouth, and on fully jointed body. 17" - $5,800.00. *Courtesy Frasher Doll Auctions.*

pg. 146.) 14" - $2,000.00; 18" - $2,600.00; 23" - $3,000.00.

#2072: Closed mouth, glass eyes, wig. 18" - $3,600.00. **Toddler:** 22" - $4,350.00.

#2097: Toddler: 15" - $700.00; 21" - $1,000.00. **Baby:** 14" - $550.00; 18" - $850.00.

Character Child: Closed mouth, painted eyes or glass eyes, jointed child body, no damage and nicely dressed.

Marked "BSW" in heart: No mold number. (See photo in Series 6, pg. 164.) 17" - $2,700.00; 21" - $3,200.00.

#529: Also marked with "BSW" in heart. Closed mouth, painted eyes. 16-17" - $5,800.00.

#2033 "Wendy": (See photo in Series 6, pg. 163.) 13" - $18,000.00; 16" - $21,000.00 up; 20" - $24,000.00 up.

Both of these 14" dolls are called "Wendy" and they are marked "2033/ BSW" in heart and "531." They have fully jointed bodies. Girl may have original clothes and wig. Each - $19,000.00; Original - $24,000.00. *Courtesy Frasher Doll Auctions.*

Franz Schmidt & Co. began in 1890 at Georgenthal, near Waltershausen, Germany. In 1902, they registered the cross hammers with a doll between and also the F.S.&Co. mark.

Mark:

1310
F.S. & Co.
Made in
Germany
10

Baby: Bisque head on bent limb baby body, sleep or set eyes, open mouth and some may have pierced nostrils. No damage and nicely dressed. (Add more for toddler body.)

#1271, 1272, 1295, 1296, 1297, 1310: 12" - $450.00; 14" - $575.00; 20" - $775.00; 25" - $1,300.00. **Toddler:** 8-9" - $675.00; 15" - $785.00; 21" - $1,150.00; 25" - $1,400.00.

#1267: (See photo in Series 5, pg. 126.) Open/closed mouth, painted eyes. 14" - $2,800.00; 19" - $3,800.00. **Glass eyes:** 16" - $3,600.00; 21" -$4,600.00.

#1285: 16" - $800.00; 22" - $1,000.00.

Child: Papier maché and composition body with walker mechanism with metal rollers on feet. Open mouth, sleep eyes. Working and no damage to head, nicely dressed.

#1250: 14" - $725.00; 20" - $950.00.

#1262: Closed mouth, almost smiling child. Painted eyes, wig, jointed body. 16" - $6,800.00; 21" - $15,000.00 up.

#1263: Closed mouth, painted eyes, rather downcast expression. 20" - $9,700.00 up; 24" - $15,000.00 up.

#1266, 1267: Child with open mouth and sleep eyes. 22" - $2,600.00.

#1286: Molded hair, ribbon, open mouth smile, glass eyes. 15-16" - $3,800.00.

Child, marked "S & C": 1890-on. 6-7" - $325.00; 14" - $500.00; 17" - $675.00; 22" - $700.00; 25" - $800.00; 30" - $1,150.00; 36" - $1,900.00; 40" - $2,800.00.

Left: 17" marked "1295 F.S.&Co." Sleep eyes, open mouth with two upper teeth, pierced nostrils, and on bent limb baby body. Right: 17" marked "C.M. Bergmann Special." Open mouth and on bent limb baby body with jointed wrists. F.S.&C. - $625.00; Bergmann - $595.00. *Courtesy Frasher Doll Auctions.*

SCHMITT & FILS

Schmitt & Fils produced dolls from the 1870's to 1891 in Paris, France. The dolls have French jointed bodies and came with closed or open/closed mouths.

Mark:

Child: 1880 – on. Bisque head with long, thin face. Jointed body with closed mouth or open/closed mouth. No damage and nicely dressed. Marked on head and body. 16" - $16,000.00 up; 18" - $18,000.00 up; 22" - $23,000.00 up; 25" - $26,000.00 up; 28" - $29,000.00.
Child: (See photo in Series 6, pg. 166.) Round face with full cheeks. 11-12" - $9,600.00; 18" - $18,000.00 up; 23" - $20,000.00 up.

10¾" tiny Schmitt & Fils, marked with shield and crossed hammers. Closed mouth, and on marked Schmitt body with straight wrists. 10¾" - $9,600.00; Parasols - $550.00; Purses - $350.00.
Courtesy Frasher Doll Auctions.

SCHOENAU & HOFFMEISTER

Schoenau & Hoffmeister began making dolls in 1901 and were located in Bavaria. The factory was called "Porzellanfabrik Burggrub" and this mark will be found on many of their doll heads. Some of their mold numbers are **21, 169, 170, 769, 900, 914, 1271, 1800, 1906, 1909, 1923, 4000, 4900, 5000, 5300, 5500, 5700, 5800, 5900** and also **Hanna.**

Mark:

Princess Elizabeth: Smiling open mouth, set eyes, bisque head on jointed five-piece body and marked with name on head or body. 16" - $1,800.00; 22" - $2,500.00; 25" - $2,800.00.
Hanna: Child with black or brown fired-in color to bisque head. Sleep or set eyes, five-piece body or jointed body. Marked with name on head. 8" - $385.00; 14" - $750.00.
Hanna Baby: Bisque head, open mouth, sleep eyes and on five-piece bent limb baby body. 9" - $325.00; 14" - $650.00; 15" - $725.00; 22" - $1,100.00; 24" - $1,300.00. **Toddler:** 7-8" - $375.00-425.00; 15" - $850.00; 19" - $1,000.00.
Character Baby: #169, 769, 1271, etc. 1910–on. Bisque head on

five-piece bent limb baby body. Can also be marked with "BURGGRUB." 13" - $385.00; 16" - $575.00; 18" - $650.00; 24" - $825.00. **Toddler:** 20" - $900.00; 23" - $1,100.00.

Child: #1800, 1906, 1909, 5500, 5700, 5900, 5800, etc. Bisque head with open mouth, sleep or set eyes, jointed body. No damage and nicely dressed. 10" - $185.00; 14" - $295.00; 17" - $365.00; 21" - $475.00; 28" - $800.00; 30" - $950.00; 34" - $1,200.00; 38" - $1,800.00. **Kid body:** Open mouth. 14" - $185.00; 17" - $265.00; 21" - $350.00.

Painted Bisque: Painted head on five-piece body or jointed body. 9" - $145.00; 12" - $225.00.

Das Lachende Baby (The Laughing Baby): 23" - $2,400.00; 26" - $2,900.00.

37" marked "S", "PB" in star, "H 1906." Very large child on fully jointed body with open mouth and glass eyes. Shown with early American carved wooden horse that is 33" wide, 26" tall. 37" - $1,800.00; Horse - $800.00. *Courtesy Frasher Doll Auctions.*

22" "Princess Elizabeth" marked "Porzellanfabrik Burggrub/Princess Elizabeth 6½ Made in Germany." Open, smiling mouth, original wig, on five-piece toddler body. **22" - $2,700.00.** *Courtesy Frasher Doll Auctions.*

Albert Schoenhut & Co. was located in Philadephia, PA, from 1872 until the 1930's. The dolls are all wood with spring joints, have holes in the bottoms of their feet to fit in a metal stand.

Marks:

(1911–1913)   **(1913–1930)**

SCHOENHUT DOLL
PAT. JAN. 17, '11, USA
& FOREIGN COUNTRIES
(Incised 1911–on)

Child With Carved Hair: May have comb marks, molded ribbon, comb or bow. Closed mouth. Original or nice clothes. **Excellent condition:** 14" - $2,500.00; 21" - $2,800.00. **Very good condition:** Some wear: 14" - $1,600.00; 21" - $1,900.00. **Poor condition:** With chips and dents. 14" - $600.00; 21" - $700.00.

Child: Rare, 1911. Looks exactly like Kammer & Reinhardt's #101 pouty. (See photo in Series 8, pg. 152.) 21" - $4,600.00 up.

Man With Carved Hair: 19", mint - $3,000.00; some wear - $1,800.00; chips, dirty - $800.00.

Baby Head: Can be on regular body or bent limb baby body. Bald spray painted hair or wig, painted de-

20" carved hair doll with center part and coiled braids around ears. All original. 15½" smiling carved hair girl that is all original. Has sculptured hairbow. Original metal doll stand. 20" - $2,800.00; 15½" - $2,400.00.
Courtesy Frasher Doll Auctions.

16" body with carved hair, painted features, and wearing original shoes with holes that are also in wooden feet to fit the stand made for the doll. 7½" Schoenhut pig that is all wood with leather ears and tail. 16" - $2,500.00; Pig - $350.00. *Courtesy Frasher Doll Auctions.*

cal eyes. Nicely dressed or original. **Excellent condition:** 12" - $550.00; 16" - $765.00; 18" - $825.00. **Good condition:** 16" - $450.00; 18" - $550.00. **Poor condition:** 16" - $200.00; 18" - $250.00.

Toddler: Excellent condition. 12" - $900.00; 16" - $965.00.

Child, character face: 1911–1930. Wig, intaglio eyes. Open/closed mouth with painted teeth. Suitably redressed or original. **Excellent condition:** 14" - $1,700.00; 21" - $2,200.00. **Good condition:** 14" - $975.00; 21" - $1,350.00. **Poor condition:** 14" - $350.00; 21" - $650.00.

Cap Molded To Head: (See photo in Series 8, pg. 152.) 16" - $3,400.00 up.

Tootsie Wootsie: (See photo in Series 6, pg. 170.) Molded, painted hair, open/closed mouth with molded tongue and two upper teeth. Toddler or regular body. 14" - $2,100.00; 20" - $2,800.00 up.

"Dolly" Face: 1915–1930. Common doll, wigged, open/closed mouth

with painted teeth, decal painted eyes. Original or nicely dressed. **Excellent condition:** 14" - $775.00; 20" - $875.00. **Good condition:** 14" - $500.00; 21" - $750.00. **Poor condition:** 14" - $150.00; 16" - $200.00.

Sleep Eyes: Has lids that lower down over the eyes and has an open mouth with teeth or just slightly cut open mouth with carved teeth. Original or nicely dressed. **Excellent condition:** 13-14" - $1,350.00; 22" - $1,500.00. **Good condition:** 16" - $700.00; 21" - $850.00. **Poor condition:** 17" - $200.00; 22" - $275.00.

Walker: 1919–1930. One-piece legs with "walker" joints in center of

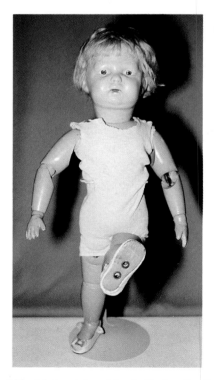

19" mint and original "baby face" Schoenhut with holes in shoes and feet to fit Schoenhut doll stand. Original teddy chemise. 19" - $1,200.00 up. *Courtesy Shirley Bertrand.*

Two Schoenhut dolls - one has "baby" face; the other a regular girl face. Both are mint and all original. Baby face - $965.00; Girl face - $985.00. *Courtesy Shirley Bertrand.*

legs and torso. Painted eyes, open/ closed or closed mouth. Original or nicely dressed. **Excellent condition:** 15" - $900.00; 18" - $1,100.00; 21" - $1,400.00. **Good condition:** 15" - $550.00; 18" - $650.00; 21" - $850.00. **Poor condition:** 15" - $125.00; 18" - $185.00; 21" - $250.00.

All Composition: Molded curly hair, "Patsy"-style body, paper label on back, 1924. 13" - $550.00.

Circus Animals: $95.00 - 500.00.

Clowns: $150.00 - 300.00.

Ringmaster: $200.00 - 350.00.

Roly-Poly Figures: 1914, marked. (See photo in Series 8, pg. 155.) $300.00 up.

14" Schoenhut boy in original uniform. Character face, wig. Flag and shoes added. 14" - $1,700.00. *Courtesy Shirley Bertrand.*

Left: Wonderful Schoenhut "dancing" doll. Doll has papier maché head, wooden body and limbs, and base is all wood. Dancing girl is attached to wire and wooden dowel that fits hole in base. Another doll, probably a boy, fits in the other hole in the base. Original. $600.00. *Courtesy Shirley Bertrand.*

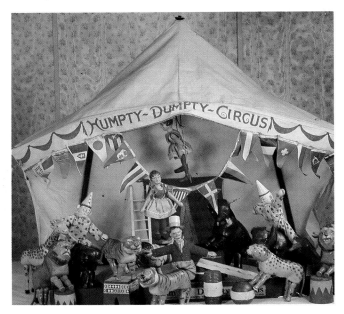

Schoenhut circus with some rare animals, such as tigers, leopard, and giraffe. Set - $2,700.00. *Courtesy Frasher Doll Auctions.*

Beautiful mint condition Schoenhut girl with original clothes and wig. Painted features, closed mouth with painted teeth. 21" - $2,200.00. *Courtesy Barbara Earnshaw-Cain.*

161

SCHUETZMEISTER & QUENDT

Schuetzmeister & Quendt made dolls from 1893 to 1898. This short term factory was located in Boilstadt, Germany.

Marks:

Child: Mold #251, 252, etc. Can have cut pate or be a bald head with two string holes. No damage and nicely dressed, open mouth. 14" - $450.00; 20" - $565.00; 23" - $685.00.

Baby: Includes mold #201 & 301. Five-piece bent limb baby body. Not damaged and nicely dressed. Open mouth. 12" - $345.00; 14" - $475.00; 17" - $550.00; 22" - $750.00. **Toddler:** 16" - $985.00; 20" - $1,250.00; 24" - $1,700.00.

22" marked "S&Q/101." Sleep eyes, open mouth, and fully jointed body. Wears old "Buster Brown Jr. Business Builders Club Member" pin. 22" - $625.00. *Courtesy Glorya Woods.*

SIMON & HALBIG

Simon & Halbig began making dolls in the late 1860's or early 1870's and continued until the 1930's. Simon & Halbig made many heads for other companies and they also supplied some doll heads from the French makers. They made entire dolls, all bisque, flange neck dolls, turned shoulder heads and socket heads.

All prices are for dolls with no damage to the bisque and only minor scuffs to the bodies, well dressed, wigged and with shoes. Dolls should be ready to place in a collection.

Marks:

1279-3
DEP

$S\ ''\ \mathcal{H}$ $S\mathcal{H}$
729 GERMANY

#130, 530, 540, 550, 570, 600, 1039, 1040, etc: Child, 1890 to 1930's, open mouth. (More for flirty eyes.) 12" - $500.00; 16" - $600.00; 19" - $800.00; 23" - $965.00; 27" - $1,300.00; 32" - $2,000.00; 35" - $2,300.00; 40" - $3,000.00.

#1049, 1078, 1079, 1099: Open mouth, jointed body. 12" - $565.00; 15" - $675.00; 19" - $725.00; 21" - $800.00; 24" - $875.00; 26" -

$1,000.00; 32" - $1,500.00; 35" - $2,000.00; 42" - $3,700.00.

#1009: With kid body. 19" - $950.00; 24" - $1,100.00; 26" - $1,400.00. **Jointed body:** 16" - $950.00; 19" - $1,300.00; 21" - $1,600.00; 24" - $1,900.00.

#1019: Open mouth, smiling. Jointed body. 16" - $6,200.00. Composition shoulder plate, ball jointed arms, cloth body and upper legs. Ball jointed lower legs. 18" - $7,500.00.

#1010, 1029, 1040, 1080, 1170, etc: Open mouth and kid body. 10" - $350.00; 14" - $465.00; 21" - $675.00; 25" - $750.00; 28" - $1,000.00.

#1109: 16" - $775.00; 23" - $1,000.00.

#1250, 1260: Open mouth, kid body. 16" - $575.00; 19" - $700.00; 25" - $975.00.

Characters: 1910 and after. Wig or molded hair, glass or painted eyes, with open/closed, closed, or open mouth. On jointed child bodies.

#IV: 20" - $22,000.00 up.

#IV: Open mouth. 23" - $5,000.00.

13" Simon & Halbig mold #150 with molded eyelids, painted eyes, closed mouth, and on jointed body. Original factory clothes. 13" - $10,500.00 up. Original - $15,000.00. *Courtesy Frasher Doll Auctions.*

14" girl marked "151 S&H 5½" has painted features with open/closed mouth, painted teeth, big smile, dimples, and on fully jointed body. 13" boy marked "150 S&H 2/0" has painted features and closed, slighty pouty mouth. Also on fully jointed body. Girl - $5,700.00; Boy - $10,500.00. *Courtesy Frasher Doll Auctions.*

#120: 16" - $1,900.00; 24" - $3,000.00; 28" - $3,900.00.

#150: (See photo in Series 7, pg. 155.) 16" - $12,000.00 up; 19" - $16,000.00 up; 23" - $21,000.00 up.

#151, 1388: (See photo in Series 7, pg. 155.) 16" - $5,000.00; 20" - $7,200.00.

#153 "Little Duke": (See photo in Series 8, pg. 157.) 16" - $33,000.00; 18" - $43,000.00; 22" - $49,000.00 up.

#540, 550, 570, Baby Blanche: 17" - $675.00; 23" - $800.00

#600: 14" - $900.00; 18" - $1,400.00; 22" - $1,900.00.

#603: 10-12" - $5,600.00.

#718, 719, 720: 16" - $2,300.00; 22" - $3,400.00. **Open mouth:** 13" - $1,300.00; 18" - $1,900.00; 25" - $2,700.00.

#729: Slight open mouth, smiling. 16" - $2,800.00 up; 19" - $4,000.00.

18" very rare character marked "S.9H./ 759/D.E.P." Swivel head on bisque shoulder plate, deep dimples, and on French style kid body. Open, smiling mouth with overbite. 18" - $14,000.00.
Courtesy Amanda Hash.

#729: Closed mouth. 16" - $2,500.00; 20" - $3,200.00. **Kid body:** 16" - $1,400.00; 20" - $1,850.00; 25" - $2,000.00.

#739: 13" - $1,150.00; 18" - $1,900.00; 26" - $2,800.00.

#740: Kid body, closed mouth. 10" - $600.00; 16" - $1,400.00; 18" - $1,600.00.

#720, 740: Jointed body. 10" - $675.00; 17" - $1,600.00; 21" - $2,200.00.

#749: Closed mouth, jointed body. 18" - $2,800.00; 22" - $3,400.00. **Open mouth:** 12" - $1,200.00; 18" - $1,900.00; 25" - $2,500.00. **Kid body:** 17" - $1,300.00; 21" - $1,900.00.

#759: Open mouth, deep cheek dimples, rare. 24" - $18,000.00 up.

#905, 908: (See photo in Series 6, pg. 173.) Closed mouth. 16" - $2,700.00; 19" - $3,200.00. **Open mouth:** 14" - $1,600.00; 20" - $1,800.00; 25" - $2,450.00.

Left: 19" marked "S&H 719 DEP." Glass eyes, open mouth with square cut teeth, and on early jointed body with straight wrists. Right: 14" marked "S&H 949." Large glass eyes, open mouth with one lower and two upper teeth. Jointed body with straight wrists. **19" - $3,200.00; 14" - $1,500.00.**
Courtesy Frasher Doll Auctions.

13½" with unusual face, mold #949. Marked "S H 3½ 949." Swivel head on bisque shoulder plate, set eyes, and closed mouth. Kid body with bisque lower arms. 13½" - $1,400.00.
Courtesy Frasher Doll Auctions.

#919: Open/closed mouth. 17" - $5,000.00; 21" - $7,000.00.

#929: Closed mouth. 17" - $3,500.00; 22" - $4,700.00. **Open mouth:** 18" - $2,400.00; 21" - $3,500.00.

#939: Closed mouth. 15" - $2,600.00; 18" - $2,900.00; 21" - $3,300.00; 26" - $4,400.00. **Kid body:** 18" - $1,600.00; 21" - $2,300.00; 26" - $2,900.00. **Open mouth:** 13" - $1,150.00; 18" - $1,900.00; 26" - $2,800.00.

#939, Black: Closed mouth. 18"- $3,500.00; 21" - $4,500.00; 26" - $5,200.00. **Open mouth:** (See photo in Series 5, pg. 132.) 18" - $1,800.00; 21" - $2,300.00; 26" - $2,900.00.

#940, 950: Kid body. (See photo in Series 7, pg. 156.) 10" - $565.00; 15" - $1,300.00; 21" - $1,700.00. **Jointed body:** 10" - $850.00; 15" - $1,700.00; 21" - $2,200.00.

#949: Closed mouth. 16" - $2,300.00; 21" - $2,600.00; 25" - $3,200.00. **Open mouth:** 18" - $1,500.00; 21" - $1,900.00; 26" - $2,400.00. **Kid body:** 15" - $1,500.00; 18" - $1,700.00; 21" - $2,100.00.

#949, Black: Closed mouth. 18" - $3,000.00; 21" - $3,700.00. **Open mouth:** 18" - $1,400.00; 21" - $1,900.00. **Kid body:** 18" - $1,400.00; 21" - $1,900.00; 26" - $2,000.00.

#969, 970: Open mouth grin, puffed cheeks. 17" - $9,800.00.

#979: Closed mouth. 13" - $2,600.00; 16" - $3,100.00; 19" - $3,450.00.

#979: Open mouth, square teeth, slight smile. 16" - $3,750.00. **Kid body:** 17" - $2,800.00; 21" - $3,200.00.

#1248, 1249, 1250, 1260, Santa: 14" - $900.00; 17" - $1,150.00; 22" - $1,400.00; 26" - $1,700.00; 34" - $2,400.00.

17" Simon & Halbig mold #949, closed mouth, has solid dome head. On fully jointed body. 17" - $2,300.00. *Courtesy Turn of Century Antiques.*

#1269, 1279: (See photo in Series 5, pg. 134.) 12" - $1,700.00; 15" - $1,900.00; 18" - $2,800.00; 22" - $3,200.00; 25" - $2,700.00; 30" - $3,000.00; 34" - $3,400.00.

#1299: 17" - $1,200.00; 21" - $1,600.00.

#1302: See Black Dolls.

#1303: Closed mouth, thin lips. 18" - $7,600.00 up.

#1304: 14" - $6,400.00; 17" - $8,000.00.

#1305: Open/closed mouth, long nose. 18" - $12,000.00.

#1308: 20" - $6,400.00 up.

#1309: Character with open mouth. 10" - $1,400.00; 16" - $1,950.00; 20" - $3,000.00.

#1310: Open/closed mouth, modeled mustache. 19½" - $19,000.00.

Left: 33" marked "S&H 1269/Germany Dep. 15." Character face with open mouth and all original wig and clothes. Fully jointed body. Rare mold number. Right: 27" "Sweet Nell" with original box, wig and clothes. Marked "ABG 1362/Made in Germany 3½." Open mouth, fully jointed body. 33" - $3,300.00; 27" in box - $1,250.00.

Courtesy Frasher Doll Auctions.

#1338: Open mouth, jointed body. 18" - $1,500.00; 24" - $2,600.00; 28" - $3,200.00.

#1339: (See photos in Series 5, pg. 135; Series 7, pg. 157.) Character face, open mouth. 18" - $1,800.00; 26" - $3,000.00.

#1339, 1358 Black: 16" - $5,800.00; 20" - $7,200.00.

#1345: 15" - $2,800.00; 17" - $4,200.00.

#1388, 1398: Lady Doll. 22" - $18,500.00 up.

#1428: 22" - $2,600.00.

#1448: Full closed mouth. 17" - $19,000.00 up; 21" - $24,000.00 up.

#1448: Open/closed mouth, laughing, modeled teeth. 16" - $14,000.00 up.

#1478: 17" - $9,500.00 up.

#1488: Child, closed mouth. 16" - $3,400.00; 20" - $4,700.00; 24" - $5,600.00.

Character Babies: 1909 to 1930's. Wigs or molded hair, painted or sleep eyes, open or open/closed mouth and on five-piece bent limb baby bodies. (Allow more for toddler body.)

#1294: 16" - $675.00; 19" - $825.00; 23" - $1,200.00; 26" - $1,800.00. **With clockwork in head to move eyes:** 25-26" - $3,000.00. **Toddler:** 22" - $1,600.00.

#1299: With open mouth. 10" - $365.00; 16" - $975.00. **Toddler:** 16" - $1,100.00; 18" - $1,300.00.

#1428 Toddler: (See photo in Series 7, pg. 158.) 12" - $1,400.00; 16" - $1,600.00; 20" - $2,000.00; 26" - $2,500.00.

#1428 Baby: 12" - $1,050.00; 15" - $1,250.00; 19" - $1,600.00.

#1488 Toddler: (See photo in Series 6, pg. 175.) 15" - $3,000.00; 18" - $3,500.00; 22" - $4,000.00. **Baby:** 15" - $1,500.00; 18" - $2,300.00; 22" - $2,600.00; 26" - $3,200.00.

#1489 Erika Baby: (See photos in Series 6, pg. 176; Series 7, pg. 159.) 20" - $3,300.00; 22" - $4,000.00; 26" - $4,700.00.

#1498 Toddler: (See photo in Series 6, pg. 175.) 16" - $6,600.00; 20" - $7,600.00. **Baby:** 16" - $6,000.00; 20" - $6,900.00.
#1039 Walker: Key wound. 16" - $1,900.00; 20" - $2,400.00; 23" - $3,000.00. **Walking/Kissing:** 20" - $1,100.00; 24" - $1,400.00.
Miniature Dolls: Tiny dolls with open mouth on jointed body or five-piece body with some having painted-on shoes and socks.
#1078, 1079, etc.: Fully jointed. 7" - $465.00; 10" - $585.00. **Five-piece body:** 7" - $375.00; 10" - $475.00. **Walker:** 10-11" - $650.00.
#1160: "Little Women" type. Closed mouth and fancy wig. 5½-6½" - $400.00; 10-11" - $550.00. **Head only:** 2-3" - $85.00-145.00.

24" Gibson Girl style adult doll marked "1159/Germany Simon & Halbig S&H." Sleep eyes, open mouth. Body has modeled bosom and narrow waist. 24" - $2,600.00. *Courtesy Frasher Doll Auctions.*

Ladies: Ca. 1910. Open mouth, molded lady-style slim body with slim arms and legs.
#1159, 1179: 12" - $925.00; 15" - $1,400.00; 19" - $1,900.00; 22" - $2,400.00; 26" - $2,800.00.
Ladies: Closed mouth. Ca. 1910. Adult slim limb body.
#1303: 15" - $10,000.00; 17" - $13,000.00.
#1305: Lady. Open/closed mouth, long nose. 18" - $9,500.00 up; 22" - $14,000.00 up.
#1307: Lady, long face. 18" - $15,500.00 up; 24" - $22,500.00 up.
#1308: Man. 13" - $5,700.00; 15" - $6,300.00.
#1398: 18" - $12,000.00 up.
#1468, 1469: 13" - $2,200.00; 16" - $2,400.00.
#1527: 18" - $9,200.00 up; 22" - $10,000.00 up.
#152 Lady: 17" - $17,800.00 up; 23" - $29,500.00 up.

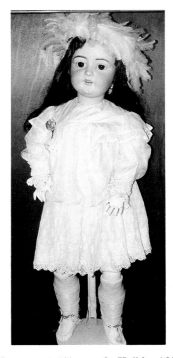

35" marked "Simon & Halbig 1079" with sleep eyes, open mouth and full cheeks. On fully jointed body. 35" - $2,000.00. *Courtesy Gloria Anderson.*

S.F.B.J.

The Société Française de Fabrication de Bébés et Jouets (S.F.B.J.) was formed in 1899 and known members were Jumeau, Bru, Fleischmann & Blodel, Rabery & Delphieu, Pintel & Godchaux, P.H. Schmitz, A. Bouchet, Jullien, and Danel & Cie. By 1922, S.F.B.J. employed 2,800 people. The Society was dissolved in 1958. There is a vast amount of "dolly-faced" S.F.B.J. dolls, but some are extremely rare and are character molds. Most of the characters are in the 200 mold number series.

Marks:

19" SFBJ 60 with body label "SFBJ Fabrication Francaise Paris." Head turns as she walks and she blows a kiss. Sleep eyes, open mouth. 19" - $1,800.00. *Courtesy Turn of Century Antiques.*

S.F.B.J.
239
PARIS

S.F.B.J.
301

S F
B J

Child: 1899. Sleep or set eyes, open mouth and on jointed French body. No damage and nicely dressed.

#60: 12" - $565.00; 14" - $625.00; 20" - $950.00; 28" - $1,300.00.

#301: 8" - $425.00; 12" - $675.00; 14" - $775.00; 20" - $1,000.00; 28" - $1,700.00.

Bleuette: 1930's–1960's. Made exclusively for Gautier-Languereau and their newspaper for children, *La Semaine de Suzette.* (Just as "Betsy McCall" was used by *McCall's* magazine.) Marked "SFBJ" or "71 Unis France 149 301" with "1½" at base of neck socket. Body marked "2" and feet marked "1." Sleep eyes, open mouth. (See photo in Series 7, pg. 36.) 10" - $800.00 up.

Jumeau Type: (See photo in Series 7, pg. 163.) Open mouth. 15" - $1,200.00; 20" - $1,700.00; 24" - $2,100.00. **Closed mouth:** 17" - $2,500.00; 21" - $3,100.00; 25" - $3,500.00.

Lady #1159: Open mouth, adult body. 24" - $2,700.00.

Character: Sleep or set eyes, wigged, molded hair, jointed body. (Allow more for flocked hair. Usually found on mold #227, 235, 237, 266.) No damage and nicely dressed.

#211: 18" - $6,000.00.

#226: 14" - $1,500.00; 19" - $2,000.00. **Painted eyes:** 16" - $1,400.00.

#227: (See photo in Series 5, pg. 136.) 16" - $2,200.00; 20" - $2,500.00.

#229: 18" - $5,000.00.

#230: 16" - $1,650.00; 22" - $2,100.00; 25" - $2,400.00.

#233: Screamer. 14" - $1,800.00; 17" - $2,800.00.

#234: 16" - $2,800.00; 21" - $3,300.00.

#235: 14" - $1,550.00; 20" - $2,100.00. **Painted eyes:** 16" - $1,400.00; 20" - $2,100.00.

#236, 262 Toddler: 12" - $1,300.00; 16" - $1,800.00; 20" - $2,200.00; 24" - $2,400.00; 26" - $2,800.00. **Baby:** 14" - $1,000.00; 19" - $1,500.00; 25" - $2,000.00.

#237: (See photo in Series 7, pg. 161.) 15" - $2,100.00; 20" - $2,500.00.

#238: 16" - $3,800.00; 24" - $4,300.00. **Lady:** 22" - $4,400.00.

#239 Poulbot: 16" - $10,000.00 up.

#242: (See photo in Series 5, pg. 137.) 14" - $2,700.00; 16½" - $2,950.00.

#247: 16" - $2,400.00; 20" - $2,950.00; 26" - $3,400.00.

#248: Very pouty, glass eyes. 14" - $4,000.00; 19" - $5,600.00.

#251 Toddler: 18"- $1,700.00; 22" - $2,200.00; 26" - $2,600.00. **Baby:** 15" - $1,300.00; 21" - $1,900.00; 25" - $2,200.00.

#252 Toddler: 16" - $6,000.00; 20" - $7,600.00; 26" - $8,400.00. **Baby:** 12" - $2,100.00; 16" - $5,200.00; 22" - $7,700.00; 26" - $8,700.00.

#257: 18" - $2,800.00.

#266: 22" - $4,400.00.

#306: Princess Elizabeth. See Jumeau section.

Googly: See Googly section.

Kiss Throwing, Walking Doll: (See photo in Series 5, pg. 138.) Composition body with straight legs, walking mechanism. When it walks, arm goes up to throw kiss. Head moves from side to side. Flirty eyes and open mouth. In working condition, no damage to bisque head and nicely dressed. 21-22" - $2,300.00.

26" "Twirp" marked "SFBJ 247 Paris." Glass eyes, open/closed mouth and on jointed toddler body. Shown with cute little 11" Kammer & Reinhardt/Simon & Halbig 126 dolls on chunky toddler bodies. Painted bisque heads. 26" - $3,400.00; 11" - $850.00 each. *Courtesy Frasher Doll Auctions.*

27" marked "SFBJ 252 Paris/21." Pouty on chubby toddler body with sleep eyes and closed mouth. Also shown is 14" white mohair Steiff elephant on wheels. 27" - $9,200.00; Elephant - $450.00. *Courtesy Frasher Doll Auctions.*

22" walking, talking, kiss throwing SFBJ 301. Sleep eyes/lashes, open mouth, and has original clothes. 22" - $2,300.00. *Courtesy Turn of Century Antiques.*

25" and 20" dolls, both with mold #251, with sleep eyes, open mouth, two upper teeth and molded tongue. Both are on jointed toddler bodies. The 25" is marked "251 Unis France." The smaller one is marked "21 SFBJ 251 Paris." 25" - $2,000.00; 20" $2,000.00. *Courtesy Frasher Doll Auctions.*

Snow Babies were made in Germany and Japan. German-made babies were made as early as 1880's on into 1920's. They can be excellent to poor in quality from both countries. Snow Babies have fired-on "pebble-textured" clothing. Many are unmarked and the features are painted. Prices are for good quality painted features, rareness of pose, and no damage to the piece.

Single Figure: 1½" - $50.00; 3" - $100.00-125.00.

Two Figures: Molded together. 1½" - $100.00-125.00; 3" - $150.00-195.00.

Three Figures: Molded together. 1½" - $145.00-185.00; 3" - $195.00-245.00.

One Figure On Sled: 2-2½" - $185.00. With reindeer: $200.00.

Two Figures On Sled: 2-2½" - $200.00.

Three Figures On Sled: (See photo in Series 6, pg. 180.) 2-2½" - $245.00.

Jointed: (See photo in Series 5, pg. 139.) Shoulders and hips. 3¼" - $165.00 up; 5" - $365.00 up; 7" - $450.00 up.

Shoulder head: Cloth body with china limbs. 9" - $385.00; 12" - $450.00.

On Sled in Glass: "Snow" scene. $225.00 up. **Sled/dogs:** 3-4" - $225.00.

With Bear: $200.00.

With Snowman: 2½" - $100.00.

With Musical Base: $185.00 up.

Laughing Child: 3" - $150.00 up.

Snow Bear with Santa: $365.00.

With Reindeer: $225.00

5" tall Snow Child that is pin jointed at shoulders and hips. Made in Gemany and marked "#3" on back. $400.00 up. *Courtesy Ellen Dodge.*

Snow Baby Riding Polar Bear: 3" - $225.00.

Snow Angel: White texturing. Pink feathered smooth bisque wings. 3" - $300.00 up.

Igloo: $90.00.

Ice Skater: 3" - $185.00 up.

Dog: Pulling sled with one figure. $225.00.

In Airplane: 4½" - $365.00.

Mother: Pushing two babies in red sled carriage. 4½" - $365.00 up.

STEIFF

Steiff started business in 1894. This German maker is better known for their plush/stuffed animals than for dolls.

Steiff Dolls: Felt, velvet or plush with seam down middle of face. Button-style eyes, painted features and sewn-on ears. The dolls generally have large feet so they stand alone. Prices are for dolls in excellent condition and with original clothes. Second prices are for dolls that are soiled and may not be original.

Adults: 16-17" - $1,900.00 up; 21-22" - $2,400.00 up.

STEIFF

Military Men: (See photo in Series 7, pg. 165.) 15" - $4,400.00 up; 17" - $4,800.00 up; 21" - $5,200.00 up.

Children: (See photo in Series 6, pg. 181.) 12" - $950.00 up; 15-16" - $1,500.00; 18-19" - $1,800.00 up.

Made is U.S. Zone Germany: Has glass eyes. 12" - $800.00 up; 16" - $1,000.00 up.

Comic Characters: Such as chef, elf, musician, etc. 14" - $2,400.00 up; 16" - $3,200.00 up.

Mickey Mouse: 9-10" - $1,200.00 up.
Minnie Mouse: 9-10" - $1,800.00 up.
Clown: 16" - $2,300.00 up.

Leprechaun: All felt, straw stuffed, carries felt cloverleaf. Red mohair beard. 12" - $500.00 up.

15" early Steiff soldier with metal button in ear and on sole of boots. Seam down middle of face, painted features and mustache. Ca. 1910. All original. 15" - $4,400.00. *Courtesy Frasher Doll Auctions.*

STEINER, JULES

Jules Nicholas Steiner operated from 1855 to 1892 when the firm was taken over by Amedee LaFosse. In 1895, this firm merged with Henri Alexander, the maker of Phenix Bébé and a partner, May Freres Cie, the maker of Bébé Mascotte. In 1899, Jules Mettais took over the firm and in 1906, the company was sold to Edmond Daspres.

In 1889, the firm registered the girl with a banner and the words "Le Petit Parisien" and in 1892, LaFosse registered "Le Parisien."

"A" Series Child: 1885. Closed mouth, paperweight eyes, jointed body and cardboard pate. No damage and nicely dressed. 8" - $2,700.00; 10" - $3,200.00; 15" - $4,300.00; 22" - $6,400.00; 25" - $7,400.00; 28" - $8,000.00.

Marks:
(See body marks in Series 7, pg. 167.)

J. STEINER
STE. S.G.D.G.
FIRE A12
PARIS

STE C3
J. STEINER
B. S.G.D.G.

172

"A" Series Child: Open mouth, otherwise same as above. 14" - $1,800.00; 18" - $2,600.00; 22" - $3,800.00.

"B" Series: Closed mouth. 24" - $5,200.00; 30" - $7,000.00.

"C" Series Child: Ca. 1880. Closed mouth, round face, paperweight eyes, no damage and nicely dressed. 18" - $5,600.00; 22" - $7,200.00; 27" - $9,200.00; 30" - $9,500.00.

Bourgoin Steiner: 1870's. With "Bourgoin" incised or in red stamp on head along with the rest of the Steiner mark. Closed mouth. No damage and nicely dressed. 18" - $6,000.00; 22" - $6,900.00; 27" - $9,200.00.

Wire Eye Steiner: Closed mouth, flat glass eyes that open and close by moving wire that comes out the back of the head. Jointed body, no damage and nicely dressed. **Bourgoin:** 18" - $5,500.00; 23" - $6,400.00; 28" - $7,900.00. **"A" Series:** 18" - $5,400.00; 22" - $6,300.00; 27" - $7,600.00. **"C" Series:** 18" - $5,300.00; 22" - $6,200.00; 27" - $7,600.00.

29" "C" Series Steiner marked "Sie C. 6. Steiner Bte SGDG Bourgoin S." Closed mouth, round face, original wig, and old clothes. On marked Steiner jointed body with straight wrists. Shown with 11¼" x 9" wooden stage with three dancing couples. When handle is turned, dolls twirl as music plays. Ca. 1900, Germany. 29" - $9,500.00; Mechanical - $2,200.00. *Courtesy Frasher Doll Auctions.*

Right: 25" marked "J. Steiner Bte SGDG Parise Fre A-17." Closed mouth and on labeled Steiner body with straight wrists. Left: 15" Kestner mold #182 with painted features, open/closed mouth with painted teeth. Jointed body. 15" marked Gebruder Heubach figurine "Girl at Helm." 25" - $7,400.00; 15" - $3,500.00; Figurine - $600.00. *Courtesy Frasher Doll Auctions.*

"Le Parisien" - "A" Series: 1892. Closed mouth: 8-9" - $2,700.00; 13-14" - $4,000.00; 18" - $5,000.00; 22" - $6,000.00; 25" - $7,000.00; 28" - $7,800.00. Open mouth: 16" - $2,500.00; 22" - $2,800.00; 25" - $3,600.00.

Mechanical: See that section.

Bisque Hip Steiner: Motschmann-style body with bisque head, shoulders, lower arms and legs and bisque torso sections. No damage anywhere. 18" - $6,800.00.

Early White Bisque Steiner: With round face, open mouth with two rows of teeth. Unmarked. On jointed Steiner body, pink wash over eyes. No damage and nicely dressed. 16" - $4,400.00; 20" - $5,200.00.

24" marked "Steiner Bte SGDG Paris/A17." Marked fully jointed body, closed mouth. 24" - **$7,200.00.** *Courtesy Frasher Doll Auctions.*

Left: 17" early white bisque, round faced Steiner with open mouth, two rows of teeth, pink wash over eyes, early Steiner body with straight wrists. Right: 9½" portrait Jumeau with closed mouth, jointed body with straight wrists. 17" - **$4,400.00;** 9½" - **$7,400.00.** *Courtesy Frasher Doll Auctions.*

"Tynie Baby" was made for Horsman Doll Co. in 1924. Doll will have sleep eyes, closed pouty mouth and "frown" between eyes. Its cloth body has celluloid or composition hands. Markings will be "1924/E.I. Horsman/Made in Germany." Some will also be incised "Tynie Baby." Doll should have no damage and be nicely dressed.

Bisque head: 13" - $365.00; 16" - $685.00.

Composition head: 15-16" - $285.00.

All bisque: Glass eyes, swivel neck. 6" - $1,000.00; 9" - $1,700.00.

Painted eyes: 6" - $565.00.

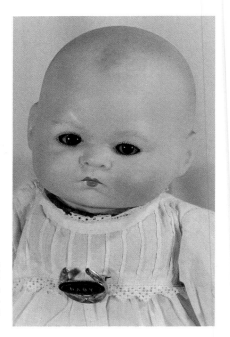

14" "Tynie Baby" marked 1924/E.I. Horsman/Made in Germany." Some will be incised "Tynie Baby." Bisque head, closed mouth with pouty look, sleep eyes, cloth body with composition or celluloid hands. 14" - $400.00.

"Unis, France" was a type of trade association or a "seal of approval" for trade goods to consumers from the manufacturers. This group of business-men, who were to watch the quality of French exports, often overlooked guidelines and some poor quality dolls were exported. Many fine quality Unis marked dolls were also produced.

Unis began right after World War I and is still in business. Two doll companies are still members, "Poupee Bella" and "Petit Colin." Other manu-facturers in this group include makers of toys, sewing machines, tile, and pens.

#60, 70, 71, 301: Bisque head, composition jointed body. Sleep or set eyes, open mouth. No damage, nicely dressed. 8-9" - $425.00; 14" - $500.00;

Marks:

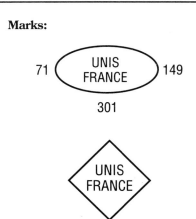

71   UNIS FRANCE   149

301

UNIS FRANCE

UNIS

17" - $600.00; 21" - $725.00; 24" - $900.00. **Closed mouth:** 16" - $2,400.00; 20" - $3,000.00. **Black or brown:** 11-12" - $375.00; 16" - $625.00.

#60, 70, 71, 301: On five-piece body, glass eyes. 6½" - $185.00; 12" - $300.00; 14" - $425.00.

Bleuette: See S.F.B.J section.

Provincial Costume Doll: Bisque head, painted, set or sleep eyes, open mouth (or closed on smaller dolls.) Five-piece body. Original costume, no damage. 6" - $200.00; 12" - $350.00; 14" - $450.00.

Baby #272: Glass eyes, open mouth, cloth body, celluloid hands. 15" - $575.00; 18" - $975.00. **Painted eyes:** Composition hands. 16" - $375.00; 19" - $565.00.

#251 Toddler: 15" - $1,450.00 up.

Princess Elizabeth: (See photo in Series 6, pg. 185.) 1938. Jointed body, closed mouth. (Allow more for flirty eyes.) 18" - $1,400.00; 23" - $1,800.00; 31" - $2,500.00.

20" marked "Unis France 301" and "79-149." Also has an "E.R." in circle, then a "T." Tin eyelids drop down over eyes, open mouth. On French fully jointed body. 20" - $700.00. *Courtesy Turn of Century Antiques.*

WAGNER & ZETZSCHE

Closed mouth: 16" - $850.00; 21" - $975.00; 24" - $1,400.00; 27" - $1,600.00.

Open mouth: 16" - $500.00; 21" - $675.00; 24" - $875.00; 27" - $1,100.00.

27" turned shoulder head with flat painted undersides to eyebrows. Glass eyes and open mouth. Kid body with bisque lower arms. 27" - $1,100.00. *Courtesy Frasher Doll Auctions.*

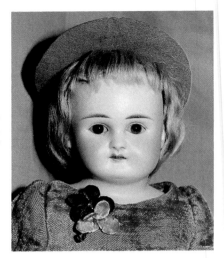

20" open mouth turned head doll with flat painted undersides to eyebrows. Made by Wagner & Zetsche. Kid body with bisque lower arms. 20" - $675.00. *Courtesy Frasher Doll Auctions.*

WAX

Poured Wax: (See photos in Series 5, pg. 144; Series 7, pg. 174.) Cloth body with wax head, limbs and inset glass eyes. Hair is embedded into wax. Nicely dressed or in original clothes, no damage to wax, but wax may be slightly discolored (evenly all over.) Not rewaxed. 16" - $1,300.00; 19" - $1,650.00; 22" - $1,850.00; 25" - $2,200.00. **Lady or Man:** 20" - $2,600.00 up; 24" - $3,600.00.

Wax Over Papier Maché or Composition: (See photo in Series 6, pg. 189.) Cloth body with wax over papier maché or composition head and with wax over composition or wood limbs. Only minor scuffs with no chipped out places, good color and nicely dressed.

Early Dolls: 1860-on.

Molded hair: 14" - $285.00; 21" - $485.00; 24" - $565.00.

Squeeker body: 14" - $325.00.

"Alice:" Headband hairdo: 14" - $450.00; 17" - $585.00. **With wig, excellent quality:** Heavy wax. 12" -

14" poured wax child stamped "London Toy Shop" in circle, "F. Aldis, 11 & 12 Belgrave Mansions, S.W." Glass eyes, mohair wig, cloth body with poured wax limbs. Old clothes. 14" - $1,200.00. *Courtesy Turn of Century Antiques.*

$265.00; 16" - $425.00; 21" - $575.00; 24" - $675.00; 29" - $725.00. **Common quality:** Wax worn or gone. 12" - $150.00; 16" - $325.00; 21" - $350.00; 24" - $465.00.

Later Dolls: 12" - $250.00; 16" - $450.00.

Bonnet or Cap: (See photo in Series 6, pg. 190.) **Hat molded on forehead:** 16" - $2,600.00. **Derby-type hat:** 22" - $2,100.00. **Bonnet-style hat:** 20" - $2,250.00. **Round face, poke bonnet:** 22" - $2,450.00. **Baby:** $16" - $1,400.00.

Pumpkin: Hair laced over ridged raised front area. 16" - $450.00; 20" - $550.00.

Slit Head Wax: (See photo in Series 6, pg. 189.) English, 1830–1860's. Glass eyes, some open and closed by an attached wire. 14" - $625.00 up; 18" - $865.00; 25" - $1,000.00 up.

Left: 16½" German poured wax shoulder head with glass eyes, human hair inserted into scalp, muslin body, and wax over composition limbs. Ca. 1870's. Original. Right: 14½" Simon & Halbig 1160 mold. Shoulder head, glass eyes, closed mouth, cloth body and bisque lower arms. Original. 16½" - **$1,300.00**; 14½" - **$800.00**. *Courtesy Frasher Doll Auctions.*

Left: 18½" wax with large sleep glass eyes. Cloth body with waxed limbs. Right: 11" "Alice in Wonderland" hairdo Parian-type with painted features and hair ribbon. Cloth with bisque limbs. 18½" - **$450.00**; 11" - **$395.00**. *Courtesy Turn of Century Antiques.*

Norah Welling's designs were made for her by Victoria Toy Works in Wellington, Shropshire, England. These dolls were made from 1926 into the 1960's. The dolls are velvet as well as other fabrics, especially felt and velour. They will have a tag on the foot "Made in England by Norah Wellings." **Child:** All fabric with stitch jointed hips and shoulders. Molded fabric face with oil painted features. Some faces are papier maché with a stockinette covering. All original felt and cloth clothes, clean condition. **Painted eyes:**

12" - $425.00; 16" - $650.00; 20" - $900.00; 24" - $1,200.00. **Glass eyes:** 14" - $550.00; 16" - $750.00; 20" - $1,100.00.

Mounties, Black Islanders, Scots, and Other Characters: These are most commonly found. Must be in same condition as child. 8" - $85.00 up; 12" - $145.00 up; 14" - $185.00 up.

Glass Eyes: White: 14" - $300.00; 17" - $450.00. Black: 14" - $250.00; 20" - $400.00; 26" - $650.00.

Babies: Same description as child and same condition. 15" - $500.00; 22" - $900.00.

The Adolf Wislizenus doll factory was located at Waltershausen, Germany and the heads he used were made by Bahr & Proschild, Ernst Heubach of Koppelsdorf, and Simon & Halbig. The company was in business starting in 1851, but it is not known when they began to make dolls.

Marks:

Child: 1890's into 1900's. Bisque head on jointed body, sleep eyes, open mouth. No damage and nicely dressed. 12" - $185.00; 14" - $325.00; 17" - $400.00; 22" - $550.00; 25" - $625.00.

Baby: Bisque head in perfect condition and on five-piece bent limb baby body. No damage and nicely dressed. 16" - $475.00; 19" - $585.00; 25" - $950.00.

#110, 115: 16" - $1,100.00. **Glass eyes:** 16" - $3,800.00 up.

Left: 23" marked "28 A.W. Special Germany." Sleep eyes, open mouth, jointed body. Right: 28" Simon & Halbig mold #1250 with open mouth, kid body with bisque lower arms. 23" - $575.00; 28" - $975.00. *Courtesy Frasher Doll Auctions.*

English: William & Mary Period, 1690's–1700. Carved wooden head, eyes. Eyebrow and eyelashes are painted with tiny lines. Colored cheeks, human hair or flax wig. Wood body, carved wood hands shaped like forks. Legs are wood and jointed. Upper arms are cloth. In medium to fair condition: 15-18" - $55,000.00 up.

English: Queen Anne Period. Early 1700's. Eyebrows and lashes made of dots. Glass pupiless eyes (some painted). Carved wooden head, jointed wooden body, cloth upper arms. Nicely dressed and in overall good condition. 14" - $9,700.00 up; 18" - $19,000.00 up; 24" - $26,000.00 up.

11½" all wood with joints at elbows and knees. Made in 1960's and 1970's by Shackman of Japan. Applied wooden nose, stub hands, poor quality painted features. 11½" - $95.00. *Courtesy Kathy Tvrdik.*

English: Georgian Period, 1750's–1800. Round wooden head with gesso coating, inset glass eyes. Eyelashes and eyebrows made up of dots. Human or flax wig. Jointed wood body with pointed torso. Medium to fair condition: 13" - $2,950.00; 16" - $4,600.00; 18" - $5,200.00; 24" - $6,550.00.

English: 1800's–1840's. Gesso coated wooden head, painted eyes. Human hair or flax wig. Original gowns generally longer than wooden legs. 12-13" - $1,450.00; 15" - $1,950.00; 20" - $2,900.00.

German: 1810's–1850's. Hair is delicately carved and painted with little curls around face. Some have decorations carved in hair. Features are painted. All wood doll with pegged or ball jointed limbs. 7" - $765.00; 12-13" - $1,400.00; 16-17" - $1,700.00.

German: 1850's–1900. All wood with painted plain hairstyle. Some may have spit curls around face. 5" - $150.00; 8" - $235.00; 12" - $375.00. Same, except wooden shoulder head, more elaborate carved hair such as buns. Wood limbs and cloth body. 9-10" - $400.00; 16-17" - $600.00; 23" - $875.00.

German: After 1900. Turned wood head with carved nose. Hair painted and painted lower legs with black shoes. Peg jointed. 10-11" - $100.00. **Child:** All wood, body is fully jointed. **Glass eyes, open mouth:** 14-15" - $450.00; 18" - $700.00; 23" - $900.00.

Nesting Dolls: Called "Matryoshka." Prices are for the set. **Old:** 1930's and before. 3" - $35.00 up; 6" - $60.00 up; 8" - $85.00 up. **New:** 4" - $10.00; 6" - $20.00. **Political:** Includes Gorbachev, Yeltsin. 4½" - $25.00; 6½" - $40.00.

MODERN DOLLS

A variety of Madame Alexander dolls – 21" "Margaret O'Brien," 12" McGuffey Ana (Lissy), 12" "Katie & Tommy" made for FAO Schwarz. Shown with #1 Barbie by Mattel. "Margaret O'Brien" - $950.00; McGuffey Ana - $1,350.00; "Katie & Tommy" $1,100.00 each; Barbie - $2,600.00. *Courtesy Frasher Doll Auctions.*

14" "Waterfall Mermaid." Fill with water and tail changes colors. Made by A&R Toys for Kay-Bee Toys, Inc. Molded-on clothes. Has ocean and stars painted in eyes. $35.00. *Courtesy Kathy Tvrdik.*

ADVANCE

26" "Winnie - Walking, Talking, and Singing Doll." Hard plastic with vinyl head, sleep eyes and plastic attached shoes with roller on bottom of feet. Battery operated. Original in box, 1959. 21" - $225.00; 26" - $365.00. *Courtesy Gloria Anderson.*

The author's separate price guide covering over 1,000 Madame Alexander dolls is available from book dealers or Collector Books.
1953–1954: 7½-8" straight leg, non-walker, heavy hard plastic. **Party Dress:** Mint and all correct - $425.00 up. Soiled, dirty hair mussed or parts of clothing missing - $95.00. **Ballgown:** Mint and correct - $1,000.00 up. Soiled, dirty, bad face color, not original - $200.00. **Nude:** Clean and good face color. $200.00. Dirty and bad face color - $40.00.
1955: 8" straight leg walker. **Party Dress:** Mint and all correct. $435.00 up. Soiled, dirty, parts of clothes missing - $75.00. **Ballgown:** Mint and all correct - $1,200.00 up. Dirty, part of clothing missing, etc. - $150.00. **Basic sleeveless dress:** Mint - $250.00. Dirty - $40.00. **Nude:** Clean and good face

color - $275.00. Dirty, not original, faded face color - $35.00.
1956–1965: Bend knee walker. **Party Dress:** Mint and all correct - $300.00 up. Dirty, part of clothes missing, etc. - $65.00. **Ballgown:** Mint and correct - $1,000.00 up. Soiled, dirty, parts missing, etc. - $150.00. **Nude:** Clean, good face color - $125.00. Dirty, faded face color - $35.00. **Basic sleeveless dress:** Mint - $200.00. Dirty, faded face color - $40.00. **Internationals:** $125.00-250.00. Dirty, parts missing - $65.00.
1965–1972: Bend knee, non-walkers: **Party Dress:** Mint and original - $275.00 up. Dirty, parts missing, etc. - $50.00. **Internationals:** Clean and mint - $125.00. Dirty or soiled - $45.00. **Nude:** Clean, good face color - $100.00. Dirty, faded face color - $30.00.
1973–1976: "Rosies." Straight leg, non-walker, rosy cheeks and

8" #447 "Tea Party at Grandma's." Bend knee walker. Shown in 1955 catalog. In this condition - $400.00.
Courtesy Sandy Johnson Barts.

8" #440 plays in "Garden with Her Dog." Straight leg walker. 1955 only. In this condition - $400.00. *Courtesy Sandy Johnson Barts.*

marked "Alex." **Bride or Ballerina:** Bend knee walker - $250.00 up. Bend knee only - $135.00. Straight leg - $60.00. **Internationals:** $60.00. **Storybook:** $70.00.

1977–1981: Straight leg, nonwalker marked "Alexander." **Bride or Ballerina:** $50.00-60.00. **International:** $50.00-60.00. **Storybook:** $50.00-60.00.

1982–1987: Straight leg, nonwalker with deep indentation over upper lip that casts a shadow and makes the doll look as if it has a mustache. **Bride or ballerina:** $45.00-55.00. **International:** $50.00-60.00. **Story-book:** $50.00-60.00.

1988–1989: Straight leg, nonwalker with new face that is more like the older dolls and still marked with full name "Alexander." **Bride or ballerina:** $45.00-55.00. **International:** $45.00-55.00. **Storybook:** $50.00-60.00.

MADAME ALEXANDER – BABIES

Prices are for mint condition dolls.

Baby Brother or Sister: 1977–1982. 14" - $80.00; 20" - $75.00.

Baby Ellen: 1965–1972. 14" - $100.00.

Baby Lynn: (Black Sweet Tears) 1973–1975. 20" - $100.00.

Baby McGuffey: Composition. 22" - $165.00. Soiled - $50.00.

Bonnie: Vinyl. 1954-1955. 19" - $80.00. Soiled - $30.00.

Genius, Little: Composition. 18" - $145.00. Soiled - $45.00.

Genius, Little: Vinyl, may have flirty eyes. 21" - $100.00. Soiled - $35.00.

Genius, Little: 8" - $225.00. Soiled - $40.00.

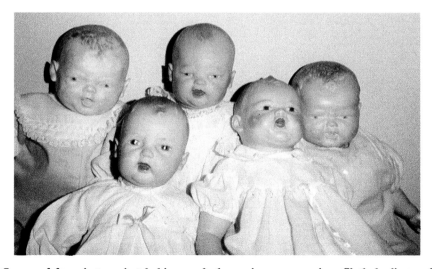

Group of frowning, crying babies made by various companies. Cloth bodies and early vinyl heads and limbs. Back row: Horsman and Madame Alexander. Front row: American Character, Arranbee, and Effanbee. All have painted features.
Courtesy Mauldin Doll Museum.

Happy: Vinyl, 1970 only. 20" - $250.00. Soiled - $75.00.

Honeybun: Vinyl, 1951. 19" - $140.00. Soiled - $40.00.

Huggums, Big: 1963–1979. 25" - $95.00. **Lively:** 1963. 25" - $125.00.

Kathy: Vinyl. 19" - $125.00; 26" - $165.00. Soiled: 19" - $35.00; 26" - $45.00.

Kitten, Littlest: Vinyl. 8" - $225.00 up. Soiled - $60.00.

Mary Cassatt: 1969–1970. 14" - $150.00; 20" - $225.00.

Mary Mine: 14" - $75.00. Soiled - $30.00.

Pinky: Composition. 23" - $165.00. Soiled - $75.00.

Precious: Composition. 12" - $145.00. Soiled - $55.00.

Princess Alexandria: Composition. 24" - $225.00. Soiled - $95.00.

Pussy Cat: Vinyl. 14" - $95.00-25.00. **Black:** 14" - $95.00. Soiled: $25.00.

Rusty: Vinyl. 20" - $350.00. Soiled - $85.00.

Slumbermate: Composition. 21" - $550.00. Soiled - $165.00.

Sweet Tears: 9" - $50.00. Soiled - $25.00. **With layette:** $150.00.

Victoria: 20" - $60.00. Soiled - $20.00.

Back row: Two 17" Madame Alexander "Genius Babies" with composition heads, hands and legs with remainder cloth. Sleep eyes and both mint and original. Front row: 1953 straight leg, non-walker "Bride" and Ginny "Square Dance Series" by Vogue. "Genius Babies," each - $250.00. Bride - $375.00; Ginny - $325.00. *Courtesy Frasher Doll Auctions.*

MADAME ALEXANDER – CISSETTE

This 10-11" doll with high heel feet was made from 1957 to 1963, but the mold was used for other dolls later. She is made of hard plastic, and clothes will be tagged "Cissette."

First prices are for mint condition dolls; second prices are for soiled, dirty or faded clothes, tags missing and hair messy.

Street Dresses: $200.00, $75.00

Ballgowns: $450.00, $150.00.

Ballerina: $425.00, $125.00.

Gibson Girl: $750.00, $200.00.

Jacqueline: $475.00 up, $150.00.

Margot: $385.00 up, $140.00.

Portrette: $425.00, $150.00.

Wigged in case: $1,200.00 up, $500.00.

Cissette dressed in #0733-1962. Also came in all white with red polka dots on top and ruffle under skirt plus red rick-rack trim on skirt. Called the "Square Dance" dress. $200.00 *Courtesy "Flip" Wilson.*

MADAME ALEXANDER – CISSY

"Cissy" was made 1955–1959 and had hard plastic with vinyl over the arms, jointed at elbows, and high heel feet. Clothes are tagged "Cissy."

Street Dress: $250.00.
Ballgown: $775.00.
Bride: $475.00 up.

Queen: $850.00.
Portrait: "Godey," etc. 21" - $1,400.00 up.
Scarlett: $1,000.00.
Flora McFlimsey: Vinyl head, in-set eyes. 15" - $575.00.

20" beautiful "Cissy Bride" #2190-1962 that has fantastic face color. In this unplayed with condition - $700.00.

MADAME ALEXANDER – CLOTH DOLLS

The Alexander Company made cloth and plush dolls and animals and also oil cloth baby animals in the 1930's, 1940's and early 1950's. In the 1960's, a few were made.

First prices are for mint condition dolls; second prices are for ones in poor condition, dirty, not original, played with or untagged.

Animals: $300.00 up, $85.00.

Dogs: $265.00, $95.00.

Alice in Wonderland: $800.00, $250.00.

Clarabelle, The Clown: 19" - $385.00, $125.00.

David Copperfield or Other Boys: $700.00-800.00.

Funny: $50.00, $15.00.

Little Shaver: 7" - $485.00; 10" - $500.00.

Little Women: $625.00-700.00 each, $225.00.

Muffin: 14" - $100.00, $30.00.

So Lite Baby or Toddler: 20" - $450.00, 150.00.

Susie Q: $650.00, $200.00.

Tiny Tim: $650.00, $200.00.

Teeny Twinkle: Has disc floating eyes. $500.00, 150.00.

MADAME ALEXANDER – CLOTH DOLLS

Large 21" "Little Shaver" made of all cloth with painted features. All original. $600.00. *Courtesy Kris Lundquist.*

MADAME ALEXANDER – COMPOSITION

First prices are for mint condition dolls; second prices are for dolls that are crazed, cracked, dirty, soiled clothes or not original.

Alice in Wonderland: 9" - $300.00, $85.00; 14" - $465.00, $100.00; 21" - $950.00, $250.00.

Babs Skater: 1948. 18" - $650.00, 200.00.

Baby Jane: 16" - $875.00, $300.00.

Brides or Bridesmaids: 7" - $250.00, $85.00; 9" - $265.00, $90.00; 15" - $275.00, $80.00; 21" - $585.00, $185.00.

"Karen Ballerina" of 1946-1947. All composition and original. Uses the "Margaret" face. $700.00. *Courtesy Green Museum.*

Dionne Quints: 8" - $175.00, $50.00; Set of five - $1,200.00. 11" - $350.00, $125.00; Set of five - $2,450.00. **Cloth Baby:** 14" - $500.00, $140.00; Set of five - $3,500.00. **Cloth Baby:** 16" - $700.00, $150.00. 19-20" - $675.00, $200.00.

Dr. DeFoe: 14-15" - $1,400.00, $500.00.

Fairy Princess: 1939. 15" - $600.00; 21" - $950.00 up.

Flora McFlimsey: (Marked "Princess Elizabeth.") Has freckles. 15" - $500.00, $150.00; 22" - $600.00-650.00, $200.00.

Flower Girl: (Princess Elizabeth) 1939-1947. 16" - $550.00, $125.00; 20" - $750.00, $300.00; 24" - $925.00, $475.00.

Internationals/Storybook: 7" - $265.00, $50.00; 11" - $325.00, $100.00.

Jane Withers: 13" - $950.00 up, $400.00; 18" - $1,300.00, $600.00.

Kate Greenaway: (Marked "Princess Elizabeth.") Very yellow blonde wig. 14" - $525.00, $175.00; 18" - $850.00, $300.00.

Little Colonel: 9" - $450.00, $150.00; 13" - $650.00, $275.00; 23" - $850.00, $400.00.

14" and 11" "McGuffey Ana." The 14" all hard plastic doll has a "Margaret" face and was made between 1948-1950. The 11" "Betty" doll is made of all composition, 1937-1939. Both dolls are all original. 14" - $625.00; 11" - $600.00.
Courtesy Shirley Bertrand.

Madelaine DuBain: 1937–1944. 14" - $575.00, $200.00; 17" - $700.00, $300.00.
Margaret O'Brien: 15" - $700.00, $300.00; 18" - $850.00, $285.00; 21" - $1,100.00, $500.00.
Marionettes: Tony Sarg: 12" - $265.00, $95.00. **Disney:** $350.00, $165.00. **Others:** 12" - $245.00, $95.00.
McGuffey Ana: (Marked "Princess Elizabeth.") 13" - $600.00, $185.00; 20" - $800.00, $350.00.
Military Dolls: 1943–1944. 14" - $750.00, $300.00.
Nurse: 1936–1940. 14-15" - $475.00 up.
Portrait Dolls: 1939–1941, 1946. 21" - $2,300.00 up, $950.00.
Princess Elizabeth: Closed mouth. 13" - $500.00, $175.00; 18" - $625.00, $250.00; 24" - $750.00, $350.00.
Scarlett: 9" - $425.00, $165.00; 14" - $850.00, $285.00; 18" - $1,000.00, $500.00; 21" - $1,400.00, $650.00.
Snow White: (Princess Elizabeth) 1939–1942. 13" - $400.00, $135.00; 18" - $600.00, $200.00.

Sonja Henie: 17" - $900.00, $350.00; 20" - $1,000.00, $450.00. **Jointed waist:** 14" - $800.00, $350.00.
Wendy Ann: 11" - $450.00, $150.00; 15" - $600.00, $200.00; 18" - $850.00, $400.00.

21" "Alice In Wonderland" with brown sleep eyes. All composition and original. (Wendy Ann) $950.00. *Courtesy Kris Lundquist.*

MADAME ALEXANDER – HARD PLASTIC

First prices are for mint condition dolls; second prices are for dolls that are dirty, played with, soiled clothes or not original.
Alice in Wonderland: 14" - $625.00, $200.00; 17" - $725.00, $300.00; 23" - $875.00, $400.00.
Annabelle: 15" - $500.00, $200.00; 18" - $600.00, $200.00; 23" - $700.00, $275.00.
Babs: 20" - $625.00, $200.00.
Babs Skater: 18" - $600.00, $200.00; 21" - $750.00, $375.00.

Ballerina: 14" - $285.00, $125.00.
Brenda Starr: 12", 1942. **Dress:** $200.00; **Gown:** $225.00 up; **Bride:** $200.00.
Binnie Walker: 15" - $185.00, $90.00; 25" - $375.00, $125.00.
Cinderella: 14" - $700.00, $285.00. **"Poor" outfit:** 14" - $650.00, $250.00.
Cynthia: Black doll. 15" - $950.00, $400.00; 18" - $1,000.00, $500.00; 23" - $1,200.00, $600.00.
Elise: 16½". **Street Dress:** $125.00, $60.00. **Ballgown:** $275.00, $125.00.

Bride: 16" - $325.00, $165.00.
Fairy Queen: 14½" - $675.00,
Godey Lady: 14" - $1,600.00, $700.00.
Man/Groom: 14" - $900.00,
$400.00.
Kathy: 15" - $750.00, $250.00.
Kelly: 12" - $425.00, $150.00; 16"
(Marybel): $300.00, $125.00.
Lissy: 12". **Street dress:** $285.00,
$165.00. **Bride:** $285.00, $150.00. **Ballerina:** $325.00, $165.00.
Little Women: 8" - $135.00,
$60.00; Set of five (bend knee) -
$700.00; Set of five (straight leg) -
$350.00. **Lissy:** 12" - $300.00, $100.00;

Set of five - $1,500.00. 14" - $425.00;
Set of five - $1,500.00.
Laurie: Bend knee. 8" - $135.00
up, $60.00; 12" - $325.00, $160.00.
Madeline: 1950–1953. Jointed
knees and elbows. 18" - $785.00, $375.00.
Maggie: 15" - $475.00, $185.00;
17" - $650.00, $250.00; 23" - $775.00,
$400.00.
Maggie Mixup: 8" - $425.00 up,
$150.00; 16½" - $350.00, $145.00. **Angel:**
8" - $1,000.00, $400.00.
Margaret O'Brien: 14½" -
$875.00, $400.00; 18" - $1,000.00,
$500.00; 21" - $1,250.00, $600.00.

Back row: 15" hard plastic "Beth" (Maggie), 18" hard plastic "Bride" (Margaret), and 16½" "Elise" hard plastic and all original. Front row: 14" "Ballgown Cinderella" and "Poor Cinderella" made of all hard plastic (Margaret) and 15" all hard plastic "Annabelle" (Maggie). Beth - **$425.00**; Bride - **$575.00**; Elise - **$275.00**; Ballgown - **$700.00**; Poor Cinderella - **$650.00**; Annabelle - **$500.00**.
Courtesy Turn of Century Antiques.

MADAME ALEXANDER – HARD PLASTIC

Mary Martin: Sailor suit or ballgown. 14" - $900.00 up, $450.00; 17" - $750.00, $385.00.
McGuffey Ana: 1948–1950. Hard plastic/vinyl. 21" - $850.00, $425.00.
Peter Pan: 15" - $800.00, $400.00.
Polly Pigtails: 14" - $650.00, $300.00; 17" - $850.00, $400.00.
Prince Charming: 14" - $775.00, $375.00; 18" - $850.00, $375.00.
Queen: 18" - $1,200.00, $600.00.
Shari Lewis: 14" - $300.00, $165.00; 21" - $475.00, $250.00.
Sleeping Beauty: 16½" - $550.00, $150.00; 21" - $875.00, $400.00.
Wendy (Peter Pan Set): 14" - $800.00, $400.00.
Wendy Ann: 14½" - $650.00, $250.00; 17" - $850.00, $365.00; 22" - $900.00, $425.00.
Winnie Walker: 15" - $245.00, $95.00; 18" - $375.00, $150.00; 23" - $425.00, $185.00.

16½" "Elise Bride" of 1959. Hard plastic head. Mint and original. Gown also made in pink. $575.00. *Courtesy Margaret Mandel.*

MADAME ALEXANDER – PLASTIC AND VINYL

First prices are for mint condition dolls; second prices are for dolls that are played with, soiled, dirty and missing original clothes.
Bellows' Anne: 1987 only. 14" - $75.00.
Bonnie Blue: 1989 only. 14" - $95.00.
Bride: 1982–1987. 17" - $125.00.
Caroline: 15" - $285.00, $100.00.
Cinderella: Pink: 1970–1981. **Blue:** 1983–1986. 14" - $75.00.
Edith, the Lonely Doll: 1958–1959. 16" - $245.00; 22" - $325.00.
Elise: 17", 1966. **Street dress:** $200.00. **Formal:** 1966, 1976–1977. $200.00. **Bride:** 1966–1986. $100.00.
First Ladies: First set of six - $800.00. Second set of six - $625.00. Third set of six - $575.00. Fourth set of six - $550.00. Fifth set of six - $475.00. Sixth set of six - $600.00.

Grandma Jane/Granny, Little: 1970–1972. 14" - $265.00, $100.00.
Ingres: 14", 1987 only. $75.00.
Isolde: 14", 1985 only. $90.00.
Jacqueline: 21". **Street Dress:** $575.00, $250.00. **Ballgown:** $700.00, $350.00. **Riding Habit:** $575.00, $250.00.
Janie: 12" - $285.00, $135.00.
Joanie: 36" - $350.00, $165.00.
Leslie: 17", black doll. **Ballgown:** 17" - $465.00, $225.00. **Ballerina:** $350.00, $100.00. **Street Dress:** $375.00, $175.00.
Little Shaver: Vinyl, 1963 only. 12" - $200.00, $85.00.
Nancy Drew: 1967 only. 12" - $375.00, $125.00.
Napoleon: 1980–1986. 12" - $60.00.
Marybel: 16" - $200.00, $90.00. **In case:** $350.00; $175.00.

Mary Ellen: 31" - $600.00, $275.00.

Melinda: 14" - $265.00, $125.00; 16" - $450.00, $200.00.

Michael with Bear: Peter Pan set. 11" - $450.00, $185.00.

Peter Pan: 14" - $385.00, $125.00.

Polly: 17" - $325.00, $145.00.

Renoir Girl: 14" - $90.00-65.00. **With watering can:** 1986–1987. $75.00-45.00. **With hoop:** 1986–1987. $75.00-45.00.

Scarlett: White gown, green ribbon. 1969–1986. 14" - $145.00, 70.00.

Smarty: 12" - $325.00, $145.00.

Sound of Music: Small set: $1,400.00. Large set: $1,700.00. **Liesl:** 10" - $200.00, $95.00; 14" - $225.00, $95.00. **Louisa:** 10" - $265.00, $125.00; 14" - $300.00, $145.00. **Brigitta:** 10" - $225.00, $95.00; 14" - $225.00, $95.00. **Maria:** 12" - $350.00, $150.00; 17" - $375.00, $160.00; **Marta:** 8" - $225.00, $75.00; 11" - $200.00, $145.00. **Gretl:** 8" - $225.00, $95.00; 11" - $200.00, $145.00. **Friedrich:** 8" - $225.00, $95.00; 11" - $200.00, $100.00.

Wendy: Peter Pan set. 14" - $300.00, $145.00.

12" "Janie" with freckles. Dress tagged "Janie" and is numbered "1122B-1965." Janie was made in 1964-1965 only. This dress also came in blue and white with red ribbon trim. $285.00
Courtesy Green Museum.

36" "Joanie" made of plastic and vinyl with sleep eyes, lashes, and smiling closed mouth. Made in 1960-1961 only. **$350.00.** *Courtesy David Spurgeon.*

Prices are for mint condition dolls. There are many 21" Portrait dolls and all use the Jacqueline face. The early ones have jointed elbows; later dolls have one-piece arms. All will be marked "1961" on head.

Agatha: 1967–1980. $450.00.

Bride: 1965. $900.00.

Coco: 21", 1966. **Portrait:** $2,200.00. **Street Dress:** $2,300.00. **Ballgown:** Other than portrait series. $2,200.00.

Cornelia: 1972–1978. $275.00-475.00.

Gainsborough: 1968–1978. $325.00-650.00.

Godey: 1965, 1967–1977. $625.00, $325.00-575.00.

Jenny Lind: 1969. $1,700.00.

Lady Hamilton: 1968: $475.00.

Madame Pompadour: 1970. $1,200.00.

Magnolia: 1977: $400.00. **1988:** $275.00.

Manet: 1982–1983. $275.00.

Melanie: 1967–1989. $350.00-575.00.

Mimi: 1971. $525.00.

Monet: 1984. $285.00.

Morisot: 1985–1986. $250.00.

Queen: 1965. $750.00 up.

Renoir: 1965–1973. $650.00-700.00.

Scarlett: 1965–1989. $300.00-1,200.00.

Toulouse-Lautrec: 1986–1987. $195.00.

21" "Agatha" of 1979 and 1980. Head will be marked "1961." Uses the "Jacqueline" doll. $450.00.

21" "Madame Doll" Portrait using the "Coco" doll of 1966 only. Mint with wrist tag. **$2,200.00.** *Courtesy Frasher Doll Auctions.*

13" "Jackie Robinson" doll made of all composition is original. Made in 1940's by Allied-Grand Doll Mfg. Co., Brooklyn N.Y. 13" - $1,000.00 up. *Courtesy Ellyn McCorkell.*

AMERICAN CHARACTER DOLL COMPANY

All American Character dolls are very collectible and all are above average in quality of doll material and clothes. Dolls marked "American Doll and Toy Co." are also made by American Character, and this name was used from 1959 until 1968 when the firm went out of business. Early dolls will be marked "Petite." Many will be marked "A.C."

First prices are for mint dolls; second prices are for dolls that have been played with, dirty, with soiled clothes or not original.

"A.C." marked child: Composition. 14" - $150.00, $50.00; 20" - $225.00, $95.00.

Annie Oakley: 1955, original, hard plastic. 17" - $400.00, $150.00.

Betsy McCall: See Betsy McCall section.

Butterball: 1961. 19" - $150.00, $75.00.

Cartwright: Ben, Joe or Hoss. 1966. 8" - $100.00, $45.00.

Chuckles: 1961. 23" - $165.00, $75.00. **Baby:** 18" - $125.00, $40.00.

Composition Babies: 1930's–1940's. Cloth bodies, marked "A.C." 14" - $95.00, $25.00. 22" - $145.00, $60.00. **Marked "Petite":** 1920's–1930's. 14" - $175.00, $80.00; 22" - $250.00, $100.00.

Cricket: 1964. 9" - $35.00, $15.00.
Growing hair: $40.00, $20.00.
Eloise: 1950's. A cloth character, yarn hair, crooked smile. (See photo in Series 7, pg. 212.) 14-15" - $250.00; 21" - $375.00.
Freckles: 1966. Face changes. 13" - $35.00, $15.00.
Hedda-Get-Betta: 1960. 21" - $100.00, $45.00.
Miss Echo, Little: 30" talker, 1964. (See photo in Series 8, pg. 190.) $225.00, $100.00.
"Petite" marked child: Composition. 16" - $200.00, $85.00; 20" - $265.00, $100.00; 24-25" - $345.00, $165.00.
Preteen: 14" child, marked "AM. Char. 63" (1963). Grow hair. $35.00, $15.00.
Puggy: All composition, painted eyes, frown, marked "Petite." 12-13" - $525.00, $165.00.
Ricky, Jr.: 1955–1956. 13" - $65.00, $30.00; 20" - $125.00, $45.00.
Sally: 1929–1935. Composition, molded hair in "Patsy" style. 12" - $185.00, $60.00; 14" - $200.00, $80.00. 16" - $265.00, $85.00; 18" - $295.00, $145.00.
Sally Says: 1965. Talker, plastic/vinyl. 19" - $75.00, $35.00.
Sweet Sue/Toni: 1949–1960. Hard plastic, some walkers, some with extra joints at knees, elbows and/or ankles, some combination hard plastic and vinyl. Marked "A.C. Amer. Char. Doll," or "American Character" in circle. Must have excellent face color and be original. Ballgown: 10½" (1958) - $165.00, $75.00; 15" - $265.00, $85.00; 18" - $345.00, $125.00. Street dress: 10½" (1958) - $125.00, $50.00; 15" - $200.00, $70.00; 18" - $325.00, $125.00; 22" - $375.00, $145.00; 24" - $450.00, $165.00; 30" - $565.00, $200.00. Vinyl: 10½" - $150.00, $45.00; 17" - $265.00, $60.00; 21" - $350.00, $100.00;

14" and 18" "Sweet Sue" by American Character. All hard plastic and original, has wrist tag with name. Both have mohair wigs. 14" - $200.00 up; 18" - $325.00 up. *Courtesy Kris Lundquist.*

21" "Sweet Sue." All hard plastic and original. 21" - $400.00 up. *Courtesy Sharon McDowell.*

25" - $465.00, $175.00; 30" - $550.00, $200.00. **Groom:** 20" - $450.00, $150.00. **Mint in box:** 14" - $350.00 up; 17-18" - $500.00 up.
Talking Marie: 1963. 18", vinyl/plastic. Record player in body, battery operated. $85.00, $30.00.
Tiny Tears: 1955–1962. **Hard plastic/vinyl:** 8" - $50.00, $20.00; 13" - $125.00, $45.00; 17" - $185.00, $90.00. **All vinyl:** 1963. 8" - $45.00, $15.00; 12" - $50.00, $25.00; 16" - $60.00, $30.00. **Mint in box:** 13" - $300.00 up.
Toodles: 1956–1960. **Baby:** 14" - $135.00, $50.00. **Tiny:** 10½" - $165.00, $50.00. **Toddler:** With "follow me eyes." 22" - $225.00, $80.00; 28" - $300.00, $130.00; 30" - $325.00, $165.00.
Toodle-Loo: 1961. 18" - $175.00, $80.00.
Tressy: 12½". **Grow Hair:** 1963–1964. (#1 heavy makeup). $55.00, $20.00. **#2 Mary/Magic Makeup:** 1965–1966. Pale face, no lashes, bend knees. $30.00, $10.00.
Whimette/Little People: 1963. 7½" - $20.00, $5.00.
Whimsey: 1960. 19" - $90.00, $35.00.

Collection of "Toodles" from baby, toddler, to child. All are mint and original. **$225.00 up.** *Courtesy Sherry Vandermeer.*

13" "Tiny Tears" with hard plastic head and vinyl body in original trunk with wardrobe. $285.00 up in case. Played with condition - $125.00. *Courtesy Ellyn McCorkell.*

The first tags were red woven lettering on white linen tape. Second tags were made of white rayon with red embroidered lettering. The third tags (around 1969) were red printing on white satin tape. The fourth tags (about 1976) had red printing on gauze-type cloth. The hair on dolls from 1934–1963 was made of yarn. From 1960–1963, hair was made of orange or yellow chicken feathers. Since 1963, the hair has been made of synthetic fur.

Animals became part of the line in 1964. On the oldest models, tails were made of the same materials as the body. During the mid-1970's, cotton bias tape was used and the ones made during the 1980's are made of cotton flannel.

Late 1980's kitten. Many kittens were made in the 1960's but none were made from mid-1970's to 1984. $50.00 up. *Courtesy Jeannie Mauldin.*

Child: 1950's: 10" - $2,000.00 up. **1960's:** 10" - $1,200.00 up. **1970's:** 10" - $300.00 up. **1980's:** $150.00.

Adults: 1950's: 10" - $3,000.00 up. **1970's:** 7" - $1,800.00.

Babies: Usually angels. **1960's:** 7-8" - $325.00. **1970's:** 7" - $275.00. **1980's:** 7" - $200.00.

Skiers: 1960's: 7" - $350.00 up. **1970's:** 7" - $200.00. **1980's:** 7" - $75.00 up.

Elf/Gnome: 1970's: 7" - $200.00; 12" - $300.00. **1980's:** 7" - $50.00; 12" - $85.00; 16" - $125.00; 22" - $165.00.

Monks: 1970's: 8" - $75.00 up.

Indians: 1970's: 7" - $200.00. **1980's:** 8" - $150.00 up; 18" - $250.00 up.

Santa/Mrs. Claus: 1970's: 7" to 26" - $75.00-200.00. **1980's:** 7 to 26" - $45.00-175.00.

Bears: 1970's: 7" - $150.00 up; 10" - $185.00 up; 18" - $265.00 up. **1980's:** 7" - $80.00 up; 10" - $150.00 up; 18" - $175.00 up.

8" rabbit of the 1980's. $50.00 up.
Courtesy Jeannie Mauldin.

Santa and Mrs. Claus standing Annalee figures. Shown with mischievous child dressed in hooded Christmas pajamas. Santa - $350.00; Mrs. Claus - $400.00; Child - $500.00. *Courtesy Nell Hudson.*

18" Ballerina Bear by Annalee. Made in 1985 in an edition of only 918. All felt and original. $225.00 up. *Courtesy Bette Todd.*

10" Valentine Panda by Annalee. Made in 1986 only with 1,940 being made. Adorable and rare. $300.00 up. *Courtesy Bette Todd.*

The Arranbee Doll Company began making dolls in 1922 and was purchased by the Vogue Doll Company in 1959. Vogue used the Arranbee marked molds until 1961. Arranbee used the initials "R & B."

First prices are for mint condition dolls; second prices are for dolls that have been played with, are cracked, crazed, dirty or do not have original clothes.

Angeline: 1951–1952. Hard plastic, mohair wig. 14" - $245.00; 18" - $300.00.

Babies: Bisque heads. See Armand Marseille section.

Babies: Original. 1930's–1940's. Composition/cloth bodies. 16" - $100.00, $45.00; 22" - $150.00, $60.00.

Bottletot: 1932–1935. Has celluloid bottle molded to celluloid hand. 18" - $225.00, $90.00.

These 10" dolls are vinyl with sleep eyes. All are from mid-1950's and original. Left: Marked "Vogue" has jointed waist. Center: Marked "ℙ" and made by Arranbee or Belle. Waist not jointed. Right: Ideal's "Little Miss Revlon." Marked "Ideal Doll VT 10½". Vogue - $135.00 up; ℙ - $95.00 up; Revlon - $85.00 up. *Courtesy Kathy Tvrdik.*

Debu-Teen: 1940. Composition girl with cloth body. 14" - $200.00, $75.00; 18" - $265.00, $95.00; 21" - $325.00, $125.00.

Dream Baby, My: (See Armand Marseille section for bisque heads.) **Composition:** 1934–1944. 14" - $265.00, $100.00; 16" - $375.00; 19" - $600.00. **Vinyl/cloth:** 1950. 16" - $65.00, $25.00; 23" - $135.00, $60.00.

Francine: Hard plastic, waist length saran wig, 1955. 14" - $250.00; 18" - $300.00.

Kewty: 1934–1936. Original. Composition "Patsy" style molded hair. 10" - $125.00, $45.00; 16" - $185.00, $85.00.

Littlest Angel: 1956, all hard plastic. 10" - $45.00, $10.00. **Vinyl head:** 10" - $30.00, $10.00. **Red hair/freckles:** 1960. 10" - $65.00, $30.00.

Miss Coty: 1958. Vinyl, marked "ℙ." ("ℙ" dolls also dressed and

21" baby marked "Arranbee" with cloth body and composition head and limbs. All original. Shown with all original "Terri Lee" cowgirl and all original Madame Alexander all composition "Sonja Henie" with sleep eyes, open mouth and dimples. 21" - $265.00; Terri Lee - $295.00 up; Sonja - $695.00 up. *Courtesy Turn of Century Antiques.*

marketed by Belle Doll Co.) 10" - $95.00, $30.00.

My Angel: 1961, plastic/vinyl. 17" - $40.00, $20.00; 22" - $65.00, $35.00; 36" - $150.00, $90.00. **Walker:** 30", 1957–1959. $100.00. **Oil cloth body/ vinyl:** 1959. 22" - $65.00.

Nancy: 1936–1940. Composition, molded hair or wig. 12" - $185.00, $65.00; 17" - $325.00, $140.00; 19" - $425.00, $165.00. **Hard plastic, vinyl arms/head:** 1951–1952 only. Wig. 14" - $135.00, $70.00; 18" - $185.00, $90.00. **Walker:** 24" - $250.00, $100.00.

Nancy Lee: 1939. **Composition:** 14" - $245.00, $100.00; 17" - $300.00, $150.00; 20" - $385.00, $165.00. **Hard plastic:** 1950–1959. 14" - $265.00, $100.00; 20" - $465.00, $150.00.

Nancy Lee: 1954. Unusual eyebrows/vinyl. 15" - $165.00, $85.00.

21" "Nancy Lee Bride" of 1950. Mohair wig and sleep eyes. In mint condition. 21" - **$465.00.** *Courtesy Sharon McDowell.*

Nancy Lee: 1952. Baby, painted eyes, "crying" look. 15" - $145.00, $70.00.

Nancy Lee: 1934–1939. Baby with composition head and limbs, open mouth with upper and lower teeth. 25" - $250.00, $95.00.

Nanette: 1949–1959. Hard plastic. 14" - $200.00, $85.00; 17" - $285.00, $100.00; 21" - $350.00, $150.00; 23" - $450.00, $165.00. **Walker:** Jointed knees, 1957–1959. 18" - $300.00, $100.00; 25" - $465.00, $200.00. **Plastic/vinyl walker:** 1955–1956. 30" - $195.00, $95.00. **Mint in box:** 17" - $400.00.

Sonja Skater: 1945. Composition. 14" - $265.00, $95.00; 17" - $300.00, $100.00; 21" - $400.00, $150.00.

Storybook Dolls: 1930–1936. All composition. Molded hair, painted eyes. 9-10" - $165.00, $45.00. **Mint in box:** $265.00.

Taffy: 1956. Looks like Alexander's "Cissy." 23" - $75.00, $40.00.

14" all hard plastic "Nanette" in original clothes. Replaced hair ribbons. Has floss-like wig. 14" - **$200.00 up.** *Courtesy Kris Lundquist.*

19-20" "Walking Raving Beauty." Came as regular doll and walker. Made by Artisan Novelty Co. about 1951. Mint with tube box but also came in regular style box. All hard plastic with large sleep eyes and open mouth. Excellent quality and clothes. 19" - $350.00 up. *Courtesy Kris Lundquist.*

20" all original and tagged "Raving Beauty" by Artisan. One doll has blue eyes; the other, brown eyes. Both are made of all hard plastic and have open mouths and glued-on wigs. Early 1950's. Each - $250.00 up. *Courtesy Patricia Woods.*

First prices are for mint dolls; second prices are for dolls in average condition, dirty, soiled, or not original.
Alfred E. Newman: Vinyl head. 20" - $200.00.
Captain Kangaroo: 19" - $125.00; 24" - $185.00.
Christopher Robin: 18" - $165.00.
Daisy Mae: 14" - $150.00; 21" - $200.00.

Emmet Kelly (Willie the Clown): 24" - $225.00.
Lil' Abner: 14" - $165.00; 21" - $225.00.
Mammy Yokum: Molded hair. 14" - $150.00; 21" - $200.00.
Mammy Yokum: Yarn hair. 14" - $185.00; 21" - $250.00.
Pappy Yokum: 14" - $150.00; 21" $200.00.

Original 13½" "Mammy Yokum" made by Baby Berry in late 1940's. Mask style face with painted features, vinyl hands, and stuffed cloth body. Marked "B.B." Clothes tag marked "Al Capp Dog Patch Family. Exclusive license Baby Berry Toy NYC." 14" $150.00. Mint in box - $400.00.
Courtesy Carol Turpin.

BARBIE

See related dolls, such as "Midge," "Ken," etc. under Mattel.
1958–1959: #1, holes in feet for metal cylinders on stand. **In box:** $3,000.00. **Doll only:** Mint. $1,700.00 up. **Very good:** $1,200.00.
1960: #3, curved eyebrows, marked 1959 body. **In box:** $550.00 up. **Doll only:** $250.00.
1961: #4, marked "Pat. Pend. 1961." $300.00. **Bubble cut:** $250.00.

1963: Fashion Queen with 3 wigs. $250.00.
1964: Ponytail with swirl bangs. No curly bangs. $250.00. **In box:** $325.00.
1965: Color 'n Curl. 2 heads and accessories. First bend knee, Dutch boy style hair, full bangs. $500.00.
1967: Twist 'n Turn. $90.00.
1968: Spanish Talking. $195.00.
1969: Twist 'n Turn in pink swim-

suit fashioned with a fan blade design. $95.00 up.

1970: Standard Barbie. Pink/green vertical striped swimsuit. $60.00.

1971: Growing Pretty Hair: $350.00 up. New Living: $75.00 up. Live Action: $85.00.

1972: Ward's Anniversary: $225.00. Busy Barbie: Long hair. $100.00. Growing Pretty Hair: Long gown, blue top, and red print skirt. $250.00. Walk Lively: $85.00.

1973: Quick Curl: $95.00.

1974: Newport: 45.00. Sun Valley: $80.00. Sweet Sixteen: $85.00.

1975: Free Moving: $70.00. Funtime: $70.00. Gold Medal Skater: $60.00. Winter Sports: $40.00. Olympic Sports: $45.00. Hawaiian: $90.00.

1976: Ballerina: $60.00. Deluxe Quick Curl: $60.00. Free Moving: $70.00. Beautiful Bride: $90.00. Gold Medal Skier: $60.00.

Mint 11½" #3 "Barbie." Doll only - $150.00 up. In box - $350.00 up.

1977: Super Star: $75.00.

1978: Super Size Barbie: $150.00 up. Fashion Photo: $60.00. In The Spotlight: $95.00.

1979: Pretty Changes: $80.00. Kissing: $60.00. Sunloving Malibu: $25.00 up.

1980: Beauty Secrets: $45.00; Black Barbie: $50.00. Roller Skater: $25.00.

1981: Western: $40.00.

1982: Pink & Pretty: $40.00. Magic Curl: $60.00. Fashion Jeans: $25.00. All Stars: $35.00.

1983: Twirly Curls: White - $35.00; Black, Hispanic - $75.00. Happy Birthday: $35.00.

1983: My First Barbie: $20.00. My First Barbie: Short dress, second issue. $25.00.

1983: Horse Loving: $40.00. Golden Dream: Department store. $60.00. Dream Date: $25.00. Angel Face: $30.00.

1984: Loving You: $15.00. Sun

#1 Barbie. Has inverted "V" eyebrows, eyes with white painted irises. Doll has metal holes in bottom of feet to fit #1 stand. Doll only - $1,000.00 up.

Gold Malibu: $15.00. Great Shape:
$35.00. Crystal: $30.00.
1985: Peaches & Cream: $50.00.
Dreamtime: $25.00. Day to Night:
$35.00.
1986: Dream Glow: $40.00. Rock-
ers: $50.00 up. Gift Giving: $20.00.
Tropical: $20.00. Astronaut: Red/silver
suit. $85.00. Magic Moves: $25.00.
Holiday Specials: 1988: Red
gown. $400.00 up. **1989:** White gown/
marabou trim. $125.00 up.
Bob Mackie: 1990. Gold sequin
gown in case. $200.00 up.
International, Specials:
1981: Royal, Parisian, Italian.
$65.00.
1982: Scottish: $165.00. Oriental:
$125.00.
1983: Hawaiian: $60.00. Eskimo:
$175.00. India: $175.00.
1984: Spanish: $150.00. Swedish:
$80.00.
1985: Swiss, Irish: $165.00.
1986: Japanese: $125.00. Greek:
$40.00. Peruvian: $40.00. German:
$40.00. Canadian: $40.00. Korean:
$40.00. Hispanic: $80.00.

"Royal Barbie" made in **1979** but
marketed in **1980. One of the first
three International Series department
store specials. $65.00.** *Courtesy Gloria
Anderson.*

**Talking Ken and Barbie in original gift set which is a very rare
item. $600.00 up.** *Courtesy Marie Ernst.*

Barbie Gift Sets:
Olympic Gymnast: $65.00.
Fur Collection: $200.00 up.
Malibu Beach Party: $95.00.
Ice Breaker: Boxed. $450.00.
Career Girl: Boxed. $350.00.
Mix 'n Match Set: 1962. $550.00 up.
Sparkling Pink: 1963. $500.00 up.
Round The Clock Wedding Party:
1964. $550.00 up.
On Parade: Majorettes. $700.00 up.

#3 ponytail "Barbie" shown in "Masquerade" outfit. Doll - **$150.00.** Outfit - **$90.00.** *Courtesy Kathy Tvrdik.*

Barbie Items:
Travel Trailer: $50.00.
Silver-vette: $50.00.
Cycle: $25.00.
Roadster: $265.00.
Sports Car: $250.00.
Dune Buggy: $90.00.
Clock: $45.00.
Family House: $165.00.
Watches: $20.00-45.00. Small dial watch: $50.00.
Airplane: $1,000.00 up.
Horse "Dancer": Brown. $150.00.
First Barbie stand: Round, two pronged. $200.00.
Heirloom Service: $85.00.
Record Tote: $25.00.
Photo Album: $40.00.
Diary: 1963. $30.00.
Autograph book: 1962. $30.00.
Barbie Clothes:
1958: #900 series. Easter Parade: $900.00. Gay Parisienne: $900.00. Roman Holiday: $900.00. Solo In Spotlight: $900.00.
Enchanted Evening: Pink gown. $185.00. Plantation Belle: $250.00. Picnic Set: $135.00. Commuter set: $150.00.
1963: Drum Majorette: $90.00. Cheerleader: $90.00. Little Theatre outfits: $85.00-200.00. Travel outfits: $40.00-80.00. Masquerade: $90.00. Sophisticated Lady: Pink gown, red cape with high collar. $200.00. Midnight Blue gown and cape: $250.00.
1964: Astronaut: $185.00. Holiday Dance: $50.00. Campus Sweetheart: $90.00. Junior Prom: $75.00. Skin Diver: $45.00.
1965: Golden Glory: $60.00. Benefit Performance: $195.00. Debutante Ball: $125.00. Riding In Park: $70.00. Reception Line: $70.00. Garden Wedding: $100.00.
1966: Patio Party: $80.00. Evening Enchantment: $165.00 up. Tropicana: $85.00. Floating Gardens: $165.00.

One of the most desirable of the the early "Barbie" outfits and accessories is "The Candy Striper." In box - $125.00. *Courtesy Bessie Carson.*

Flocked hair "Ken" shown in "Barbie's Sports Car." $250.00. *Courtesy Kathy Tvrdik.*

First prices are for mint condition dolls; second prices are for played with, dirty, soiled or not original dolls. **8":** 1958. All hard plastic, jointed knees. Made by American Character Doll Co. **Street Dress:** $175.00, $70.00. **Ballgown:** $200.00 up, $90.00. **Bathing Suit or Romper:** $125.00, $40.00. **Ballerina:** $185.00; $65.00. **Riding Habit:** $185.00, $80.00.

11½": Brown sleep eyes, reddish rooted hair, vinyl/plastic. Original, made by Uneeda but unmarked. $125.00, $50.00.

13": Made by Horsman, 1975, but doll is marked "Horsman Dolls, Inc. 1967" on head. $50.00, $30.00.

14": 1961. Vinyl with rooted hair, medium high heels, round sleep eyes. Made by American Character Doll Company, marked "McCall 1958." $245.00, $100.00.

14": Vinyl head, rooted hair, rest hard plastic marked "P-90 body." Made by Ideal Doll Company. $285.00, $85.00.

22": Unmarked, made by American Character. Extra joints at waist,

Left: 8" "Betsy McCall" made of all hard plastic with jointed knees. Has sleep eyes, and all original clothes. This outfit is an extra boxed one and came with or without the vest and with various hats. Right: 8" "Betsy McCall" in play dress. Black leotards, shoes, and original dress. Each - $175.00.

ankles, wrists and above knees.
$250.00, $85.00.

20": Vinyl with rooted hair, slender limbs and made by American Character Doll Company. (Allow more for flirty eyes.) $300.00, $100.00.

22": Vinyl/plastic with extra joints and made by Ideal Doll Company. $325.00, $125.00.

29-30": All vinyl, rooted hair and made by American Character Doll Company. $400.00, $165.00.

29": Marked "McCall 1961." Has extra joints at ankles, knees, waist and wrists. Made by American Character. $450.00, $140.00.

8" "Betsy McCall" in rare "Glamour Girl" outfit. 8" in this outfit - $195.00.
Courtesy Sandy Johnson Barts.

29": Marked "B.M.C. Horsman 1971." $200.00, $70.00.

36": All vinyl with rooted hair and made by American Character Doll Company. $650.00 up, $300.00.

36": Marked "McCall 1959." Made by Ideal Doll Company. $550.00 up, $225.00.

39": Boy called "Sandy McCall." Marked same as above girl. Made by Ideal Doll Company. $700.00 up, $350.00.

14" "Betsy McCall" made of hard plastic with vinyl head. All original with sleep eyes. Never used pattern came with doll. 14" - $285.00 up. *Courtesy Ellen Dodge.*

BLOCK DOLL CORPORATION

10" all hard plastic walker made by Block Doll Corporation in mid-1950's. Jointed knees and very much like the Arranbee's "Little Angel" except face is different enough to distinguish. Original with replaced shoes. Mint - $85.00; played with condition - $35.00. *Courtesy Kathy Tvrdik.*

BUDDY LEE

"Buddy Lee" dolls were made in composition to 1949, then changed to hard plastic and discontinued in 1962–1963. "Buddy Lee" came dressed in two "Coca-Cola" uniforms. The tan with green stripe outfit matched the uniforms worn by delivery drivers while the white with green stripe uniforms matched those of plant workers. (Among Coca-Cola employees the white uniform became more popular and in warmer regions of the country, the white outfit was also worn by outside workers.)

"Buddy Lee" came in many different outfits.

Engineer: $275.00 up.
Gas Station attendant: $265.00 up.
Cowboy: $350.00 up.
Coca-Cola uniform: White with green stripe - $350.00 up. Tan with green stripe - $400.00 up.
Other soft drink companies uniforms: $300.00 up.
Hard Plastic: Original clothes. $350.00 up.

All composition "Buddy Lee" with jointed shoulders only. Painted-on boots, original cowboy outfit. $350.00 up. *Courtesy Ellyn McCorkell.*

CAMEO DOLL COMPANY

Annie Rooney, Little: 1926. All composition, legs painted black, molded shoes. 12" - $425.00; 17" - $800.00

Baby Bo Kaye: 1925. Bisque head, open mouth. 16" - $2,550.00; 19-21" - $3,100.00. **All bisque:** 4½" - $1,300.00; 6½" - $1,700.00. **Celluloid head:** 12" - $375.00; 15" - $685.00. **Composition head:** Mint: 14" - $550.00. Light craze and not original: 14" - $125.00.

Baby Mine: 1962–1964. Vinyl/cloth, sleep eyes. Mint: 16" - $125.00; 19" - $165.00. Slightly soiled and not original: 16" - $60.00; 19" - $75.00.

Bandy: Wood/composition. Ad doll for General Electric. Large ears. Majorette uniform painted on. Tall hat (non-removable). 17" - $425.00 up.

Betty Boop: 1932. Composition head, wood jointed body. Mint: 12" - $625.00. Light craze and a few paint chips: 12" - $300.00.

Champ: 1942. Composition/freckles. Mint: 16" - $600.00. Light craze, not original: 16" - $300.00.

Giggles: 1946. Composition, molded loop for ribbon. Mint: 11" - $300.00; 14" - $565.00. Light craze: 11" - $145.00; 14" - $200.00.

Ho-Ho: 1940. **Plaster:** In excellent condition. 4" - $50.00. **Vinyl:** in excellent condition: 4" - $10.00.

Joy: 1932. Composition, wood jointed body. Mint: 10" - $300.00; 15" - $450.00. Slight craze: 10" - $145.00; 15" - $200.00.

Kewpie: See Kewpie section.

Margie: 1935. **Composition:** Mint: 6" - $200.00; 10" - $265.00. Slight craze and not original: 6" - $90.00; 10" - $125.00. **Segmented wood/composition:** 1929. 9½" - $300.00, 145.00.

Miss Peep: 1957 and 1970's. Pin jointed shoulders and hips. **Vinyl:** Mint and original: 1960's. 18" - $45.00. **Black:** 18" - $80.00. Slightly soiled and not original: 18" - $28.00. **Black:** 1972. 18" - $35.00. **Ball jointed shoulders and hips:** 1970's–1980's. 17" - $60.00; 21" - $95.00.

Miss Peep, Newborn: 1962. Plastic and vinyl. Mint and original: 18" - $35.00. Slight soil and not original: 18" - $20.00.

Peanut, Affectionately: 1958. Vinyl. Mint and original: 18½" - $70.00. Slight soil and not original: 18½" - $35.00.

14½" **"Joy"** by Cameo. Wood and composition. Hole in molded hair for bow. Painted-on slippers. In mint condition. **$450.00 up.** *Courtesy Shirley Bertrand.*

15" **"Margie"** by Cameo. Wood and composition segmented body and limbs. Original dress. Molded hair band. Note strange cut of slippers. **$450.00 up.** *Courtesy Shirley Bertrand.*

Pete the Pup: 1930–1935. Composition, wood jointed body. Mint: 9" - $250.00. Slight craze and few paint chips: 9" - $100.00.
Pinkie: 1930-1935. **Composition:** Mint and original. 10" - $300.00. Slight craze: 10" - $145.00. **Wood jointed body:** 10" - $325.00. **Vinyl/plastic:** 1950's. Mint: 10-11" - $165.00. Slight soil and not original: 10-11" - $100.00.
Plum: 1952–1954. Body hinged like "Miss Peep." Dimples. 18" - $65.00; 23" - $90.00.
Scootles: 1925, 1930's. **Composition:** Mint and original. 8" - $400.00 up; 12" - $450.00 up; 15" - $575.00 up; 20" - $775.00. Light craze and not original: 8" - $100.00; 12" - $225.00; 15" -

$285.00; 20" - $350.00. **Composition:** Sleep eyes, mint. 15" - $600.00; 21" - $800.00 up. Slight craze: 15" - $350.00; 21" - $385.00. **Black, composition:** Mint. 15" - $775.00. Slight craze: 15" - $300.00. **Vinyl:** 1964. Mint, original. 14" - $185.00 up; 19" - $350.00 up; 27" - $500.00 up. Lightly soiled and not original: 14" - $80.00; 19" - $125.00; 27" - $200.00. **All Bisque:** See that section.
Pretty Bettsie: Composition, one piece body and limbs. Molded hair, smile. Molded-on yellow, pink, or blue short dress with white ruffles at hem. Painted-on shoes and socks. Separate wooden neck joint. Chest paper label marked "Pretty Bettsie/Copyright J. Kallus." 9" - $200.00; 14" - $285.00 up.

21" "Skootles" that is all composition and original. Rare sleep eyes. In mint condition - $785.00 up. *Courtesy Shirley Bertrand.*

10" tall and all cloth with soft sculptured face. Wooden stand with label "Made in the Philippines." Looks like Fidel Castro or could represent Confederate soldier. 10" - $85.00.
Courtesy Cecil Kates.

17" brown toaster cover doll. Homemade from pattern. Pattern also will make a "topsy-turvy" style two-headed doll. 17" - $25.00.

Beautiful 15" cloth child of World War II. Mask face that is oil painted, yarn hair, and all original. $85.00. *Courtesy Gloria Anderson.*

Late 1920's - early 1930's all cloth doll with painted features. When examined, appears to be factory made, but may be a pattern to cut and sew at home. Original. $30.00.

CREATA

11½" "Flower Princess" called "Fancy Fashions" of 1982. Made by Creata International, Inc. All vinyl teen with painted features. This doll is named "Lissette." The "Flower Princess" dolls and their clothes were extremely well designed and made. Very collectible. 11½" - $45.00. *Courtesy Marie Ernst.*

14" porcelain "Shirley Temple" in Scots outfit made by Danbury Mint. Glass eyes, high bisque color, but extremely fine mouth detail. Marked "20th Century/Film Corp/All Rights Reserved. D/M Shirley Temple. 14" - $335.00. *Courtesy Kathy Tvrdik.*

18" "Princess Diana" made by Danbury Mint. Porcelain and cloth, metal tiara and earrings. Train on gown is over a yard long. Rather high face color and lacks artist detail to eyes. 18" - $250.00.

This company also used the names Topper Toys, Topp Corp., and Topper Corp. They were well known for making dolls that did things and were battery operated during the 1960's and 1970's. These dolls have become highly collectible as they were well played with and not many dolls survived.

Penny Brite: 8" child. Mint - $30.00. Played with - $20.00 up.

Susie Cute: 1964. 7" - $18.00.

Baby Boo: Battery operated, 1965. 21" - $50.00.

Baby Magic: 1966. 18" - $60.00.

Baby Tickle Tears: 14" - $45.00.

Party Time: Battery operated, 1967. 18" - $50.00.

Lil' Miss Fussy: Battery operated. 18" - $50.00.

30" "Betty Bride" from 1957. One-piece stuffed vinyl body and limbs, high heel feet. Vinyl head with rooted hair. Also came as "Rosemary" in blue, lavender, yellow, or pink ballgown with silver threads running through it. These dolls were sold in grocery stores. Many of these dolls survived and show up in flea markets, shows, and auctions. Mint - $125.00; Played with - $75.00.
Courtesy Ellyn McCorkell.

6" "Private Ida," one of the "Go-Go" set and made by Topper Toys. One piece body and limbs with wire so limbs are posable. 1965–1966. $35.00 in box. *Courtesy Kathy Tvrdik.*

Baby Catch A Ball: Battery operated, 1969. 18" - $55.00.

Baby Peek 'N Play: Battery operated, 1969. 18" - $45.00.

Smarty Pants: Battery operated, 1971. 19" - $40.00.

Dawn: 6". Mint - $15.00. In original box - $20.00. Played with - $6.00.

Dawn Model Agency Dolls: Mint - $35.00. In box - $45.00. Played with - $18.00.

Boys of Dawn Series: Mint - $28.00. In box - $35.00. Played with - $15.00.

6" "Dawn" and two of the "Model" dolls. 1970–1971. Dawn - $20.00; Models - $35.00. *Courtesy Gloria Anderson.*

DOLL ARTIST

16" pre-1986 "Honey" that was limited to 25. A wonderful example of the quality that flows from the designer's fingers. Made by Susan Dunham of Dunham Art Studios. 16" - $1,800.00 up.

21" "Mary, Queen of Scots" from the Royal Collection of 1982–1983. Designed and made by Susan Cathey Dunham of Dunham Art Studios. 21" - $1,200.00. *Photo by John Lynch.*

28" "Hillary" made by Ruth Belaire of Wisconsin. Cloth and bisque with pouty mouth and glass eyes. Original - $2,600.00. *Courtesy Shirley Bertrand.*

7" jointed wooden dolls of historical figures are made by Frances Bringloe of Seattle, Washington. Very detailed and rare. $800.00 up. *Courtesy Shirley Bertrand.*

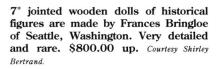

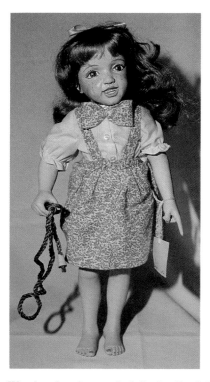

Wooden hand carved dolls by Paul Spencer. Right: Adorable child "Becky" that is jointed with open/closed mouth, two rows of teeth, and painted features. Left: Delightful boy figure entitled "Playing Hooky." Carved hair and painted features. Girl - $800.00; Boy - $675.00.

Standing: 19" "Baby #1" with cloth body, wax over bisque head and limbs, and glass eyes. Sitting: "Ida #2/250" is of the same construction. Both were made by Brigid Deval in 1988. Baby - $4,900.00. *Courtesy Shirley Bertrand.*

The name of this company was made up from the name of the founder E.G. Goldberger. Founded in 1917, the early dolls were marked "E.G.", then E. Goldberger" and now the marks of "Eegee" and "Goldberger" are used.

Andy: Teen type. 12" - $35.00.
Annette: Teen type. 11½" - $55.00. 1966, marked "20/25M/13." 25" - $60.00; 28" - $75.00; 36" - $100.00.

19" "Annette" made of plastic and vinyl. Has sleep eyes, rooted hair. Marked "Eegee/15/PM/19." Also came in 25" size marked "20/25/13 Eegee." Made in 1966. Was released in 1970's as "Carol." 19" - $55.00. *Courtesy Kathy Tvrdik.*

12" "Andy" made of plastic and vinyl. Has molded hair and painted features. Marked "Eegee 1961" on head. Can also be marked "Eg. 1961." $35.00. *Courtesy Kathy Tvrdik.*

Annette: 1966, plastic/vinyl walker. 25" - $50.00; 28" - $75.00; 36" - $100.00.
Baby Luv: 1973, cloth/vinyl, marked "B.T. Eegee." 14" - $45.00.
Baby Susan: 1958, name marked on head. 8½" - $20.00.
Baby Tandy Talks: 1960, foam body/vinyl, pull string talker. $70.00.
Babette: 1962, Barbie look-alike. 11½" - $85.00 up.

Ballerina: 1958, hard plastic/vinyl head. 20" - $50.00.
Ballerina: 1964, hard plastic/vinyl head. 31" - $135.00.
Ballerina: 1967. Foam body and limbs, vinyl head. 18" - $40.00.
Boy Dolls: Molded hair, rest vinyl. 13" - $35.00; 21" - $50.00.
Composition: Sleep eyes, open mouth girls. 14" - $185.00 up; 18" - $235.00 up. **Babies:** Cloth and composition. 16" - $100.00 up; 20" - $160.00 up.
Debutante: 1958, vinyl head, rest hard plastic, jointed knees. 28" - $125.00.
Dolly Parton: 1980. 12" - $35.00; 18" - $70.00.

15" "Barbara Cartland," famous romance novelist. Made in 1983 and marked "Eegee Co." on head, "1963-Eegee" on body. Uses the "Gemmette" plastic body and vinyl arms. Painted features on rather adult face. Original - **$48.00.** *Courtesy David Spurgeon.*

Flowerkins: 1963, 16", plastic/vinyl, marked "F-2" on head. (7 in set.) In box - $90.00. Played with, no box - $30.00.
Gemmette: 1963, teen type. (See photo in Series 8, pg. 216.) 14" - $45.00.
Georgie or Georgette: 1971, red-headed twins. Cloth and vinyl. 22-23" - $55.00.
Gigi Perreaux: 1951, hard plastic, early vinyl head. 17" - $250.00 up.
Granny: from "Beverly Hillbillies." Old lady modeling, grey rooted hair, painted or sleep eyes. 14" - $75.00.
Miss Charming: 1936, all composition Shirley Temple look-alike. 19" - $385.00 up. Pin - $25.00.
Miss Sunbeam: 1968, plastic/vinyl, dimples. 17" - $35.00.

Eegee's "Susan Stroller" that is made just like the Ideal doll "Saucy Walker" but will be unmarked. This one is mint and original. Pin hip walker, sleep eyes, and all hard plastic. 20" - $60.00.
Courtesy Ellyn McCorkell.

EEGEE DOLL COMPANY

Musical Baby: 1967, has key wind music box in cloth body. 17" - $30.00.

My Fair Lady: 1956, all vinyl, jointed waist, adult type. 10½" - $50.00; 19" - $85.00.

Posey Playmate: 1969, foam and vinyl. 18" - $30.00.

Puppetrina: 1963. 22" - $40.00.

Shelly: 1964, "Tammy" type. Grow hair. 12" - $25.00.

Sniffles: 1963, plastic/vinyl nurser. Marked "13/14 AA-EEGEE." 12" - $20.00.

Susan Stroller: 1955, hard plastic/vinyl head. 15" - $48.00; 20" - $60.00; 23" - $70.00; 26" - $80.00.

Tandy Talks: 1961, plastic/vinyl head, freckles, pull string talker. 20" - $75.00.

EFFANBEE DOLL COMPANY

First prices are for mint condition dolls; second prices for dolls that are played with, soiled, dirty, cracked or crazed or not original. Dolls marked with full name or "F & B."

Alyssia: 1958, walker. Hard plastic/vinyl head. 20" - 285.00, $100.00.

American Children: (See photo in Series 8, pgs. 217-218.) 1938. Marked with that name, some have "Anne Shirley" marked bodies, others are unmarked. All composition, painted or sleep eyes. **Closed Mouth Girls:** 19-21" - $1,400.00. **Closed Mouth Boy:** 15" - $1,200.00; 17" - $1,400.00. **Open Mouth Girl:** (Barbara Joan) 15" - $750.00; (Barbara Ann) 17" - $800.00; (Barbara Lou) 21" - $975.00 up.

Anne Shirley: 1936-1940. Marked with name. All composition. 15" - $250.00; 17" - $285.00; 21" - $365.00; 27" - $475.00.

Armstrong, Louis: 1984-1985 only. 15½" - $95.00.

Babyette: 1946, cloth/composition. Sleeping. 12" - $265.00, $125.00; 16" - $350.00; $175.00.

Babykin: 1940. **All composition:** 9-12" - $185.00, $85.00. **All vinyl:** 10" - $35.00.

Baby Cuddleup: 1953, oil cloth body, vinyl head and limbs. Two lower teeth. 20" - $50.00, $20.00; 23" - $85.00, $40.00.

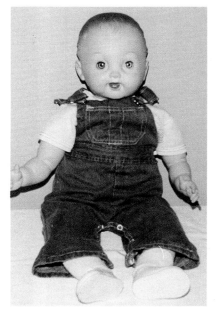

25" "Baby Cuddleup" of 1953. Oil cloth body with vinyl head and limbs. Open mouth with two lower teeth. Nicely molded, painted hair. 25" - $55.00.
Courtesy Jeannie Mauldin.

Baby Dainty: 1912-1922. Marked with name. Composition/cloth. 15" - $250.00, $95.00; 17" - $300.00, $125.00.

Baby Evelyn: 1925, marked with name. Composition/cloth. 17" - $300.00, $125.00.

EFFANBEE DOLL COMPANY

Baby Grumpy: See Grumpy.
Baby Tinyette: 1933-1936. Composition. 7-8" - $245.00, $100.00. **Toddler:** 7-8" - $265.00; $100.00.

Betty Brite: 1933, marked with name. All composition, fur wig, sleep eyes. 16-17" - $285.00, $100.00.

Bright Eyes: 1938, 1940's. Same doll as Tommy Tucker and Mickey. Composition/cloth, flirty eyes. 16" - $275.00; 18" - $325.00; 22-23" $375.00.

Brother or Sister: 1943. Composition head and hands, rest cloth, yarn hair, painted eyes. 12" - $175.00, $70.00; 16" - $200.00, $80.00.

Bubbles: 1924, marked with name. Composition/cloth. 15" - $275.00, $125.00; 19" - $325.00, $145.00; 22" - $425.00, $200.00; 25" - $450.00, $200.00. **Black:** 16" - $550.00; 20" - $865.00.

Button Nose: (See photo in Series 8, pg. 218.) 1936–1943. **Composi-**

27½" "Bubbles." Composition and cloth with rare toddler legs. Sleep eyes, open mouth, and molded hair. 27½" - **$695.00.** *Courtesy Turn of Century Antiques.*

tion: 8-9" - $185.00, $75.00. **Vinyl/cloth:** 1968. 18" - $45.00, $25.00.

Candy Kid: 1946, all composition. 12" - $265.00, $95.00. **Black:** 12" - $325.00, $95.00.

Churchill, Sir Winston: 1984. $85.00.

Charlie McCarthy: Composition/cloth. 15" - $325.00; 19-20" - $565.00, $200.00.

Coquette: Composition, molded hair (some with loop for ribbon), painted eyes, smile. 10" - $225.00; 14" - $285.00.

Composition Dolls: Molded hair, all composition, jointed neck, shoulders and hips. Painted or sleep eyes. Open or closed mouth. Original clothes. All composition in perfect condition. Marked "Effanbee." 1930's. 9" - $200.00, $85.00; 15" - $225.00, $100.00; 18" - $285.00, $125.00; 21" - $350.00, $150.00.

Composition Dolls: 1920's. Cloth body, composition head and limbs, open or closed mouth, sleep eyes. Original clothes and in perfect condition. Marked "Effanbee." 18" - $175.00, $90.00; 22" - $225.00, $125.00; 25" - $325.00, $125.00; 27-28" - $400.00, $150.00.

Currier & Ives: Plastic/vinyl. 12" - $45.00, $15.00.

Disney Dolls: 1977–1978. Cinderella, Snow White, Alice in Wonderland and Sleeping Beauty. 14" - $250.00, $95.00.

Emily Ann: 1937. 13" puppet, composition. $165.00, $60.00.

Dydee Baby: 1933 on. Hard rubber head, rubber body. Later versions had hard plastic head. Perfect condition. 14" - $165.00, $60.00.

Dydee Baby: 1950 on. Hard plastic/vinyl: 15" - $150.00, $50.00; 20" - $225.00, $150.00.

Fields, W.C.: 1938. Composition/cloth. 22" - $695.00, $200.00. Plastic/vinyl: 15" - $225.00.

224

Fluffy: 1954. All vinyl. 10" - $50.00, $15.00. **Girl Scout:** 10" - $60.00, $15.00. **Black:** 10" - $70.00, $15.00. **Katie:** 1957, Molded hair. 8½" - $70.00, $25.00.

Garland, Judy: 1984, as "Dorothy of Oz." $50.00.

Gumdrop: 1962 on. Plastic/vinyl. 16" - $30.00, $15.00.

Grumpy: 1912–1938. Frown, painted features, cloth and composition. 12" - $250.00, $100.00; 14" - $300.00, $125.00. **Black:** 12" - $350.00, $165.00; 14-15" - $425.00, $200.00.

Hagara, Jan: First dolls designed. **Laurel:** 1984. 15" - $150.00. **Cristina:** 1984 only. $200.00. **Larry:** 1985. 15" - $100.00. **Lesley:** 1985. $95.00. **Originals:** As George Washington, Uncle Sam, Amish, etc. 12" - $225.00 up.

Half Pint: 1966 on. Plastic/vinyl. 10" - $30.00, $10.00.

Happy Boy: 1960. All vinyl, freckles, molded tooth. 10" - $45.00, $20.00.

17" "Honey" made of all hard plastic with mohair wig, sleep eyes, and is all original. One of the "Glamour Girl" series. 17" - $400.00.

One of the "Honey" all hard plastic dolls with clothes designed by Schiaparelli. All original, including gloves. 21", in this outfit and condition - $800.00. *Courtesy Gloria Anderson.*

Hibel, Edna: Designer. 1984 only. **Flower girl:** $150.00. **Contessa:** $175.00.

Historical Dolls: 1939. All composition, original. 14" - $650.00, $250.00; 21" - $1,500.00, $700.00.

Honey: All composition. 14" - $250.00, $95.00; 20" - $400.00, $150.00; 27" - $600.00, $200.00.

Honey: 1949–1955. Must have excellent face color. All hard plastic, closed mouth. (Add more for unusual, original clothes.) 14" - $300.00, $90.00; 18" - $400.00, $150.00; 21" - $550.00, $175.00.

Honey: 1947–1948. Composition, flirty eyes: 21" - $450.00, $125.00. **Walker:** 14" - $245.00, 19" - $345.00. **Jointed knees:** 19" - $365.00.

Howdy Doody: 1947. Composition/cloth. String operated mouth. 16-17" - $185.00. Composition head and limbs puppet on string. 17" - $145.00; 20" - $185.00. **1947-1949:** Composition/cloth, puppet mouth formed but not moveable. 18" - $250.00. **1950's:** Hard plastic/cloth doll. 18" - $185.00.

Humpty Dumpty. 1985. $85.00 up.

Ice Queen: 1937. Skater outfit, composition, open mouth. 17" - $800.00, $250.00.

Lamkins: 1930, cloth/composition. 15" - $365.00 up; 18" - $500.00 up; 22" - $650.00.

Lil Sweetie: 1967. Nurser with no lashes or brow. 16" - $50.00, $25.00.

Limited Edition Club:
1975: Precious Baby - $550.00. **1976:** Patsy - $375.00. **1977:** Dewees Cochran - $200.00. **1978:** Crowning Glory - $165.00. **1979:** Skippy - $350.00. **1980:** Susan B. Anthony - $165.00. **1981:** Girl with watering can - $165.00. **1982:** Princess Diana - $125.00. **1983:** Sherlock Holmes - $185.00. **1984:** Bubbles - $125.00. **1985:** Red Boy - $125.00. **1986:** China head - $125.00.

Little Lady: 1939–1947. All composition. (Add more for original clothes.) 15" - $300.00, $90.00; 17" - $425.00, $125.00; 21" - $500.00, $165.00; 27" - $650.00, $225.00.

Little Lady: 1943. Cloth body, yarn hair: 21" - $365.00 up. Pink cloth body, wig: 17" - $285.00 up. With magnets in hands: 15" doll only. $350.00. Doll/accessories: $450.00.

Hard-to-find character "Lamkins" that is composition and cloth. Fingers curled with molded painted-on center finger ring. 18" - $500.00. *Courtesy Turn of Century Antiques.*

14" "Little Lady" that is strung and made of all composition. Mint and all original with wrist tag. 14" - $300.00 up. *Courtesy Kris Lundquist.*

18" "Little Lady Majorette" that is mint and original. All composition, sleep eyes, and mohair wig. 18" - $450.00 up. *Courtesy Patricia Woods.*

21" all composition "Little Lady" dressed in original nurse's uniform. Sleep eyes and mohair wig. 21" - $500.00 up.

Lovums: 1928. Marked with name. Composition/cloth, open mouth smiling. 15" - $235.00, $100.00. 20" - $300.00, $150.00; 23" - $350.00.

Mae Starr: Marked with name. Composition/cloth. Record player in torso. 30" - $450.00, $200.00.

Marionettes: Composition/wood. 14" - $175.00, $80.00.

Martha and George Washington: 1976. 11" - $200.00.

Mary Ann or Lee: 1928–1937. Marked with name. Open smile mouth, composition and cloth and all composition. 16" - $265.00, $95.00; 18" - $285.00,

$125.00; 20" - $325.00, $150.00; 24" - $425.00, $175.00.

Marilee: 1920's. Marked with name. Composition/cloth, open mouth. 13" - $250.00, $100.00; 16" - $300.00, $125.00; 23" - $365.00, $150.00; 28" - $475.00; $200.00.

Mary Jane: 1960. Plastic/vinyl, walker and freckles. 31" - $265.00, $100.00.

Mary Jane: 1917–1920. Composition, jointed body or cloth, "Mama" type. 20-22" - $275.00.

Mickey: 1946. (Also Tommy Tucker and Bright Eyes.) Composition/cloth, flirty eyes. 16" - $275.00; 18" -

$325.00, $100.00; 22-23" - $375.00, $125.00.

Mickey: 1956. All vinyl. Some with molded on hats. 11" - $100.00, $45.00.

Miss Chips: 1965 on. Plastic/vinyl. **White:** 18" - $50.00. **Black:** 18" - $65.00.

Pat-O-Pat: Composition/cloth, painted eyes. Press stomach and pats hands together. 13-14" - $165.00, $70.00.

Patricia: 1932-1936. All composition: 14" - $385.00, $145.00. Original: $450.00 up.

Patricia-kin: 1929-1930's. 11" - $325.00, $125.00.

14" **"Miss Liberty."** Has metal Statue of Liberty pin dated **1886-1986.** Limited to **750** made for Meyer's stores. Came with history of Statue of Liberty and doll stand. She is fastened onto cardboard flag background which comes out of box. 14" - **$75.00.**

13" **wigged, all composition, "Patsy" with sleep eyes, all original. Original w/pin - $500.00. Played with - $365.00.** *Courtesy Shirley Bertrand.*

Patsy: 1927-1930's. All composition. 14" - $365.00, $150.00. Composition/cloth: 14" - $375.00, $175.00. Original: $425.00 up.

Patsy Babyette: 1930's, 1940's. 9" - $245.00, $90.00. Original: $300.00 up.

Patsyette: 1930's. 9" - $265.00, $100.00. Original: $350.00 up.

Patsy Ann: 1930's. 19" - $465.00, $165.00. Original: $525.00 up. **Vinyl:** 1959. 15" - $165.00, $60.00. Original: $200.00 up.

Patsy Joan: 1927-1930. Reissued 1946-1949. 16" - $450.00, $175.00. Original: $500.00 up. **Black:** 16" - $750.00 up, $225.00. Original: $550.00 up.

Patsy, Jr.: 11" - $285.00, $100.00. Original: $350.00 up.

Patsy Lou: 1929-1930's. 22" - $485.00, $175.00. Original: $575.00 up.

Patsy Mae: 1932. 30" - $785.00, $325.00. Original: $865.00 up.

Patsy Ruth: 1935. 26-27" - $765.00, $325.00. Original: $850.00 up.

Patsy, Wee: 1930's. 5-6" - $300.00, $125.00. Original: $365.00 up.

Polka Dottie: 1953. 21" - $165.00, $60.00.

Portrait Dolls: 1940. All composition. 12" - $265.00, $100.00.

Presidents: 1984. Lincoln: 18" - $55.00. Washington: 16" - $55.00. Teddy Roosevelt: 17" - $65.00. F.D. Roosevelt: 1985. $60.00.

Prince Charming or Cinderella: All hard plastic. 16" - $425.00 up, $165.00.

Pum'kin: 1966 on. All vinyl, freckles. 10½" - $40.00, $20.00.

Blonde "Patsy Baby" with sleep eyes, all composition, original flannel sacque, and Effanbee bracelet. 9" - $245.00. *Courtesy Shirley Bertrand.*

Rootie Kazootie: 1953. 21" - $185.00, $80.00.

Roosevelt, Eleanor: 1985. 14½" - $60.00.

Rosemary: 1925 on. Marked with name. Composition/cloth. 13" - $250.00, $125.00; 16" - $300.00, $150.00; 23" - $365.00, $150.00; 28" - $475.00, $200.00.

Santa Claus: 19", composition with molded beard and hat. (See photo in Series 8, pg. 223.) $1,200.00 up.

Skippy: 1929, 1940's. All composition. 14" - $445.00, $165.00. Soldier: $500.00. Sailor: $565.00.

Suzanne: 1940. Marked with name. All composition. 14" - $275.00, $125.00.

Suzie Sunshine: 1961 on. Freckles. 17-18" - $45.00-20.00. Black: 17-18" - $65.00, $35.00.

Suzette: 1939. Marked with name. All composition. 12" - $245.00, $100.00.

16½" rare "Patsy Joan" made of all composition and is original, 1946. $750.00. *Courtesy Mary Jane and Francis Anicello.*

EFFANBEE DOLL COMPANY

Sweetie Pie: 1938–1940's. Composition/cloth. 14" - $165.00, $50.00; 19" - $265.00, $90.00; 24" - $365.00, $125.00.
Tommy Tucker: 1946. (Also Mickey and Bright Eyes.) Composition/cloth, flirty eyes. 16" - $275.00, 18" - $325.00, 22-23" - $375.00, $125.00.
Twain, Mark: 1984. 16" - $70.00.
Wayne, John: 1981, in western outfit. 17" - $125.00 up. As soldier: 1982. 18" - $100.00 up.
West, Mae: 1982. 18" - $100.00 up.
Witch: Designed by Faith Wick. 18" - $95.00 up.

11½" "Young Betsy." Plastic/vinyl with sleep eyes. Original outfit designed by Rachel Shea especially for Carson Pirie Scott & Co. Ltd. Productions. Head marked "Effanbee 1976/1176." $60.00. *Courtesy Marie Ernst.*

FRANKLIN MINT DOLLS

1987: Gibson Bride - $400.00.
1988: Swan Lake - $285.00; Queen Galadril - $300.00; Scarlett & Rhett - $200.00 each; Amy (Little Women) - $200.00; Christmas Angel - $265.00.
1989: Mary, Mary - $195.00; Cinderella - $275.00; Snow White (marked 1988) - $265.00; Bo Peep - $195.00.
1990: Snow Queen - $450.00; Rapunzel - $275.00; Jewels of Month Dolls - $185.00; Country Store figures - $225.00; Glenda, The Good Witch - $225.00; Victorian Bride - $600.00; Baby (Days of Week) - $200.00; Marilyn Monroe - $245.00; Promenade (Mother & Child) - $285.00.
1991: Gibson Girl - $265.00; Disney Cinderella - $285.00; Rose Princess - $300.00; John Wayne - $265.00; Evil Witch of Oz - $285.00; Cyrena/Atlantis - $325.00; Scarlett/case - $500.00.

22" "Gibson Bride" with bisque shoulder head and limbs on cloth body. Marked "Franklin Heirloom Doll 1987." $400.00.
Detail photo on cover of this book.

19" "Snow White" in Disney Crest colors. Bisque shoulder head and limbs with cloth body. Marked "Franklin Heirloom Doll 1988." 19" - $265.00.

GALOOB

These "Baby Face Dolls" made by Galoob are real characters and adorable dolls. They are jointed at neck, shoulder, hips, elbows, and knees. Made in 1990. Each - $45.00. *Courtesy Jeannie Mauldin.*

GERBER BABY

1936: 8", all printed cloth. Holds can of baby food and toy dog. Rare. $400.00.

1954: 12", rubber, by Sun Rubber Co. Mint - $55.00 up; Mint in box - $200.00 up.

1966: 14", soft vinyl, Arrow Industries. Lopsided smile. $45.00 up.

1972: 10", plastic/vinyl. Uneeda Doll Co. $30.00 up.

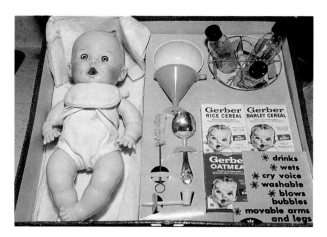

12" pristine mint in box Gerber baby that is all rubber and just like new. Inset glassene eyes, open mouth, molded top knot. Made by Sun Rubber in 1954. **$200.00 up.** *Courtesy Patricia Woods.*

GIRL'S WORLD

7" "Emerald The Witch" marked "1971/Girl's World/Pat. Pend./Made in Japan." Dress tagged "Emerald Witch." Battery operated glowing eyes. **Mint/original - $65.00.** *Courtesy Kathy Tvrdik.*

Hartland Industries made many figures with horses during the mid to late 1950's. These are extremely collectible as they are rare, especially when the horses have saddles. Most came from the Warner Brothers television productions. The figures included:

James Arness as "Matt Dillon" on *Gunsmoke.* (Sept. 1955 to Sept. 1975)

James Garner as "Bret Maverik" on *Maverik.* (See photo Series 8, pg. 228.)

John Lupton as "Tom Jefords" on *Broken Arrow.* (Sept. 1956 - Sept. 1960)

Gail Davis as "Annie Oakley." (April 1953 – Dec. 1956)

Hugh O'Brien as "Wyatt Earp." (Sept. 1955 – Sept. 1961)

Dale Robertson as "Jim Hardie" on *Wells Fargo.* (March 1957 – Sept. 1962)

Pat Conway as "Clay Hollister" on *Tombstone Territory.* (Oct. 1957 – Oct. 1959)

Wayde Preston as "Capt. Chris Colt" on *Colt 45.* (Oct. 1957 – Sept. 1960)

Richard Boone as "Paladin" on *Have Gun Will Travel.* (Sept. 1957 – Sept. 1963)

John Payne as "Vint Bonner" on *The Restless Gun.* (Sept. 1957 – Sept. 1959)

Clint Walker as "Cheyenne" (Sept. 1955 – Sept. 1963)

Ward Bond as "Major Seth Adams" on *Wagon Train.* (Sept. 1957 – Sept. 1965)

Chief Thunderbird with horse "Northwind."

Robert E. Lee with horse "Traveler."

General George Custer and horse "Bugler."

Brave Eagle with horse "White Cloud."

General George Washington with horse "Ajax."

"Lone Ranger" with horse "Silver."

Left: 7-8" Roy Rogers on horse, "Trigger." Figure molded in one piece. Removable saddle, molded stand-up mane on horse. Both marked "Hartland Industries." Right: 7-8" Dale Evans on horse, "Buttercup." This horse is modeled differently from other Hartland (note leg placement) but also has stand-up mane. Each figure with horse - $225.00 up. *Courtesy Shirely Bertrand.*

HARTLAND INDUSTRIES

"Tonto" with horse "Scout."
Jim Bowie with horse "Blaze."
"Sgt. Preston of the Yukon" with horse.
Roy Rogers with horse "Trigger."
Dale Evans with horse "Buttercup."
Cochise with pinto horse.
Buffalo Bill with horse.

Other figures made by the company include baseball notables Mickey Mantle, Ted Williams, Stan Musial, Henry Aaron, Ed Mathews, and George "Babe" Ruth.
Figure and horse: $225.00 up.
Figure in box with horse and accessories: $365.00.
Figure alone: $95.00.
Horse alone: $150.00.
Baseball figure: $250.00 up.

HASBRO

All prices are for mint condition dolls.
Adam: 1971. Boy for World of Love series. 9" - $15.00.
Aimee: 1972. Plastic/vinyl. 18" - $50.00.
Charlie's Angels: 1977. 8½" Jill, Kelly, or Sabrina. $20.00 each.
Defender: 1974. One-piece arms and legs. 11½" - $85.00 up.
Dolly Darling: 1965. 4½" - $9.00.

4" **"Daisy Darling"** marked **"Hasbro 1966."** Doll fits into flower stand. **$30.00.** *Courtesy Kathy Tvrdik.*

Flying Nun: Plastic/vinyl, 1967. 5" - $45.00.
(Add $50.00 more in mint in box on G.I. Joe's.)
G.I. Joe, #1: 12", marked "G.I. Joe Copyright 1964 by Hasbro Patent Pending Made in U.S.A." **1964–1966:** (4 models.) White only. Scar, molded hair, no beard. #1 marking. $90.00 up. **1965–1966:** (5 models.) **Black:** #1 marking. $90.00 up. **1966–1967:** No scar on face. $125.00 up. **1966:** Russian, German, Japanese, British, Australian. Each - $265.00 up. In box, each - $400.00.
G.I. Joe, #2: 1967-1974. 12", marked "G.I. Joe Copyright 1964 by Hasbro Pat. No. 3,277,602 Made in U.S.A." **1967:** (6 models) #2 marking. Design same as #1. **Talking Commander:** No scar, blonde, brown eyes. $150.00 up.
G.I. Joe, #3: 1975. 12", body marked same as #2 model; head marked "Hasbro Ind. Inc. 1975 Made in Hong Kong." **1968:** Same style (6 models). Scar on face. #2 marking. $85.00 up.
G.I. Joe, #4: 1975. 12", marked in small of back "Hasbro Pat. Pend. Par. R.I." Talking 1975 version has #2 marked body. **1970:** (9 models.) Flocked hair and/or beard. Black and white. **Land Adventurer:** $200.00 up. **Sea Adven-**

234

12" "Duke, The Hall of Fame G.I. Joe Hero." Has electronic light and sound weapon, stand, manual, and dog tags. Numbered Collector's Edition and sold through Target Stores in 1991 only. More figures will be seen in 1993. $65.00.

Mountain Troops set #7530. There was also a "Ski Patrol" with two piece ski parka that does not have the extra equipment (ice axe, robes, grenades). $400.00 up. *Courtesy Don Tvrdik.*

G.I. Joe helicopter from the "Search For The Stolen Idol/The Secret of the Stolen Idol" adventure set. 1976. $250.00. *Courtesy Don Tvrdik.*

turer: $225.00 up. **Air Adventurer:** $250.00 up. **Astronaut:** $250.00 up. **Talking:** $350.00 up.

G.I. Joe, #5: 1974. (8 models.) #2 & #3 markings. Has Kung Fu grip. $200.00 up.

G.I. Joe, #6: 1975. (7 models.) #3 and #4 markings. White. **Mike Powers, Atomic Man:** $75.00 up. **Eagle Eye:** $85.00. **Fire Fighter:** $175.00. **West Point:** $200.00 up. **Military Police:** $175.00 up. **Ski Patrol:** $400.00 up. **Secret Agent:** Unusual face, mustache. $250.00 up. **Foreign:** (See photo in Series 7, page 235.) $300.00 up. **Green Beret:** $125.00 up. **Negro Adventurer:** No beard. $350.00 up. **Frogman:** 1973. With 17" sled. $300.00 up. **G.I. Joe Nurse:** In box - $1,000.00 up.

G.I. Joe Accessories:
Armored Car: 20" - $100.00 up. **Motorcycle and side car:** By Irwin.

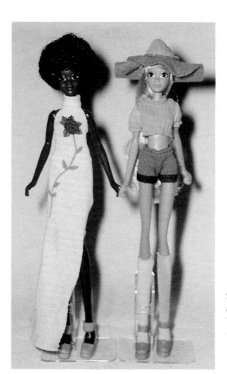

$125.00 up. **Desert Jeep:** Tan. $250.00 up. **Turbo Swamp Craft:** $75.00 up. **Space Capsule:** $200.00 up. **Foot Locker:** $30.00 up. **Sea Sled:** $80.00 up. **Tank:** $175.00 up. **Jeep:** $145.00 up. **Helicopter:** $250.00 up. **All Terrain Vehicle:** $150.00 up.

G.I. Joe Boxed Uniforms and Accessories:
Boxed figure in uniform: $125.00 up. **Adventure Team outfit:** $300.00 up. **Diver:** "Eight Ropes of Danger." $400.00 up. **Scuba Diver:** "Jaws of Death." $200.00 up. **Safari:** "White Tiger Hunt." $200.00 up. **Test Pilot:** $650.00 up. **Jungle Explorer:** "Mouth of Doom." $400.00 up. **Secret Agent:** "Secret Mission To Spy Island." $600.00 up. **Space Man:** "Space Walk Mystery." $400.00 up. "The Hidden Missle" $450.00 up. **Polar Explorer:** "Fight For Survival." $465.00 up. **Shark's Surprise:** $300.00 up.

Leggie: 1972. 10" - $20.00. **Black:** $30.00.

Little Miss No Name: 1965. 15" - $90.00.

Mamas and Papas: 1967. (See photo in Series 8, pg. 230.) $45.00 each.

Monkees: Set of four. 4" - $95.00 up.

Show Biz Babies: 1967. $35.00 each. Mama Cass: $45.00.

Storybooks: 1967. 3" - $45.00-65.00 in boxes.

Sweet Cookie: 1972. 18" - $40.00.

That Kid: 1967. 21" - $85.00.

World of Love Dolls: 9", 1971. **White:** $12.00. **Black:** $18.00.

10" "Leggie." All vinyl with painted features, long bendable legs. Unique dolls and hard-to-find originals. Marked "Hasbro 1972 Hong Kong." White - $20.00; Black - $30.00. *Courtesy Kathy Tvrdik.*

3" "Sleeping Beauty." All vinyl, rooted hair, painted features. One of the Storybook figures made in 1967 only. $45.00. *Courtesy Kathy Tvrdik.*

15" "Little Miss No Name." Plastic/vinyl. Marked "1965 Hasbro" on head. Penny added to upturned palm. Redressed near original, which is like this, but has cotton patch on skirt. $90.00. *Courtesy Kathy Tvrdik.*

HORSMAN DOLL COMPANY

First prices are for mint condition dolls; second prices for ones that have been played with, are dirty and soiled or not original. Marked "Horsman" or "E.I.H."

Angelove: Made for Hallmark, 1974. Plastic/vinyl. 12" - $35.00.

Answer Doll: 1966. Button in back moves head. 10" - $20.00, $10.00.

Billiken: Composition head, slant eyes, plush or velvet body. 1909. 12" - $345.00, $125.00; 16" - $425.00.

Baby Bumps: 1910. Composition/cloth. 12" - $185.00, $75.00; 14" - $245.00, $95.00. **Black:** 11" - $265.00, $90.00; 15" - $300.00, $125.00.

Baby First Tooth: 1966. Cloth/vinyl, cry mouth with one tooth, tears on cheeks. 16" - $40.00, $15.00.

Baby Tweaks: 1967. Cloth/vinyl, inset eyes. 20" - $40.00, $18.00.

Ballerina: 1957. Vinyl, one-piece body and legs, jointed elbows. 18" - $85.00.

Betty: All composition. 16" - $245.00, $90.00. All vinyl, one-piece body and limbs: 1951. 14" - $65.00. Plastic/vinyl: 16" - $30.00, $15.00.

Betty Jo: All composition. 16" - $245.00, $90.00. Plastic/vinyl, 1962: 16" - $30.00, $15.00.

Betty Ann: (Add more for original clothes.) All composition: 19" - $300.00, $150.00. Plastic/vinyl: 19" - $50.00, $25.00.

Betty Jane: All composition. 25" - $350.00, $150.00. Plastic/vinyl: 25" - $75.00, $40.00.

Blink: (Also called "Happy.") 1916 Gene Carr designed character. Cloth body, composition head and limbs. Painted eyes are almost closed. "Watermelon" style open/closed mouth with one lower tooth. Very prominent ears, painted hair. 14-15" - $325.00 up.

Bye-Lo Baby: Cloth/vinyl. 100th anniversary for Wards, 1972. 14" - $55.00. Reissued 1980–1990's. 14" - $25.00.

20" **"Baby Dimples"** with tin sleep eyes, molded hair. Composition head and limbs with cloth body. Open mouth and dimples. 20" - **$325.00.** *Courtesy Kathy Tvrdik.*

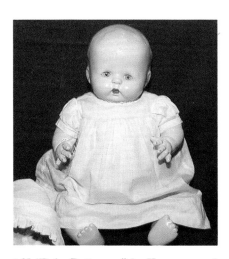

18" **"Baby Buttercup"** by Horsman and marked **"EIH"** on back of head. Original clothes tagged **"EI Horsman."** Tin sleep eyes, molded hair. A rare Horsman doll. 18" - **$325.00.** *Courtesy Patricia Woods.*

Body Twist: 1929–1930. All composition. Top of body fits down into torso. 11" - $185.00, $75.00.

Bright Star: (See photo in Series 8, pg. 233.) 1937–1946. All composition: 18-19" - $350.00, $125.00. All hard plastic: 1952. 15" - $250.00, $95.00.

Brother: Composition/cloth. 22" - $250.00 up, $100.00. Vinyl: 13" - $45.00, $20.00.

Campbell Kids: Marked "E.I.H." Ca. 1911. Composition/cloth, painted features. 14" - $500.00 up. "Dolly Dingle" style face: 13": 1930–1940's. All composition. $350.00 up.

Celeste Portrait Doll: In frame. Eyes painted to side. 12" - $30.00, $15.00.

Christopher Robin: 11" - $30.00, $10.00.

Child Dolls: 1930–1940's. All composition: 14" - $165.00, $80.00; 16" -

$225.00, $95.00; 18" - $300.00, $100.00. All composition, very chubby toddler: 14" - $135.00, $50.00; 17" - $185.00, $85.00. All hard plastic: 14" - $125.00, $50.00; 18" - $225.00 up, $100.00.

Cindy: Marked "170." All hard plastic. 1950's. 15" - $100.00 up, $50.00; 17" - $145.00 up, $80.00. All early vinyl: 1953. 18" - $50.00, $15.00. Lady type, jointed waist: 1959. 19" - $85.00, $40.00.

Cindy Kay: All vinyl, long legs. Child, 1950-on. 15" - $75.00, $55.00; 20" - $95.00; 27" - $165.00.

Cinderella: 1965, plastic/vinyl. Painted eyes to side. 11½" - $30.00, $15.00.

Composition Dolls: 1910's– 1920's. "Can't Break Em" composition/ cloth body, marked "E.I.H." 12" - $165.00, $60.00; 16" - $195.00, $100.00. 1930's: 16" - $160.00, $70.00; 18" - $225.00, $90.00; 22" - $285.00, $125.00.

Crawling Baby: Vinyl, 1967. 14" - $25.00, $10.00.

Dimples: 1928–1933. Composition/cloth. 16" - $225.00, $90.00; 20" - $325.00, $125.00; 24" - $350.00, $145.00. **Toddler:** 20" - $365.00, $145.00; 24" - $400.00, $165.00. **Laughing:** Painted teeth. 22" - $400.00, $185.00.

Disney Exclusives: "Cinderella," "Snow White," "Mary Poppins," "Alice in Wonderland." 1981. 8" - $45.00 each.

Gold Medal Doll: 1930's. Composition/cloth, upper & lower teeth. 21" - $200.00, $90.00. Vinyl/molded hair: 1953. 26" - $185.00, $85.00. Vinyl Boy: 1954. 15" - $75.00, $30.00.

Ella Cinders: 1925. Comic character. Composition/cloth. 14" - $425.00; 18" - $700.00.

Elizabeth Taylor: 1976. 11½" - $50.00, $20.00.

Floppy: 1965. Foam body and legs/vinyl. 18" - $20.00.

Flying Nun: (Sally Field) Original, 1965. 12" - $70.00, $15.00.

Hansel & Gretel: 1963. Sleep eyes, unusual faces. (See photo in Series 7, pg. 238.) $185.00 each.

Hebee-Shebee: All composition. 10½" - $465.00, $200.00

Jackie Coogan: 1921. Composition/cloth, painted eyes. 14" - $465.00, $165.00.

Jackie Kennedy: 1961. Marked "Horsman J.K." Adult body, plastic/vinyl. 25" - $145.00, $70.00.

Jeanie Horsman: 1937. All composition. 14" - $225.00, $90.00. Composition/cloth: 16" - $185.00, $80.00.

27" "Cindy Kay" from 1955. Early stuffed vinyl with disk joints at shoulders and hips. Glued-on wig, sleep eyes. A hard-to-find early vinyl example in mint condition. 27" - $165.00.
Courtesy Kathy Tvrdik.

12" "Flying Nun" (Sally Field). Plastic and vinyl, made by Horsman Dolls. The little one is 4½" tall, all vinyl, and made by Hasbro in 1967. Both have painted features. 12" in box - $70.00. 4½" in box - $45.00. *Courtesy David Spurgeon.*

Hard plastic/cloth: 16" - $75.00; $35.00; 22" - $90.00, $40.00. Vinyl/cloth: 16" - $20.00, $8.00; 22" - $30.00, $15.00.

Michael: (Mary Poppins) 1965. 8" - $25.00, $15.00.

Mousketeer: 1971. Boy or girl. 8" - $20.00, $10.00.

Patty Duke: 1965. Posable arms. 12" - $45.00, $18.00.

Peggy: 1957. All vinyl child, one-piece body and legs. 25" - $75.00, $40.00.

Jojo: 1937. All composition. 12" - $200.00, $90.00. 16" - $265.00, $125.00.

Life-size Baby: Plastic/vinyl. 26" - $250.00, $100.00.

Lullabye Baby: 1964, 1967. Cloth/vinyl. Music box in body. 12" - $20.00, $8.00. All vinyl: 12" - $15.00, $5.00.

Mary Poppins: 1964. 12" - $35.00, $15.00; 16" - $70.00, $30.00; 26" (1966) - $200.00, $100.00; 36" - $350.00, $175.00. In box with Michael and Wendy: 12" & 8" - $150.00.

Mama Style Babies: 1920's and 1930's. Composition/cloth. Marked "E.I.H" or "Horsman." 14" - $165.00, $85.00; 18" - $225.00, $100.00. **Girl Dolls:** 14" - $250.00, $90.00; 18" - $300.00, $125.00; 24" - $385.00, $165.00.

28½" "Peggy Ann" by Horsman, 1930. Tin sleep eyes, open mouth, composition head and limbs with cloth body. All original with original long curl human hair wig. Mint condition - $475.00 up. *Courtesy Patricia Woods.*

Peggy Pen Pal: 1970. Multi-jointed arms. Plastic/vinyl. 18" - $40.00, $20.00.

Pippi Longstocking: 1972. Vinyl/cloth. 1972. 18" - $35.00, $15.00.

Polly & Pete: 1957. Black dolls, molded hair, all vinyl. 13" - $225.00, $60.00.

Poor Pitiful Pearl: 1963, 1976. 12" - $50.00, $25.00; 17" - $100.00, $50.00.

Peterkin: 1915–1930. All composition, painted googly-style eyes. 12" - $350.00, $125.00.

Pudgie Baby: 1978. Plastic/vinyl. 12" - $35.00, $15.00. 24" (1980) - $50.00, $30.00.

Pudgy: 1974. All vinyl, very large painted eyes. 12½" - $35.00, $15.00.

Roberta: 1928. All composition. Molded hair or wigs, 1937. 14" - $250.00, $90.00; 20" - $325.00, $125.00. 24" - $325.00, $150.00.

Rosebud: 1928. Composition/cloth. Marked with name, dimples and smile. Sleep eyes, wig. 14" - $250.00, $90.00; 18" - $300.00, $125.00. 24" - $385.00, $165.00.

Ruthie: 1958–1966. All vinyl or plastic/vinyl. 14" - $22.00, $8.00; 20" - $38.00, $12.00.

17" "Thirstee Baby" made of plastic and vinyl. Has sleep eyes and open mouth. Marked "3437/15 EXE" high on head and "Horsman Dolls" on back. 17" - $45.00. *Courtesy Kathy Tvrdik.*

Sleepy Baby: 1965. Vinyl/cloth, eyes molded closed. 24" - $50.00, $25.00.

Tuffie: 1966. All vinyl. Upper lip molded over lower. 16" - $65.00, $25.00.

Tynie Baby: See that section.

HOYER, MARY

The Mary Hoyer Doll Mfg. Co. operated in Reading, Pa. from 1925. The dolls were made in all composition, all hard plastic, and last ones produced were in plastic and vinyl. Older dolls are marked in a circle on back "Original Mary Hoyer Doll" or "The Mary Hoyer Doll" embossed on lower back.

First price is for perfect doll in tagged factory clothes. Second price for perfect doll in outfits made from Mary Hoyer patterns and third price is for redressed doll in good condition with only light craze to composition or slight soil to others.

Composition: 14" - $475.00, $385.00 up, $165.00.

Hard Plastic: 14" - $425.00 up, $400.00, $195.00; 17" - $565.00 up, $500.00, $250.00.

Plastic and Vinyl: 14-15" (Margie) Marked "AE23." 12" - $145.00, $70.00, $15.00; 14" - $200.00, $95.00; $30.00.

Above: Hard plastic and composition Mary Hoyer dolls. Mint, all tagged, some having extremely rare outfits. $425.00-800.00. *Courtesy Patricia Woods.*

Left: 13-14" Mary Hoyer doll made of all composition with sleep eyes. Dressed in outfit made from Mary Hoyer pattern. $475.00 up. *Courtesy Kathy Tvrdik.*

IDEAL NOVELTY AND TOY COMPANY

First prices are for mint condition dolls. Second prices are for cracked, crazed, dirty, soiled or not original dolls.

April Showers: 1968. Battery operated, splashes with hands, head turns. (See photo in Series 7, pg. 242.) 14" - $30.00, $15.00.

Baby Belly Button: 1970. 9" plastic/vinyl. **White:** $18.00, $7.00. **Black:** $25.00, $12.00.

Baby Crissy: 1973–1975. 24", pull string to make hair grow. **White:** $85.00, $35.00. **Black:** $100.00, $45.00. 1981 re-issue: No grow hair. 24" - $40.00, $15.00.

Baby Snooks (Fannie Brice) and Other Flexies: Wire and composition. 12" - $275.00 up, $125.00.

Bam-Bam: 1963. Plastic/vinyl or all vinyl. 12" - $15.00, $8.00; 16" - $25.00, $10.00.

Batgirl and Other Super Women: Vinyl. (See photo in Series 7, pg. 243.) 12" - $150.00, $60.00.

Betsy McCall: See that section.

Betsy Wetsy: 1937 on. Composition head, excellent rubber body. 13" - $95.00, $20.00; 16" - $125.00, $35.00. **Hard plastic/vinyl:** 12" - $75.00, $20.00; 14" - $90.00, $35.00. **All vinyl:** 12" - $25.00, $9.00; 18" - $55.00, $20.00.

Betty Big Girl: 1968. Plastic/vinyl. 30" - $235.00, $95.00.

Betty Jane: 1930's–1944. Shirley Temple type. All composition, sleep eyes, open mouth. 14" - $185.00, $90.00; 16" - $265.00, $100.00; 24" - $300.00, $145.00.

Blessed Event: 1951. Called "Kiss Me." Cloth body with plunger in back to make doll cry or pout. Vinyl head with eyes almost squinted closed. 21" - $145.00, $50.00.

Bonnie Braids: 1951. Hard plastic/vinyl head. (See photo in Series 7, pg. 245.) 13" - $60.00, $25.00. **Baby:** 13" - $50.00; $10.00.

Bonnie Walker: 1956. Hard plastic, pin jointed hips, open mouth, flirty eyes. Marked "Ideal W-25." 23" - $85.00, $35.00.

Brandi: 1972. Of Crissy family. 18" - $65.00, $35.00.

Brother/Baby Coos: 1951. Composition/cloth with hard plastic head. 25" - $100.00, $60.00. Composition head/latex: 24" - $35.00, $10.00. Hard plastic head/vinyl: 24" - $65.00, $20.00.

Busy Lizy: 1971. 17" - $30.00, $15.00.

Bye Bye Baby: 1960. Lifelike modeling. 12" - $185.00, $60.00; 25" - $385.00, $175.00.

16" "Betsy Baby" by Ideal from 1965. All vinyl, mint, and original in box. Mint in box - $165.00; Played with - $55.00. *Courtesy Patricia Woods.*

Captain Action: 1966. Extra joints. (Add $50.00 if mint in box.) 11½" - $75.00 up. As Batman, etc.: $95.00 up.

Cinnamon: 1971. Of Crissy family. 12" - $55.00, $25.00. **Black:** $75.00, $40.00. **Hair Doodler:** $45.00. **Curly Ribbons:** $50.00.

Composition Child: All composition girl with sleep eyes, some flirty, open mouth, original clothes and excellent condition. Marked "Ideal" and a number or "Ideal" in a diamond. 14" - $165.00, $70.00; 18" - $250.00, $90.00; 22" - $300.00, $100.00. **Cloth body:** With straight composition legs. 14" - $125.00, $45.00; 18" - $185.00, $70.00; 22" - $200.00, $80.00.

Composition Baby: 1930's–1940's. (Also see "Mama Dolls.") Composition head and limbs with cloth body and closed mouth. Sleep eyes (allow more for flirty eyes), original and in excellent condition. 16" - $200.00, $85.00; 18" - $225.00, $90.00; 22" - $285.00, $125.00; 25" - $365.00, $150.00. **Flirty eyes:** 16" - $225.00, $90.00; 18" - $285.00, $100.00.

...t: 1970–1971. Of Crissy fam-...$45.00, $20.00. **Black:** $65.00, ...0. **Look-a-round:** $50.00, $25.00. **Crissy:** 1968–1971. 18" - $50.00, $20.00. **Black:** $70.00, $35.00. **Look-a-round:** 1972. $45.00, $20.00. **Talking:** 1971. $60.00, $30.00. **Floor length hair:** First, 1968. $145.00, $60.00. **Moving:** $50.00, $25.00. **Swirls Curler:** 1973. $45.00, $20.00. **Twirly Beads:** 1974. $40.00, $15.00. **Hair Magic:** No ponytail, 1977. $40.00, $15.00.

Daddy's Girl: 1961–1962. 42" - $850.00 up, $300.00 up.

Deanna Durbin: 1939. All composition. 14" - $475.00, $200.00; 17" - $550.00, $185.00; 21" - $625.00, $300.00; 24" - $765.00, $325.00; 27" - $900.00 up, $400.00.

Diana Ross: Plastic/vinyl. 18" - $165.00, $80.00.

Dina: 1972. Of Crissy family. 15" - $70.00, $35.00.

Doctor Evil: 1965. Multi joints. Came with face masks. 11" - $55.00 up, $15.00.

Dodi: 1964. Of Tammy family. Marked "1964-Ideal-D0-9E." 9" - $40.00, $10.00.

Dorothy Hammill: 1977. 11½" - $30.00, $10.00.

Eric: 1976. Tuesday Taylor's boyfriend. 12½" - $30.00, $15.00.

Flatsy: 1968–1970. Set of nine in frames. 5" - $12.00 each, $5.00. **Fashion:** 1969. 8" - $15.00, $6.00.

Flexies: 1940's. Composition and wire, soldier, children, Fanny Brice, etc. 12" - $275.00 up, $125.00.

Flossie Flirt: 1938–1945. Composition/cloth. **Flirty eyes:** 20" - $265.00, $95.00; 24" - $350.00, $125.00. **Black:** $400.00, $150.00.

Giggles: Plastic/vinyl. 16" - $45.00, $20.00; 18" - $70.00, $35.00. **Black:** 18" - $125.00, $75.00. **Baby:** 16" - $40.00, $20.00.

Goody Two Shoes: 1965. 18" - $150.00, $45.00. **Walking/talking:** 27" - $225.00, $70.00.

Harmony: 1971. Battery operated. 21" - $50.00, $35.00.

Harriet Hubbard Ayer: 1953. Hard plastic/vinyl. 15" - $200.00 up, $70.00; 17" - $300.00 up, $125.00.

Honey Moon: 1965. From "Dick Tracy." White yarn hair, magic skin body. 15" - $60.00, 10.00. **Cloth/vinyl:** $65.00, $30.00

5" posable "Flatsy" made of all vinyl. Painted features, rooted hair. Marked "Ideal/1967/Pat. Pending/Hong Kong." Original - $12.00. *Courtesy Kathy Tvrdik.*

Beautiful, mint "Ferdinand the Bull" from 1939. All composition jointed legs and neck. Decal outline of bee, "Ideal" name on side. Hole in mouth holds flowers. Pipe cleaner tail. $500.00.

15" "Honey Moon" with yarn hair and painted features. Original clothes. Also had plastic bubble that head was encased in. Cloth and vinyl. Marked "1965 C.T. N.Y. 6/Ideal Toy Corp. H-M-14-2-24." From Dick Tracy comics. 15" - $60.00. *Courtesy Kathy Tvrdik.*

King Little: 1940. Composition/ wood. 14" - $300.00, $100.00.
Kiss Me: 1951. See "Blessed Event."
Kissy: 22" - $50.00, $35.00. **Black:** $100.00, $40.00. **Cuddly:** 1964. Cloth/ vinyl. 17" - $40.00, $20.00.
Kissy, Tiny: 1962. 16" - $40.00, $15.00. **Black:** $75.00, $30.00. **Baby:** 1966. Kisses when stomach is pressed. 12" - $30.00, $10.00.
Liberty Boy: 1918. 12" - $325.00, $100.00.

16" "Huggee Girl" marked "Ideal Doll/ G-17." From 1952. Molded hair, open/ closed mouth. Stuffed vinyl body and limbs with cardboard disk joints at shoulder and hips. Vinyl head, sleep eyes. Also came with cloth body, vinyl head and limbs. $40.00. *Courtesy Kathy Tvrdik.*

Joan Palooka: 1952. 14" - $85.00, $45.00.
Joey Stivic (Baby): 1976. One-piece body and limbs. Sexed boy. 15" - $55.00, $25.00.
Jiminy Cricket: 1939–1940. Composition/wood. 9" - $275.00, $125.00.
Judy Garland: 1939. All composition. 14" - $1,000.00, $400.00; 18" - $1,200.00 up, $500.00. Marked with backward "21" (1941): 21" - $575.00, $225.00.
Judy Splinters: 1951. Cloth/ vinyl/latex, yarn hair, painted eyes. 18" - $145.00, $45.00; 22" - $225.00, $75.00; 36" - $365.00, $125.00.
Katie Kachoo: 1968. Raise arm and she sneezes. $35.00; $15.00.
Kerry: 1971. Of Crissy family. 18" - $50.00, $25.00.

9" plastic/vinyl "Jody" with bendable legs and floor length hair. Original, marked "1965/Ideal." 9" - $32.00. *Courtesy Kathy Tvrdik.*

18" all original, all composition Hawaiian "Marama." Marked on back "18." Original raw silk dress with matching panties. Original caracul wig and beautiful painted features. Flowers and beads are original. A very rare doll. 18" - $975.00 up. *Courtesy Patricia Woods.*

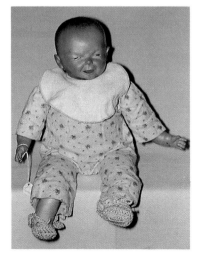

18" "Kiss Me" with early vinyl head and limbs with cloth body. Painted eyes, wide open mouth with molded tongue. Mouth opens and closes by pressing back. Marked "S3/Ideal Doll/ Pat. Pending" on head. From 1951. 18" - $145.00. *Courtesy Kathy Tvrdik.*

Little Lost Baby: 1968. Three-faced doll. (See photo in Series 7, pg. 249.) 22" - $80.00, $45.00.

Magic Lips: 1955. Vinyl coated cloth/vinyl. Lower teeth. 24" - $65.00, $35.00.

Mama Style Dolls: 1920–1930's. **Composition/cloth:** 16" - $200.00, $85.00; 18" - $285.00, $95.00; 24" - $325.00, $125.00. **Hard plastic/cloth:** 18" - $85.00, $35.00; 23" - $125.00, $45.00.

Mary Hartline: 1952 on. All hard plastic. (See photo in Series 8, pg. 241.) 15" - $400.00, $100.00; 21-23": $650.00 up, $250.00.

Mary Jane or Betty Jane: All composition, sleep and/or flirty eyes, open mouth. Marked "Ideal 18": 18" - $250.00 up, $100.00. 21" - $325.00, $175.00.

Mia: 1970. Of Crissy family. 15½" - $50.00, $25.00.

Mini Monsters: (Dracky, Franky, etc.) 8½" - $25.00, $15.00.

Miss Clairol (Glamour Misty): 1965. Marked "W-12-3." 12" - $35.00, $15.00.

Miss Curity: 1952 on. **Hard plastic:** 14" - $300.00 up, $100.00. **Composition:** 21" - $450.00, $125.00.

Miss Ideal: 1961. Multi-jointed. 25" - $375.00 up, $100.00; 28" - $425.00, $165.00.

Miss Revlon: 1956 on. 10½" - $85.00, $35.00; 17" - $165.00 up, $65.00. 20" - $200.00, $95.00. **In box or trunk:** 20" - $450.00; $125.00.

Mitzi: 1960. Teen. 12" - $85.00 up, $45.00.

Mortimer Snerd and Other Flexie Dolls: 1939. Composition and wire. 12" - $275.00 up, $125.00.

Patti Playpal: 1960-on. 30" - $200.00, $100.00; 36" - $300.00, $135.00.

18" "Miss Revlon" that is mint in original box. All vinyl with jointed waist and sleep eyes. Marked "Ideal Doll/VT-18" on head and body. 18" doll only - $165.00; 18" in box - $300.00 up. *Courtesy Ellyn McCorkle.*

Black: 30" - $350.00, $150.00; 36" - $450.00, $200.00.
Pebbles: 1963. Plastic/vinyl and all vinyl. 8" - $18.00, $8.00; 12" - $30.00, $15.00; 15" - $45.00, $25.00.
Penny Playpal: 1959. 32" - $150.00, $75.00.
Pepper: 1964. Freckles. Marked "Ideal - P9-3." 9" - $40.00, $25.00.
Pete: 1964. Freckles. Marked "Ideal - P8." 7½" - $40.00, $25.00.
Peter Playpal: 1961. 36-38" - $425.00, $200.00.
Pinocchio: 1938–1941. Composition/wood. 12" - $300.00, $100.00; 21" - $650.00, $200.00.

12" **"Samantha The Witch"** from TV show, *Bewitched* (1964-1972), played by Elizabeth Montgomery. Green painted eyes to side or straight ahead. Original, marked "Ideal Toy Corp./M-12-E-2" on head, "1965/Ideal (in oval) M-12" on hip with a "1" lower on hip. 12" - **$125.00 up.** *Courtesy David Spurgeon.*

Pixie: 1967. Foam body. 16" - $25.00, $10.00.
Posey (Posie): 1953–1956. Hard plastic/vinyl head, jointed knees. Marked "Ideal VP-17." 17" - $100.00, $45.00.
Real Live Baby: 1965. Head bobs. 20" - $30.00, $15.00.
Sally-Sallykins: 1934. Cloth/composition, flirty eyes, two upper and lower teeth. 14" - $150.00, $75.00; 19" - $225.00, $95.00; 25" - $300.00, $125.00.

18" mint and original **"Peggy"** by Ideal from 1918. Tin sleep eyes, closed mouth, composition head and limbs, and cloth body. Short arms are typical of this period of dollmaking. Long stockings added. 18" - $350.00. *Courtesy Gloria Anderson.*

Samantha The Witch: 1965. Green eyes. Marked "M-12-E-2." 12" - $125.00, $45.00.

Sandy McCall: See Betsy McCall section.

Sara Ann: 1952 on. Hard plastic. Marked "P-90." (See photo in Series 7, pg. 248.) Saran wig: 14" - $185.00 up, $75.00. 21" marked "P-93": $350.00 up, $125.00.

Saralee: 1950. Cloth/vinyl. **Black:** 18" - $285.00, $145.00.

Sara Stimson: (Little Miss Marker) 1980, marked "1979." $25.00, $10.00.

Saucy Walker: 1951 on. 16" - $100.00, $50.00; 17" - $165.00, $60.00; 20" - $185.00, $70.00. **Black:** 18" - $225.00, $100.00.

Shirley Temple: See that section.

Snoozie: 1933. Composition/cloth, molded hair, sleep eyes, open yawning mouth. Marked "B Lipfert." 13" - $175.00, $50.00; 16" - $245.00, $100.00; 20" - $365.00, $150.00.

Snow White: 1937 on. All composition, black wig, on marked Shirley Temple body, sleep and/or flirty eyes. 12" - $475.00, $200.00; 18" - $545.00, $225.00. **Molded hair:** Eyes painted to side, 1939. 14" - $185.00, $85.00; 18" - $450.00, $145.00.

Sparkle Plenty: 1947. 15" - $50.00, $25.00.

Suzy Playpal: 1960–1961. Chubby, vinyl body and limbs. Marked "Ideal O.E.B. 24-3." 24" - $150.00, $60.00.

Tabitha: 1966. Cloth/vinyl. Eyes painted to side. Marked "Tat-14-H-62" or "82." 15" - $50.00, $30.00.

Tara: 1976. Grows hair. Black. 16" - $45.00, $20.00.

Tammy: 1962. 12" - $50.00, $20.00. **Black:** $60.00, $25.00. **Grown-up:** 1965. 12" - $45.00, $20.00.

Tammy's Mom: 1963. Eyes to side. Marked: "Ideal W-18-L." 12" - $60.00, $35.00.

12½" "Ted," brother of "Tammy." Marked "Ideal Toy Corp/B-12-U-2" on head. Shown with 9" "Dodi" that is marked "1964/Ideal Toy Corp/Do-9-E" on head. Both are plastic/vinyl and have painted features. "Ted" - $50.00; "Dodi" - $40.00. *Courtesy Kathy Tvrdik.*

Ted: 1963. Tammy's brother. Molded hair. Marked "Ideal B-12-U-2." 1963. 12½" - $50.00, $25.00.

Thumbelina: 1962 on. **Kissing:** 10½" - $20.00, $8.00. **Tearful:** 15" - $30.00, $12.00. **Wake Up:** 17" - $45.00, $20.00. **Black:** 10½" - $50.00, $20.00.

Tickletoes: 1930's. Composition/cloth. 15" - $150.00, $85.00; 21" - $225.00, $100.00. **Magic Skin body:** 1948. **Hard plastic head:** 15" - $60.00, $15.00.

Tiffany Taylor: 1973. Top of head swivels to change hair color. 18" - $60.00, $20.00. **Black:** 18" - $75.00, $35.00.

Tippy or Timmy Tumbles: 16" - $25.00, $15.00. **Black:** $40.00, $20.00.

Toni: 1949 on. 14" (P-90): $325.00 up, $85.00. 15" (P-91): $375.00 up, $95.00. 17-18" (P-92): $475.00 up, $100.00. 21" (P-93): $500.00 up, $165.00. 23" (P-94): $650.00 up, $200.00. **Walker:** $300.00 up, $75.00.

Tressy: Of Crissy family. 18" - $50.00, $25.00. **Black:** $80.00, $40.00.

Tribly: Composition: 1940's. Mint/ original. 15" - $295.00. Cloth/vinyl: 1951, 3 faced baby. 20" - $50.00, $25.00.

Tubbsy: 1966. Plastic/vinyl, battery operated. 18" - $35.00, $15.00.

Tuesday Taylor: 1977. 11½ - 12" - $45.00, $15.00.

Uneeda Kid: 1914-1919. Composition head and limbs, cloth body. molded-on black boots. Painted eyes and hair. Has look of Schoenhut. 16" - $465.00.

Upsy Dazy: 1972. Foam body, stands on head. 15" - $25.00, $10.00.

P-90 "Toni" made of all hard plastic. Mint in original box with playset. The dress does not have an attached slip and although unusual, there are other mint in box dolls that also do not have the attached slip. Mint in box - $385.00 up; Played with - $95.00 up. *Courtesy Patricia Woods.*

All mint and original Ideal "Toni" dolls from P-90 to P-93, except second from left top and bottom. These two are "Sweet Sue" dolls by American Character and the last doll on bottom is first issue of "Elise" ballerina. All are hard plastic. **$325.00–650.00.** *Courtesy Patricia Woods.*

Velvet: 1970–1971. Of Crissy family. 16" - $45.00, $15.00. **Black:** $85.00, $30.00. **Look-a-round:** $50.00, $20.00. **Talking:** $50.00, $30.00. **Moving:** $45.00, $15.00. **Beauty Braider:** 1973. $40.00, $15.00. **Surely Daisy:** 1974. $40.00, $15.00.

Wingy: From Dick Tracy comics. Hard plastic, vinyl head. (See photo in Series 8, pg. 247.) 14" - $125.00 up.

16" "Uneeda Kid" advertising doll for Uneeda Biscuits, made from 1914 to 1919. Composition head and limbs with molded-on boots. Cloth body. Original including small box of biscuits. Made by Ideal Novelty and Toy Co. Mint, original - $525.00. *Courtesy Jeannie Mauldin.*

14" "Lively Thumbelina" made of vinyl and cloth with painted features and rooted hair. Has wooden knob on back that when turned makes doll move. Marked "Ideal Toy Co./OTT-14." 14" - $30.00 up. *Courtesy Kathy Tvrdik.*

15" mint three-faced "Tribly." Face not seen is crying. Composition head with cloth body and limbs. Knob on top of head to rotate faces. Original felt bunny outfit which is rare. 15" - $295.00. *Courtesy Shirley Bertrand.*

KAMAR

13" "J.F. Kennedy" with vinyl head, hands, and shoes. Posable arms and legs. Sits in rocking chair. Has music box that is key wound. Made by Kamar in 1962. 13" - $145.00. *Courtesy Kathy Tvrdik.*

KENNER

First prices are for mint condition dolls; second prices are for played with, dirty or missing clothing and accessories.

Baby Bundles: 16"-$15.00, $10.00. **Black:** $22.00, $15.00.

Baby Yawnie: Cloth/vinyl, 1974. 15" - $20.00, $10.00.

Big Foot: All rigid vinyl. (See photo in Series 7, pg. 253.) 13" - $20.00, $9.00.

Butch Cassidy or Sundance Kid: 4" - $20.00, $9.00 each.

Blythe: 1972. Pull string to change the color of eyes. 11½" - $35.00, $10.00.

Charlie Chaplin: All cloth with walking mechanism. 1973. 14" - $65.00, $30.00.

Cover Girls: (Darci, Erica, Dana, etc.) 12½", white. $35.00, $12.00. **Black:** $40.00, $15.00.

Crumpet: 1970. Plastic/vinyl. 18" - $35.00, $20.00.

Dana: Black doll, 1978. 12½" - $40.00, $15.00.

Darci: Blonde, 1978. 12½" - $35.00, $12.00.

Dusty: 12". $20.00, $8.00.

Erica: Red hair, 1978. 12½" - $35.00, $12.00.

Gabbigale: 1972. 18" - $35.00, $15.00. **Black:** $45.00, $20.00.

Garden Gals: 1972. Hand bent to hold watering can. 6½" - $10.00, $4.00.

Hardy Boys: 1978. Shaun Cassidy and Parker Stevenson. 12"-$20.00, $8.00.

International Velvet: 1976. Tatum O'Neill. 11½" - $25.00, $10.00.

Jenny Jones and Baby: All vinyl, 1973. 9" Jenny and 2½" baby. $15.00, $6.00. Set - $25.00, $8.00.

252

Skye: Black doll. 12"-$20.00, $10.00.
Star Wars: 1974–1978. Large size figures. **R2-D2:** 7½"-$90.00 up, $30.00. **C-3PO:** 12"-$100.00 up, $35.00. **Darth Vader:** 15" - $100.00 up, $25.00. **Boba Fett:** 13"-$150.00 up, $30.00. **Jabba:** 8½"-$55.00, $20.00. **IG-88:** 15"-$185.00 up, $50.00. **Stormtrooper:** 12" - $90.00 up, $25.00. **Leia:** 11½"-$90.00 up, $25.00. **Han Solo:** 12" - $85.00, $25.00. **Luke Skywalker:** 13½" - $85.00, $25.00.

Chewbacca: 15" - $85.00 up, $25.00. **Obi Wan Kenobi:** 12" - $90.00, $30.00.
Strawberry Shortcake: 1980's. 4½-5", each - $12.00 up. **Sleep eyes:** $25.00 each. **Sour Grapes, etc.:** 9" characters. $15.00.
Steve Scout: 1974. 9"-$15.00, $8.00. **Black:** $25.00, $10.00.
Sweet Cookie: 1972. 18" - $25.00, $10.00.

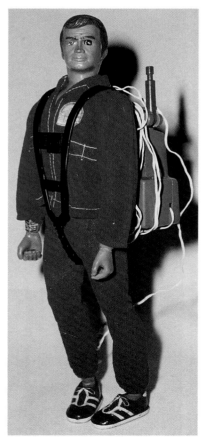

Left: 13" "Six Million Dollar Man" with gripper hand and bionic eye. Made by General Mills Fun Group/Kenner in 1977. Right: 12" "Jamie Sommers/Bionic Woman." Extra joints and painted features. Made by Kenner. "Six Million Dollar Man" - $22.00; "Bionic Woman" - $20.00. *Courtesy Don Tvrdik.*

KENNER

12" "Blythe" made in 1972. Small body and large head. Pull string and eyes change color and position. Vinyl and plastic. 12" - $35.00. *Courtesy Kathy Tvrdik.*

8" "Dr. Terror" - half man, half Cyborg. From the Centurions Power Team. Marked "K.P.T. 86. Kenner Parker Toys 1986." 8" - $18.00. *Courtesy Don Tvrdik.*

KEWPIE

First prices are for mint condition dolls; second prices are for dolls played with, crazed or cracked, dirty, soiled or not original.

Bisque Kewpies: See antique Kewpie section.

All Composition: Jointed shoulder only. 9" - $150.00, $60.00; 14" - $235.00, $90.00. **Jointed hips, neck and shoulder:** 9" - $225.00, $85.00; 14" - $350.00, $150.00. **Black:** 12" - $350.00.

Talcum Powder Container: 7-8" - $195.00.

Celluloid: 2" - $40.00; 5" - $85.00; 9" - $165.00. **Black:** 5" - $145.00.

Bean Bag Body: Must be clean. 10" - $45.00, $15.00.

3½" "Kewpie Thinker" made of all vinyl and marked on back "Kewpie/Rose O'Neill/Cameo. Made in 1971. 3½" - $20.00. *Courtesy Kathy Tvrdik.*

Cloth Body: Vinyl head and limbs. 16" - $200.00, $95.00. Composition head: $465.00 up.

Kewpie Gal: With molded hair/ribbon. 8" - $65.00, $25.00.

Hard Plastic: 1950's. One-piece body and head. 8" - $95.00, $25.00; 12" - $225.00, $95.00; 16" - $350.00, $145.00. Fully jointed at shoulder, neck and hips: 12-13" - $385.00, $175.00; 16" - $500.00, $225.00.

Ragsy: 1964. Vinyl one-piece, molded-on clothes with heart on chest. 8" - $50.00, $28.00. Without heart: 1971. 8" - $30.00, $15.00.

Thinker: 1971. One-piece vinyl, sitting down. 4" - $20.00, $8.00.

8½" original all vinyl "Kewpie" made in 1950's by Cameo. Jointed neck, shoulders, and hips. 8½" - $45.00 up. *Courtesy Gloria Anderson.*

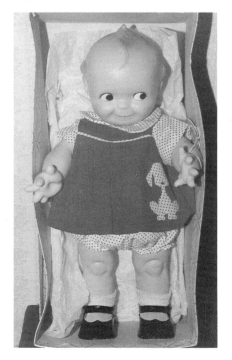

19" vinyl jointed "Kewpie" in original box marked "Made by Blumberg." Original wrist tag, squeaker in body. Tag marked "Kewpie/designed and copyright by/Rose O'Neill/A Cameo Doll. 19" - $300.00. *Courtesy Patricia Woods.*

Kewpie: Vinyl, jointed at shoulder only. 9" - $45.00, $15.00; 12" - $75.00, $20.00; 14" - $90.00, $30.00. Jointed at neck, shoulders and hips: 9" - $80.00, $25.00; 12" - $135.00, $35.00; 14" - $185.00, $50.00; 27" - $350.00, $165.00. Not jointed at all: 9" - $25.00, $10.00; 12" - $45.00, $15.00; 14" - $60.00, $20.00. Black: 9" - $50.00, $15.00; 12" - $75.00, $25.00; 14" - $125.00, $45.00. Bean Bag Type Body: 1970's. Vinyl head. 10" - $35.00, $15.00.

Ward's Anniversary: 1972. 8" - $80.00, $25.00.

All Cloth: Made by Kreuger. All one-piece including clothing. 12" - $185.00, $90.00; 16" - $350.00, $100.00;

KEWPIE

20" - $485.00, $175.00; Removable dress and bonnet: 12" - $265.00, $85.00; 16" - $400.00, $145.00; 20" - $600.00, $200.00; 25" - $1,200.00, $500.00.

Kewpie Baby: 1960's. With hinged joints. 15" - $195.00, $80.00; 18" - $265.00, $95.00.

Kewpie Baby: With one-piece stuffed body and limbs. 15" - $165.00, $80.00; 18" - $185.00, $70.00.

Plush: Usually red with vinyl face mask and made by Knickerbocker. 1960's. 6" - $45.00, $20.00; 10" - $60.00, $25.00.

KLUMPE

 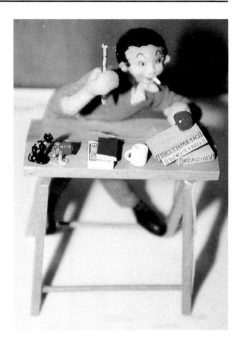

Left: 9" "Klumpe Butcher" made of felt and cloth and has oil-painted features. Wire runs throughout so arms and legs are posable. Right: 9" "Klumpe" working at wooden desk. Posable figure is smoking a cigarette, has coffee cup, plus an apple for the teacher. "Butcher" - $90.00; At desk - $95.00. *Courtesy Jeannie Mauldin.*

KNICKERBOCKER TOY COMPANY

First prices are for mint condition dolls; second prices are for dolls played with, crazed or cracked, dirty, soiled or not original.

Alexander: Comic character from "Blondie." All composition, painted hair and features. 9" - $375.00 up, $125.00.

Bozo Clown: 14" - $30.00; 24" - $65.00.

256

Cinderella: With two heads; one sad; the other with tiara. 16" - $20.00.

Clown: Cloth. 17" - $25.00.

Composition Child: 1938 on. Bent right arm at elbow. 15" - $225.00 up.

Daddy Warbucks: 1982. 7" - $15.00, $9.00.

Dagwood: Composition, painted hair and features. 14" - $650.00, $275.00.

Flintstones: 17" - $30.00 each.

Kewpie: See Kewpie section.

Levi Rag Doll: All cloth. 15" - $15.00.

Little House on the Prairie: 1978. 12" - $20.00 each.

Little Orphan Annie: 1982. 6" - $18.00, $6.00.

Lord of Rings: 5" - $15.00 each.

Mickey Mouse: 1930–1940's. 18" - $1,600.00.

Miss Hannigan: 7" - $15.00, $9.00.

Molly: 5½" - $15.00, $15.00.

Pinocchio: All plush and cloth. 13" - $185.00 up. All composition: 13" - $350.00 up.

Punjab: 7" - $20.00, $9.00.

Scarecrow: Cloth. 23½" - $165.00 up.

16" "Annie" doll made of all cloth. Original with dog in pocket. Tag is marked "Columbia Pictures. 1982. Knickerbocker." 16" - $18.00. *Courtesy Kathy Tvrdik.*

10" "Carrie," "Holly," and "Amy" of Holly Hobbie set. Plastic and vinyl. Marked "American Greeting Cards 1974. Knickerbocker Toys Inc." Each - $18.00. *Courtesy Kathy Tvrdik.*

Seven Dwarfs: 10", all composition. Each - $265.00 up. All cloth: 14" - $300.00 each.

Sleeping Beauty: 1939. All composition, bent right arm. 15" - $300.00 up; 18" - $465.00.

Snow White: 1937. All composition, bent right arm. Black wig. 15" - $300.00 up; 20" - $465.00 up. Molded hair and ribbon: 13" - $285.00.

Soupy Sales: 1966. Vinyl and cloth, non-removeable clothes. 13" - $135.00.

Two-headed Dolls: 1960's. Vinyl face masks; one crying, one smiling. 12" - $20.00.

5½" "Robotech" figures by Matchbox, 1985. Made of rigid vinyl. Note oversized hands. Marked "1985 H G USA/Tatsu/Matchbox Ind. Ltd./Made in China." Top left: "Khyron." Top right: "Miriya." Bottom left: "Exedore." Bottom right: "Breetai-Zentraedi." Top row figures - $12.00; Bottom row figures - $16.00. *Courtesy Don Tvrdik.*

First prices are for mint condition dolls; second prices are for dolls that have been played with, are dirty, soiled, not original and/or do not have accessories.
Allen: 12" - $85.00. In box - $200.00 up.
Baby First Step: 1964. 18" - $25.00, $12.00. Talking: $35.00, $15.00.
Baby Go Bye Bye: 1968. 12" - $18.00, $9.00.
Baby's Hungry: 1966. 17" - $30.00, $15.00.
Baby Love Light: 1970. Battery operated. 16" - $20.00, $10.00.
Baby Pataburp: 13" - $30.00, $15.00.
Baby Play-A-Lot: 1971. 16" - $30.00, $10.00.
Baby Say 'n See: 1965. 17" - $30.00, $10.00.
Baby Secret: 1965. 18" - $40.00, $15.00.
Baby Small Talk: 1967. 11" - $20.00, $8.00. As Cinderella: $25.00, $10.00. **Black:** $35.00, $15.00.
Baby Tenderlove: 1969. **Newborn:** 13" - $15.00, $5.00. **Talking:** 1969. 16" - $20.00, $10.00. **Living:** 1970. 20" - $30.00. **Molded hair piece:** 1972. 11½" - $35.00. **Brother:** 1972. Sexed. 13" - $40.00.
Baby Teenie Talk: 1965. 17" - $30.00, $12.00.
Baby Walk 'n Play: 1968. 11" - $20.00, $8.00.
Baby Walk 'n See: 18" - $25.00, $15.00.
Barbie: See that section.
Bozo: 18" - $30.00, $10.00.
Bucky Love Notes: 1974. Press body parts for tunes. 12" - $18.00.
Buffie: 1967. With Mrs. Beasley. 6" - $45.00, $12.00; 10" - $60.00, $20.00.
Capt. Lazer: 1967. 12½" - $250.00 up, $50.00.
Casey: 1975. 11½". $125.00 up.
Casper, The Ghost: 1964: 16" - $30.00, $20.00. **1971:** 5" - $15.00, $5.00.

12½" "Capt. Lazer" with jointed knees at boots. Battery operated pack on back. Marked "1967/Mattel Inc." on head; "1967 Mattel Inc./Made in Mexico" on body. **$250.00 up.** *Courtesy Don Tvrdik.*

Charlie's Angels: 1978, marked "1966." 11½" - $20.00, $8.00.
Charmin' Chatty: 1961. 25" - $145.00, $50.00.
Chatty Brother, Tiny: 1963. 15" - $30.00, $10.00. **Baby:** 1962. $30.00, $10.00. **Black:** $55.00, $20.00.
Chatty Cathy: 1962 on. 20" - $75.00, $40.00. Brunette/brown eyes: $100.00, $50.00. **Black:** $200.00, $55.00.
Cheerleader: 1965. 13" - $20.00, $9.00.
Cheerful Tearful: 1965. 13" - $25.00, $8.00. **Tiny:** 1966. 6½" - $15.00, $6.00.

12" "Colonial Pilot" from large "Battlestar Galactica" set. **1978** only. **All original. 12" - $95.00 up.** *Courtesy Don Tvrdik.*

Fluff: 9" - $45.00 up.
Francie: 1966. 11½" - $85.00 up.
Black: $400.00 up. **Malibu:** $35.00.
Twist n' Turn: 1967. $65.00. **Busy Hands:** 1972. $50.00. **Quick Curl:** 1973. $40.00.
Grandma Beans: 11" - $15.00, $8.00.
Gorgeous Creatures: 1979. Mae West style body/animal heads. Each - $20.00, $10.00.
Grizzly Adams: 1971. 10" - $25.00, $10.00.

Molded hair #1 "Ken" shown in sports jacket outfit. **$125.00 up.** *Courtesy Kathy Tvrdik.*

Christie: 1968. Black doll. 11½" - $75.00 up.
Cynthia: 1971. 20" - $45.00, $25.00.
Dancerina: 1968. 24" - $45.00, $20.00. **Black:** $70.00, $30.00. **Baby: Not battery operated:** $35.00, $15.00. **Black:** $50.00, $25.00.
Debbie Boone: 1978. 11½" - $20.00, $9.00.
Dick Van Dyke: 25" - $85.00, $40.00.
Donny Osmond: 1978, marked "1968." 12" - $15.00, $9.00.
Drowsy: 1966. Pull string talker. 15" - $20.00, $8.00.
Dr. Doolittle: 1967. Talker. Cloth/vinyl: 22½" - $50.00, $25.00. **All vinyl:** 6" - $25.00, $7.00.

Guardian Goddesses: 1979. Each: 11½" - $185.00 up.
Herman Munster: 16" - $35.00, $15.00.
Heros In Action: (Set of 14) 1975. Marked "Mattel Hong Kong. Pat Pending." Each: 3" - $20.00.
Hi Dottie: 1969. 17" - $30.00, $15.00.
Honey Hill Bunch: 1975. (Set of six.) 6" - $12.00, $3.00.
How West Was Won: 1971. 10" - $30.00. Indians: 10" - $35.00.
Hush Lil Baby: 15" - $15.00, $8.00.
Jamie, Walking: With dog, 1969. 11½" - $325.00 up.
Jimmy Osmond: 1979. 10" - $25.00, $10.00.
Julia: 1969. 11½" nurse - $200.00 up. Talking: $225.00 up.
Lil Big Guy: 13" - $20.00, $10.00.
Kelley: Quick Curl: 1973. $85.00. Yellowstone: 1974. $70.00.
Ken: Flocked hair: $145.00 up. Molded hair: Non-bending knees. $125.00 up. Malibu: $30.00 up. Live Action: $60.00 up. Mod hair: $30.00 up. Busy: $45.00 up. Talking: $150.00 up.

Half-inch tall doll in plastic child's ring. One of the "Kiddles." $18.00. *Courtesy Kathy Tvrdik.*

Kiddles: 1966 on. With cars: $50.00 up. With planes: $55.00 up. In ice cream cones: $25.00 up. In jewelry: $30.00 up. In perfume bottles: $20.00 up. In bottles: $20.00 up. With cup and saucer: $100.00 up. Storybooks: With accessories. $125.00 up. Baby Biddle: In carriage. $175.00 up. Santa: $50.00 up. Animals: $40.00.

12" "Kitty O'Neill" with green painted eyes and uses Barbie body. Marked "Mattel Inc., 1966." 11½" "Debbie Boone" marked "Resi. Inc. 1978" on head; "Mattel, Inc. 1966" on body. Kitty - $30.00; Debbie - $20.00. *Courtesy David Spurgeon.*

Circus necklace: 1968. $50.00 each.
Kitty O'Neill: 1978. 11½"" - $30.00, $9.00.
Midge: 1963. 11½", freckles. $185.00 up. 1965: Bendable legs. $85.00 up.
Mother Goose: 20" - $40.00, $15.00.
Mrs. Beasley: Talking, 16". $60.00, $25.00.
Peachy & Puppets: 1972. 17" - $20.00, $8.00.
P.J.: 11½" - $80.00 up. Talking: $100.00 up.
Randy Reader: 1967. 19" - $65.00, $20.00.
Real Sister: 14" - $20.00, $10.00.
Ricky: 1965, red hair and freckles. $145.00 up.

"Ricky" made in 1964 to 1967 and is friend of "Skipper," Barbie's little sister. $145.00 up. *Courtesy Kathy Tvrdik.*

19" "Randy Reader" marked "1967 Mattel." Battery operated. Holds book, eyes move from side to side. $65.00. *Courtesy Kathy Tvrdik.*

Rockflowers: 1970. 6½" - $25.00, $10.00.
Rose Bud Babies: 6½" - $20.00, $10.00.
Saucy: 1972. 16" - $55.00. Black: $75.00.
Scooby Doo: Vinyl and cloth girl, 1964. 21" - $65.00, $25.00.
Shaun: 1979. 12" - $15.00, $9.00.
Shrinking Violet: (See photo in Series 7, pg. 265.) 1962. Pull string talker, features move. Cloth, yarn hair. 15" - $50.00 up, $15.00.

Singing Chatty: 1964. Pull string. 17" - $40.00, $10.00.

Sister Belle: 1961. 17" - $40.00, $15.00.

Skediddles: 1966 on. 4" - $40.00 up. **Disney:** $85.00 up. **Cherry Blossom:** 1967. $85.00. **Cartoon:** $60.00.

Skipper: 1963. $125.00 up. **Growing up:** 1976. $75.00 up.

Skooter: 1963, freckles. $90.00 up.

Small Talk: 1967. Pull string. 11" - $20.00, $8.00. **Sister:** 1967. 10" - $20.00, $8.00. **Cinderella:** 1968. $25.00, $10.00.

Small Walk, Sister: 1967. 11½" - $25.00, $10.00.

Stacey, Talking: $165.00.

Swingy: 20" - $35.00, $15.00.

Tatters: 10" - $45.00, $20.00.

Teachy Keen: 1966. 17" - $30.00, $15.00.

Teeners: 4" - $30.00, $15.00.

Timey Tell: (Chatty Tell) 1964, watch attached to wrist. 17" - $35.00, $15.00.

Tinkerbelle: 19" - $45.00, $15.00.

"Growing Up Skipper" marked "1967/ Mattel, Inc./Hong Kong/U.S. & For. Pat." on hip. Put on market in 1975. By rotating arm, waist gets longer and small breasts appear. $75.00. *Courtesy Gloria Anderson.*

8" "Skooter" on the left has freckles and a smile. Mattel marketed this doll in the 1960's as a friend to "Barbie's" sister, "Skipper," shown on the right. "Skooter" - $90.00 up; "Skipper" - $75.00 up. *Courtesy Gloria Anderson.*

Tippy Toes: 1967. 16" - $20.00, $9.00. Tricycle or horse: $20.00, $5.00.
Truly Scrumptious: Original. 11½" - $250.00 up. **Doll only:** $175.00 up. **Talking:** 1968. $200.00.
Tutti: 1965. 6" - $75.00 up. Packaged sets: $100.00 up.
Todd: 1965. 6" - $75.00 up.
Twiggy: 1967. 11½" - $175.00 up.
Upsy-Downsy: 1969. 3" - $20.00, $6.00.
Welcome Back, Kotter: 1973. 9" figures - $12.00-20.00.

4" "Annabelle's Autodiddle Skediddle" with "Lickety Spiddle" doll in it. Marked "1967/Mattel Inc./Mexico/US Pat. Pend" on back. $40.00. *Courtesy Kathy Tvrdik.*

9½" original "Tarzan" marked "1971 Mattel Inc. Hong Kong." Multi-jointed action figure. $25.00. *Courtesy Kathy Tvrdik.*

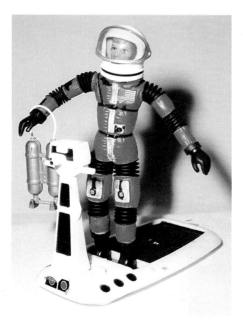

6" "Sgt. Storm" in astronaut suit. Circular sections are joints. Light brown molded hair. Only helmet is removable. Marked "1966 Mattel Inc./U.S. and Foreign Patent Pending." 6" - $60.00 up. *Courtesy Don Tvrdik.*

The Mdvanii doll was the dream and design of the genius Billyboy™ of Paris, who is world renowned for his designer jewelry and clothes collections. Each doll is entirely handmade, anatomically correct, and each has a gold metal tag on the back of the head to ensure her authenticity. The hair is human and the hairstyles are by famous hairdresser Alexandre de Paris. Most of the dolls have wigs with some having rooted hair. The wigged models can be changed just by changing the wig.

Mdvanii was first introduced in the fall of 1989, and her high quality made her news in several international magazines and papers, such as the *Wall Street Journal, Vogue, London Sunday Times, Elle,* and *New York Times,* among other publications.

The wardrobe for this doll is the finest ever created for any 11½" doll. Clothes are all hand made from finest materials and are labeled. Clothes range from street clothes to ballgowns. Her wardrobe and hairdos reflect Parisian high fashion.

The first market prices on these dolls can range from $165.00 to $850.00 and the secondary market has reflected prices above these. An average Mdvanii doll (wigged, shoes, and dressed in shirtwaist print dress) on secondary market sells for $300.00. Dolls in ballgowns run from $950.00 to $1,500.00 on the secondary market.

"Mdvanii" is shown in afternoon, evening, and night clothes designed and produced by Billyboy™ of Paris, France. Part of the 1991 line. $500.00-950.00.
Courtesy Claudia Meeker.

MDVANII

"Mdvanii" is shown in basic dresses available for her that can be in different designs or colors. The wardrobe for this doll is totally amazing in its quality and design. Credit goes to designer and manufacturer Billyboy™. $300.00 up.
Courtesy Claudia Meeker (Claudia's Collectables.)

MEGO CORPORATION

First prices are for mint condition dolls; second prices are for ones that are dirty or not original. For full listings, see *Modern Collector Dolls*, Volume 4, page 172-177.

Action Jackson: 1971–1972. Beard and no beard. 8" - $185.00 up.

Batman: 1974. Action figure. 8" - $25.00, $8.00. Arch enemy set: (4 in series) 8" - $25.00, $8.00.

Camelot: 1974. (5 in series) 8" - $55.00, $15.00.

Captain & Tenille: 1977. 12" - $20.00, $9.00.

Cher: 12" - $20.00 up, $6.00. Dressed in Indian outfit: $25.00, $10.00.

CHIPs: Ponch and Jon, 1977. 8" - $15.00, $6.00.

Diana Ross: 12½" - $50.00 up, $20.00.

Dinah Mite: 1973. 7½" - $10.00, $5.00. **Black:** $15.00, $7.00.

Haddie Mod: 1971. Teen type, 11½" - $15.00, $6.00.

Happy Days Set: 1974. **Fonzie:** $15.00, $6.00. **Others:** $10.00, $3.00.

Jaclyn Smith: 1975. 12½" - $20.00, $9.00.

Joe Namath: 1971. 12" - $65.00, $25.00.

KISS: 1978. (4 in series) 12½" - $45.00, $10.00.

Lainie: 1973. Jointed waist, battery operated. 19" - $30.00, $15.00.
Laverne & Shirley: 1977. 11½" - $20.00, $9.00. **Lenny & Squiggy:** 12" - $25.00, $10.00.
One Million BC: 1974–1975. (5 in series) 8" - $15.00, $6.00.
Our Gang Set: 1975. 5" (Six in series). **Mickey:** $22.00, $10.00. **Others:** $12.00, $6.00.
Planet of Apes: 1974–1975. (5 in series) 8" - $15.00, $7.00.
Pirates: 1971. (Four in series) 8" - $55.00, $20.00.
Robin Hood Set: 1971. (Four in series) 8" - $55.00, $20.00.
Soldiers: 8" - $25.00, $10.00.
Sonny: 12" - $20.00 up, $9.00.
Starsky or Hutch: 1975. $15.00, $6.00. **Captain or Huggy Bear:** $20.00, $8.00.
Star Trek Set: (See photo in Series 8, pg. 269.) 1974–1975. (Six in series) 8" - $35.00, $15.00.
Star Trek Aliens: 1974–1977. (Four in set) 8" - $20.00, $8.00.

Super Women: 1973. Action figures (4 in series). 8" - $15.00, $6.00.
Suzanne Somers: 1975. 12½" - $25.00, $10.00.

8" "Fonzie and Richie" from *Happy Days* television series. Marked "Mego 1976." $10.00 up. *Courtesy Don Tvrdik.*

9" "Kojack" from television series starring Telly Savalas. Action figure with multi-joints. Made by and marked "Mego." $20.00 up. *Courtesy Don Tvrdik.*

7½" "Mr. America" and "Falcon." Mego's superheroes of 1974. Both are original. Each - $25.00. *Courtesy Don Tvrdik.*

MEGO CORPORATION

Waltons: 1975. (Six in series) 8" - $15.00, $6.00. **Wild West Set:** 1974. (Six in series) 8" - $45.00, $15.00. **Wonder Woman:** (Lynda Carter) 1975. 12½" - $20.00, $9.00. **World's Greatest Super Heros:** 1974–1975. (Eight in series) 8" - $20.00, $8.00. **Arch Enemy Set:** (Eight in series) 8" - $20.00, $8.00.

World's Greatest Super Heros: 1975–1976. Second set (Six in series.) $15.00, $7.00. **Wizard of Oz:** 1974. **Dorothy:** $25.00, $9.00. **Munchkins:** $15.00, $6.00. **Wizard:** $20.00, $8.00. **Others:** $10.00 - $4.00. **15" size:** Cloth/vinyl. Each: $100.00, $40.00.

MOLLYE DOLLS

First prices are for mint condition dolls; second prices are for crazed, cracked, dirty dolls or ones without original clothes.

Mollye Goldman of International Doll Company and Hollywood Cinema Fashions of Philadephia, PA made dolls in cloth, composition, hard plastic and plastic and vinyl. Only the vinyl dolls will be marked with her name, the rest usually have paper wrist tag. Mollye purchased unmarked dolls from many other firms and dressed them to be sold under her name. She designed clothes for many makers, including Horsman, Ideal and Eegee (Goldberger). **Airline Doll:** Hard plastic. 14" - $275.00 up, $100.00; 18" - $400.00 up, $125.00; 23" - $450.00 up, $100.00; 28" - $600.00 up, $250.00.

Babies: Composition: 15" - $175.00, $65.00; 21" - $250.00, $95.00. Composition/cloth: 18" - $95.00, $40.00. All composition toddler: 15" - $200.00, $80.00; 21" - $275.00, $100.00.

Babies: Hard plastic: 14" - $95.00, $65.00; 20" - $165.00, $90.00. Hard plastic/cloth: 17" - $95.00, $55.00; 23" - $165.00, $85.00.

Babies: Vinyl: 8½" - $15.00, $7.00; 12" - $20.00, $8.00; 15" - $35.00, $12.00.

18" extremely rare "Grouchy Baby" of 1946. Cloth body, composition head and arms, molded brown hair. Sleep eyes, grumpy expression. Completely original. Doll made for Mollye Goldman by Arranbee and dressed/marketed by Mollye. Tag on leg seam marked "Mollye." $485.00. *Courtesy Patricia Woods.*

Cloth: Children. 15" - $145.00, $65.00; 18" - $185.00, $75.00; 24" - $225.00, $80.00; 29" - $300.00, $100.00.
Cloth: Young ladies. 16" - $195.00, $80.00; 21" - $285.00, $100.00.
Cloth: Internationals. 13" - $85.00, $40.00; 15" - $125.00 up, $50.00; 27" - $275.00 up, $85.00.
Composition: Children. 15" - $150.00, $45.00; 18" - $185.00, $75.00.
Composition: Young lady. 16" - $365.00, $100.00; 21" - $525.00, $150.00.
Composition: Jeanette McDonald. 27" - $800.00 up, $250.00.
Composition: Thief of Bagdad Dolls. 14" - $300.00, $95.00; 19" - $475.00, $125.00. **Sultan:** 19" - $650.00, $200.00. **Sabu:** 15" - $600.00, $200.00.
Vinyl Children: 8" - $30.00, $10.00; 11" - $50.00, $20.00; 16" - $75.00, $25.00.

Beautiful all hard plastic doll created for Mollye International Doll Co. in 1954. Dress designed and made by Mollye Goldman. Upturned nose, large sleep eyes, and mohair wig. 17" - **$285.00 up.** *Courtesy Kris Lundquist.*

Hard Plastic: Young ladies. 17" - $285.00 up, $95.00; 20" - $350.00 up, $100.00; 25" - $400.00, $125.00.
Little Women: 9" vinyl. $40.00, $15.00.
Lone Ranger/Tonto: Hard plastic/latex. 22" - $200.00, $75.00.
Raggedy Ann or Andy: See that section.
Beloved Belindy: See Raggedy Ann section.

12" "Angeleen" made in 1938 by Mollye. All composition, mint and original. Doll is unmarked and has wrist tag. Painted features. $165.00.
Courtesy Patricia Woods.

MONICA STUDIOS

Very rare little 11" "Monica" that is all original except for replaced shoes. Hair embedded into scalp, large painted eyes. 11" - $175.00 up; 15" - $385.00 up; 19" - $500.00 up. *Courtesy Patricia Woods.*

NABER KID

Mr. Harold Naber began carving wooden figures of Eskimos while living and working mainly as a bush pilot for 22 years in Alaska. The early works of this very talented man are highly prized by those who own them. Many of his early carvings were done for his Indian friends and some were sold through stores.

There is a newspaper called *Naber Kids News Report* put out by the company that can be ordered from *Naber Kids News Report* Subscription Service, 8915 S. Suncoast Blvd., Homosassa, FL 32646. Included in the newpaper are dolls for sale or trade, plus new information, list of dealers, and list of places Mr. Naber will be visiting.

Retirement dates:

06-21-87: "Molli" - $1,000.00.

01-16-88: "Jake" - $965.00.

05-04-88: "Max" - $925.00.

03-04-89: "Ashley" - $700.00.

07-15-89: "Milli" - $500.00.

09-28-90: "Maurice" - $600.00.

03-04-90: "Maxine" - $450.00.

19-28-90: "Sissi" - $700.00.

11-30-90: "Frieda" - $475.00.

12-17-90: "Walter" - $485.00.

05-03-91: "Peter" - $325.00.

05-03-91: "Pam" - $325.00.

07-28-91: "Darina" - $365.00.

Early handcarved figures:
Marked on head or foot. $900.00 up.
Later 1980's figures: Marked,
plus tag. $250.00 up.

Right: 9½" "Eskimo" purchased in 1987
in Homer, Alaska but was carved much
earlier. One of Naber's very early dolls.
Has early yellow tag, rabbit and seal fur.
$250.00. *Courtesy Mauldin Museum.*

Below, left: 17" "Ashley" of 1986-1987.
Wooden resin and cloth body. Painted
features. Marked "Ashley 1986 Naber"
on head. Also marked "Naber" on bottom
of feet and under each arm. $650.00 up.
Courtesy Kathy Tvrdik.

Below, right: "Henry" is an unique design
by Harold Naber and joined the Naber
Kids in 1992. His mold was accidentally
damaged beyond repair and only 557
were made. Of this number, only 200
were dressed as a diver, which is very
rare. "Henry" - $325.00 up.

The painted bisque Nancy Ann Dolls will be marked "Storybook Doll U.S.A." and the hard plastic dolls marked "Storybook Doll U.S.A. Trademark Reg." The only identity as to who the doll represents is a paper tag around the wrist with the doll's name on it. The boxes are marked with the name, but many of these dolls are found in the wrong box. Dolls were made 1937–1948.

First prices are for mint condition dolls; second prices are for played with, dirty dolls.

Bisque: 5" - $50.00-75.00 up, $15.00; 7½-8" - $60.00 up, $15.00. **Jointed hips:** 5" - $70.00 up, $18.00; 7½-8" - $75.00 up, $18.00. **Swivel neck:** 5" - $75.00 up, $20.00; 7½-8" - $80.00 up, $20.00. **Swivel neck, jointed hips:** 5" - $75.00, $20.00; 7½-8" - $85.00, $20.00. **Black:** 5" - $145.00 up, $50.00; 7½-8" - $175.00 up, $65.00. **White painted socks:** $160.00 up.

"Queen of Hearts" is a painted bisque doll. This molded sock example dates from 1940. In box - $150.00. *Courtesy Margaret Mandel.*

5½" and 7" "Nancy Ann" painted bisque storybook dolls. Left is #190 "A Shower Girl For April." Each - $65.00; In box - $150.00. *Courtesy Gloria Anderson.*

272

Plastic: 5" - $45.00 up, $10.00; 7½-8" - $50.00, $15.00. Black: $65.00, $20.00.
Bisque Bent Leg Baby: 3½-4½" - $125.00 up, $35.00.
Plastic Bent Leg Baby: 3½-4½" - $85.00 up, $20.00.
Judy Ann: Name incised on back. 5" - $325.00 up, $100.00.
Audrey Ann: 6" heavy doll, toddler legs, marked "Nancy Ann Storybook 12." $1,000.00 up, $300.00.
Margie Ann: 6" bisque, in school dress. $150.00 up, $45.00.
Debbie: Name on wrist tag/box. Hard plastic in school dress. $145.00 up, $40.00.
Debbie: Hard plastic, vinyl head. $90.00, $30.00.
Debbie: In dressy Sunday dress, all hard plastic. $165.00, $45.00. Same, vinyl head: $100.00, $20.00.

Teen Type (Margie Ann): Marked "Nancy Ann." All vinyl. 10½" - $90.00 up, $20.00.
Muffie: 8", all hard plastic. **Dress:** $200.00 up, $85.00. **Ballgown:** $250.00 up, $95.00. **Riding Habit:** $225.00 up, $95.00. **Walker:** $175.00 up.
Muffie: 8" hard plastic, reintroduced doll. $95.00 up, $25.00.
Nancy Ann Style Show Doll: 17-18" unmarked. All hard plastic. All in ballgown. $500.00 up, $200.00.

Beautiful strung "Muffie" of 1952–1953. $250.00. *Courtesy Peggy Millhouse.*

18" "Gigi" by Nancy Ann. All hard plastic, sleep eyes, and overall a beautiful doll. 18" - **$500.00.** *Courtesy Kris Lundquist.*

"Muffie's Pal" poodle made by Steiff of Germany. Dog - $85.00; In box - **$100.00.** *Courtesy Maureen Fukushima.*

NANCY ANN STORYBOOK

Walker trio of "Muffies." All hard plastic and original, ca. 1954. Each - $175.00 up. *Courtesy Peggy Millhouse.*

RAGGEDY ANN and ANDY

Designed by Johnny B. Gruelle in 1915, these dolls are still being made. Early dolls will be marked "Patented Sept. 7, 1915." All cloth, brown yarn hair, tin button eyes (or wooden ones), thin nose, painted lashes far below eyes and no white outline around eyes. Some are jointed by having knees or elbows sewn. Features of early dolls are painted on cloth.

First prices are for mint condition dolls; second prices are for played with, dirty, missing clothes or redressed dolls. **Marked with patent date:** 15-16" - $1,200.00 up; 23-24" - $1,500.00 up; 30" - $2,000.00. Worn and dirty: 15-16" - $600.00; 23-24" - $900.00; 30" - $1,000.00.

Applause Dolls: Will have tag sewn in seam. 1981. 12" - $20.00; 17" - $35.00; 25" - $55.00; 36" - $75.00 up.

Averill, Georgene: Red yarn hair, painted features and have sewn cloth label in side seam of body. Mid-1930's. 15" - $400.00 - $125.00 up; 19" - $650.00. **Asleep/Awake:** 13-14" - $600.00 up. Worn and dirty: $250.00 up. **1940's:** 18" - $165.00. **1950's:** 18" - $135.00. **1960-1963:** 15" - $75.00; 18" - $95.00.

Beloved Belindy: Black doll. **Knickerbocker:** 1965. (See photo in Series 7, pg. 276.) 15" - $500.00 up, $300.00. **Volland Co.:** Smile mouth, two rows of teeth, button eyes. Red/white legs, red feet. 15" - $1,500.00-800.00. **Averill:** (See photo in Series 8, pg. 276.) 15" - $1,400.00 up.

Hasbro: 1983 to date. Under Playskool label. Still available.

Knickerbocker Toy Co.: 1963–1982. Printed features, red yarn hair. Will have tag sewn to seam. **1960's:** 12" - $165.00; 16" - $225.00; 23-24" - $350.00; 30-36" - $400.00-500.00. **1970's:** 12" - $45.00; 16" - $60.00; 23-24" -

274

18" Mollye Outfitter's "Raggedy Ann" that was made only three years. Eyes to side, outlined nose. Mollye's name on chest. Very rare. 18" - $800.00 up. *Courtesy Ellen Dodge.*

9" "Raggedy Hugger." Arms are wrapped around each other and sewn so they can not be removed. Made by Knickerbocker. 9" - $30.00.

18" Georgene Averill "Raggedy Ann and Andy." Both are original; both have outlined noses. Pair - $900.00 up. *Courtesy Ellen Dodge.*

$100.00; 30-36" - $195.00-250.00. **1980's:**
16" - $25.00; 23-25" - $60.00; 30-36" -
$85.00-125.00. **Talking:** 1974. 12" -
$45.00. 1960's - $265.00.

Mollye Dolls: Red yarn hair and
printed features. Heavy outlined nose.
Lower lashes closer to eyes. Most will
have multicolored socks and blue shoes.
Will be marked in printed writing on
front of torso "Raggedy Ann and Andy
Doll/Manufactured by Mollye Doll Out-
fitters." First company to imprint solid
red heart on chest. 15" - $700.00 up,
$200.00; 22" - $900.00 up, $300.00.

Nasco/Hobbs-Merrill: 1973. Plas-
tic/vinyl with rooted yarn hair. 24" -
$165.00-60.00.

Vinyl Dolls: 8½" - $12.00, $3.00;
12" - $18.00, $6.00; 16" - $22.00, $8.00;
20" - $28.00, $10.00.

16" "Raggedy Ann and Andy" made by
Ideal. They have bisque heads, arms
and legs, cloth bodies, and yarn hair.
Painted features and seam lines. Each -
$95.00. *Courtesy Sandra Cummins.*

**17" original Volland dolls. Boy has hole in chest where candy heart was; girl has
wooden heart. Some dolls have brown hair; others red hair. Marked "Pat. Sept.
7, 1915." Each - $850.00 up.** *Courtesy Ellen Dodge.*

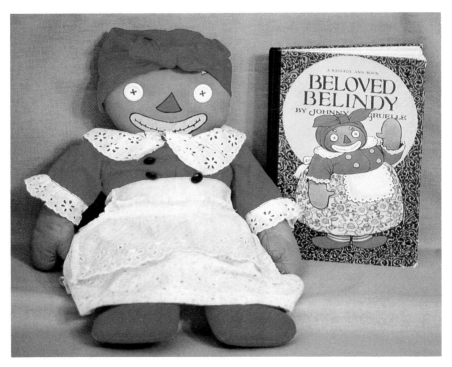

19" "Beloved Belindy" by Georgene Averill. Has "Georgene" green stamp on head. The book shown with doll is rare. Doll - $1,400.00 up; Book - $75.00 up. *Courtesy Ellen Dodge.*

Volland Co.: (See photo in Series 8, pg. 277.) 1920–1934. Lashes low on cheeks. Feet turn outward. Can have brown yarn hair. Some have oversized hands with free-standing thumbs. Long thin nose, lines low under eyes. Different mouth appearances are:

15" - $1,200.00 up; 18" - $1,300.00 up; 22" - $1,500.00 up; 24" - $1,800.00 up; 29" - $2,000.00 up.

Group of "Raggedy Ann and Andy" dolls with two in center being the oldest. All are made by Knickerbocker. $25.00-165.00. *Courtesy Ellen Dodge.*

RAGGEDY ANN and ANDY

Left to right: All original 20" "Beloved Belindy" with button eyes, oil-painted features, and outlined nose. 25" Kammer & Reinhardt mold #116a. Original 19" "Raggedy Ann" by Georgene Averill with outlined nose. 20" "Princess Elizabeth" made by Schoneau & Hoffmeister and a rare brown "Hilda" baby by Kestner. "Beloved Belindy" - $1,400.00; #116a - $3,200.00; "Raggedy Ann" - $650.00; "Princess Elizabeth" - $2,400.00; "Hilda" - $2,800.00. *Courtesy Frasher Doll Auctions.*

REMCO

First prices are for mint condition dolls; second prices are for played with, dirty or not original dolls.

Addams Family: 5½" - $15.00, $8.00.

Baby Crawlalong: 1967. 20" - $20.00, $10.00.

Baby Grow A Tooth: 1969. 14" - $20.00, $10.00. **Black:** $30.00, $12.00.

Baby Know It All: 1969. 17" - $20.00, $10.00.

Baby Laugh A Lot: 1970. (See photo in Series 7, pg. 277.) 16" - $20.00, $7.00. **Black:** $30.00, $15.00.

Baby Sad or Glad: 1966. 14" - $25.00, $15.00.

Baby Stroll-A-Long: 1966. 15" - $20.00, $10.00.

Dave Clark 5: 1964. 4½" - $50.00, $20.00.

Heidi: 1965. 5½" - $9.00, $3.00. **Herby:** 4½" - $12.00, $5.00. **Spunky:** Has glasses. 5½" - $14.00, $5.00. **Jan:** Oriental. 5½" - $14.00, $5.00.

Winking Heidi: 1968. $10.00, $4.00.

Jeannie, I Dream Of: 6" - $20.00, $5.00.

Jumpsy: 1970. (See photo in Series 7, pg. 277.) 14" - $20.00, $8.00. **Black:** $22.00, $10.00.

Laura Partridge: 1973. 19" - $55.00, $25.00.

Lindalee: 1970. Cloth/vinyl. 10" - $20.00, $9.00.

L.B.J.: 1964, portrait. 5½" - $30.00, $10.00.

Littlechap Family: 1963. Set of four. $200.00, $60.00. **Dr. John:** 14½" - $50.00, $20.00. **Lisa:** 13½" - $40.00,

$12.00. **Libby:** 10½" - $35.00, $10.00.
Judy: 12" - $35.00, $10.00.
  Mimi: 1972–1973. Battery operated singer. 19" - $45.00, $20.00. **Black:** $60.00, $20.00.
  Orphan Annie: 1967. Plastic/vinyl. 15" - $30.00, $10.00.
  Sweet April: 1971. All vinyl baby. 5½" - $10.00, $3.00. **Black:** 5½" - $15.00, $3.00.
  Tippy Tumbles: 1966. 16" - $20.00, $8.00.
  Tumbling Tomboy: 1969. 16" - $15.00, $8.00.

5¾" "Karate Kid" and "Mr. Miyagi." Two levers in back operate arms and legs. Marked "1986 Columbia Pictures/ Industries, Inc. Remco Toys, Inc. Made in China." Each - $10.00. *Courtesy Don Tvrdik.*

19" "Mimi" made of plastic/vinyl with painted features. Made in 1972-1973. Battery operated, record insert in side. Outfits sold separately along with record *I'd Like To Teach The World To Sing* in six languages. This is the French outfit. 19" - $45.00. *Courtesy Kathy Tvrdik.*

5½" "Jan" marked "2/KJ 250/Remco Ind. Inc. 1965." (Can also have numbers "2/FJ 112.") Vinyl with painted features. 5½" - $15.00. *Courtesy Kathy Tvrdik.*

The 8" "Sandra Sue" doll has a slim body and limbs. She is a walker, but the head does not turn as she walks. The doll and her clothes are of excellent quality and she was first made in the late 1940's and into the 1950's. A large wardrobe of clothing was available for the doll along with accessories and scaled furniture of the finest quality. She is unmarked except for a number under an arm or leg.

Close-up of beautiful face on the "Sandra Sue" doll. Thin body and limbs. All hard plastic and sleep eyes. Original dress. $250.00. *Courtesy Peggy Millhouse.*

Left: Exceptional "Sandra Sue" that is all hard plastic and original. Side part wig, sleep eyes. Mint in dress - $250.00 up; Mint in ballgown - $300.00 up. Right: "Sandra Sue" skier with wrist tag. Original, mint condition. *Courtesy Karen and Sheila Stephenson.*

Sasha dolls were made by Trenton Toys, Ltd., Reddish, Stockport, England from 1965 to 1986, when they went out of business. The original designer of these dolls was Sasha Morgenthaler in Switzerland. The dolls are made of all rigid vinyl with painted features. The only marks will be a wrist tag. All dolls are 16" tall.

Boy or Girl in box: $200.00
Boy or Girl in cylinder: $325.00
Boy: "Gregor" - $185.00.
Girl: $185.00.
Black Boy: "Caleb" - $285.00.
Black Baby: $250.00
Cora: #119 (Black) - $285.00; #111 (White) - $200.00.
White Baby: $165.00
Sexed Baby: Pre-1979. $250.00
Early Dolls: Tube/sack packaging, girl or boy. $300.00 each.
Limited Edition Dolls: Limited to 5,000, incised #763, dressed in navy velvet. **1981:** $250.00. **1982:** Pintucks dress. $325.00. **1983:** Kiltie Plaid. $350.00. **1985:** Prince Gregor. $365.00. **1986:** Princess. $1,600.00. **1986:** Dressed in sari from India. $1,200.00 up.
Pre-1965: Originals. **White:** 16-18" - $1,200.00 up. **Black:** $2,800.00 up. **Eskimo:** $4,500.00 up.

Early rare red head in braids, original. **$200.00 up.** *Courtesy Shirley Bertrand.*

SHIRLEY TEMPLE

First prices are for mint condition dolls; second prices are for played with, dirty, cracked or crazed or not original dolls. Allow extra for special outfits such as "Little Colonel," "Cowgirl," "Bluebird," etc. (Allow 25% to 50% more for mint in box dolls. Price depends upon clothes.)

All Composition:
11" - $725.00, $450.00. **Cowgirl:** $825.00, $500.00.
13" - $650.00, $400.00.
15-16" - $675.00, $425.00.

17-18" - $725.00, $500.00.
20" - $865.00, $500.00.
22" - $925.00, $550.00.
25" - $1,000.00, $600.00. **Cowgirl:** $1,200.00, $650.00.
27" - $1,150.00, $650.00. **Cowgirl:** $1,350.00, $675.00.
Vinyl of 1950's: Allow more for flirty eyes in 17" and 19" sizes.
12" in box - $200.00. Mint, not in box - $165.00. Played with, dirty - $40.00.
15" in box - $325.00. Mint, not in box - $265.00. Played with, dirty - $85.00.

17" in box - $450.00. Mint, not in box - $365.00. Played with, dirty - $95.00.

19" in box - $500.00. Mint, not in box - $450.00. Played with, dirty - $125.00.

36" in box - $1,800.00. Mint, not in box - $1,500.00. Played with, dirty - $800.00.

1972: Reissue from Montgomery Ward. In box - $200.00; Mint, not in box - $165.00; Dirty - $45.00.

1973: Has box with many pictures of Shirley on it. Doll in red polka dot dress. 16" in box - $165.00. Mint, no box - $125.00. Played with, dirty - $45.00.

27" "Shirley Temple" with flirty eyes, tagged dress, button, and original hair set. Mint - $1,300.00. *Courtesy Turn of Century Antiques.*

1982–1983: Plastic/vinyl. Made by Ideal. 8" - $30.00, 12" - $35.00.

Shirley Display Stand: Mechanical doll. $2,300.00 up.

"Hawaiian": Marked Shirley Temple (but not meant to be a Shirley Temple.) 18" - $850.00, $400.00.

Japan: All bisque (painted) with molded hair. 6" - $225.00. Composition: 7-8" - $265.00.

German: 1936. 16", marked "GB42." All composition, sleep eyes, open mouth smile. $650.00 up.

Babies: Marked on head, open mouth with upper and lower teeth, flirty, sleep eyes. 16" - $950.00, $565.00; 18" - $1,000.00, $650.00; 22" - $1,200.00, $700.00; 25" - $1,400.00, $800.00; 27" - $1,600.00, $900.00.

Look-Alike Dolls: Composition, with dimples. 16" - $200.00; 20" - $350.00; 27" - $600.00. Vinyl: 36" - $800.00.

22" "Shirley Temple" as "Little Colonel." Mint and all original including hair set. Also has original button pin. $1,300.00. *Courtesy Turn of Century Antiques.*

Shirley Temple Accessories:
Script Name Pin: $18.00-25.00.
Pin Button: Old 1930's doll pin.
$90.00. Others - $15.00.
Boxed outfits: 1950's: $35.00 up.
1970's: $30.00 up.
Tagged 1930's dress: $125.00 up.
Purse with name: $12.00-15.00.

Buggy: Made of wood. 26" -
$385.00 up; 32" - $450.00 up; 34" -
$500.00 up. Wicker: 26" - $500.00 up.
Trunk: $145.00 up. Gift set/doll
and clothes. **1950's:** $450.00 up.
1930's: $175.00.
Statuette: Chalk in dancing dress.
7-8" - $265.00; 4½" - $185.00.

36" "Shirley Temple" in unplayed with
condition, 1960. Excellent face color, mint
in box. 30" "Mimi" by Madame Alexander
with flirty eyes. Multi-jointed and original.
Bottom row: 15" hard plastic, all original,
Mary Hoyer doll; "Jerri Lee" in cowboy
outfit; 8" "Ginny" and 8" "Easter" doll by
Madame Alexander. 36" - $1,800.00; 30" -
$600.00; 15" - $450.00; "Jerri Lee" -
$350.00; "Ginny" - $225.00; "Easter" -
$1,200.00. *Courtesy Frasher Doll Auctions.*

Three "Shirley Temple" dolls. 16" German
marked "485." Composition, glass flirty
sleep eyes, mohair wig, open mouth, five-
piece body, redressed. Original 19" Ideal
all vinyl with flirty eyes from 1950's. 15"
vinyl made for Montgomery Ward's
anniversary in 1972, original. 16" -
$300.00; 19" - $450.00; 15" - $265.00.
Courtesy Frasher Doll Auctions.

SHIRLEY TEMPLE

8" "Shirley Temple" made of vinyl and plastic. All original, marked "1982" on body; "1982 Ideal Toy Corp/S.T. ?-8-N-8371" on head. $30.00. *Courtesy Kathy Tvrdik.*

TERRI LEE

First prices are for mint condition dolls, which could be higher due to the outfit on the doll. Second prices are for soiled, poor wig or not original. **Terri Lee: Composition:** $350.00, $100.00. **Hard plastic:** Marked "Pat. Pend." $285.00 up, $100.00. **Others:** $265.00 up, $100.00. **Black:** "Patti Jo." $550.00 up, $250.00. **Vinyl:** $200.00, $75.00. **Talking:** $500.00, $185.00. Mint in box: $500.00 up.

Jerri Lee: 16", hard plastic, caracul wig. $300.00, $185.00. **Black:** "Benjamin." $550.00, $250.00. Mint in box: $500.00 up.

Tiny Terri Lee: 10" - $165.00, $80.00.

Tiny Jerri Lee: 10" - $185.00, $80.00.

Connie Lynn: 19" - $385.00 up, $150.00.

Gene Autry: 16" - $1,600.00 up, $700.00.

Linda Baby: (Linda Lee) 10-12" - $200.00 up, $95.00.

So Sleepy: 9½" - $285.00 up, $100.00.

Clothes: Ballgown: $100.00 up. **Riding Habit:** $100.00 up. **Skaters:** $100.00 up. **School Dresses:** $50.00 up. **Coats:** $35.00 up. **Brownie Uniform:** $40.00 up.

Clothes for Jerri Lee: Two-piece pants suit: $100.00 up. **Short pants suits:** $100.00 up. **Western shirt/ jeans:** $70.00 up.

Mary Jane: Plastic walker, Teri Lee look-alike with long molded eyelids. 16" - $265.00 up.

"Jerri Lee" dolls with caracul wigs and all original cowboy outfits. Each - $365.00. *Courtesy Susan Girardot.*

16", all hard plastic, "Terri Lee" in Easter outfit with purse and matching bonnet. All original, mint in box. $500.00. *Courtesy Patricia Woods.*

Group of completely original and mint "Terri Lee" and "Jerri Lee" dolls. Lower far right is a mint and original "Mary Jane." All are hard plastic. $285.00-550.00. *Courtesy Patricia Woods.*

Mint in box "Talking Terri Lee." Original cord and record. Cord plugs into record player. $500.00. *Courtesy Turn of Century Antiques.*

Group of "Jerri Lee," "Tiny Jerri Lee," and black "Benjie." All original. $300.00-550.00. *Courtesy Susan Girardot.*

All vinyl "Linda Baby" in nursery chair and "Connie Lynn" is holding very rare "So Sleepy" that has vinyl head with painted sleepy eyes and stuffed body and limbs. All original. "Linda Baby" - $200.00; Chair - $150.00; "Connie Lynn" - $385.00; " So Sleepy" - $285.00. *Courtesy Susan Girardot.*

Trolls: 2½"-3" - $15.00 up; 5" - $20.00-25.00; 7" - $30.00-40.00; 10" - $50.00; 12" - $60.00; 15" - $80.00 up.

Troll animals: Cow - $65.00; Donkey - $80.00; Ape - $80.00; Turtle - $55.00; Giraffe - $70.00.

10" pink inset hair Troll that is all original with lavender inset eyes. **$50.00.** *Courtesy Gloria Anderson.*

Left: 4" "Scuba Troll" made in 1965. Inset eyes and hair. Right: 7½" Santa Claus Troll bank with hole in back for coins. Inset eyes and unmarked. 4" - $25.00; 7½" - **$45.00.** *Courtesy Gloria Anderson and Kathy Tvrdik.*

First prices are for mint condition dolls; second prices are for soiled, dirty or not original dolls.

Baby Dollikins: 1958. 21" - $30.00, $15.00.

Baby Trix: 1964. 16" - $20.00, $10.00.

Ballerina: Vinyl. 14" - $20.00, $7.00.

Blabby: 1962. $20.00, $9.00.

Bare Bottom Baby: (See photo in Series 7, pg. 289.) 12" - $20.00, $12.00.

Bob: 1963. 10½" - $15.00, $9.00.

Coquette: 1963. 16" - $20.00, $10.00.

Dollikins: 1957. 8" - $25.00, $8.00; 11" - $30.00, $10.00; 19" - $50.00, $20.00.

Fairy Princess: 32" - $90.00, $40.00.

Freckles: 1960. 32" - $90.00, $45.00.

Freckles Marionette: 30" - $65.00, $30.00.

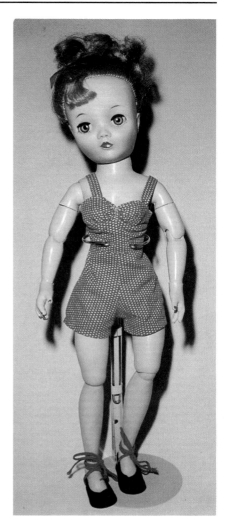

18" "Dollikin" with extra joints at waist, above elbows, at elbows, knees, and ankles. Vinyl head with sleep eyes and rooted hair. Hard plastic body and limbs. **1957. $50.00.** *Courtesy Kathy Tvrdik.*

10" "Blue Fairy" from the story "Pinocchio." All vinyl. Rooted blue hair, sleep eyes, and high heel feet. Marked "Uneeda." $65.00. *Courtesy Kathy Tvrdik.*

Grannykins: 1974. Painted-on half-glasses. 6" - $8.00, $3.00.

Lucky Lindy: (Lindbergh) Composition. 14" - $375.00, $225.00.

Magic Meg: 1971. Grow hair. 16" - $20.00, $9.00.

Pollyanna: 1960. 10½" - $30.00, $9.00; 17" - $45.00, $15.00; 31" - $100.00, $50.00.
Pri-Thilla: 1958. 12" - $15.00, $8.00.
Purty: 1961. (See photo in Series 7, pg. 289.) Press stomach to make eyes squint. 15" - $20.00, $12.00.
Rita Hayworth: 1948. Composition. 14" - $365.00, $175.00.
Serenade: 1962. Battery-operated singer. 21" - $50.00, $15.00.
Suzette: 1959–1960, 1962. 10½" - $50.00, $25.00; 11½" - $50.00, $25.00; 11½" with sleep eyes: $75.00, $40.00.
Tiny Teens: 1957. 5" - $10.00.

14" **"Posey Twins."** All composition with glassene sleep eyes. Made in 1947 by Uneeda Doll Co. Girl's underclothes are stapled on. Both are original. Each - $95.00. *Courtesy Jeannie Mauldin.*

VOGUE DOLLS, INC.

First prices are for mint condition dolls; second prices are for played with, dirty, crazed, messed up wig or not original.
Baby Dear: 1960–1961. 12" - $60.00, $20.00; 17" - $95.00, $40.00. 1964: 12" - $50.00, $20.00. **Newborn:** 1960. Sleep eyes. $75.00.
Baby Dear One: 25" - $145.00, $85.00.
Baby Dear Two: 27" - $155.00, $75.00.
Baby Wide Eyes: 1976. Very large brown sleep eyes. All vinyl. 16" - $30.00, $10.00.
Brickette: 1960. 22" - $60.00, $25.00. **Reissued:** 1979–1980. 18" - $35.00.
Ginny: 1948–1949. Composition "Toddles." $235.00 up, $90.00.

17" **"Baby Dear"** made by Vogue in 1959. Both are signed **"E. Wilkins"** on upper legs. Painted features, cloth bodies, and rooted baby hair. Each - **$95.00 up.** *Courtesy Kathy Tvrdik.*

Ginny: 1954–1957. Hard plastic molded lash walker. $165.00 up, $75.00.
Ginny: 1957–1962. Hard plastic, jointed knee, molded lash walker. $145.00 up, $60.00.
Ginny Hawaiian: 8" brown-black doll. $725.00 up, $365.00.
Ginny Queen: $1,600.00 up, $600.00.
Ginny Crib Crowd: Bent leg baby with caracul (lamb's wool) wig. $650.00 up, $300.00.
Crib Crowd Easter Bunny: $1,400.00 up, $600.00.
Ginny: 1977. All vinyl Internationals. $50.00 up. Other: $35.00 up.

17" "Dearest One" made of all vinyl with rooted hair, sleep eyes/lashes. Open mouth nurser, posable head. Doll is strung. Marked "Vogue Doll Inc./ 1967" on head and body. $60.00.
Courtesy Kathy Tvrdik.

Ginny: 1950–1953. 8" hard plastic, strung, painted eyes. $375.00 up, $100.00.
Ginny: 8" hard plastic, sleep eyes, painted lashes and strung. $325.00 up, $100.00.
Ginny: Caracul (lamb's wool) wig. Child, not baby. $400.00 up, $200.00.
Ginny: 1954. Painted lashes, sleep eyes, hard plastic walker. $225.00 up, $95.00.

Composition "Toddles" as "Mary Had A Little Lamb." Original in original box. $425.00. *Courtesy Sandy Johnson Barts.*

All of these "Ginny" dolls are strung. Left to right: "Julie," 1952, "Frolicking Fables Series;" "Ginger," #64, "Debutante Series;" (sitting) "Sister" of "Brother & Sister Series," missing cap; "Easter," #8-12D, traditional doll from 1949-1950; #36 from the 1952 "Brother & Sister" series. Each - $325.00. *Courtesy Margaret Mandel.*

"Ginny" 1953 "Tiny Miss Series." Top row: #41 "June" with replaced hat; #43 "Beryl;" #39 "Lucy" with replaced hat. Bottom row: #44 "Cheryl;" #40 "Wanda;" #42 "Glad." Each - $325.00. *Courtesy Peggy Millhouse.*

Ginny Exclusives: 1986–1991. **Shirley's Doll House:** Goes Country/Country Fair - $90.00; Black - $100.00; Santa/Mrs. Claus - $70.00; Babysitter: $65.00; Sunday Best (boy or girl) - $55.00. **Gigi and Sherry Meyer's:** Favorite Ginny - $60.00; Clown - $55.00; Cowgirl - $55.00; Prince Charming - $65.00; Cinderella - $60.00. **Little Friends:** Alaska - $60.00. **Toy Village:** Ashley Rose - $55.00. **Enchanted Doll House**: Enchanted Ginny - $55.00.

    Ginny Accessories: Ginny Gym: $275.00 up. **Ginny Pup:** Steiff. $165.00 up. **Luggage Set:** $100.00 up. **Shoes/Shoe Bag:** $35.00 up. **Furniture:** Chair, bed, dresser, wardrobe, rocking chair. $60.00 each. **Name Pin:** $55.00. **Book:** *Ginny's First Secret* - $135.00. **Parasol:** $15.00. **School Bag:** $70.00.

"Ginny" as "Roller Skater" (#1800). All hard plastic with painted eyes and mohair wig. $375.00. *Courtesy Peggy Millhouse.*

    Hug A Bye Baby: 1975. 16" - $25.00, $15.00. **Black:** $35.00, $15.00. **Jan:** 1957. 12" - $135.00, $50.00. **Jeff:** 1957. 10" - $75.00, $35.00. **Jill:** 1957. 10" - $150.00, $55.00. In box/ballgown: $300.00 up. **Lil Imp:** 11" - $45.00, $20.00. **Love Me Linda:** 15" - $30.00, $10.00. **Miss Ginny:** 1967–1970's. Young lady type. 11-12" - $25.00, $10.00; 15" - $40.00, $15.00. **Star Bright:** 1966. 18" - $100.00, $40.00. **Baby:** 18" - $65.00, $25.00. **Welcome Home or Welcome Home Baby Turns Two:** 20-24" - $75.00, $40.00. **Wee Imp:** 8", red wig. $400.00 up, $100.00.

"Toddles" in "Valentine's Day" special made in late 1940's for Wanamaker's Department Store. Outfits tagged and dolls marked. Each - $365.00. *Courtesy Susan Giradot.*

10" "Jill" by Vogue, all original. Hard plastic, sleep eyes, heeled feet. $150.00 up. *Courtesy Sandy Johnson Barts.*

UNIQUE

12" "Elly Mae Clampett" played by Donna Douglas on the television series, *The Beverly Hillbillies* (1962–1971). Made by Unique in 1960's. Original with painted features and made of plastic and vinyl. Marked on head. Had two dresses - one of yellow print; the other, green with pink check. (Buttons of blouse shown in photo can also be black.) Doll also called "Calico Lass." $40.00. *Courtesy David Spurgeon.*

The dolls designed and made by the Robin Woods Company over the years have been some of the finest quality dolls available in their price range. These dolls stand out in a crowd because Robin Woods used imagination and creative talent that bears her signature. The dolls are beginning to show up on the secondary market and more will appear as time goes on. The last "pure" Robin Woods doll appeared on the market during 1991. In 1992, Robin Woods became the creative designer for the Alexander Doll Company and will be designing dolls under the name of "Alice Darling."

The following are a few of the dolls that can be found on the secondary market.

1989: Hope - $165.00; **Lorna Doone** - $175.00; **Heidi** - $165.00; **William Noel** - $185.00; **Elizabeth St. John** - $200.00.

1990: "Camelot Series." **Kyliegh Christmas** - $185.00; **Melanie Phebe** - $175.00; **Tess Circus** - $160.00; **Bobbi** - $165.00; **Marjorie** - $165.00; **Meaghan** - $200.00; **Tess Durbervilles** - $225.00.

1991: Laurel - $165.00; **Delores** - $225.00; **Victoria** - $185.00; **Miss Muffet** - $175.00; **Sleeping Beauty** set - $385.00; **Pumpkin Eaters** - $225.00; **Eliza Doolittle** - $200.00; **Mistress Mary** - $150.00; **Bette Jack** - $275.00; **Alena** - $275.00; **Tennison** - $275.00.

Robin Woods Limited Editions:
Merri: 14", limited edition, 1991 Doll Convention, Disneyworld. $500.00.

Mindy: 14", limited to 300 for Disney's "Robin Woods Day." $325.00.

Rainey: 14", 1991 Robin Woods Club doll. Limited to 300. $300.00.

Angelina: 14", 1990 limited edition Christmas angel made for J.C. Penney's. $550.00.

Noelle: 14", limited edition Christmas angel for J.C. Penney's. $275.00.

Julianna: 14", 1991 J.C. Penney's limited edition. Little girl shopping for holidays. $235.00.

Robin Woods Specials:
Gina, The Earthquake Doll: For Ann's of Burlingame, CA. $650.00.

Christmas Tree Doll: Doll becomes the tree. For Disney. $675.00.

14" Christmas dolls made by Robin Woods for 1987. Both have green sleep eyes. Only 300 sets made. Each - $300.00. *Courtesy Shirley Bertrand.*

14" "Violet" with painted violet
tinted eyes. All original. $200.00.
Courtesy Shirley Bertrand.

14" "William Noel," 1989 Christmas
doll. Has painted blue eyes and
came with sled. $185.00. *Courtesy
Shirley Bertrand.*

"Emma and Seth" made by R. John Wright in the mid-1980's. Each - $1,700.00-1,900.00. *Courtesy Mary Lu Trowbridge.*

The Enchanted Doll House Exclusives: "Rachael" (1985–1986); "Edward" (1986–1987).) "Rachael" - $1,400.00-1,500.00; "Edward" - $1,300.00-1,400.00. *Courtesy Mary Lu Trowbridge.*

Left: "Christopher Robin & Pooh." Series 1, sold as set in 1985. Right: "Tad" and "Lillian" from the "Little Children Series 1." Sold separately in 1984–1985. "Pooh" Series - $1,400.00-1,800.00; "Children" Series, each - $1,000.00-1,400.00. *Courtesy Mary Lu Trowbridge.*

"Scott" is a wonderful boy made in 1987–1988. $975.00-1,100.00. *Courtesy Mary Lu Trowbridge.*

INDEX

301

NUMBERS

314

LETTERS AND SYMBOLS

Other Doll Books By
America's Leading Doll Author
PATRICIA SMITH

Antique Collector's Dolls, Volumes I & II, each $17.95

Collector's Encyclopedia of
Madame Alexander Dolls $24.95

French Dolls in Color, 3rd Series $14.95

Madame Alexander Dolls $19.95

Madame Alexander Price Guide #18 ....$ 9.95

Modern Collector's Dolls Volumes I-V, each $17.95

Modern Collector's Dolls Price Guide for
Volumes I-V..$ 9.95

Shirley Temple Dolls, Volumes I & II, each.................$17.95

World of Alexander-kins $19.95

Order from your favorite dealer or

COLLECTOR BOOKS
P.O. Box 3009
Paducah, KY 42002-3009

When ordering by mail, please add $2.00 postage and handling
for the first book, 30¢ for each additional book.

Schroeder's
ANTIQUES Price Guide

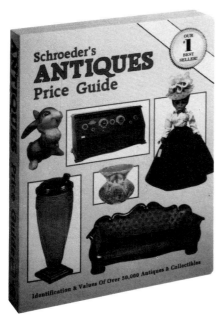

Schroeder's Antiques Price Guide is the #1 best-selling antiques & collectibles value guide on the market today, and here's why . . . More than 300 authors, well-known dealers, and top-notch collectors work together with our editors to bring you accurate information regarding pricing and identification. More than 45,000 items in almost 500 categories are listed along with hundreds of sharp original photos that illustrate not only the rare and unusual, but the common, popular collectibles as well. Each large close-up shot shows important details clearly. Every subject is represented with histories and background information, a feature not found in any of our competitors' publications. Our editors keep abreast of newly-developing trends, often adding several new categories a year as the need arises. If it merits the interest of today's collector, you'll find it in Schroeder's. And you can feel confident that the information we publish is up to date and accurate. Our advisors thoroughly check each category to spot inconsistencies, listings that may not be entirely reflective of market dealings, and lines too vague to be of merit. Only the best of the lot remains for publication. Without doubt, you'll find Schroeder's Antiques Price Guide the only one to buy for reliable information and values.

8½x 11", 608 Pages **$12.95**

COLLECTOR BOOKS
A Division of Schroeder Publishing Co., Inc.

Dinosaurs, the Lost World, and You

by John Morris

A tremendous teaching tool, this booklet meets evolutionary stories about dinosaurs head-on. Written by one of the leading creationist/geologists of our time, *Dinosaurs, the Lost World, and You* explores what we really know about these great beasts. Since dinosaurs are used to promote evolutionary concepts to an unsuspecting public, Morris refutes much of the prevailing thought by pointing out that the Bible does indeed fit nicely with much modern evidence for real science, such as the vast dinosaur fossil graveyards around the world. No home or church should be without this booklet.

ISBN: 0-89051-256-6 • 48 pages
$3.99

Available at Christian bookstores nationwide